THE INDEPENDENT PARALEGAL'S HANDBOOK

by Ralph Warner

Edited by Karen Chambers
Illustrated by Mari Stein

ACCESS
TO LAW

NOLO PRESS • 950 PARKER ST., BERKELEY, CA 94710

Your Responsibility When Using A Self-Help Law Book

We've done our best to give you useful and accurate information in this book. But laws and procedures change frequently and are subject to differing interpretations. If you want legal advice backed by a guarantee, see a lawyer. If you use this book, it's your responsibility to make sure that the facts and general advice contained in it are applicable to your situation.

Keeping Up to Date

To keep its books up to date, Nolo Press issues new printings and new editions periodically. New printings reflect minor legal changes and technical corrections. New editions contain major legal changes, major text additions or major reorganizations. To find out if a later printing or edition of any Nolo book is available, call Nolo Press at (510) 549-1976 or check the catalog in the *Nolo News,* our quarterly newspaper.

To stay current, follow the "Update" service in the *Nolo News.* You can get the paper free by sending us the registration card in the back of the book. In another effort to help you use Nolo's latest materials, we offer a 25% discount off the purchase of any new Nolo book if you turn in any earlier printing or edition. (See the "Recycle Offer" in the back of this book.)

This book was last revised in: **April 1993**

Second Edition

Second Printing: April 1993

Editors: Karen Chambers
Mary Randolph
Stephen Elias

Production: Stephanie Harolde
Terri Hearsh

Warner, Ralph E.
    The independant paralegal's handbook / Ralph Warner.
      p. cm.
    ISBN 0-87337-119-4 : $24.95
    1. Legal assistants--United States--Handbooks, manuals, etc.
I. Title.
KF320.L4W37   1991
340' . 023'73--dc20   91-17632
                                            CIP

recycled &
recyclable

Dedication

For my friend Ed Sherman, whose creative genius contributed so much to the formation of the Wave Project, and with it, the modern independent paralegal movement. Over 20 years ago, Ed understood that the average American is fully competent to gather and understand the information necessary to make his or her legal decisions.

About the Author

Along with Charles "Ed" Sherman, Ralph Warner founded Nolo Press in 1971 and the Wave Project in 1972. The Wave Project originally consisted of 18 nonlawyer divorce typing services offices located throughout California. (Many still exist, under the name "Divorce Centers of California.") Both Nolo and the Wave Project were pioneer efforts to allow nonlawyers direct access to the legal system.

Ralph Warner is currently the publisher of Nolo Press as well as author of several of its self-help law books. He continues to be active in the independent paralegal movement and the larger political movement to break the lawyers' monopoly over the delivery of routine legal services.

Recycle Your Out-of-date Law Books
And Get 25% Off Your Next Purchase

OUT OF DATE = DANGEROUS

Using an old edition can be dangerous if information in it is wrong. Unfortunately, laws and legal procedures change often. Generally speaking, any book more than two years old is of questionable value. Books more than four or five years old are a menace.

To help you keep up-to-date, we extend this offer:

If you cut out and deliver to us the title portion of the cover of any old Nolo book, we'll give you a 25% discount off the retail price of any new Nolo book. For example, if you have a copy of *Tenants' Rights*, 4th edition and want to trade it for the latest *California Marriage and Divorce Law*, send us the *Tenants' Rights* cover and a check for the current price of *California Marriage and Divorce Law*, less a 25% discount.

Information on current prices and editions is listed in the preceding pages of this book and in the catalog in the Nolo News (see offer at the back of this book).

This discount offer is to individuals only.

Acknowledgements

Of the many wonderful people who helped me with this new edition, two special friends come first—Stephen Elias, Nolo Press Associate Publisher, and Catherine Jermany, Executive Director of the National Association for Independent Paralegals, in Sonoma, California. Over the last ten years, I have talked about the independent paralegal movement with Steve and Catherine so many times, I have long since lost track of where my ideas stop and theirs start. Fortunately, as with any of life's exciting collaborations, it makes no difference to any of us, as long as we collectively deepen our understanding of this truly fascinating subject.

My special thanks to Karen Chambers, who helped greatly with legal research and rewriting for Chapter 2, and did much to make this new edition better throughout.

I am deeply appreciative of the help I received from Rosemary Furman, Toni Ihara, Jolene Jacobs, Bob Mission, Robin Smith, Glynda Mathewson, Bob Anderson and Virginia Simons. These people truly pioneered the independent paralegal movement, and their willingness to share their experiences and insights with me give this book a depth it would otherwise lack.

Thank you to Rose Palmer and Judy Lamb, two brave and enthusiastic women who head nonprofit organizations that provide legal and advocacy assistance to women on issues of child support, custody, visitation and domestic violence. Both greatly deepened my understanding about how nonlawyers can successfully bring legal information and services to large groups of people bypassed by lawyers.

Over many years, I have received much valuable counsel from my very good friends at HALT—Americans for Legal Reform. Executive Director, Glen Nishimura, has helped by consistently reminding me that government regulation often protects incompetent, price-gouging providers, not consumers. And Debbie Chalfie, HALT's Legislative Director, has given me so many great ideas on how to break down the lawyer's monopoly that I've long since lost count.

I am also indebted to Afroditi Price, President of the California Association of Freelance Paralegals, Inc., in Berkeley, California, for many good suggestions on improving the chapter on freelance para-legals.

Finally, I would like to thank a number of other friends who extended a helping hand along the way, including Tony Mancuso, Kay Ostberg, Michael Phillips, Salli Rasberry and, most especially, Stephanie Harolde, who contributed many helpful editorial suggestions.

Table of Contents

Introduction

*H*ere is a book for people who want to work in our legal system but do not wish to work for a lawyer or to become one. Completely revised in this second edition, it is designed as a resource for those who wish to help consumers prepare their own paperwork in uncontested actions such as bankruptcy, divorce, small business incorporations, landlord-tenant, or probate. I refer to these people as "independent paraegals" (IPs), although they are also commonly called "legal technicians" and "legal typists." Unfortunately, many lawyers use none of these terms, instead referring to nonlawyers who help consumers prepare legal paperwork as "criminals."

Of course, these days most Americans aren't particularly horrified by the criminal offense of practicing law without a license. In fact, compared to a real crime, like burglary or arson, unauthorized practice is a bit of a joke. Before you laugh too hard, however, remember that independent paralegals still face a number of lawyer-designed laws, court decisions, and rules of court whose sole purpose is to suppress their activities. And remember, too, that should an IP be accused of the crime of practicing law without a license, the people who will prosecute and judge her will all be lawyers.

Have you stopped laughing? If you haven't, consider Rosemary Furman, a pioneering Florida independent paralegal, who was sentenced to four months in jail (even though she was never charged with a crime and was denied the right to trial by jury) in 1984 by a trial judge, who said, "Only her imprisonment will provide the sting to preserve the integrity of the court." And don't assume that what happened to Furman was an isolated instance. In 1989, a Louisiana independent paralegal, Jerome Papania, was arrested by seven officers and charged with unauthorized practice for helping consumers type bankruptcy forms. In 1990, Mershan Shaddy, an independent paralegal in San Diego, California was sentenced to jail for providing customers information about divorce law. And as this book goes to press, in the spring of 1991, another IP, Dennis Ridderbush, has been in jail for 20 days for typing bankruptcy forms in Wisconsin.

Enter this guidebook, designed to help independent paralegals carry on their business competently (and, I hope, make a good living), steer clear of organized lawyerdom's monopolistic rules defining who can practice law, and stay out of jail. Unfortunately, when it comes to this last goal (the crucial part about not getting locked up), I can make no guarantees. Although I will teach you a method to prepare legal paperwork that has been widely judged not to constitute unauthorized practice, anyone who begins a career as an independent paralegal must accept the fact that it is possible to deliver excellent, honest services at a reasonable price and still end up being harassed by lawyers.

Enough negatives. Despite the obstacles created by the legal profession, the independent paralegal movement is growing rapidly all across America. The average American, faced with almost daily news stories about the glut of lawyers (close to 800,000 at last count), at the same time that he finds even routine legal services prohibitively expensive, is increasingly supportive of high-quality, low-cost paralegal alternatives. For example, in states such as Arizona and California more than 60% of divorces and 30% of bankruptcies are now done without lawyers. The rapid growth in popularity of self-help law books, legal services delivered by telephone, and self-help law computer programs are other manifestations of what amounts to a major change in how ordinary Americans gain access to the legal system. Indeed, it's probably fair to say that the only group still shocked by the growth of the nonlawyer legal form preparation business is lawyers.

As a co-founder of both Nolo Press, the publisher of close to eighty self-help law products, and the Wave Project, one of the first self-help divorce typing businesses, I have been involved in the independent paralegal movement for over 20 years. This doesn't mean I have all the answers about how to survive and prosper as an independent paralegal. It does mean that I have a number of suggestions which should ease the task of the nonlawyer determined to deliver competent services in the hostile shadow of the American legal profession. By way of example, this book covers:

- What types of legal paperwork an independent paralegal can safely and profitably prepare;

- How to get the necessary training to work as an independent paralegal;

- What to call your business;

- How to market your services in a cost-effective way;

- How to let customers know you are not a lawyer;

- How to work with lawyers when necessary;

- How to minimize the chance of harassment by the bar;

- What to do if you are threatened by the bar;

- How much to charge;

- How to think about working with computers.

In addition, this book contains interviews with eleven prominent people in the independent paralegal field. Many of these are IPs who have been successfully delivering services to the public for many years. Others are involved in IP training, the development of self-help law materials used by IPs, or the effort to get states to adopt legislation to legalize the occupation. In many ways, these interviews, which you will find in the Appendix, are the most important part of the book and I urge you to take the time to read them carefully.

Many of the suggestions in this book are aimed at helping you to deal with problems you are sure to face as part of starting any new business. These range from choosing a business name, to finding the right location for the business, to getting a business license, to buying equipment, and so on. Sometimes it is necessary to borrow money to begin. Certainly, once your doors are open, it is important to quickly generate a positive cash flow. None of this is easy, especially when you remind yourself that embarking on a career as an independent paralegal involves not only putting yourself through normal "new business trauma," but simultaneously coping with the hostility of the legal profession.

This raises the question of why anyone would want to become an independent paralegal. Or, asked more directly, why are you even considering a field where persecution, or at least official harassment, is a distinct possibility, and criminal conviction, including even a jail sentence, is not out of the question? One obvious answer is that running an independent paraegal business is potentially profitable. Lawyers' fees are so outrageous that independent paralegals can significantly undercut them (often by as much as 70%) and still make an excellent living. Indeed, a few farsighted business commentators predict that independent paralegal businesses will be one of the major success stories of the next decade.

But the prospect of making good money doesn't begin to explain why so many pioneer paralegals have been willing to assume the risk inherent in challenging organized lawyerdom. In talking to dozens, some of whom have been in business for almost 20 years, I sense that, for most, the determination to persevere is drawn from the same sort of stubborn conviction that motivated Massachusetts colonists to toss chests of tea into the Boston Harbor in 1767. Like their colonial forefathers, angered by King George III's nasty monopoly on tea, these men and women stand up to organized lawyerdom's even nastier monopoly over the delivery of legal services, because they believe they are right.

While obviously I don't minimize the problems inherent in embarking on a career as an independent paralegal, I believe that with a lot of determination and a little luck, you can establish a profitable business and provide a valuable service helping nonlawyers with their own legal paperwork. This should become easier in the future, as public support for deregulation of the legal profession is almost sure to grow.

A Few Words About Terminology

Because lawyers in private practice, legislatures, bar associations, prosecutor's offices, and judge's robes have all been trained to defend their monopoly to deliver legal services, I often refer to them here with the shorthand term "organized lawyerdom," except when it's important to distinguish among them.

Also, as noted, for convenience I refer to nonlawyers who help other nonlawyers deal with the legal system as "independent paralegals" (IPs) even though some people in the field describe themselves in other ways— as "legal technician," "form preparer," "legal typing service," "legal information specialist," "divorce counselor" or "public paralegal."

When describing the people who hire independent paralegals, I use the word "customer," rather than "client." I do this both because I believe it is wise for paralegals to distinguish themselves from lawyers as much as possible and because I personally don't like the word client, which has Latin roots in the terms "to hear" and "to obey." "Customer," on the other hand, conjures up the image of a powerful person, someone who expects good and conscientious service and who won't patronize a business again if she isn't satisfied.

And then there is the pesky personal pronoun. My solution to the problem of how to handle gender is to use "he" and "she" more or less alternatively throughout the book. While this solution isn't perfect, it makes more sense to me than only using "he" or adopting other cumbersome schemes such as writing "he and she," "he/she" or "s(he)" every time an abstract person must be identified.

Finally, a few words about Nolo Press, the National Association for Independent Paralegals (NAIP) and Americans for Legal Reform—HALT are appropriate. Throughout this text, you will find many references to Nolo's self-help law materials, NAIP's independent paralegal training programs and HALT's political organizing efforts. You may even begin to wonder why I plug these groups so much. The simple answer is that the activities of Nolo, NAIP and HALT are at the heart of so many aspects of the independent paralegal movement that the references are unavoidable. Just the same, by way of full disclosure, I want to make it clear that I have a financial interest in Nolo, that my long-time close associates, Catherine Jermany and Stephen Elias, are principal owners of NAIP, and that I have worked closely for many years with a number of staffers at HALT and am proud to be a member of that organization.

Chapter 1

The Historical Background

A person who decides on a career as an independent paralegal almost by definition must engage in a struggle with organized lawyerdom, a powerful adversary. Before you do this, you should learn some history—that is, understand the historical forces that have led to the current confrontation between independent paralegals and organized lawyerdom. Second, while you should respect these lessons, you should not allow them to control your strategy or tactics. Does this sound paradoxical? It isn't. Because we live in an age of unprecedented change, the lessons of history, while important, should be only one element in your strategy to keep your business from being suppressed by organized lawyerdom.

Reading history and not being ruled by it is never easy. Unfortunately, the natural human response is to draw such inflexible lessons from past events that history is repeated. Thus, it is a cliche that the best-trained generals tend to refight the last war, learned economists make predictions based on yesterday's recession, and baseball managers repeatedly rely too much on aging players who hit last year's home runs.

Independent paralegals, however, do have one dubious advantage over generals and coaches, who are trying to extrapolate past successes into future victories: IPs don't have many past victories to cloud their vision. Indeed, an independent paralegal who slavishly applies history's lessons is likely to conclude that a career as an independent paralegal is hopeless. Why? Because the IP will learn that in the nineteenth and early twentieth centuries, organized lawyerdom, relying on superior financial, organizational and political resources, effectively crushed America's once vibrant self-help law tradition. Does this mean that the current independent paralegal movement will also be suppressed by a vastly more powerful legal profession? Not at all. For reasons I develop in this chapter, I think that if paralegals as a group are willing both to learn from past mistakes and adopt new strategies, they can win the legal right to exist.

A. An American Tradition: "Every Man His Own Lawyer"

Let's look back four-and-one-half centuries. What can we say about the practice of law in colonial America? Very little, because in the early days of the American experience neither a lawyer elite nor a lawyer-dominated dispute resolution system existed in most colonies. Especially in Puritan New England, the Quaker communities in Pennsylvania, and the Dutch settlements in New York, there was a strong religious and egalitarian spirit hostile to the very notion of lawyers. Colonists solved their disputes within the community, which in those early days was heavily influenced by the church. Church elders were expected to guide disputing members of their congregations to a "just" result. The ultimate punishment for deviant behavior was exile from both church and community. For example, Anne Hutchinson, a woman who challenged several orthodox views in the Massachusetts Bay Colony, was tried by the church for heresy and exiled to the wilderness; she eventually ended up in Rhode Island.

When a particular dispute threatened to prove intractable, formal mediation techniques, similar to those newly popular today, were often used to help the disputants arrive at their own compromise. In 1635, a Boston town meeting ordered that no congregation member could litigate before trying arbitration, and Reverend John Cotton, the leading Puritan minister of the time, stated that to sue a fellow church member was a "defect in brotherly love." In 1641, the "Body of Liberties" adopted by the Massachusetts Bay Colony prohibited all freemen from being represented by a paid attorney:

> *Every man that findeth himselfe unfit to plead his own cause in any court shall have libertie to employ any man against whom the court doth not except, to help him, Provided he give him noe fee or reward for his pains.*

In the second half of the seventeenth century, England increasingly asserted its political authority over the colonies, with the result that the common law tradition—complete with courts, trial by jury, and inevitably, lawyers—began to take hold. As you might guess, once established, it didn't take these first American lawyers long to try to suppress competition. Indeed, in Virginia, as early as 1642, legislation prohibited pleading a case without license from the court. Apparently, however, the egalitarian, every-man-his-own-spokesman tradition was strong even in relatively affluent Virginia; lawyers who charged for their services were banned from Virginia courts in 1645. They were allowed back in 1647, licensed in 1656, again prohibited from receiving compensation in 1657 and finally again allowed to practice with pay, if licensed, in 1680. Similar legislative ambivalence toward lawyers was evident in other colonies.[1]

One hundred years later, by the middle 1700s, lawyers were in evidence in all colonial commercial centers. Their prominence reflected the fact that although respect for religion still ran strong in America, ecclesias-

---

[1] I am indebted to Charles Warren, *A History of the American Bar* (Boston, Little Brown) and Roscoe Pound, *The Lawyer From Antiquity to Modern Times* (West Publishing Co., 1953), for much of this historical background.

tical control of nearly all aspects of colonial life had receded before new waves of colonists more interested in secular than heavenly success.

In 1750s' America, there were as yet no law schools as we know them today. Young lawyers served an apprenticeship with an established practitioner and when they had learned enough legal ropes were questioned by a local judge (who had very likely received much the same sort of catch-as-catch-can training) and admitted to practice. When it came to legal knowledge, the gap between an attorney and the average educated citizen, never great in the cities, was almost non-existent in rural America. Even James Mason and Thomas Jefferson, authors of many of the important documents leading up to American independence, thought of themselves as farmers who had happened to study some law.

Many notable patriots of the Revolutionary War, including John Adams, Alexander Hamilton, Aaron Burr, and Patrick Henry, had legal training. Indeed, depending on how you define the term, about 40% of those who signed the Declaration of Independence were lawyers. Despite the prominence of these lawyer-patriots, the American Revolution marked the beginning of a long period of declining prestige for the legal profession. Much of the reason for this is traceable to the fact that the majority of the established bar sided with King George III rather than George Washington, and when the war was lost left the colonies for England or Canada. As Thomas Jefferson remarked in a letter to James Madison, "Our lawyers are all Tories."

It should also be noted that a number of patriots with legal training, such as Jefferson and Madison, were radical ideologists, interested in legal theory as it contributed to the creation of a new social order but not enamored with the traditional practice of law. Many patriot-lawyers saw the English legal system with its formal rules of pleading and courts of equity, as fundamentally undemocratic and opposed its wholesale adoption after independence.[2] In this context, the creation of a written constitution guaranteeing citizens certain fundamental rights can be seen as a reaction against the English common law system, which consisted of a collection of laws and court decisions that could be changed, willy-nilly, by Parliament and King.

Despite the fact that there were plenty of lawyers in late eighteenth century America, there is strong evidence that most citizens did not rely on them as a primary source of legal knowledge. Eldon Revare James, in *A List of Legal Treatises Printed in the British Colonies and the American States Before 1801,* found that:

> *In the hundred years between the publication in 1687 of William Penn's gleanings from Lord Coke and the issuance of the American editions of Buller's Nisi Pruis and Gilbert's Evidence in 1788, not a single book that could be called a treatise intended for the use of professional lawyers was published in the British Colonies and American States. All of the books within this period which by any strength of definition might be regarded as legal treatises were for the use of laymen.*

One of the most popular of these law books directed at the nonlawyer was entitled *Every Man His Own Lawyer,* which was in its ninth edition by 1784. Published in London, but widely distributed in the colonies, this was

---

[2]Much the same thing happened during Franklin Roosevelt's New Deal and again in the years of social and political ferment in the late 1960s, when a minority of radical lawyers broke with the legal establishment to argue that the legal system, itself, had become repressive.

a comprehensive guide to both civil and criminal law, divided into seven sections covering the following diverse topics:

I. Of Actions and Remedies, Writs, Process, Arrest and Bail.

II. Of Courts, Attorneys and Solicitors therein, Juries, Witnesses, Trials, Executions, etc.

III. Of Estates and Property in Lands and Goods, and how acquired; Ancestors, Heirs, Executors and Administrators.

IV. Of the Laws relating to Marriage, Bastardy, Infants, Idiots, Lunaticks.

V. Of the Liberty of the Subject, *Magna Charta,* and *Habeas Corpus* Act and other statutes.

VI. Of the King and his Prerogative, the Queen and Prince, Peers, Judge, Sheriffs, Coroners, Justices of Peace, Constables, etc.

Use of this book was sufficiently widespread that it appears in a historical vignette featuring the second President of the United States, John Adams. It seems that before the Revolution, Adams, then a Boston lawyer and farmer, campaigned against "pettifoggers" (a derogatory term for independent paralegals and even some marginal lawyers) and led lawyer efforts to suppress the practice of law by "untrained" persons. Adams, like so many members of the profession today, worried about the loss of fees when he remarked that "looking about me in the country I found the practice of law grasped into the hands of deputy sheriffs, pettifoggers and even constables who filled all the writs upon bonds, promissory notes and accounts, received the fees established for lawyers and stirred up many unnecessary suits."

Apparently to prove the extent of the problem presented by the proliferation of nonlawyer practitioners, Adams relates this story about a pettifogger and tavern keeper named Kibby: "In Kibby's barroom, in a little shelf within the bar, I spied two books. I asked what they were. He said, '*Every Man His Own Lawyer* and *Gilbert on Evidence.*' Upon this, I asked some questions of the people there and they told me that Kibby was a sort of lawyer among them; that he pleaded some of their cases before justices, arbitrators, etc."[3]

As the new nation took shape, lawyers, with a number of conspicuous exceptions, tended to be poorly trained if they were trained at all. Indeed, except in Eastern commercial centers such as Boston, where at times an apprentice lawyer was required to work in a law office for as long as seven years before gaining admission to the bar, an American lawyer was little more than a man who could read and write and who owned a fire-proof box. Still, in the last years of the eighteenth century and first decade of the nineteenth, urban lawyers were able to hold onto many of the pre-rogatives of their profession, thanks to laws in a number of states that established professional licensure requirements. This hard-won prominence was not to last, however. Along with a number of other "establishment" groups, from bankers to Freemasons, the legal profession did not fare well as America moved west. According to Daniel Lewolt, writing in *Americans for Legal Reform,* Vol. 5, No. 1 (Fall 1984):

> *The final blows were administered to legal professionals during the Andrew Jackson years. Frontiersmen, whose muddy boots had been allowed to trample White House rugs during Jackson's inaugural celebration, believed that justice should be popular and egalitarian and that experience was the best teacher. After 1830, even the requirement of reading [law] with a lawyer as a condition of practicing law was eliminated, and virtually anyone could practice law.*

Lewolt's view is supported by Leonard Tabachnik, who finds in *Professions for the People* (Schenkman Publishing, 1976) that:

> *The belief that professionalism advances science and protects the public from quackery was completely rejected by state legislators*

---

[3]See Roscoe Pound, *The Lawyer From Antiquity to Modern Times* (West Publishing, 1953).

during the Age of Jackson: ... By 1840, only 11 of 30 states main-tained regulations for admission to the Bar.

With the legal profession in retreat during these years, how did people settle disputes? The average citizen settled many on his own, without formal legal help, relying on one of several lay legal guides, such as Thomas Wooler's *Every Man His Own Attorney,* published in 1845.[4] In an interesting parallel to modern self-help law books, Wooler wrote in his introduction:

> *When attorneys are employed, they must be paid; and their charges are not always regulated whether by their abilities or their services to a client, but by their own desire to make as much as they can. This evil can only be remedied by making their clients well informed on common subjects, and able to see what course they are taking in matters of more intricacy.*

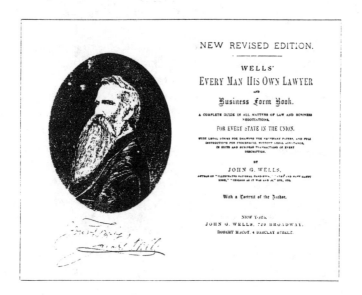

---

[4] I am indebted to a fascinating article by Mort Reber, entitled "A Return to Self-Reliance," which appeared in the *People's Law Review* (Nolo Press, 1980), for much of this information.

In addition, John Wells' *Every Man His Own Lawyer* (a different book than the one of the same title behind Kibby's bar that so annoyed John Adams and the members of the other, more powerful, bar), was sold as "a complete guide in all matters of law and business negotiations for every State of the Union, containing legal forms and full instructions for proceeding, without legal assistance, in suits and business transactions of every description." Apparently the popularity of this book was widespread. The author writes in the introduction to the 1879 edition:

> *The original edition of this work was prepared and presented to the public many years ago and was received with great favor, attaining a larger scale [hundreds of thousands according to Wells] it is believed, than any work published within its time."* [5]

One might imagine that during the middle years of the nineteenth century, when almost any American could practice law and there was widespread interest in and support for self-help alternatives to lawyers, that the intellectual quality of work done by the legal profession was low and individual lawyers were members of an endangered species. Just the opposite was true. As noted by Barlow Christensen in his article, "The Unauthorized Practice of Law: Do Good Fences Really Make Good Neighbors—Or Even Good Sense?" in the American Bar Foundation Research Journal (1980, No. 2):

> *The history of the profession during this period is paradoxical. On the one hand, this time is generally acknowledged to have been the great formative era in American law, during which were produced the great institutional cases that formed the foundation for the legal system as it exists today. It was also an era of great lawyers—Luther Martin, William Pinkney, William Wirt, Jeremiah*

---

[5] *Ed. Note:* Although you can't always trust authors when it comes to assessing the popularity of their work, I have been able to find Wells' book in a number of collections of nineteenth century books, giving some credence to his claims.

Mason, Daniel Webster, Rufus Choate.[6] In addition, it was an era of great judges, including James Kent, John Marshall and Joseph Storey. On the other hand, however, it was, as well, an era of decentralization and deprofessionalization of the profession, a return to the virtually unregulated profession of the colonial period.

B. The Lawyers Take Over

By now, you are probably asking, "So what happened?" How did lawyers develop their stranglehold over almost every aspect of making, administering and carrying out our laws? The full answer to this question is complex, a subject worthy of a book of its own. Here I can only suggest some of the historical forces that combined to produce the political climate conducive to letting lawyers assert a virtual monopoly over our legal system. These include:

- **Non-English Speaking Immigrants:** In the late nineteenth and early twentieth centuries, huge numbers of non-English speakers immigrated to the United States. These new Americans had a stiff language barrier to overcome. In addition, they had not been brought up in the comparatively democratic, always argumentative, every person on his feet having his say, tradition of the English protestant church and, to a lesser extent, English common law. In short, this influx of humanity created a huge group that was, at least initially, at a considerable disadvantage when dealing with the American legal system. In an age when unsuspecting new immigrants really were sold shares in the Brooklyn Bridge, many people were taken advantage of by all sorts of quick buck artists, including the legal variety. As a result, confidence that the average citizen could competently handle her own legal affairs began to erode, and calls for better professional standards began to be heard.

---

[6]For some reason Christensen leaves out Abraham Lincoln and Stephen Douglas.

- **Rapid Urbanization:** The decline of communities where people knew each other also had a negative effect on legal self-reliance. The New England town meeting style of local government, so much a part of rural small town America in the eighteenth and nineteenth centuries, didn't work in the urban America of the twentieth century. Similarly, the power of many nineteenth century spiritual and immigrant communities dedicated to solving disputes without the intervention of lawyers began to wane.[7] After the Civil War, New York, Chicago and a dozen more big, anonymous cities that had been growing for decades came to dominate the states in which they were located, and, through their newly-huge banks, insurance companies and stock exchanges, the commercial and political life of the nation. In the large cities, family and church ties had little power to bind people and help them settle their disputes outside of court. Increasingly, disputes now had to be dealt with in the public arena of the civil and criminal courts—the traditional spider webs of the professional bar—complete with their arcane language, obfuscatory procedures and long delays.

- **New Technology and Business Concentration:** Unprecedented development of new technologies in almost every industry, particularly energy, transport and telecommunications, changed the relationship of Americans to their employers, spurred the growth of big labor unions to protect workers' rights and required more and

---

[7]In the nineteenth century, all sorts of groups, including Shakers, Seventh Day Baptists, Swedenborgians, the Socialist followers of Owen and Fourier, Orthodox Jews, and literally hundreds of others, established communities that handled disputes without lawyers. Rather typically, John Noyes, the founder of the Oneida community, considered litigation "as the private equivalent of war," and it was said that the members of the Amana community in Iowa "live[d] in such perpetual peace that no lawyer is found in their midst." For more on the story of how a number of American communities tried to do without lawyers entirely, see Jerold Auerbach, *Justice Without Law: Resolving Disputes Without Lawyers,* Oxford University Press (1983).

better trained lawyers to invent, administer (and all too often manipulate) the business and legal infrastructure that held it all together. For example, within the relatively few years between the end of the Civil War and the beginning of the first World War, modest factories clustered mostly in areas with access to water and power gave way to institutions such as Standard Oil, the Ford Motor Company, General Electric, railroads that spanned half a continent, and yes, even the Coca Cola Company. In this brave new corporate world, disputes that would have been settled face to face in simpler times were now routinely turned over to big city law firms.

- **The Closing of the Frontier:** In the last decade of the nineteenth century, America ran out of free farm and range land. No longer could the average person realistically hope to pack up the wagon, gather the kids, hitch up old Dobbin and head west to homestead a free 160 acres. This is important because the American tradition of always moving west had helped prevent establishment groups, including lawyers, from dominating American political and legal institutions. No sooner did one city gain economic clout and its professionals start building themselves mansions on the hill, than the center of gravity of the entire country lurched west. When America ran out of open land, lawyers and other establishment figures, including bankers, insurance agents, physicians, and brokers, had a chance to catch up with western migration for the first time in almost 300 years. Before long, they were able to control the political and economic life of the new states, just as they already did in the old, and the winds of legal change which had usually blown from the west were substantially stilled.

- **Consumer Reform:** The early consumer movement, which fought for reasonable standards of product safety, honest and accountable business practices and opposed price-fixing and other monopolistic practices, paradoxically played an important role in the increase in organized lawyerdom's power. The reformers (often called "muckrakers"), inspired by authors like Upton Sinclair (*The Jungle*) and

Lincoln Steffens (*The Shame of the Cities*), broke with the common law tradition of *caveat emptor* ("let the buyer beware") to argue that in an industrial society dominated by large scale capitalism the government must intervene in the commercial life of the nation to see that the ordinary citizen has a reasonable opportunity to avoid cynical exploitation by big business. This consumer crusade resulted in much of the progressive legislation adopted during the presidencies of Theodore Roosevelt and Woodrow Wilson, and laid the foundation for later reforms that have resulted in all sorts of good things, from purer food to safer workplaces. But it often produced negative results as it related to traditional professional groups such as lawyers and doctors. These "professionals" used the consumer reform movement to sell the nation on the rationale of "professional responsibility" and to justify organizing themselves into publicly-sanctioned monopolies. For example, when it came to training new lawyers, the legal profession now emphasized formal schooling over the traditional apprenticeship method, and pushed required written examinations as an alternative to being admitted to practice on the recommendation of a practitioner or judge.

All of these changes quickly worked to the pecuniary benefit of American lawyers. Already by the turn of the century, lawyers had gained substantially in wealth, power and community standing. Among the presidents elected between 1890 and 1932, Cleveland, Harrison, McKinley, Taft, Coolidge, Harding[8], and Franklin Roosevelt were members of the bar, and Supreme Court justices Oliver Wendell Holmes and Louis Brandeis were among the most respected men in America. Even Teddy Roosevelt spent a year at Columbia law school before concluding that the practice of law was too boring.

It was particularly remarkable how quickly lawyers were able to use the new educational and certification requirements to eliminate nonlawyer

---

[8]Warren Harding was as unsuccessful as a lawyer as he was as president, quitting the profession early on to go into the newspaper business.

competition. As late as 1890, less than half of the states and territories had meaningful educational requirements for lawyers. But by 1915, only 13 states and one of the remaining territories allowed admission to law practice without attending law school. By 1940, all states effectively required professional study to be a lawyer.[9] Perhaps because it was so easy for organized lawyerdom to sell the American public on the image of an educated professional bar dedicated to high standards of integrity and service, lawyers had little incentive to actually back up this image with substantive consumer protection. For example, once new lawyers passed a general knowledge examination that had little to do with the day-to-day work of a practicing lawyer, there were absolutely no requirements for continuing skills testing or education. And legal consumers who were cheated or overcharged by the professional incompetence of individual lawyers, were then, as now, provided with little meaningful recourse.

It wasn't until the depression of the 1930s that lawyers really had to defend their newly-minted monopoly. Bad economic times hit the legal profession particularly hard, striking as they did at the roots of its new power base as the protector of corporate America. Suddenly, from skyscraper to street corner, there were too many lawyers chasing too few clients—at least those who could pay their bills. The result might have been a legal profession that made a concerted effort to try to make good cheap legal help available to millions of newly poor Americans. In fact, despite lip service to helping widows and orphans, organized lawyerdom did just the opposite, banding together as never before to fix prices by use of a number of anti-competitive devices. These included, most prominently, bar association-mandated minimum fees, "treaties" with other professions, including bankers, accountants and real estate brokers, designed to respect each other's service monopolies, and a concerted campaign to eliminate all nonlawyer competition.

---

[9]Willard Hurst, *The Growth of American Law: The Law Makers* (Little Brown & Co., 1950).

Just as the depression caused a lot of people to consider handling their own legal work, or to seek help from more reasonably-priced non-lawyer practitioners, the bar adopted a surprisingly militant campaign to rid the nation of the last vestiges of the self-help law movement that had survived from the nineteenth century.[10] If you doubt the accuracy of this assertion, consider that the first American Bar Association committee ever to deal specifically with unauthorized practice was formed in 1930, and by 1938, over 400 state and local bar associations had formed similar committees.

The great increase in interest in unauthorized practice by bar associations led naturally to an increase in the number of nonlawyers who were prosecuted. As noted by Deborah Rhode in her fascinating 1981 study of unauthorized practice published in the Stanford Law Review,[11] a 1937 survey of reported unauthorized practice cases devoted 94 pages to all pre-1930 decisions and 619 pages to unauthorized practice suits decided between 1930 and 1937. Much of the reason for this increase in enforcement was the passage of new unauthorized practice statutes with tougher penalties. Most of this new legislation was orchestrated by the newly-organized local and state bar unauthorized practice committees, all of which claimed their activities were designed not to feather the nest of the legal profession but to protect the public from unqualified and incompetent law practitioners. Interestingly, Deborah Rhode's in-depth study finds almost no evidence that the public ever asked for, or needs, this "protection."

---

[10]The American Bar Association also lead a fifty-state effort to close down unaccredited mostly night law schools which, in the previous several decades, had produced the majority of American lawyers. The idea was frankly to limit the supply of new lawyers in an effort to push up legal fees. For the fascinating story of the suppression of America's unaccredited law schools, see Richard Abel's *American Lawyers* (Oxford University Press, 1989).

[11]Rhode, "Policing the Professional Monopoly: A Constitutional and Empirical Analysis of Unauthorized Practice Prohibitions," 34 Stan. L. Rev. 1 (1981).

When good economic times returned after the Second World War, the legal profession suddenly found that there weren't enough lawyers to go around. This isn't surprising when you realize that relatively few lawyers were trained during the depression. This shortage of lawyers, coinciding as it did with the unprecedented expansion and prosperity of the American middle class, resulted in an economic golden age for lawyers. Or, put simply, in the 1950s it was a snap to make big bucks in the law business. And just in case any nonlawyers were tempted to try to participate in this bonanza, the tough unauthorized practice statutes passed in the 1930s were still on the books to keep out interlopers.

In fairness, it should be noted that during the Eisenhower years, the average American's new-found admiration for "professionalization" also contributed to the maintenance of organized lawyerdom's monopoly. In the prosperous 1950s, it seemed as if everyone wanted their kids to be lawyers, doctors or orthodontists (as popular as law school was, learning to straighten middle class children's teeth was surely the growth profession of the decade). Against this background, it wasn't hard for the legal profession to convince most people that "a person who represents himself has a fool for a client."

C. The Modern Movement Away From Lawyers

Paradoxically, just as the legal profession reached the zenith of its power in the early 1960s, the first hints of its present vulnerability were becoming apparent. In its effort to clamp down on potential competitors, organized lawyerdom acted as if it, and it alone, was equipped to serve the legal needs of the broad American public. Although many lawyers believed it (and despite two generation's accumulation of evidence to the contrary, a few still do), this was far from true. Lawyers had gained status and wealth serving corporate America, the growing bureaucracy of federal and state governments, and, to a lesser extent, individuals in upper income brackets. Except for a few profitable (to lawyers), but very limited, legal areas, such as personal injury litigation and probate, the legal profession barely dealt with the average American of 1965.

That the majority of middle-class Americans were underserved by the legal profession (and that blue collar and ethnic Americans weren't served at all) became embarrassingly obvious in the late-1960s. This widespread recognition was triggered in part by the Johnson administration's sponsorship of federally-funded legal services for the poor (legal aid), the first ever coordinated delivery of legal help nationwide. Everyone who worked in a legal services office in those years (and increasingly reporters who covered the war on poverty) was struck by an incredible fact—despite the bargain basement ambience of the largely ghetto-based offices, each had to employ a number of people who did nothing but turn away middle-class Americans not poor enough to qualify for legal aid, but not affluent enough to retain a lawyer under the traditional fee for services model. In short, when middle class Americans lined up on the streets of Watts, Bedford-Stuyvesant, and the South Side of Chicago (places they had gone previously only after rolling up the windows and locking the doors of their Pontiacs) to wait in line to talk to a lawyer, the fiction that American lawyers served the average American was revealed to be just that.

But it wasn't only the discovery that lawyers had priced their services out of the financial reach of most Americans that resulted in the profession's great fall in the public regard. Widespread latent dissatisfaction with the legal profession also surfaced during the investigation of the Watergate break-in in 1973. Many, if not most, of the people accused of illegal conduct—including Dean, Erlichmann, Colson, Chapin, Segretti, Mitchell, and Nixon himself, were lawyers. Instead of admitting they were wrong, these men first told a series of whopping lies and then, even after they were forced to admit their culpability, tried to wriggle off the hook on one or another legal technicality. In short, almost every American with a TV set learned that being a lawyer had little to do with the bar association's image of a profession dedicated to the pursuit of truth and justice. Woody Guthrie, it seemed, had been right all along when he sang about a profession which did its robbing not with a six-gun but a fountain pen.

After Watergate, most Americans understood that a majority of lawyers were out to make a pile of money fast, and if ignoring the rules they were supposed to respect helped them achieve their goal quicker, so be it. And when it came right down to it, why should this be shocking? Wasn't this trend of "life in the fast lane," "damn the rights of others," "winning is everything" approach equally fashionable among stock brokers, doctors, football coaches, morticians, bankers, car salespeople and others? Yes, but since these other groups hadn't tried so hard to put their occupation on a pedestal, they were less vulnerable to attack.

Not only did the public, as a whole, lose respect for the legal profession, some individuals with legal questions and problems began to look for ways to solve them without lawyers. One consequence was that America began to rediscover its strong historical tradition of legal self help. By the middle 1970s, Norman Dacey's *How To Avoid Probate* and Charles Sherman's *How To Do Your Own Divorce in California* were best sellers. In California, Nolo Press had been established, and had published over 20 successful self-help law books. And of particular interest to readers of this book, non-lawyer (independent paralegal) typing services began to offer legal form preparation services directly to the public.

Specifically, in California, the Wave Project, which was staffed by dropped-out teachers, social workers, legal secretaries and business people, began advertising that it would type forms for people who wanted to do their own divorces for a fee of $50-$75. And in Florida, Rosemary Furman, a former court clerk disgusted with the money-grubbing hypocrisy she found in the courthouse, did much the same thing (see the interview with Rosemary Furman in the Appendix for details). The Wave Project, which was begun by Ed Sherman and myself in 1972, operated about 20 independent paralegal legal form preparation offices throughout California. Many of these businesses still exist. Several are run by their original owners, although they have dropped the Wave Project name in favor of the more prosaic California Divorce Center.

Soon after the Wave Project began to list its services in the classified sections of newspapers, organized lawyerdom took notice. As you can probably imagine, the bar's reaction wasn't to applaud. Organized lawyerdom attacked the Wave Project in two principal ways. The first involved local bar associations or judges complaining to county district attorneys that the nonlawyer proprietors of the Wave Project offices were guilty of the crime of practicing law without a license. As a result, almost every Wave Project office was confronted by a hostile deputy district attorney. In a number of counties, the district attorney's office went so far as to send an investigator with a hidden recording device into the office and try to trick the independent paralegal operator into giving what they defined as "legal advice." (See Jolene Jacobs' interview in the Appendix.) Assuming the IP did say something a deputy D.A. thought amounted to the practice of law, the visit would normally be followed by a citation letter (occasionally an immediate arrest was made) ordering the IP to present herself at the D.A.'s office at a certain date and time. The D.A. would then usually inform the independent paralegal that she could be prosecuted for the crime of practicing law without a license unless she shut down her business. (See Chapter 2 for details of how this happens.)

Most independent paralegals refused to close down. Several, including Bob Mission (see interview in the Appendix), were arrested and formally charged with unauthorized practice. A number of IPs who were cited but not prosecuted eventually ended up working out a compromise with the district attorney under which they promised to restrict the content of advertisements or otherwise limit the scope of their businesses in exchange for being allowed to continue operating. Of the formal prosecutions, some were dropped on the basis of the sort of settlement just mentioned, several resulted in victory for the independent paralegal, and a number, perhaps the majority, ended when the independent paralegal became so exhausted and/or scared that he agreed to close up shop.

The second way organized lawyerdom attacked the Wave Project focused on several of the people who founded or coordinated it. For example, Charles Sherman, whose *How To Do Your Own Divorce in California* launched the self-help law movement on the west coast, was dragged through a two-year battle during which the bar association tried to seize his license to practice law based on his Wave Project activities. (The actual charges included advertising legal services and aiding and abetting the unlicensed practice of law.) Phyllis Eliasberg, who took over coordination of the Wave Project from Ed Sherman and myself in 1974, faced similar charges.

Sherman's license was eventually ordered suspended, but oddly, at the last moment the California Bar backtracked and the suspension never took effect. Part of the reason for this was undoubtedly the U.S. Supreme Court's decision in *Bates v. State Bar of Arizona,* 433 U.S. 350 (1977), which made attorney advertising legal. Probably of as much importance, however, was the fact that organized lawyerdom was shocked by the bad publicity they were generating for themselves by prosecuting Sherman and Eliasberg. By deciding to stop harassing Sherman, the California Bar showed more savvy than did the Florida Bar, which persisted in prosecuting Rosemary Furman for UPL, even after this resulted in CBS's "60 Minutes" featuring her as a national folk heroine for typing $50 divorces.

By the early 1980s, about one-hundred independent paralegals existed in Florida, California and several other western states. In addition to divorce, those pioneers began preparing legal forms for other problems, including bankruptcy, step-parent adoption, and change of name. As more form preparation services were added, many IPs began to prosper. By 1990, California had close to one thousand IPs, many of whom were loosely organized into a statewide association, the California Association of Independent Paralegals. Although the movement was slower to catch on in other parts of the country, by 1990, the Sonoma, California-based National Association for Independent Paralegals now reports members in all 50 states.

 See Chapter 15 for a brief history of recent events in California and Florida.

Chapter 2

The Law

his chapter is concerned with the laws, court rules, and powers claimed by bar associations that, taken together, define the unauthorized practice of law. Mastering this information is crucial to your success as an independent paraiegal because the unauthorized practice laws are organized lawyerdom's principal way to attack nonlawyers who challenge its monopoly power to deliver legal services. As we go through this chapter, it's important to keep in mind the general truth that it's one thing to know what any law says and quite another to understand what the words mean in the real world. Especially in the context of regulations governing the unauthorized practice of law, which are incredibly vague, it is necessary to understand the nuances of both community and law enforcement attitudes in your city and state.

 In Chapter 3, I discuss in detail what an independent paralegal can do to avoid charges of unauthorized practice of law. Basically, as an IP, you should do three things: tell the world you are not a lawyer, give your customers the information they need to make their own decisions and limit yourself to legal form preparation.

A. Introduction to the Concept of Unauthorized Practice of Law (UPL)

What exactly is the practice of law and how can you avoid doing it? Unfortunately, the term "practice of law" is nowhere clearly and unambiguously defined. Courts in many states prescribe who can deliver legal services under their inherent power to regulate law practice. Unfortunately, the reasoning in their decisions tends to be circular: only lawyers can practice law. Statutes that make unauthorized practice a crime in the majority of states are no more helpful, defining the practice of law as "what lawyers do" or "what lawyers are trained to do," terms which are impossible to interpret by any meaningful objective standard.

But all hope is not lost. Although you probably can't get much help from definitions of the practice of law, you may be able to get some guidance from finding out what is not considered to be the practice of law. Probably the best place to look is at the court decisions of your own state, the rules that regulate your state's bar, and any pronouncements on the subject issued by your state's supreme court.[1] For example, in the aftermath of the Rosemary Furman affair, the Florida Supreme Court amended the Rules Regulating the Florida bar to read:

> *It shall not constitute the unlicensed practice of law for nonlawyers to engage in limited oral communications to assist individuals in the completion of legal forms approved by the Supreme Court of Florida. Oral communications by nonlawyers are restricted to those communications reasonably necessary to elicit factual information to complete the form(s) and inform the individual how to file such form(s)."*

Since then, the Florida Supreme Court has gone on to approve hundreds of pages of legal forms, thus opening wide the window for Florida independent paralegals to help consumers prepare these forms, free of worry that they will be charged with UPL.[2]

Let's take a look at some recent case decisions that will give you a sense of the approaches different state courts have taken in deciding what constitutes UPL. In *The People v. Landlords Professional Services,*[3] a California case involving an eviction service that helped people prepare and file unlawful detainer actions, the court, applying a statute that made UPL a crime, found that the service was engaged in the unauthorized practice of law because:

---

[1] You will find tips for doing legal research throughout this chapter. For a thorough guide, see *Elias, Legal Research: How to Find and Understand the Law* (Nolo Press). Nolo also publishes a 2-1/2 hour videotape, entitled *Legal Research Made Easy: A Roadmap Through the Law Library Maze,* by Bob Berring.

[2] In another example, a Nevada court said that stenographic and scrivener services that provided their customers with simple and straightforward kits so that the customers could make self-informed decisions would not be considered UPL. *State Bar of Nevada v. Johnson* (No. CV89-5814, Nev. 2nd Dist. Ct., April 12, 1990).

[3] 215 Cal.App.3d 1599 (4th Dist.,1989).

1. The advertisement suggested that the eviction service did more than simply provide clerical assistance. The ad implied that the service actually accomplished evictions.

2. "Call and talk to us" on the ad and "counselor" on the business card were general invitations for discussion and suggested that the service sells expertise.

3. The service provided specific information and advice directed to the client's personal problems and concerns.

The court found that the service provided by the IP business would not amount to the "practice of law" as long as the service was "merely clerical," because:

- It is not UPL to make forms available for clients' use.

- It is not UPL to fill in forms and file and serve them at the specific direction of the client.

- It is not UPL to give a client a detailed manual containing specific advice.

- It is not UPL as long as the service doesn't personally advise the client with regard to her particular case.

An opinion written by the Washington Supreme Court illustrates just how unpredictable application of UPL regulations to any specific situation can be.[4] Here the court invoked its own inherent power to regulate the practice of law to find that the preparation of certain real estate forms necessary to buy and sell houses, which had, in the past, always been prepared by lawyers, could now be drawn up by nonlawyers. In allowing nonlawyer involvement in real estate transactions, the court relied on the public's interest in freedom of choice, convenience and the lower costs provided by nonlawyers. In doing so, the court specifically ruled that:

---

[4] *Cultum v. Heritage House Realtors, Inc.*, 103 Wash. 2d 623 (1985).

There are sound and practical reasons why some activities that fall within the broad definition of the "practice of law" should not be unauthorized simply because they are done by laypersons.

B. Criminal Penalties for Unauthorized Practice

More than two-thirds of the states have criminal statutes that make unauthorized practice a misdemeanor, which typically means that fines are limited to about $1,000, and jail time to one year or less in a county correctional facility. For example, in California, the UPL statute reads like this:

Any person advertising or holding himself or herself out as practicing or entitled to practice or otherwise practicing law who is not an active member of the State bar is guilty of a misdemeanor."

In states where UPL is a crime, public prosecutors play a key role in UPL enforcement. It's a deputy district or state attorney who first decides if a particular independent paralegal is committing unauthorized practice and should either be prosecuted or pursued in a civil action. (See Section D, below, for more on enforcement of UPL laws.)

HOW TO LOOK UP YOUR STATE'S UPL STATUTE

Obviously, it's important to find out how courts have defined the unauthorized practice of law in your state. Go to a large public library or, better yet, a law library (often found at county court houses or publicly-funded law schools). Find the book containing your state's laws (often referred to as statute books or code books). If possible, use the "annotated" version of your legal code, which contains not only the laws themselves but also useful information about relevant court cases, articles and other secondary sources that discuss each law. Locate the volume entitled General Index and look up the Unauthorized Practice of Law, which will refer you to the appropriate code and section.

Once you have found and read the law in the hardbound volume, check the same statute number in the inserted "pocket part" (just inside the back cover). This will contain any changes passed by your state's legislature from the time the hardbound book was published up to about six months to one year ago. If your legislature has met since then, ask a law librarian to show you how to check to see if there have been even more current changes.

C. Judicial Penalties for Unauthorized Practice—the Inherent Powers Doctrine

Courts in most states assert the power to define and regulate the practice of law. In legal parlance, this is often referred to as the "inherent powers doctrine."[5] Courts claim this power comes from their authority to regulate courts, and by extension lawyers, as officers of the court. (See "How Powerful are a Court's Inherent Powers," in this chapter.) The inherent powers

---

[5]For a more in-depth discussion, see Wolfram "Lawyer Turf and Lawyer Regulation—The Role of the Inherent-Powers Doctrine", University of Arkansas at Little Rock Law Journal, Volume 12, Number 1 (1989-90).

doctrine is often used by courts to limit the power of the legislature to regulate the practice of law. For example, if a state legislature passes a law or regulation that affects lawyers or the practice of law, the state supreme court has the power to find it unconstitutional because it invades the exclusive province of the judiciary. They almost never do, as long as the law strictly limits what nonlawyers can do. Courts are far more likely to overrule legislation when they believe it is too liberal in allowing nonlawyers to perform legal tasks. In the following sections, we will review some court decisions that will give you an idea of how the inherent powers doctrine is applied and how it might be relevant to you as an IP.

HOW POWERFUL ARE A COURT'S INHERENT POWERS?

The concept of inherent powers goes back hundreds of years to a time when most legal matters were brought before courts. Judges, who were assumed to have broad "inherent" powers over their own courts, didn't have to expand this doctrine much to regulate the conduct of lawyers and the practice of law. Today the legal system bears little resemblance to that of the 18th century. For one thing, the majority of legal matters never get near a court. Nevertheless, lawyers and judges, eager to protect their historical monopoly, stretch the doctrine of inherent judicial power far beyond its historical meaning to justify judicial regulation of every aspect of our legal system, including even the activities of independent paralegal form preparers. In the long run, this attempt to inflate the inherent powers doctrine out of all reasonable recognition will probably fail; in the short run, it could be dangerous to your livelihood.

1. Court Regulation of Independent Paralegals Who Appear Before State Administrative Hearings

Administrative agencies are created by statute and basically exist to facilitate some legislative purpose, such as administering health, labor or retirement programs. Many of these agencies have mechanisms to hear appear before it. And if this isn't confusing enough, consider that courts in some states acquiesce to this so-called unauthorized practice while others do not. With this in mind, let's look at a few cases.

In a decision by the Florida Supreme Court, the court found that the preparation of documents and presentation of non-contested juvenile dependency cases by lay counselors was unauthorized practice.[6] The court said if advice involved important rights and required knowledge of law greater than that of the average citizen, it constituted unauthorized practice. Apparently applying this rule, the Florida Supreme Court has also stated that preparing a living trust constitutes unauthorized practice.[7] But in a more positive move, the Florida Supreme Court has also recently used the inherent powers doctrine to approve the use of many divorce and landlord-tenant forms by nonlawyers free from fear of UPL charges. (See Chapter 15, Section B.)

In Rhode Island, the supreme court considered two statutes that allowed nonlawyers to represent people in informal hearings within the Department of Worker's Compensation.[8] The purpose of these nonlawyer "employee assistants" was to give help and advice to employees under the Workers' Compensation Act. The court concluded that although the activities subject to the statutes could be considered the practice of law, they were okay because any definition of the practice of law must be responsive to the public interest. The court explicitly states that the

---

[6] *Florida Bar Re: Advisory Opinion HRS Nonlawyer Counselor,* 547 So.2d 909 (1989).

[7] *The Florida Bar Re: Advisory Opinion—Nonlawyer Preparation of Living Trusts,* Case No. 78,358. However, in this opinion, the Florida Court allowed nonlawyers to gather necessary information to prepare a living trust. This may allow IPs to continue to do form typing for customers who have obtained their own forms and instructions and simply want the IP to assemble them.

[8] *Unauthorized Practice of Law Committee v. State of Rhode Island, Department of Workers' Compensation,* 543 A.2d 662 (1988).

legislature may aid the court's inherent power to define the practice of law and determine who may practice, but the legislature must abide by the court's standard. The court points out that it has not interfered with a number of legislative acts which, in effect, carved out exceptions to the practice of law because they constituted a response to a public need.

In short, while theoretically the Rhode Island legislature's power to regulate state administrative proceedings is second to the courts, in practice, the court will not upset the legislature's decision if it agrees with the public policy being advanced. This approach, which leaves the final decision up to the courts, is the prevailing approach in the United States,[8] according to legal commentator Gregory T. Stevens.[9]

Because of the differences between what a state law or agency regulation says and what actually happens, it is not always easy to know whether an independent paralegal can appear before a particular agency on behalf of a claimant or not. Probably the best approach is to simply call any agency you are interested in and ask.

2. Federal Administrative Agency Hearings

The federal system gives exclusive regulatory control of federal agencies to Congress. The Administrative Procedure Act authorizes federal agencies to allow nonlawyers to practice before them without regard to whether the activities would be unauthorized practice in the state where the agency proceeding occurs. This does not mean that all federal agencies allow nonlawyers to do this, only that each agency has the power to allow nonlawyer representation if it so chooses. According to one U.S. Supreme Court decision, states cannot restrict the right of any person to perform a

---

[8]"The Proper Scope of Nonlawyer Representation in State Administrative Proceedings: A State Specific Balancing Approach," 43 Vand. L. Rev. 245 (January 1990).

[9]For example, see *UPL Comm. v. Employers Unity, Inc.* 716 P.2d 460 (Colo. 1986); *UPL Comm. v. State Dept. of Workers Comp.*, 543 A.2d 662 (RI 1988).

function that falls within the scope of federal authority.[10] However, to guarantee the right of nonlawyers to appear, the agency in question must explicitly allow nonlawyer representation. If it fails to do so, states can prohibit UPL in a federal agency proceeding.

For example, in Florida, the state bar's committee on the unauthorized practice of law wanted the court to find that certain nonlawyer involvement in preparing pension plans was unauthorized practice.[11] In this instance, federal statutes and regulations authorized nonlawyers to practice before federal agencies. The Florida Supreme Court ruled that because the federal agency granted such authority, the states could not use their own definition of UPL to limit it, and thus, the court did not find unauthorized practice in this instance.

a. Bankruptcy Court— Who Regulates Unauthorized Practice?

There is no clear federal law or regulation dealing with whether or not nonlawyers can appear before a federal bankruptcy court or prepare paperwork for consumers who wish to represent themselves. In the absence of a federal law on the subject, state unauthorized practice laws and rules of court apply. This means a state prosecutor or court can go after independent paralegals who provide customers with legal advice in the bankruptcy field.

What about the inherent power of federal bankruptcy court judges to regulate unauthorized practice in their own courts? This doctrine is alive and well, and many federal bankruptcy judges assert it. Does this mean state UPL authorities are likely to voluntarily defer to the local federal bankruptcy judge to regulate UPL in its jurisdiction? Yes, and as a practical

---

[10] *Sperry v. U.S., 373 U.S. 379 (1963).*

[11] *The Florida Bar Re: Advisory Opinion—Nonlawyer Preparation of Pension Plans,* No. 74, 479 (1990).

matter, they often do. Most bankruptcy enforcement is carried out by United States Bankruptcy judges.[12]

 In Chapter 3, I discuss how an independent paralegal can run a bankruptcy typing service in a way that largely avoids the risk of being found guilty of the unauthorized practice of law. I discuss the regulation of fees charged by independent paralegals for preparing bankruptcy forms in Chapter 9.

D. Enforcement of Unauthorized Practice Rules

Is there a way to predict whether a UPL action is likely in a particular area? Not with any accuracy. This is because most UPL proceedings, civil and criminal, are triggered by an individual lawyer, bar association or judge, often because the IP is perceived to be infringing on what many lawyers believe is their exclusive domain. In some states, bar associations are authorized to bring court UPL actions directly against IPs. Often, the bar is seeks an injunction to prohibit all or some activities of the paralegal service. Because of the uncertain definition of "practicing law," some courts will provide guidelines that the IP is directed to follow, and as long as the IP agrees to do this, he or she will usually be able to remain in business. Bar associations may also refer cases to the state or local prosecutor to demand that UPL charges be filed against a particular IP. A prosecutor or court may also initiate UPL proceedings on their own.

What happens if you do run afoul of the enforcement division of your state supreme court, or a bar association committee that threatens to turn

---

[12]Two recent Bankruptcy Court decisions, both finding an IP guilty of UPL, are *In re Webster et al v. Larson,* 120 Bankr. 111 (1990) and *In re Bachman* (Case No. 88-04588—Southern District of Florida).

you into a court or to the local prosecutor? Deborah Rhode, in her *Stanford Law Review* study,[13] finds that normally no formal action is taken. Typically, what happens is this:

1. The bar association or court contacts the independent paralegal—often by letter, but sometimes personally—and asks her to cease what it considers the offending conduct.

2. If the IP doesn't comply, the bar may subpoena her to appear before a bar association hearing, at which point she is likely to be formally told to stop preparing forms for nonlawyers. This sort of intimidation causes many people to close down.

But what happens if the independent paralegal politely but firmly insists on her constitutional right to continue helping nonlawyers do their own legal paperwork? Depending on the make-up of the particular bar committee or the attitude of the state supreme court, and on the law of the particular state, the bar association or court may:

1. Do nothing.

2. Initiate its own civil court proceeding to try to put the independent paralegal out of business. As touched on earlier, this generally takes the form of an action in a trial court to enjoin the IP from engaging in whatever activity organized lawyerdom alleges constitutes the unauthorized practice of law. If a resulting injunction is violated, the IP is typically held in contempt of court and jailed or fined, or both. (This is basically what happened to Rosemary Furman in Florida.)

---

[13]Rhode, "Policing the Professional Monopoly: A Constitutional and Empirical Analysis of Unauthorized Practice Prohibitions," 34 Stanford Law Rev. 1 (1981). Although this study is dated, it is the only one of its kind that is currently available. See also Rhode, "The Delivery of Legal Services by Nonlawyers," Georgetown Journal of Legal Ethics, Vol. 4:209 (1990).

3. In the approximately 36 states where UPL is a crime, the matter may potentially be referred to a criminal prosecutor. Prosecutors, who are normally overloaded with higher profile criminal cases, such as those involving drugs and violence, will generally only prosecute a UPL case when they think they have a good chance of winning. Practically, this means that they most often go after nonlawyers who either incompetently practice law or fraudulently misrepresent their skills or status, as when an unlicensed person claims to be a lawyer. In either of these situations, the prosecutor can legitimately claim that he is putting out of business someone who is a danger to the public.

To see how a typical UPL complaint might be handled, let's take a fairly typical example. Suppose a prosecutor is told by a bar associate that Mary Smith, a nonlawyer, prepared divorce forms for Leroy Jackson. First, acting as a public stenographer is not a crime anyplace. At the very least, the prosecutor would have to establish that Smith transferred some legal expertise to Jackson (remember that states differ as to amount and types of legal information that must be transferred to constitute UPL). Assuming the prosecutor believed that Smith transferred enough legal expertise or advise to Jackson to constitute UPL, the prosecutor would next likely look to see if Smith's advice was inaccurate or resulted in any harm. Assuming this was not the case, and Jackson was pleased with Smith's service, the prosecutor would be faced with trying to convict a person who is providing a good service at a reasonable price. Assuming Smith requests a jury trial, as she is almost sure to do, this sort of case can be difficult for the prosecutor to win.

Faced with this sort of situation, many prosecutors are likely to decide to wait until they have a stronger case, one where an independent paralegal misrepresented her credentials or services, or where her legal advice resulted in customer harm. Smith will probably not be prosecuted and her file will become inactive. Sometimes, however, the prosecutor may try to work a case up a bit, especially if the complaint has come from lawyers or judges who have political clout. If the prosecutor does decide to pursue Smith further, the next step will probably be to anonymously contact her typing service and request legal information. Often this means an investigator posing as a customer, and almost certainly carrying a concealed tape recorder, will ask Smith a number of broad questions designed to get her to give what the District Attorney's office considers to be legal advice.

 As we discuss in Chapter 3, the best way for an independent paralegal who fears this sort of investigation to protect herself is to consistently avoid answering broad customer questions about substantive law. To stay out of legal hot water, the independent paralegal wants to present herself as a typing service and no more.[14]

Assuming a prosecutor decides to continue working up a UPL case against Smith, the next step, short of actually prosecuting, is usually to request a meeting. Normally, it happens something like this. Smith receives a letter (often called a "citation" or "cite" letter in the trade) asking her to show up at the prosecutor's office on a certain date to meet with deputy district attorney so-and-so to discuss the allegation that she has engaged in illegal activities—to wit, practicing law without a license. The first thing Smith or any other IP should know about this sort of letter is that it is often part of a campaign to intimidate the IP into giving up her business, not the first step in a formal prosecution. A prosecutor who has already decided to prosecute an IP will probably not bother to write a cite letter.

The second thing Smith should know about the citation letter process is that even though she is not required to show up, it's wise to do so.

---

[14]I discuss a number of techniques to avoid giving what organized lawyerdom considers to be legal advice throughout this book. An obvious problem in this area, however, is that some lawyers define unauthorized practice so broadly that it includes almost any interaction between an independent paralegal and the public where money changes hands but doesn't end up in a lawyer's pockets. As I discuss later in this chapter, many, if not most, of organized lawyerdom's efforts to characterize law practice so expansively have been rejected by courts.

When a district attorney is unsure of her legal ground (which is often the case if she sends a cite letter), she looks for a reason to either pursue a formal action or forget the matter. Smith's failure to show up may well be reason enough for her to decide to get tough. Of course, Smith is entitled, but not required, to have a lawyer present at any conference with law enforcement personnel.

At the meeting, a deputy district attorney may try to scare Smith into voluntarily abandoning her business. In the past, many independent para-legals have done just that, concluding that even though they haven't done anything illegal, they don't have the resources to "fight city hall." Assuming Smith was operating a quality business and following the advice contained in this book on how to empower her customers without engaging in UPL, there is no reason for her to be intimidated into quitting. And surely, she will be comforted to know that most people who have refused to close down haven't, in fact, been prosecuted. (See Virginia Simons' and Jolene Jacobs' interviews in the Appendix.)

What's Smith's best alternative strategy to outright capitulation? First, she should try to get the prosecutor to talk about the issues she believes justify a prosecution. In this context, Smith should try to get the deputy prosecutor to agree that it's legal for nonlawyers to use self-help law books to carry out legal tasks. Next, Smith should try to get her to con-cede that the act of typing forms for lay people doesn't constitute the prac-tice of law. Finally, Smith should see if the prosecutor will agree that typing forms following a customer's instructions gleaned from a self-help law book does not constitute unauthorized practice. Since this is now the legal view of many state courts (see Section E, below), it shouldn't be dif-ficult, especially if Smith does some legal research and come to the meeting armed with her state's court decisions.

Assuming Smith can get a prosecutor to concede that typing legal forms following the instructions of nonlawyers is not in and of itself ille-gal, she has laid the groundwork for a compromise that will allow her to continue her business without further hassle. Why do I say this? Because once the prosecutor concedes that her core form typing activity is not illegal, her next step should be to cooperate with the prosecutor so that it's clear her future activities will be limited to this type of operation. In short, unless the prosecutor's requests are so outrageous that they will amount to Smith going out of business, she will be wise to try to find some common ground on which to compromise, even if she feels she is giving up important legal rights. The reason for this is that a compromise recognizes Smith's right to exist. It gets the prosecutor off her back and allows her crucial time to make the sort of alliances in the community that will make it difficult to prosecute her in the future. Later, once Smith feels she is sufficiently established and has the allies (e.g., media people, prominent citizens, and maybe even judges and lawyers) necessary to fight back, she can always challenge what she feels are organized lawyerdom's illegal restrictions on her business.

As part of a settlement, Smith might agree to change her classified ads from "Divorce—$150" to "Self-Help Divorce Typing—$150." Or maybe, in an extreme situation, not to advertise in the local paper at all. (As I point out in Chapter 10, there are many other good ways to market your services.) Further, Smith might agree that all her customers will be given or sold a copy of a relevant self-help law book so each has the legal information necessary to make his own informed decisions.

But suppose no compromise with the prosecutor is possible and Smith is told flat out that if she doesn't close up shop in ten days, she will be charged with the crime of practicing law without a license. Based on the rarity of recent prosecutions in this area and my own conversations with a number of people faced with this sort of ultimatum, there is still a fairly good chance that she won't be prosecuted. Of course, I can't give her any such a guarantee. But, if she feels that her business has been conducted with integrity and competence, and especially if she has some support from the media or the local legal community, she will probably want to keep operating at the same time that she makes the types of changes in her ads and operating policies discussed above to make her business as bulletproof as possible.

Finally, even if UPL charges are filed, Smith should know that this doesn't mean that either a trial or conviction will result. In many instances, she will again be given a chance to close her business in exchange for having the prosecution dropped at a pre-trial conference or meeting. Why? Because, as I have emphasized repeatedly, organized lawyerdom is anxious not to create any more national heroes, as it did with Rosemary Furman in Florida. (See interview in the Appendix.) Unless Smith is plainly guilty of consumer fraud, lawyers will usually be almost as anxious to keep her out of the courtroom as she is to stay out.

HOW TO LOCATE UPL COURT CASES

There are a number of ways to find relevant court cases. The first place to check is the case notes, which you will find with the your state's UPL statute in the annotated code. (See "How to Look Up Your UPL Statutes," earlier in this chapter.) Once you locate at least one relevant case and read it, you will almost surely be referred to other UPL cases. Also, with the case citation you have, use Shepard's Case Citations to get citations to all other cases that mention that case.

Another way to check for UPL cases is to check a case digest for your state. (All populous state have them.) A digest is a collection of case summaries that are organized by subject matter and indexed. To use a digest for your state, check the subject-matter index under unauthorized practice of law.

A third way to identify cases in your state is to read all the cases mentioned in the text and footnotes of this chapter. Typically, these will refer to (cite) UPL cases from other states, one of which may be yours.

Also, law review articles on UPL cite a number of cases. The important articles are:

- Rhode, "Policing the Professional Monopoly: A Constitutional and Empirical Analysis of Unauthorized Practice Prohibitions," 34 Stanford Law Rev. 1 (1981).

- Michelman, "Guiding the Invisible Hand: The Consumer Protection Function of Unauthorized Practice Regulation," *Pepperdine L. Rev.,* Vol. 12, No. 1 (1984).

- Wolfram, "Lawyer Turf and Lawyer Regulation—The Role of the Inherent-Powers Doctrine," University of Arkansas at Little Rock Law Journal, Volume 12, Number 1 (1989-90).

- Rhode, "The Delivery of Legal Services by Nonlawyers," Georgetown Journal of Legal Ethics, Vol 4: 209 (1990).

Finally, check the *Index of Legal Periodicals* under the heading "Unauthorized Practice." This publication lists all law review and law journal articles in the unauthorized practice area. You may well find a current one that discusses the case law of your state. Once you know the case name and citation, you are ready to actually look up the case. Cases are compiled in volumes called "case reports," "reports" or "reporters." Ask you librarian where these reports are located and how to find the case you're looking for.

Legal Research Note: Nolo's *Legal Research: How To Find and Understand the Law* (Elias) and its video, *Legal Research Made Easy: A Roadmap through the Law Library Maze,* thoroughly explain how to accomplish all the tasks mentioned here.

E. A Review of Unauthorized Practice Litigation of the Past Twenty-Five Years

Before you can use the legal system to fight back, it's wise to learn what others in a similar situation have accomplished. To this end, let's go back a couple of decades and briefly outline how the unauthorized practice battle has unfolded. Note that while 25 years ago most judicial decisions involved the sale of self-help law books and kits, as we get closer to the present, this type of activity is no longer subject to official question, and courts and prosecutors have become more concerned with IPs providing legal advice.

1967 The New York Court of Appeals (the highest N.Y. court) overturns the conviction of Norman Dacey, the nonlawyer author of *How to Avoid Probate* (Crown Books), holding that the publication and sale of a book about how a lay person can accomplish legal procedures did not constitute unauthorized practice. *N.Y. County Lawyers' Association v. Dacey*, 234 N.E.2d 459 (1967).

1973 The Florida Supreme Court holds that the inclusion of printed instructions along with legal forms constitutes the unlawful practice of law, but that the sale of naked forms by nonlawyers without instructions is okay. *Florida Bar v. American Legal and Business Forms, Inc.*, 274 So.2d 225 (1973).

1975 Advertisement, publication and sale of legal forms and instructions was upheld as long as there was no personal contact between purchaser and seller. *Oregon State Bar v. Gilchrist*, 538 P.2d 913 (1975).

1976 The Michigan Supreme Court arrives at the same conclusion as *Gilchrist*, but several justices write extraordinary separate opinions. One of these cogently argues that offering personal help in filling out divorce forms, in addition to selling them, should not constitute unauthorized practice. *State Bar v. Cramer*, 399 Mich. 116 (1976).

1976 Colorado allows the preparation of divorce forms by an independent paralegal if the functions carried out are only those of a scrivener. In other words, if the form preparer sticks absolutely to the role of a public stenographer and takes down the customer's words verbatim, she is not guilty of practicing law without a license. While this case is worded conservatively, it basically allows independent paralegals to operate above ground in Colorado. *Colorado Bar Assn. v. Miles,* 557 P.2d 1202 (1976).

1978 A California Superior Court arrives at substantially the same conclusion, allowing scrivener services, as did the Colorado court in the *Miles* case. *State Bar v. Benson,* EA-C 16879 (Superior Court Los Angeles County, 1978).

1978 The Florida Supreme Court reverses its 1973 ruling discussed above and allows the sale of legal forms along with written instructions and personal contact between buyer and seller, provided the seller only copies information supplied by customers. *Florida Bar v. Brumbaugh,* 355 So.2d 1186 (1978).

1978 Missouri, Kansas and New York courts refuse to allow personal contact between an independent paralegal and customers, although both say sale of forms and explanatory materials is okay. In *McGiffert v. State ex rel. Stowe,* 366 So.2d 680 (1978), an Alabama court holds that advertising services to obtain divorce "without attorney's fee" by a nonlicensed person is unauthorized practice.

1984 The Arizona state legislature repeals its statute that prohibits UPL. Although there is still a court rule prohibiting UPL, there has essentially been no UPL enforcement since 1984 and independent paralegals and publishers of self-help legal form books and kits have captured much of the business of preparing legal forms for divorce and other basic legal services.

1984 California disbands its state unauthorized practice office and leaves enforcement of unauthorized practice laws to local district attorneys. Except in cases of fraud or misrepresentation, this means that in the years ahead, little enforcement of unauthorized practice will take place in California outside of a few counties where the bar is able to influence the district attorney to initiate criminal prosecutions.

1984 Independent paralegal Rosemary Furman is held in contempt of court and sentenced to jail for violating an injunction ordering her not to engage in unauthorized practice, which among other things consisted of giving nonlawyers procedural advice and typing forms.

Furman's request for a jury trial is denied. *Florida Bar v. Furman,* 451 So.2d 808 (1984). Giving up on Florida's outrageously pro-lawyer procedures, she takes her campaign against lawyers' monopolistic practices to a national audience via television, personal appearances, etc. (See Furman interview in the Appendix.) The Florida governor eventually commutes Furman's sentence on condition that she cease running her typing service.

1985 The State Bar of Wisconsin stops handling both attorney discipline and unauthorized practice cases because it fears that to continue to do so would place it in jeopardy of being sued for violating antitrust laws.

1985 A number of states begin to follow the lead of California and enact simplified procedures for divorce, child support collections, will preparation, and other tasks, specifically designed to eliminate the need for lawyers. This trend towards state-sponsored self-help legal remedies gives increased validity to the argument of independent paralegals that many routine legal services can be safely accomplished without lawyer help.

1985 The Washington State Supreme Court concludes that the drafting of contracts to buy and sell real estate by brokers does not constitute the unauthorized practice of law. The public, the court reasons, is better served by the freedom to choose from a range of providers, even if this means nonlawyers perform functions traditionally reserved by the legal profession. *Cultum v. Heritage House Realtors, Inc.,* 694 P.2d, 630 (1985).

1986 The American Bar Association's Commission on Professionalism recommends the limited licensing of paralegals to provide such services as real estate closings, simple wills, etc. Although there is little active follow-up, the fact that the ABA no longer seems interested in crusading against nonlawyer form preparers is important.

1987 Recognizing the huge, unmet need for moderately-priced immigration counseling, California authorizes non-lawyer immigration consultants to operate as long as they disclose in writing that they are not lawyers. Cal. Business & Professions Code § 27420.

1987 The Florida Supreme Court states that it is not UPL for IPs to engage in limited oral communications to help individuals complete court-approved legal forms.

1988 The California Public Protection Committee, appointed in 1986 by the state bar to investigate public harm from nonlawyer legal services and to determine if regulation of the nonlawyer providers would be appropriate, concluded that the state UPL laws should be repealed and that "legal technicians" (IPs) should be allowed to perform certain legal services provided that the IPs register and inform clients that they are not lawyers.

1989 In 1989, the California State Bar acknowledges that a vast number of Californians do not have reasonable access to the legal process and thus, authorizes the Commission on Legal Technicians to determine guidelines for the practice and regulation of IPs. When this commission issued its report in 1990, it recommended that qualified (meaning regulated) IPs should be allowed to engage in the limited practice of law in the areas of bankruptcy, family, and landlord and tenant law. (As this book goes to print, the Commission's proposal is being reviewed by the state bar and no final determination has been made.)

reliance by the customer. However, if the customer relies on the express or implied expertise of the IP form preparation service, it is unlawful practice. *State Bar of Nevada v. Johnson et al.,* No. CV89-5814 (Nev. 2nd Dist. Ct., April 12, 1990).

1990 A Wisconsin bankruptcy court, invoking its own inherent power to determine what constitutes UPL, states that unauthorized actions include providing counseling, advice and recommendations with respect to any provision of the Bankruptcy Code. In this case, although the IP claimed to do nothing more than sell forms and provide a typing service, the court found that the IP exercised legal judgment in counseling the customer, among other things, as to which property exemptions should be chosen. *In Re: John M. Webster v. Rodney A. Larson,* 120 Bankr. 111 (1990).

1990 HALT, a national public interest group fighting for better consumer legal access, sponsors legislation that would allow IPs to provide out-of-court legal services. This bill has been introduced in the California and Oregon legislature and is expected to be introduced in other states soon. (See Chapter 15 for more details.)

1991 The Florida Supreme Court (Rule 10-1.1(b)) approves a series of basic divorce and other legal forms specifically designed to be prepared by nonlawyers.

1992 Legislation to legalize IPs is defeated in Oregon, California and other states. Supporters vow to keep fighting.

1993 The American Bar Association, in a publication entitled "Self-Representation in Divorce Cases," finds that in Maricopa County, Arizona (the area of the ABA study), at least one party was not represented by a lawyer in 90% of divorce cases. And in 52%, both parties represented themselves.

F. The Constitution and the Independent Paralegal[15]

This is not the place for a detailed scholarly treatise weighing all the constitutional theories that underlie the bar's efforts to proscribe the activities of non-lawyer competitors, including independent paralegals. The subject has already been ably covered by a number of law review articles. Again, one of the best of these is "Unauthorized Practice," by Deborah Rhode, in Volume 34:1 of the *Stanford Law Review.*[16] In addition, what is ultimately judged to be constitutional in this area is almost sure to be influenced more by changing societal views as to the right of the average person to gain affordable access to legal services than it will by the study of old cases.

Just the same, it's wise for all independent paralegals to understand a little about how the constitution relates to organized lawyerdom's continuing drive to protect its monopoly power over the legal system. Let's start our discussion by asking a basic question. Where does the United States Constitution say that only lawyers can legally help the public prepare their own legal paperwork or, for that matter, accomplish other "legal" tasks?

The answer, of course, is that the Constitution doesn't mention the subject. Why, then, haven't organized lawyerdom's activities long since been held as an obvious restriction of the free speech right of indepen-

---

[15]A number of legal commentators believe that direct enforcement actions by state and local bar associations also violate the Sherman Anti-Trust Act. We do not discuss this here because of the rapid move by most bar associations to back off from direct enforcement of unauthorized practice actions, instead referring these proceedings to state supreme courts or to the local prosecutor.

[16]Another excellent general article challenging the bar's assertion that it needs to regulate independent paralegals is Christensen, "The Unauthorized Practice of Law: Do Good Fences Really Make Good Neighbors—or Even Good Sense?, " *American Bar Foundation Research Journal* (Spring 1980).

dent paralegals, or an unwarranted intrusion on the right of the public to petition their government by representing themselves in court?[17]

Organized lawyerdom justifies its right to regulate independent paralegals under the rather vague umbrella of the Constitution's police power. Legislatures and courts, lawyers contend, have a legitimate interest in regulating the quality of legal services available to the public. This public interest rationale, it should be noted, has long been accepted as establishing a constitutional basis to regulate the First Amendment rights (freedom of speech, etc.) of all sorts of other groups, from teachers and bill collectors to operators of toxic waste dumps.

Specifically, when it comes to justifying their right to ban independent paralegals, lawyers claim that because independent paralegals are not subject to bar association rules of conduct, examinations for competence, educational standards and the protections guaranteed clients by the lawyer-client relationship (whatever they are), there is a substantial risk that IPs will provide the public with an unacceptably low quality of service.

This rationale falls apart for two principal reasons. First, there is little evidence that paralegals, unregulated, pose a greater threat to the public than do lawyers, as they are now regulated (loosely at best) by bar associations. Second, the fact that paralegals are not subject to regulation is an argument for regulation, not absolute prohibition of their entire business.

Given that lawyers do not learn basic form preparation skills in law school, and are not tested on these skills on the multistate bar exam, the

---

[17]In this context, the United States Supreme Court has ruled that if prisoners are denied the right to legal help in preparing habeas corpus petitions, they must be afforded a reasonable alternative. *Johnson v. Avery,* 393 U.S. 483 (1969). Shouldn't ordinary citizens who can't afford the high prices charged by lawyers be allowed to take advantage of low cost alternatives to gain access to the legal forum their tax dollars support? For more on this access argument, see "On Letting the Laity Litigate: The Petition Clause and Unauthorized Practice Rules," Univ. of Penn. Law Review, Vol. 132 (1984).

fact that lawyers are loosely regulated in other ways is not evidence that lawyers can competently handle form preparation services. Indeed, with formal consumer complaints against lawyers currently being filed at close to 100,000 per year, there is considerable basis to conclude that lawyers should be better trained and tested.

In addition, in several states, including California, attempts by bar investigators to unearth complaints among thousands of *pro se* plaintiffs have been notably unsuccessful. Indeed, at several public hearings by the California Bar's Public Protection Committee, and the Commission on Legal Technicians, far more members of the public showed up to complain about lack of lawyer competence than testified against IPs. In its report of April 1988, the Public Protection Committee found that "there are a number of highly qualified and dedicated legal technicians [IPs] who deliver valuable assistance for fair consideration."

Similarly, a number of years ago, when title companies began to fill out real estate documents, the Colorado Supreme Court found "no convincing evidence that the massive changeover in the performance of this service from attorneys to title companies has been accompanied by any great loss, detriment or inconvenience to the public. The uncontroverted evidence was that lawyers for this simple operation considerably slowed the loan closings and cost the persons involved a great deal of money."[18]

Barlow Christensen, in his study of unauthorized practice published in the American Bar Foundation's Research Journal (Spring 1980) concludes:

> *Suppression of the practice of law by nonlawyers has been proclaimed to be in the public interest, a necessary protection against incompetence, divided loyalties, and other evils. But this interest of the public is one that has been defined, articulated, promulgated, and enforced not by the public but by the legal profession. And nowhere, in all of the literature or in any of the court decisions, is*

---

[18] *Conway-Bogue Realty Investment Co. v. Denver Bar Association*, 312 P.2d 998 (1957).

*there evidence of a public voice with respect to this supposed public
interest.*

Even if we assume that the independent paralegal movement does
present a threat to American consumers because an occasional paralegal
might provide poor service, is this a sufficient constitutional justification
for the prohibition against all independent paralegal activity currently
advocated by organized lawyerdom? Probably not. More reasonably, it
supports regulating paralegals with legitimate and fair rules that really do
protect the public, not the legal profession.

 In Chapter 15, I discuss the HALT-sponsored Legal Technicians
Bill, which provides a regulatory scheme for independent paralegals.

There are two reasons why current unauthorized practice regulations
are unconstitutional and should have been adjudged to be so long ago.
The first has to do with the vague and self-serving nature of the basic
statutory definition of the unauthorized practice of law. As noted earlier in
this chapter, most states define the practice of law as either being something lawyers customarily do, or something it takes a lawyer's knowledge
to do, or something it takes more than ordinary intelligence and knowledge to do, or something you have to get a license to do, or all four.
These definitions are hopelessly circular, vague and ambiguous.[19] They
neither fairly put the independent paralegal on notice as to what conduct
is prohibited, nor protect the public.

---

[19]To illustrate, consider that in some states (let's call them "Type A" states), real
estate brokers have traditionally prepared property deeds, while in others ("Type
B" states) this task has customarily been accomplished by lawyers. Does this mean
Type B states can constitutionally charge a real estate broker who prepares a deed
with unauthorized practice because lawyers normally do this work, but State A
states can't, because lawyers haven't traditionally handled it?

A second and even more powerful reason why traditional unauthorized practice regulations are unconstitutional has to do with the manner in which bar associations prosecute people who they believe are guilty of the unauthorized practice of law. Even assuming that legislatures, and in some circumstances courts, are entitled to regulate how IPs fill out legal forms, organized lawyerdom must still meet a reasonable standard of fairness (due precess) when it comes to enforcing its rules. Today this is nowhere being done.

As outlined above, actions against independent paralegals are commonly instituted not in a criminal proceeding in which the IP has the right to a jury trial, but by bar committees made up primarily or exclusively of lawyers or, more typically, by judicial officials acting on bar association complaints. This was the situation faced by Rosemary Furman in Florida. (See Rosemary Furman interview in Appendix.) In either instance, the complaint leading to bar or court action is almost always from a member of the legal profession angry at low-cost competition, not from a consumer with a legitimate beef. And in some situations, especially where bar associations try to order IPs out of business on their own initiative, everyone involved in the process of investigating and sanctioning the independent paralegal (a decision usually made in secret) is an attorney with a pecuniary interest in suppressing nonlawyer competition. In other professions, courts have not allowed such interested parties to have absolute regulatory power. For example, in *Gibson v. Berryhill,* 331 F.Supp. 122 (1971) *aff'd,* 411 U.S. 564 (1973), a federal court held that a board made up of optometrists in private practice wasn't sufficiently impartial to be allowed to prohibit another optometrist from working for a corporation.

Also, as noted earlier, in many instances, before official action to go after an IP is taken, a bar committee or court first threatens the independent paralegal in an "informal" proceeding. Thus, the independent paralegal often finds herself in the surreal situation of being called to account by a group of lawyers, told to stay off their turf, and threatened with a fine and jail, all as part of an extra-judicial proceeding in which the independent paralegal has no fair way to defend her conduct. (See Judy Lamb interview in Appendix.) It's worthy of note that in other areas of

American life, including the regulation of books claimed to be pornographic, where First Amendment rights were being restricted by quasi-official, but essentially private, review boards, the U.S. Supreme Court has found a constitutional violation.[20]

If actions by lawyers to suppress non-lawyer competition are so obviously biased, why aren't there court decisions saying they are unconstitutional? Partly because lawyers' groups are adept at backing off in situations when a court case might produce a bad precedent, and partly because very few independent paralegals have had enough financial resources to fully litigate the issue. But mostly, because judges, blinded by their claim of absolute power over the legal system based on the "inherent powers" doctrine (see Section C above), have so far applied a biased standard of what constitutes fair procedure. Indeed, the current legal standards and procedures are so unfair that, sooner or later, they are bound to be ruled in violation of basic due process when it comes to regulating the legal profession.

Let's assume that to be constitutional, regulation of paralegals must be strictly limited to rules necessary to protect American people from incompetent work done by untrained people and that these rules must be both fairly and impartially administered. What might such a regulation scheme look like?[21]

- Legal recognition of the fact that every citizen's right to self-representation and reasonable access to the courts necessarily includes the right to get competent help from reasonably-priced service providers.

- State unauthorized practice of law regulations should be limited so that they do not prohibit the preparation of routine legal forms,

---

[20]*Bantam Books Inc. v. Sullivan,* 372 U.S. 58 (1963).

[21]See Chapter 15 for a discussion of the HALT bill currently being considered in California and Oregon.

and the giving of common sense procedural and factual advice needed to prepare such forms.

- Reasonable registration and licensure procedures for independent paralegals who want to prepare routine legal forms should be limited to legal areas where there is a high probability of consumer harm.

- If regulation includes the requirement that an IP pass a test as a condition of qualifying for a license, the test should be closely based on the skill the IP needs to carry out the particular form preparation task. For example, an IP who wishes a license to help customers prepare guardianship papers should be tested on that skill and not on general legal knowledge or principles. In other areas (name changes, simple divorces with no children or property), independent paralegals should have to do little more than register with the state agency.

- Administration of any regulatory system dealing with independent paralegals should not be left in the hands of bar associations, state supreme courts or other lawyers' groups who have a clear bias in favor of suppressing competition. Instead, regulations should be administered by a consumer agency in the public interest. Adding a minority of lay people to existing bar association unauthorized practice committees or turning enforcement power over to the judiciary does not accomplish this goal.

Chapter 3

How To Do Your Job And Stay Out of Jail

*G*iven the inherently fuzzy boundaries of what constitutes the "unauthorized practice of law," how do you protect yourself? There are no foolproof ways to avoid attacks by organized lawyerdom, but you can greatly reduce your vulnerability if you consistently do three things:

1. Tell the world you are not a lawyer,

2. Provide your customers access to the basic legal information necessary to make their own decisions, and

3. Limit yourself to legal form preparation—don't give legal advice.

A. Tell the World You Are Not a Lawyer

Making it clear that you are not licensed to practice law is not only an honest way to run your business, it protects you from the charge that you have fraudulently misrepresented your services. In addition, a strong statement making it clear that you are an IP typing service or legal technician, not a lawyer, will establish one essential part of your defense should you ever be charged with unauthorized practice.

If organized lawyerdom, through a bar association, public prosecutor, state court, or a state regulatory body, such as the Department of Consumer Affairs or Bureau of Professional Standards, ever scrutinizes your business, the first thing it will look at is whether you make it absolutely clear you are not a lawyer. In this context, it's not enough that you don't use the word "lawyer" or "attorney" in your advertisements. The thing organized lawyerdom will look for is whether a potential customer reading your promotional material, or coming to your place of business, is clearly and unequivocally put on notice that you are not a lawyer, and that you do not provide legal expertise.[1]

I AM NOT A LAWYER!

---

[1]In *State Bar of Nevada v. Johnson,* No. CV89-5814 (Nev. 2nd Dist. Ct., April 12, 1990), the judge repeatedly emphasizes the importance of legal typing services (IPs) making it clear to the public that they are not lawyers and do not practice law.

When you think about it, making sure you are squeaky clean when it comes to informing the public that you help consumers prepare legal forms, but are not a member of the bar and do not give legal advice, is reasonable. Incidentally, you have absolutely no business motive to be shy about doing this because many, if not the majority, of your customers will seek you out precisely because you don't charge lawyer prices or have lawyer attitudes.

Think of it this way. If you consult a person who claims to be a CPA, or a chef "trained in Paris," or a "juggler" who used to work for the Ringling Brothers Circus, you expect that person to tell the truth about his background. If the "CPA" in fact turns out to be a tax preparer who has taken a few accounting courses, the "chef" worked for a week washing dishes at a fast food place in Paris, Illinois, and the "juggler's" job at Ringling Brothers involved following an elephant with a shovel, you are likely to feel ripped off, and justifiably so. This isn't to say that you might not choose a non-CPA tax preparer in the first place. You well might. But you're entitled to the information that lets you make the choice knowingly.

Here are some detailed suggestions as to how to tell the world you are not a lawyer:

Business Name: I present a detailed discussion of good and bad business names in Chapter 5. For now, the main point is to choose a name for your business that cannot possibly be read to imply that you are a lawyer. The best way to do this is to emphasize "self-help" in your title.

Promotional Materials: All brochures and flyers you distribute should clearly state that you are not a lawyer. This message should not be buried in the text, but set out, near the top, in at least 10-point boldface type. Something like this works well: "The ABC Self-Help Typing Service is not staffed by lawyers and does not give legal advice."

Logos and Stationery: Your stationery and, if you use one, your logo, should reinforce your message that you are a self-help typing service. Prominent use of the term "self-help" is an excellent way to do this. Thus, The Jefferson County Typing Service might add to its stationery a line such as this: "Quality Nonlawyer Form Preparation for Self-Help Divorce and Bankruptcy."

In choosing a logo, you'll particularly want to avoid using the scales of justice or similar symbols associated with lawyers. Instead, why not choose a graphic image that reinforces the idea of people helping themselves.

Advertisements and Circulars: If you use print, radio or TV ads (see Chapter 10, "Marketing Your Services"), you will probably not be able to afford to include a lengthy statement that you are not a lawyer and do not provide legal expertise. Fortunately, there are several other ways to get your point across. One is to emphasize the self-help aspect of your service. For example, instead of titling an ad "Divorce" or "Bankruptcy," you might say "Divorce Yourself" or "Do Your Own Bankruptcy," incorporating the concept of self-help directly into your sales message. If your business name already embodies this concept, so much the better.

Here is a newspaper advertisement for an independent paralegal business that I feel does a poor job of notifying the public that no lawyers are involved:

The problem with this ad is that it nowhere informs the public that it is a nonlawyer typing service. Although it can be argued that the name "Legal Alternatives, Inc." informs the public that no lawyers are involved, this is far from obvious (there are lots of alternatives in the world, including alternative lawyers), and a prosecutor or bar association would likely contend that the prominent use of the word "legal" is likely to confuse the public.

Here is an excerpt from a flyer that does a much better job of informing the public that the paralegal business doesn't involve attorney services:

SELF-HELP DIVORCE CENTER

A sensible non-lawyer alternative since 1972

You Make The Decisions, We Do The Paperwork

- We type forms for: Legal divorce, annulment and legal separation
- Our fees are reasonable: our basic charge is $90-180 (+ court filing fee)
- Our typing service is efficient and reliable

If you have already decided on divorce and have a good grasp of the legal and practical rules and procedures you face, you do not necessarily need the services of an attorney. If you can make your own decisions about property, custody, support; and if your spouse does not hire an attorney to contest the divorce, you can sensibly get your own legal divorce without a lawyer.

Employees at the Self-Help Divorce Center are trained to record your decisions on the proper divorce forms. Taking it step-by-step, we type your divorce papers under your guidance and instruction and send them to you as you need them. We rely on the books *How To Do Your Own Divorce in California,* by Attorney Charles E. Sherman and *California Marriage and Divorce Law,* by attorneys Warner, Ihara and Elias, and recommend that you carefully read both.

SELF-HELP DIVORCE CENTER

870 Main Street, Suite 10

Lexington, CA 94450

(In the Bradley Building across from Macys Park at Eighth and Main)

Monday-Friday • Evening and Saturday appointments available

904-5757 • 432-4485

Office Signs: It is essential that you prominently display a sign in your office making it clear who you are and what you do. A straight-forward plaque mounted on your waiting room or office wall that says something like the following will do the job.

ACME TYPING:
A NONLAWYER FORM PREPARATION SERVICE

The Acme Typing Service is designed to help non-lawyers prepare their own paperwork to file their own bankruptcy, divorce, step-parent adoption, and other uncontested legal actions. You make all legal and practical decisions. Our role is to prepare the necessary paperwork under your direction. We are not lawyers and do not give legal advice. If you are unsure about any of the legal aspects of your case, please see a lawyer.

Why is it necessary to display a sign if your ads and flyers make it clear that you are not a lawyer? Because it is an extremely convenient way to document that you've made every effort to tell the public that you are not a lawyer and do not provide legal services. If you still aren't convinced, think of it this way: lawyers, who after all are past masters at elevating form over substance, truly believe in the power of disclaimers. Remember, they are the ones who get paid to write all those little warnings on the back of everything from parking lot tickets to new car purchase agreements by which customers must disclaim all sorts of rights and accept dozens of unpalatable responsibilities. Again, the point is simple—lawyers will have a difficult time claiming (and more important, a judge will have even more trouble concluding) that you are misleading the public if you constantly and obviously emphasize that you aren't a lawyer and that your customers must accept the responsibility that comes with doing their own legal work.

Signed Statements: While office signs, truth in advertising and promotional materials emphasizing that you are not a lawyer are important, they are not a substitute for your most important self-protection device. This is a written statement signed by all your customers clearly acknowledging three things:

1. You aren't a lawyer,

2. Your customers are representing themselves and have access to the legal materials necessary to make their own informed decisions, and

3. Your role is limited to preparing legal forms under your customers' direction.

Each statement should be signed in duplicate (or immediately photocopied) during the initial customer interview, with one copy given to the customer and the other retained in your permanent file. If you deal with customers who aren't fluent in English, all statements, signs, information and disclaimers should also be available in Spanish, Chinese, Vietnamese, or other relevant languages or dialects. You may find it convenient to make this signed statement part of a more detailed information sheet, which establishes the price of your services and some details about how your business works. However you present it, it should read something like this:

IMPORTANT INFORMATION ABOUT THE ACME TYPING SERVICE

The Acme Typing Service is a secretarial service designed to assist people who want to do their own legal paperwork, for _____[divorces]_____, _____[incorporations]_____, and _____[bankruptcies]_____. We are not lawyers and do not give legal advice. It is up to you to inform yourself as to the laws and procedures that affect your situation and to make your own legal decisions. To this end, we recommend the following publications: ___[enter names of best self-help manuals]_____.

The role of the Acme Typing Service is solely to prepare legal paperwork following your instructions.

I have read and accept the foregoing statement of Acme Typing Service policy.

I have a copy of *How To Do Your Own Divorce in California,* by Charles Sherman, and *California Marriage and Divorce Law,* by Warner, Ihara & Elias, and have read it carefully.

_____   _____
Date   Signature

As an alternative, here is a disclaimer that Rosemary Furman (see interview in Appendix) used for many years as part of her Northside Typing Service in Jacksonville, Florida:

Nobody at Northside Secretarial Service has represented herself to be an Attorney. I have neither sought nor received legal advice. It is my intention to represent myself in Court and I have paid my fee for secretarial service ONLY.

_____   _____
Date   Signature

Get information in the customer's own handwriting: In Chapter 8, I discuss many of the techniques necessary to running a quality legal typing business. One of these is either to get all factual information in the customer's own handwriting or, if it's necessary to employ an oral interview technique, to have your customer check all the information you collect and sign a statement that it is correct.

Why is it best to have your customers provide information in their own handwriting? Because if you are ever charged with unauthorized practice, your best line of defense will be that you prepared legal forms under the direction of your customer. Being able to produce all key information in your customer's handwriting will make it far easier to document that your customer, not you, supplied the necessary information.

If you don't believe this can be important, consider these guidelines set out in U.S. Bankruptcy Judge A. Jay Cristol's opinion in the case of *In re: Bachman* (# 881-04588, Southern District of Florida, 1990):

> *Typing services...may type bankruptcy forms for their clients, provided they only copy the written information furnished by clients...A problem arises when information is taken orally...it is suggested that typing services may take information from clients orally, provided that they record the conversations and preserve the tapes.*

B. Provide Your Customers Access to the Basic Legal Information Necessary to Make Their Own Decisions

Legal form preparers who run afoul of organized lawyerdom usually do so because they directly transfer legal expertise to their customers. Or put another way, they act like junior lawyers.[2] Fortunately, because of the wealth of good quality self-help legal information currently on the market, there is no need to do this. The IP's role should be to identify, gather and sell the legal material their customers will need to make their own

---

[2]In Florida, by order of the Florida Supreme Court, a nonlawyer, subject to disclosing that he or she isn't a lawyer, may prepare court-approved divorce, child support, landlord-tenant and some other forms free of fear of UPL charges.

informed decisions. If the IP limits himself to typing forms under his customers' directions, he should not be vulnerable to charges of UPL.

Several years ago, because of the lack of legal material directed to the nonlawyer, referring the customers to written information to answer questions was difficult. Today, however, as a result of the proliferation of self-help law articles, books, and computer software, as well as the simultaneous development of many simplified materials for lawyers that are reasonably accessible to nonlawyers, it is much easier. To follow this approach, your first job as an independent paralegal is to locate legal information that will answer the common substantive legal questions your customers ask. Once you do, it's best to keep this material in your office for your customers to look at or, if for some reason doing this is impossible, you will want to tell them where to get it. Sometimes even one or two good books will answer most questions in a particular field. For example *How to File for Bankruptcy,* by Elias, Leonard & Renauer (Nolo Press), is a detailed "how-to" guide for people who wish to file a Chapter 7 bankruptcy. It does not deal with every complication that can arise in a bankruptcy, but it does very thoroughly answer routine questions. Because it is such a good resource, it makes sense to require that every bankruptcy customer own it, even if you must supply the book yourself and add a few dollars to your typing fee to cover it.

But isn't the approach of referring customers to written materials so that they can get answers to questions more cumbersome than simply answering them in the first place? Sure, but especially in the parts of the country where organized lawyerdom is determined to suppress independent paralegals, it is also an essential strategy to your survival. In addition, you should understand that many of the self-help legal materials currently on the market are of good quality and will empower your customers to do better legal work. In other words, taking the little bit of extra trouble to help your customers use good self-help law materials as part of your business will not only provide you with a good measure of legal protection, it will enhance your customer satisfaction, and therefore your business.

As you take the time to help your customers educate themselves, consider that this approach can be markedly superior to that followed by most lawyers. Traditionally, lawyers have often preferred to tell their clients what to do, while denying them the basic legal information necessary to sensibly question the advice. For example, should a client ask how much spousal support is reasonable in a given situation, a typical lawyer will provide a dollar figure, with no explanation of the laws and practice that make that number (and probably a range of alternative numbers) sensible. Even worse, the fact that the lawyer has a financial incentive to choose a dollar figure high enough to inflame the other spouse and result in extended litigation (and therefore a higher lawyer fee) will never be disclosed. By contrast, an IP who answers the same question by providing the customer with an up-to-date written discussion of spousal support laws and practices provides a superior service. This is especially true if the written materials are keyed to a number of different fact situations and present a reasonable range of support amounts appropriate for each.

Okay, let's assume that I have convinced you of the desirability of making written materials available to your customers and that you have located the necessary books, articles, or software. The next question is, how do you get them into the hands of your customers? Here are several strategies:

Sell the book: If an excellent self-help book is available in a particular legal area, such as an up-to-date, easy-to-understand, small business incorporation manual designed specifically for your state, you will want to sell it. In fact, for your own self-protection, you will probably wish to require every customer to buy it and state in writing that they have read it. Because I am a long-time publisher of self-help law books and make most of my living selling them, you may want to discount this advice as being self-interested and hence unreliable. I am convinced, however, that if you do, you are likely to regret your decision. Why? Because, again, at the risk of being repetitive, the self-help law book allows you not only to put solid information into the hands of your customers, but to lay the groundwork in advance for one of the few effective defenses available should you be prosecuted for unauthorized practice. This is simply that an independently-published book and the information it contains is protected by the First Amendment to the U.S. Constitution.

If you face a particularly uptight situation with the local bar, you may not want to sell any legal material yourself on the theory that the more separate you are from the way in which your customer gets legal information, the better off you are should there be a lawyer-initiated investigation of your operations. While this extra degree of care is no longer necessary in the many states where IPs are well-established, it is still a good idea in states where stamping out unauthorized practice is still a maniacal concern of organized lawyerdom. Following this approach, you would arrange for a local book store or office supply store (many already carry legal forms), or another nearby merchant, to stock the book in volume, and then refer customers to that store.

Set up your own small library: Most IP's report that they hear the same legal questions over and over again. For example, people who are filing for divorce, and who have minor children, will often ask what rules govern child custody. If there are self-help law books available that detail these rules, you should have them in your own library. In addition, you will want to gather other legal materials suitable for use by your customers. In Oregon, Robin Smith of People's Paralegal Service keeps copies of a court decision and several articles from Oregon legal publications that clearly set out child custody rules. In other legal areas, People's Paralegal has similar materials available, thus allowing customers the opportunity to educate themselves.

Use legal information phone lines: A number of companies have established legal information phone services. For two or three dollars per minute, charged to a credit card, a caller can have a lawyer answer legal questions. In theory, these services are a wonderful resource for the independent paralegal as they provide a ready source of legal information for confused customers and free the independent paralegal from the temptation of providing legal information. Sadly a number of these phone answer services are essentially scams run by lawyers who profit not by answering questions, but by talking clients into buying their services or referring them to other lawyers for a fee. When a self-helper calls, the service tries to talk them out of handling their own action.

Fortunately, there are at least two phone services that do provide reliable, up-to-date legal information and are supportive of self-help efforts.

Tele-Lawyer: Offers information on a wide range of consumer law areas, including bankruptcy, credit problems and, for many but not all states, divorce and other family law concerns:

(800) 442-5529 (credit card calls in California)

(800) 283-5529 (credit card calls outside of California

Divorce Helpline: A California-only service that specializes in helping people to do their own California divorces including help in calculating child support obligations, pension fund values and the ownership interests of each spouse in marital property:

(800) 359-7004

Incidentally, many independent paralegals not only recommend that customers who have legal questions call these services, they arrange for them to do so from their office so they can listen in and use the information as part of their own continuing education effort.

Use the Law Library: In states with smaller populations there may be few, if any, published self-help law materials. If you face this situation, you will have no book to sell unless you work in legal areas such as bankruptcy, copyright, patent or Social Security appeals, which are under federal jurisdiction. And even in states where there are self-help materials available, some may be procedure-oriented, and not deal in sufficient detail with substantive law.

In either situation, you will want to do your own research at the local law library and prepare a list of relevant materials for future use by your customers. Law libraries are located in most county courthouses and are open to the public. Many law school libraries, especially those at publicly-funded universities, are similarly open to all. Your main goal will be to locate the practice books or court decisions lawyers rely on to answer the same routine questions your customers will ask. The reference librarian, if so disposed, can surely put your hand on the best materials. In this context, it's worthy of note that the American Association of Law Librarians has been working hard to make law libraries more accessible to the public, and some law librarians have already collected and organized materials of interest to nonlawyers.

HOW TO IMPROVE LEGAL RESEARCH SKILLS

Independent paralegals who have attended a formal paralegal school already know basic legal research skills. For others, it's an essential skill that should be promptly mastered. Because legal materials are organized in unique ways, it's almost essential that you either take a course or spend time with good self-help teaching tools. Here are a couple of excellent ones:

- *Legal Research: How to Find and Understand the Law,* by Stephen Elias (Nolo Press): A basic text, designed for paralegals, which follows a step-by-step approach to mastering legal research techniques.

- Legal Research Made Easy, by Robert Berring (Nolo Press/Legal Star): An entertaining 2-1/2 hr. video by an experienced law librarian that provides a comprehensive introduction to legal research techniques.

Once you have located the materials you know your customers will want to refer to, create a short reading list. Typically a list for people doing their own divorce should contain five to ten entries which focus on substantive law, such as rules governing child support and child custody and visitation. You may also want to include these information sources on your customer information sheet along with basic information, such as the amount of court filing fees and what forms are necessary to file for divorce.

Let's now look at an example of how this approach to helping your customers educate themselves might work in practice.

Example: Cathy P. is a resident of Red Bluff, California. She has been employed on a temporary basis by several lawyers as a typist and has prepared several dozen sets of divorce forms. Recently she got her own divorce, handling the whole thing herself without problem and then helped her boyfriend prepare his own divorce papers. She has just decided to set up a part-time typing service to type divorces for others.

To deepen her knowledge, Cathy first attends courses in family law and how to organize an independent paralegal business, sponsored by the National Organization for Independent Paralegals, in Sonoma, California. In addition, she follows a number of the learning techniques discussed in Chapter 8, Section A, and in the interviews with Catherine Jermany and Glynda Mathewson in the Appendix of this book.

As part of preparing herself to deal with customers' questions about divorce, Cathy checks several local books stores. She finds several books on self-help divorce in California. Two, *How To Do Your Own Divorce in California*, by Charles Sherman, and *California Marriage and Divorce Law*, by Warner, Ihara and Elias, are particularly good. They not only contain all the forms and instructions necessary for a person to represent herself in an uncontested divorce, but also the background information necessary to make sensible decisions about how to divide property and debts. Cathy decides to require every customer to purchase and read both. To make this clear, she adds a sentence to this effect to her general disclaimer form that tells people that she is not a lawyer. It looks like this:

"I have a copy of *How To Do Your Own Divorce in California*, by Charles Sherman, and *California Marriage and Divorce Law*, by Warner, Ihara & Elias, and have read it carefully."

_____   _____
Date   Signature

Cathy then locates additional books on divorce, especially those pertaining to California. These include:

- *Mediate Your Divorce,* by Joan Blades (Prentice Hall), a good general guide to how to turn a potentially contested divorce into an uncontested one through mediation techniques;

- *California Family Law: Practice and Procedure,* by Christian E. Markey, Jr., ed. (Matthew Bender), a thorough multi-volume treatise on California divorce law, complete with forms. Probably the best comprehensive source of information for both lawyers and laypersons.

- *California Practice Guide,* by William P. Hogoboom (The Rutter Group), a two-volume set that is excellent when it comes to explaining the procedures and paperwork requirements of divorce.

- *Continuing Education of the Bar,* California Marital Dissolution Practice, a two-volume legal text covering all basic laws and procedures necessary to dissolve a marriage.

- *California Divorce Solutions,* by Charles Sherman (Nolo Press), deals with the practical financial and emotional aspects of a California divorce.

- *Divorce and Money,* by Violet Woodhouse, Victoria Felton-Collins & M.C. Blakeman (Nolo Press), explains how to evaluate such major assets as pensions, investments, family homes and businesses, and how to arrive at a division of property that is fair to both sides.

C. Limit Yourself to Legal Form Preparation: Don't Give Legal Advice

Even if you include a dozen disclaimers in your promotional material and wallpaper your office with signs stating that you don't practice law and are not a lawyer, you must live up to your statements or you are likely to end up in legal hot water. In other words, if despite your assurances that you don't give legal advice you in fact advise people on how to solve complicated legal problems or help them deal with problems arising out of contested lawsuits, you may very well be charged with the criminal offense of practicing law without a license or cited by a court in a civil contempt proceeding involving the same charge.

This directly raises the question of what types of oral advice will trigger a charge of unauthorized practice of law. There is no definitive answer. The difference between explaining general consumer information and transferring legal expertise is an extremely fine one. Depending on the geographical location, the factual context, and perhaps even on the sophistication of the customer, communicating a particular type of information may be judged to be the practice of law in one prosecution and not to be in another. For example, many judges would say that telling a customer who has already completed a Chapter 7 bankruptcy that they must wait six full years to file another is general consumer information, which is widely available and hence does not constitute the practice of law. However, a few judges might still claim this information is legal in nature, and therefore, a nonlawyer explaining it to a customer is a criminal offense.

A few years ago, if an independent paralegal was prosecuted (this was rare for other reasons—see Chapter 2), a judge would normally rule that explaining any information about the law to a consumer (e.g., "you file the long white form and fill it out with black ink") constituted UPL. By contrast, today it is becoming increasingly recognized that explaining basic legal facts widely known in the community (e.g., "it's a crime to lie on tax forms, or, the speed limit is 55-mph") does not constitute the practice of law and therefore won't result in an unauthorized practice conviction. I call this the "general knowledge" exception to the rule that only lawyers can give legal advice and I believe that in the next decades it will be greatly expanded to cover wide areas of information. Logically, any information widely available to the public through self-help law books, videos, software, consumer information packets and magazines should eventually fall into this category.

Two areas where this "general knowledge" rule has already expanded the types of information an IP can transfer to a customer are bankruptcy and family law. In large part, this is because consumer reporters, consumer action columns and self-help books, to mention but a few information sources, routinely explain the basics of divorce, adoption, change of name and bankruptcy. For example, it's possible to learn that a consumer is only eligible for a Chapter 7 bankruptcy once in seven years, or that all parents who have the ability to do so must pay child support, from literally dozens of non-lawyer sources. Even lawyers' groups have begun to recognize the value of the public getting this information, to the extent that they often bestow community service awards on the reporters who prepare or present these materials.

Given this strong trend towards providing the public with better and more in-depth legal information, it seems inevitable that organized lawyerdom will be unable to successfully prosecute independent paralegals for explaining this same information to their customers. Indeed, I know of several cases that were dismissed or dropped because the prosecution couldn't sufficiently prove that the information transferred from the IP to the customer was legal in nature. (See Virginia Simons' interview in the Appendix.)

And now for a face full of cold water. Despite the trend towards liberating the law from lawyers, there is no certain way to know what information a local bar association, prosecutor or judge will regard as being general public knowledge as opposed to legal information, the transfer of which is enough to trigger unauthorized practice charges. In short, despite the broad national trend towards allowing IPs to communicate basic consumer law information to their customers, particular individuals who do so are still vulnerable.

Given this, what general guidelines should an independent paralegal follow to be in the best position to defend herself should organized lawyerdom prosecute? As I have emphasized throughout this book, the conservative answer is to do nothing but type forms in uncontested actions, best accomplished by following the customer's instructions after providing him or her with the self-help law information materials necessary to make sensible choices. If customers still have substantive legal questions, even routine ones, the independent paralegal should religiously refer them back to the self-help law materials that discuss the areas of their concern, or to a lawyer-staffed law phone service, or directly to a lawyer.

When it comes to very routine questions about subjects that are common knowledge in the community (e.g., "Is a parent legally responsible to support his or her minor child?"), IPs who work in areas where the likelihood of prosecution is low may conclude that they can safely answer. But before an IP, even one who feels legally secure, goes too far down the road of personally providing customers with legal information, I believe she should take a hard, critical look not only at what she is doing, but why she is doing it. Is she really answering legal questions and providing legal information because this is the only efficient way to legally inform the customer, or is it because she enjoys being an authority figure and secretly yearns to be a "junior lawyer." Too often, when I have examined a particular independent paralegal's operations, I have found that the independent paralegal deliberately chose to put herself in legal jeopardy and to deny her customers access to the best legal information, all because she enjoyed the lawyer-like role of telling the customers what to do.

A good compromise between never giving oral information or answering customers' sensible questions and acting like a lawyer is to back all oral information you give with high-quality self-help legal written materials, preferably those published by someone other than yourself. For example, if you are typing divorces in Houston, Texas and provide the book *How To Do Your Own Divorce in Texas,* by Charles Sherman, as part of doing every divorce, you can sensibly argue that the information you are giving orally is simply a summary of the written materials.

Chapter 4

Legal Areas Open to Independent Paralegals

*M*ost people who open businesses as independent paralegals have a good idea of the type of legal paperwork they want to help people with. Often they just want to continue doing what they did when they worked for a private attorney, a legal clinic, or a court clerk's office. Or, occasionally the independent paralegal has become interested in a particular area because of a personal experience with the legal system. For example, I know two IPs who got involved with handling landlord problems after several of their own tenants refused to pay the rent. One works part-time for a county apartment owner's association specializing in counseling landlords on their legal rights; the other runs a small eviction form typing service. It is also fairly common for people to get started in the divorce typing business after successfully handling their own.

Because so many uncontested divorces and bankruptcies are processed each year, and because independent paralegals have been successfully preparing paperwork in these fields for some time, the majority of fledgling IPs initially choose these legal areas. This makes sense, unless the geographical area where the new IP wishes to work is already saturated with divorce and bankruptcy typing services, as is the case in a number of West Coast communities.

However, just because a number of independent paralegals have done well doing divorces and bankruptcies, don't be fooled into thinking that to be a success in the independent paralegal business, you are limited to helping people fill out these types of forms. There are, in fact, dozens of legal areas open to you. Before listing a number of these, let's take a moment to understand why some types of legal tasks offer great potential to independent paralegals, while others do not.

A. Avoid Contested Cases

As I repeatedly emphasize throughout this book, a basic rule for survival as an independent paralegal is normally to refrain from working with customers who have contested disputes or whose disputes are likely to become contested. (See the sidebar, below, for an exception.) Legal literacy in the U.S. is so miserably low that the average citizen doesn't know enough about the law or legal procedures to handle a contested dispute without considerable help. If, as an independent paralegal, you are the nearest thing to a legal expert in the life of a person who is confused, and perhaps intimidated by a contested lawsuit, she will almost inevitably ask you for legal advice and information. This in turn will put you in an awkward position. Unlike uncontested actions, such as bankruptcy, where there are high-quality self-help law materials to which you can refer your customers, few, if any, reliable materials exist to help nonlawyers cope with a contested lawsuit, especially if the other party is represented by a lawyer. If in attempting to respond to your customers' anxious questions you provide legal information, you run a substantial risk of being charged with practicing law without a license. On the other hand, if you refuse to provide customers with the information they think they need to deal with an immediate problem, they are likely to become demanding and perhaps angry. At the very least, trying to deal with this will be a drag on your business. And, of course, there is always the risk that an unhappy customer will complain to the bar association or a consumer agency.

The best and probably the only way to avoid this sort of problem is to strictly limit your work to uncontested actions, unless, of course, you work in a cause-related, nonprofit setting, such as advising women on how to collect child support, trying to defend the environment or helping tenants deal with a local rent control ordinance. As I discuss in more detail in Chapter 14, IPs who work in a nonprofit setting, even one that involves contested cases, are at less risk of being challenged by the bar, at least in part because lawyers don't get much in the way of fees from these areas and so are less concerned about nonlawyers getting involved.

SIMPLIFIED COURT PROCEDURE ALLOWS IPS TO PREPARE PAPERWORK IN CONTESTED CASES

In California, where over 60% of divorces are handled pro per, courts have begun establishing simplified procedures to handle contested disputes over issues such as child custody, property division, child support and visitation. Operating in this consumer-friendly atmosphere, IPs find they can type the paperwork necessary to get both spouses in a contested divorce case into court. Here is how Bakersfield IP Virginia Simons puts it: "The fact that the court has set up a way for people who are representing themselves to present their contested case means the consumer is much less apprehensive. When they come to me asking if I can help them with a contested divorce, I tell them I just type the papers and don't give legal advice. Since there are good self-help law materials available, people who argue about child support and custody without a lawyer really do fine, now that the courts make them welcome.

Fortunately, deciding to limit your work to uncontested matters does not involve much sacrifice, as the great majority (surely over 80%) of all legal matters presented to American courts and administrative tribunals do not involve a dispute. For example, despite the impression you may have gained from watching daytime TV dramas, where every divorcing couple has a small mansion, two BMW's and a herd of horny lawyers who make house calls, the great majority of modern divorces are not contested and do not require expensive lawyers or, for that matter, in most instances, any lawyer at all. This makes sense when you remember that the majority of people who divorce are relatively young, don't have much property, and often don't have children. With little to fight about, most avail themselves of the opportunity that no-fault divorce laws and standardized divorce forms offer to end their legal relationship with as little hassle as possible.

This isn't to say that every divorce is uncontested. Obviously, the trauma of a couple separating can occasionally be so powerful that it spills over into the legal arena. Indeed, several established divorce typing services report that about 5% of the seemingly uncontested divorces they prepare end up being contested, at least to some degree. This points up the need for independent paralegals working in the divorce area to emphasize in their promotional material that they only handle uncontested actions. Even more important, it indicates the necessity for tight customer screening at the initial customer interview, designed to weed out cases that are likely to become contested. Finally, the IP should plan in advance to efficiently deal with those few customers who, despite good screening, end up involved in a fight. (See Chapter 7, Section A.) For example, here is an excerpt from a flyer used by one divorce typing service.

DIVORCE YOURSELF
A NONLAWYER DIVORCE TYPING SERVICE!

With our form preparation help, you can file your own uncontested divorce. To be uncontested, you and your spouse must agree on the main issues of divorce, including:

- Custody of the children
- Visitation Rights
- Child support
- Spousal Support
- Division of Property

Important: We do not work with people involved in contested divorces. If you believe that your divorce is likely to be contested, please see a lawyer. If after you engage our services to help you prepare your uncontested divorce, your spouse files court papers to contest it, we reserve the right to refer you to a lawyer.

In addition to adopting written policies stating that you don't handle contested actions, it's important that you learn to recognize and respect the almost inevitable warning signals that will alert you when a contest is likely. For example, if a potential divorce customer tells you he doesn't plan to pay child support, wants to make his spouse pay all the bills, and that if she gives him any trouble, he will find a way to convince her, you will want to decline to type the papers. In this situation, the couple obviously hasn't agreed on much, and the other spouse is almost sure to end up with a lawyer to protect her interests.

Turning away customers can be a tough task for the new businessperson who is understandably anxious to develop business quickly. The danger is, of course, that a business-hungry IP will talk himself into helping a customer prepare paperwork in situations in which a later contest is likely. Unfortunately there is no detailed advice I can give you except to pay attention to any warning signals your customers give. You will lose much more than you gain if you take on a customer who has a messy contested problem.

Consumer bankruptcies are another area in which most filings are not contested. In bankruptcy, the underlying problem is normally painfully simple—the debtor owes a lot of money and has very little. Because there isn't much to discuss, except the holes in the debtor's pocket, few creditors are likely to challenge the bankruptcy. Very occasionally a creditor will surface with a claim that must be defended. One that is not too unusual is a creditor's assertion that the debtor submitted a fraudulent financial statement to get credit in the first place. If this occurs, or indeed, if a similar legal hassle develops in any other area in which you are working, whether it be divorce, incorporation, or probate, you will want to be able to refer your customer to a lawyer.

B. Type Legal Forms in High Demand

In addition to avoiding contested actions, you obviously want to work in areas of legal form preparation for which there is steady consumer demand. Fortunately, there is an added benefit in doing this for legal areas where the volume of paperwork is high—the legal bureaucracy has almost always worked out step-by-step protocols for handling that paperwork. Think of it this way: If a state court gets one stepparent adoption filing per calendar quarter, they may informally make up at least some of the paperwork requirements as they go along. But if they receive twenty a week, you can be sure that rules for forms and procedures will be clearly defined. And once they are, it's not difficult for the IPs to help their customers conform.

At this point you may be wanting to interrupt and ask something like this: "Doesn't each person's unique legal problem require a high degree of customization when it comes to filling out paperwork?" The simple answer is "No." Whenever a society has to deal with a great many people who need to accomplish the same task, whether it's applying for a driver's license, filing income tax, or applying for a business permit, the only cost-effective approach is to reduce the procedural steps to rote. This generally amounts to requiring the person who wants to accomplish the particular task (or their lawyer or typing service) to insert "magic words" in boxes and blanks on forms. And this is exactly the same approach courts use when it comes to filing for divorce or a change of name. The fact that lawyers think of divorce and name changes as "legal tasks" does not change the fact that, in uncontested situations, if you put the correct words in the correct boxes and blanks, you get the result you desire, and if you don't, you don't.

To sum up, in deciding whether a particular legal area is a good one for a paralegal approach, determine if:

- most filings are uncontested,

- volume is reasonably high,

- the paperwork is routine,

- you can charge enough to make a living (see Chapter 9), and

- resources are available for you to educate yourself as to how to do the particular task. (See the interview with Catherine Jermany in the Appendix).

C. Legal Areas Open to Independent Paralegals

Now let's examine some of the specific legal form preparation tasks that have worked well for independent paralegals. As mentioned, divorces and bankruptcies have long been popular with IPs because there are a lot of them and because many people who need one or the other can't afford to pay a lawyer. But these aren't the only areas where an IP can prosper.

Consider that every year there are more than a quarter million evictions, at least half a million small business incorporations and, taken together, hundreds of thousands of step-parent adoptions, name changes and conservatorships for people (most of them elderly) who aren't competent to manage their own financial affairs. In addition, hundreds of thousands of copyright applications are filed, millions of wills and living trusts are prepared, a substantial number of Social Security disability appeals are filed, and the estates of the majority of people who die must be probated. All of these legal areas and lots more are suitable for the independent paralegal because, for the most part, they involve the preparation of routine, and usually fairly repetitive, paperwork.

Here is a list of areas in which paralegals currently practice.

- **Divorce** (and annulments). This is the big one, with about 90% of IPs handling divorce petitions.

- **Bankruptcy** (Chapter 7 and Chapter 13). Nationally, this is the fastest growing IP area. About 700,000 bankruptcies are filed in the U.S. each year, and pre-printed forms and easily available self-help law books make doing the paperwork routine.

- **Evictions and other landlord services**. This is a fast growing, high-profit area that paralegals may well take over almost entirely.

- **Guardianships.** This usually routine legal action gives a grandparent or other relative or friend, who typically already has physical custody of a child who isn't their own, legal status that is often demanded by schools, hospitals, banks and others. About 25% of IPs handle guardianships.

- **Paternity actions.** When unmarried couples separate, a judicial decree of paternity is a necessary part of getting a court order for child support and custody.

- **Conservatorships.** A usually routine action brought by family members when an older person can no longer handle their own business and financial affairs.

- **Tenants' rights.** Most opportunity in this area is with nonprofit tenants' advocacy organizations, or public agencies such as rent boards or mediation services.

- **Probate.** Absent a probate-avoiding living trust or other pre-established plan to avoid probate, probate is normally required to get necessary court approval to transfer assets from the deceased person to his inheritors.

- **Debt collection.** An established industry that unfortunately never lacks growth potential—not my personal favorite. In most states, bill collectors are regulated, so don't choose this one until you check out your state's rules.

- **Debt counseling.** Many debtors don't know how to take advantage of legal protections while they reorder their affairs and get back on their financial feet. As Catherine Jermany reports in her interview in the Appendix, a number of IPs are meeting this demand by successfully combining credit counseling with the preparation of bankruptcy forms.

- **Incorporation.** Helping small business people incorporate is an area of almost unlimited potential for the independent paralegal who can afford to computerize the form preparation. (See Chapter 11.) If you doubt this, consider the view of William K. West, writing in *Case and Comment,* Vol. 90, No. 5, 1985, a publication which calls itself the "national magazine for practicing lawyers":

> *One area that normally calls for a standardized approach is incorporation. With more than 600,000 new corporations established in the United States in 1984 alone, it is a high-volume business. And yet much of it can, and should, be handled by paralegals, not lawyers. This is particularly true because standardized incorporation kits are available from a number of vendors. With proper training, a paralegal can take over the bulk of the paperwork involved in setting up a corporation, referring to the attorney only when the incorporation in question differs from routine.*

- **Parental relationship action.** Today, millions of parents aren't married. If they separate, paperwork must often be prepared for custody, support and visitation orders. In California, for example, preparing the paperwork necessary to establish a parental relationship under the Uniform Parentage Act makes up a significant portion of the business of many IPs.

- **Deed and other real estate transfers.** In many states, real estate people, title companies and other nonlawyers already control this business when residential and commercial property is bought or sold. However, consumers often need help in arranging private real estate transfers between friends and family, and this is a potential area for IP involvement.

- **Adoptions.** Many IPs prepare adoptions that occur when a parent with custody of children from a former marriage or living together relationship remarries and the new spouse wants to legally adopt the children. If the absent natural parent consents, or is out of the picture, the paperwork is routine.

- **Small claims court procedures.** Many IPs who currently work in this area concentrate on running group seminars and classes aimed at small businesspeople who use the court regularly. The idea is primarily to teach them how to use small claims court to sue customers who have failed to pay bills. But as small claims dollar limits increase in many states, the small claims counseling business is beginning to focus on helping individual consumers prepare their cases. Yes, this raises the issue of an IP helping a consumer prepare for a contested action, but since it's in the context of a court where people are encouraged to represent themselves, non-lawyers should be able to provide this information free of unauthorized practice of law charges.

- **Child support increases**. In many states, parents are entitled to petition for increases based on inflation or changed circumstances. In some states, court personnel will help with those petitions, and in many others, women's groups provide help through nonprofit organizations. But in lots of communities, IPs prepare much of this mostly routine paperwork. The National Association for Independent Paralegals estimates that over half of IPs are active in this area.

- **Restraining orders.** As with child support increases discussed just above, many women's groups provide this help. But especially when a customer is filing for divorce, IPs often prepare these protective orders in addition to typing divorce papers.

- **Simple wills**. Using the Nolo Press *Simple Will Book,* combined with will form software from the National Association for Independent Paralegals, many IPs are helping customers prepare their own wills.

- **Living trusts.** Lawyers advertise these probate avoidance devices for $1,500-$4,000. Many IPs will prepare them for $200-$400, often relying on Denis Clifford's book *Plan Your Estate With a Living Trust* to inform the customer and protect the IP from charges of unauthorized practice.

- **Name changes**. These are truly routine and easy. There are lots more of them than you might expect—check the number with your state court's office or Department of Vital Statistics.

- **Social security disability appeals.** A number of nonprofit groups who work with seniors and the disabled do this work using paralegals.

- **Copyright applications:** This is a routine, by-the-numbers job already handled by nonlawyers at most publishing companies. It's an area paralegals are sure to invade soon.

- **Partnership agreements.** Nolo Press publishes a book entitled *The Partnership Book: How to Write a Partnership Agreement,* and software, *Make Your Own Partnership Agreement,* that makes it easy for IPs to help small business people prepare their own partnership agreements.

- **Nonprofit corporations.** Several groups that work with arts groups are active in this area, but there is room for lots more paralegal form preparation work.

- **Workers compensation.** In California and a few other states where you don't have to be a lawyer to handle these contested disputes, IPs are getting into the act. Many lawyers have abandoned this area because, by their standards, fees are low. The result is a shortage of providers—a vacuum being filled by IPs.

CAN INDEPENDENT PARALEGALS REPRESENT CUSTOMERS APPEARING BEFORE ADMINISTRATIVE AGENCIES?

The Federal Administrative Procedure Act (see Chapter 2, Section C) allows Federal agencies to specifically permit nonlawyers to appear before them. Many do. For example, social security disability appeals, Medi-care appeals, Veterans programs and Federal housing programs can be handled by nonlawyers. State UPL laws can apply to Federal agencies and programs. If the agency has not explicitly stated that nonlawyers may appear before it, check in your state to see what the situation is.

At the state agency level, things are more confused. In some states, nonlawyers have the right to appear before many types of administrative agencies under state law. In others, only lawyers can appear before most agencies. In a few, state courts have used the inherent powers doctrine (see Chapter 2) to restrict the right of state legislatures to empower nonlawyers to appear before agencies. This means you will have check with each agency you are interested in individually to see if nonlawyers are allowed.

After reading this list you may be tempted to prepare several types of paperwork. There is nothing inherently wrong with this, as long as you have the detailed knowledge to handle each, and don't spread yourself too thin. Especially if you are new to the business, however, it's best to concentrate on one area, learn it thoroughly and then branch out.

When you are ready to expand, look for areas that are a natural extension of the one you already handle. Not only does this facilitate your learning process, but it makes it much easier to market your services as a coherent package. For example, Irene Zepko, a long-time paralegal in Fresno, California, defines her form preparation business around family problems. Thus, she types guardianships, conservatorships, stepparent adoptions, name changes, minor's emancipation petitions, child custody and support modifications, paperwork to establish a parental relationship for unmarried couples, as well as divorces. Indeed, divorce typing, which once made up the great majority of Zepko's business, now amounts to no more than half. Zepko takes pleasure in this diversity, both because her work is now more varied and interesting, and because, with 20 competing IPs working in Fresno, there isn't enough divorce typing to go around.

At a glance, it sounds as if Zepko has taken on a lot. But since all her work is family related, and California has adopted easy-to-use pre-printed forms, there are many similarities and procedural overlaps from one type of action to the next. Zepko is also aided by the fact that Nolo Press publishes step-by-step guides for completing paperwork in most of these areas.

Chapter 5

Naming Your Business

*N*aming a new business is fun. You free your imagination, let your creative juices flow, and come up with a name that tells the world exactly who you are. Right? Unfortunately, things are usually not that simple, especially when it comes to naming an independent paralegal business.

If you choose a name that describes the services your business offers (e.g., "Probate Form Typing Service"), people will know what you do. However, since the name isn't unique, you may have difficulty preventing a competing business with a similar name from opening up in the next town. If your name sounds too much like a lawyer's ("Divorce Law Consultants") you are likely to have the organized bar on your case in a hurry. If you pick a unique name that has nothing to do with lawyers ("Unicorn Enterprises" or "XYBOR Form Preparation Service"), your name will be easy to protect from use by competitors and will probably not trigger hostility from organized lawyerdom, but most people won't have a clue as to what you do.

HOW TO TRADEMARK YOUR NAME

In this chapter, and especially in Section G, I briefly discuss basic concepts of trademark law. I don't have the space to show you how to protect a name under Federal and state Trademark law. Doing this involves a number of steps, including choosing a protectible name, conducting a trademark search and formally registering your name. In February of 1992, Nolo Press will publish a step-by-step guide to show you how to accomplish this.

As you can see, coming up with a good name for an independent paralegal business involves juggling a number of variables. Here are a few suggestions.

A. Avoid Buzz Words That May Antagonize Organized Lawyerdom

As you should now clearly appreciate, the ability of an independent paralegal clinic to survive depends in large part on the ability of the operator to avoid the wrath of organized lawyerdom. The first place to practice this skill is in the selection of your name. The best way to avoid grief with the legal profession is to choose a name that carefully avoids such lawyer buzz words as "lawyer," "attorney," "counsel," "counsellor," "legal," "legal services," "legal information," "legal resource center," "legal clinic," "law" or "paralegal." There is an obvious reason for my advice. It amounts to illegal misrepresentation to use a name that suggests you are a lawyer if you are not.

When Ed Sherman and I initiated a group of self-help divorce typing services in California in 1973, we used the name "Wave Project." While this name was a little too fanciful for the taste of some of the people we worked with, and was eventually changed, it had one great advantage. By choosing a fanciful name rather than a descriptive one, we allowed the divorce typing business to define the "Wave Project," with the result that organized lawyerdom could never claim that our name misled the public into thinking that we provided attorney services.

When the Wave Project members changed their name, many chose "Divorce Centers of California," a name they have now successfully used for over 10 years. While it's hard to argue with success, I wouldn't have chosen this name because it doesn't sufficiently emphasize self-help. In more tradition-bound areas of the country, organized lawyerdom might claim that potential customers could be misled into thinking that Divorce Centers offered attorney services.

B. Choosing a Name That Emphasizes Self-Help Law

In my opinion, the best approach to naming your business is to adopt a name that emphasizes that you prepare paperwork for people who are handling their own legal affairs. In this context, the Latin terms for self-representation—*"In pro per"* (in one's own person) and *"pro se"* (on one's own behalf)—have been used by several independent paralegals. Although technically accurate, using somewhat obscure terms such as these is counterproductive for three reasons. First, many potential customers don't know what these Latin phrases mean. Second, some wrongly believe such phrases have something to do with lawyers, and may even wrongly conclude that you provide legal advice. Third, and most important, because Latin gobbledygook is negatively associated with lawyers and their seeming addiction to hiding behind jargon, at least some potential customers are likely to be turned off.

By pleasant contrast, however, the rough English equivalents of "in pro per" and "pro se," such as "self-representation," "self-help" and "do your own," work well as names when combined with a description of the actual service offered. Thus, "Self-Help Bankruptcy Typing Service" and "Do Your Own Divorce Typing Center" are both relatively safe and informative names.

It is not wise to use the word "help" without further defining it by adding a word such as "self." Otherwise, names like "Divorce Help" or "Bankruptcy Help" make it sound as if you provide legal expertise and information in these areas. Since doing this risks a charge that you are practicing law without a license, these are counterproductive names.

C. Using Descriptive Names

I have suggested that names that accurately describe what you do have an advantage from a marketing point of view and also help keep you out of trouble with organized lawyerdom. Thus you might end up with "South Boston Divorce Typing Service" or "Quality Incorporation Form Typing Service." Rosemary Furman, the pioneering Florida paralegal (see interview in the Appendix), who did business for years in Jacksonville, Florida under the nose of a hostile bar, called her business the "Northside Typing Service." The point of this approach is, of course, to let potential customers have some idea of what you do, but to avoid giving organized lawyerdom a convenient stick with which to beat you. In this context, remember, as I discuss in detail in Chapter 2, there is no law against simply typing forms for customers who wish to represent themselves in court, as long as it's the customer who makes all significant decisions.

The downside of using a descriptive name is that, under trademark law, descriptive names can be difficult to protect from use by potential competitors. For example, terms such as "typing," "form preparation," "word processing," "stenographer," and "secretarial" are in such general use that they are considered "public domain," and can be used by anyone, except in a few limited situations in which they are likely to result in customer confusion. (I discuss this concept in more detail in Section G, below.)

D. Combining a Unique and Descriptive Name

A good approach to naming an IP business that gets around the problem that a descriptive name is often hard to protect legally is to combine a unique or fanciful name with descriptive terminology. Thus, White Rose Divorce Typing Service would be protectible as a trademark if no one else had previously claimed or used it, and at the same time it tells your customers what you do.

E. Using Your Own Name

Yet another approach to naming your business is to use your own name, perhaps combining it with a term that describes what you do. Thus, Kwan Lee might use "Lee Probate Form Preparation Services."

One advantage of using your own name is that, in many states, it eliminates the need to file a fictitious business name statement. On the other hand, a potential disadvantage is that you can't claim exclusive use of your name under the trademark laws should someone else with the same name also wants to use it, unless over a period of time it has become so well-known and identified with your business that it clearly defines it in the public mind. (See Section G, below.)

This means if your own name is a common one, you may wish to choose a more distinctive name for your business. However, if your name is somewhat unusual, such as Pladsen, Hodovan, or Ihara, using it as part of your business name is probably fairly safe, since the chances of another independent paralegal with the same name going into competition with you seems fairly remote. For the same reasons, you might call yourself the P & K Lee Probate Form Preparation Business, a name that would likely be distinctive even if another person named Lee opened a similar business.

What about using your own name along with a vague-sounding term such as "Associates," "Consultants" or "Organization"? This is often a poor idea for two reasons. You are likely to end up with a name that sounds like a law firm, at the same time that it doesn't inform potential customers about what you do. For example, "Jones & Lee, Associates" may sound prestigious, but it is a lousy name for a typing service that helps people prepare their own wills and living trusts. Also, without a qualifier like "Jones & Lee Typing Service," or the addition of initials, you run the risk of infringing the trademark of some other business already using that name, especially if your name is similar to a famous one, like Firestone, Sears or Champion.

If despite my advice you are determined to use a vague term like associates, you can make it far more safe and effective by using it in conjunction with a term that describes what you do. Thus, if Jones and Lee, Associates adds "A self-help typing service for wills and living trusts," their name fairly and accurately describes their business. Of course, they may find that this is bit cumbersome and expensive, when it comes to listing their services in classified ads.

F. Using "Paralegal" as Part of Your Name

Let's now briefly discuss "paralegal," the term many, if not most, nonlawyers who run legal form typing services use to describe themselves. Like "midwife," "computer consultant" and "financial planner," "paralegal" can mean almost anything. Because most states have no official certification programs for paralegals, people with all sorts of training and experience quite properly and legally use this term. Some base their claim to be a paralegal on the fact that they took several paralegal courses at a business school. Others have a degree in paralegal studies from a university or business school that requires several years of study and which may or may not be accredited by the American Bar Association or some other group. Still others are former law firm employees who establish their own business to market specialized "freelance paralegal" services to lawyers. (See Chapter 13.) And, of course, there are also many "independent paralegals" who teach themselves how to type and market legal form preparation services directly to the public.

So far, so good, you are probably thinking. If the term paralegal can mean a variety of things, why shouldn't I use it to describe my independent typing service? Simply put, because the great majority of people who call themselves paralegals currently work for lawyers. This means that in the view of organized lawyerdom, shortsighted though it may be, paralegals are an extension of their empire. Your use of the term may give rise to their charge that you are representing yourself to the public as working under lawyer supervision. If this is hard to swallow, consider the parallel reality of the medical profession, where many doctors believe that "nurses" are people put on the earth to serve them, and the very word nurse conjures up, in the public mind, the image of a person who takes orders from a physician.

At least one trial court decision, *State Bar of Nevada v. Johnson,*[1] has specifically disapproved of the use of "paralegal" as a name for a legal typing service. In establishing guidelines for typing service operation, that court stated:

> *...The court probably cannot keep the defendants from appropriating a business name [Paralegal] which is not elsewhere prohibited in an as yet unregulated field. The court does feel, however, that it is within its power to limit advertising a status as "para-*

---

[1] Case No. CV89-5814 (Nev. 2nd Dist. Ct., April 12, 1990)

legals," as well as advertising the firm's ability to furnish "para-legal" services, because the term misleads the public into believing that the defendants are in the business of providing legal and non-scrivener services.

What about attempting to define the term paralegal with a second term, such as "Everyone's," "People's" or "Public," to eliminate the suggestion that lawyers are involved? This helps, but I would still advise avoiding a term that is likely to annoy lawyers. At this point, you may wonder what difference this makes, if lawyers are out to shut you down anyway. I don't have a definitive response to this query, except to suggest that whenever you deal with a large, unpredictable beast with long claws, it makes sense to avoid needlessly pulling its tail.

G. Legal Protection Against Copiers

So far I have briefly mentioned the legal concept of protecting your business name from use by competitors. Now let's look more thoroughly at the legal rules that are relevant to protecting the name of any business, including yours. As part of doing so, it will be necessary for you to read the following material on both trade names and service marks before drawing any conclusion.

1. Trade Names

The name that you select for your business is considered your "trade name." Trade names are subject to one major restriction. Your trade name can't be so similar to another trade name used by the same type of business in your area as to cause customer confusion. For instance, if "Speedy Divorce Form Preparation Service" has been open down the street for a year or two, you cannot legally open your own business under this, or a very similar, name.

What this often means, in practice, is that if you form a corporation, your proposed trade name will be reviewed by the state agency in charge of corporate registrations to see whether it is too similar to existing corporate names. If it is, it will be rejected and you'll have to come up with another. Likewise, if you have a sole proprietorship or a partnership, you will have to file a fictitious business statement with the county (or the state, in some places). Your proposed name will be checked against other names in your county and rejected if it is identical or too similar to an existing one.

In addition, unincorporated businesses can defend their trade names from use by others under state laws prohibiting unfair competition. These laws generally only require that businesses not engage in conduct that creates a likelihood of confusion. Thus, assuming you (or a competing business) isn't incorporated, if another "Speedy Divorce Form Preparation Service" opens up in another part of your county, or maybe even your state, you probably could challenge them under unfair competition laws, if you could show the likelihood that some of your customers would be confused by the new business's identical trade name. And the same laws can be applied against you if you select a name identical (or too similar) to a rival's.

2. Service Marks

Now suppose you chose a highly distinctive name, such as White Rose Divorce Typing Service. As a result of one of those sleights of hand for which the law is famous, a distinctive trade name such as this is entitled to much more protection than a descriptive trade name the instant it is used to identify the services being offered by the business. Why? Because when a trade name is used to identify services, it magically becomes a service mark, and distinctive service marks, as I explain immediately below, are fairly easy to protect against use by others.[2]

---

[2]While trademarks refer to products and service marks refer to services, they mean the same thing for purposes of this discussion.

This need not be confusing, because your trade name (that is, the name you select for your business) will most likely be the same as your "service mark" (any name or symbol that is used to market a particular service.) For instance, "Hyatt Legal Services," is both the name of the business and its service mark. Or, to take a more relevant example, if you use "South Bay Probate Typing Specialists" to market South Bay Probate Typing Specialists form preparation services, you have chosen both a trade name and a service mark.

In practice, your trade name becomes your service mark as soon as you use it to market your services. The only difference between them as far as you are concerned is that trade names are entitled to slightly less and different protections than are service marks. So while trade names have protections under unfair competition laws, service marks have both that *and* protection under trademark laws, which are stronger and provide stiffer penalties for infringement.

The wrinkle is that only service marks and trademarks that are distinctive or unique get protection from copiers under trademark laws. To return to the "Speedy Divorce Form" example, because Speedy is a common promotional term, and because Divorce Form says what the business does, the mark is too descriptive or not unusual enough to get protection as a trademark. Other words that are not unique enough to act as trademarks are common surnames and geographic terms, unless they gain secondary meaning. (See box, below.)

On the other hand, White Rose Divorce Form Typing Service is distinctive because it applies a term not usually associated with such a business. That makes it unique, and therefore fully protectible as a trademark. Other ways to create a unique service mark are to make up a word (like Zoline Forms Preparation), or to use a term in a suggestive way (like Ethereal Probate Services), as long as it's not too close to the subject matter of the services to become descriptive. Distinctive or unique marks are registrable with the state trademark office (or the federal office, if you do business across state lines). Once registered, the mark is exclusively yours to use within the state (or the country.)

A SECONDARY MEANING RULE: Descriptive Business Names Can Eventually Become Protected as Service Marks

---

A service mark that starts out in the public domain because it is descriptive or already in common use, including surnames or geographic terms, can sometimes gain the right to legal protection later. Called the "secondary meaning" rule, this legal concept allows a business to gain exclusive use of a descriptive or other common mark once the business becomes so well known by that name that the name comes to signify the business in the public mind. For example, McDonald's is no longer a common surname to most people; instead, we all know it as a trademark for the fast food chain. Likewise, "Ace Hardware" is protectible as a trademark because it has become so famous that we know exactly what stores the mark refers to. But note: Proving that your mark has acquired secondary meaning can take years and cost lots, due to customer surveys and attorney fees. This concept is discussed in detail in Nolo's new trademark book, to be published in 1992.

3. Improper Use of the Name of a Well-Known Business

There is one more factor to consider when you're thinking about service marks: "dilution" of famous marks. For example, suppose that you decide to name your independent paralegal clinic "Tiffany Scriveners." As it happens, the trademark "Tiffany" is owned by the company selling Tiffany jewelry. Under general trademark/service mark law, you would only be prevented from using the Tiffany mark if customers would be likely to confuse your product or service with that attached to the mark. However, another legal rule, which operates in a number of states, allows the owner of a mark to prevent its use by another if the qualities associated with the mark would be diluted in some significant way. For instance, if a company called "Tiffany Chimney Cleaners," or "Tiffany Bankruptcy Form Preparation Service," opened its doors, the first person through them would probably be a lawyer representing the Tiffany jewelry company, with court papers alleging dilution of the Tiffany mark. In short, our advice on this one is simple: don't use or play on the unique trade name or service mark of a large business. For example, Godiva Chocolates made Dogiva Dog Biscuits change its name under this rule.

4. Summing Up the Law of Trade Names and Service Marks

Suppose Speedy Divorce Form, a sole proprietorship, was the first to use this name in connection with a divorce-form typing business that only operates within one state. If it used its name locally and just filed a fictitious business name statement, Speedy Divorce Form would be entitled to protection only against other businesses operating in the same area because of the likelihood of consumer confusion. If Speedy Divorce Form were able to register its name as a service mark with the proper state agency, it might be able to prevent a rival business from using the same mark anywhere in that state. However, this would depend on the law of the particular state. The term might be viewed as too descriptive to gain even statewide protection.

If Speedy Divorce Form operated in at least two states, then it might be entitled to some national protection for the mark by registering it with the U.S. Patent and Trademark Office. Again, because this name is so descriptive, courts would be much less willing to protect it against use by others than if it were highly distinctive, such as, say, "Klingon Divorce Typing Service" or "White Rose Self-Help Bankruptcy Typing Service."

H. Summing Up: Names You Shouldn't Use

So far, we've covered factors you should try to incorporate into a business name—the degrees of distinctiveness and descriptiveness. We have also discussed why it's a good idea to identify your business in a way that prevents lawyers from claiming you are misleading the public into thinking you are a law office or provide legal advice or help. Now, let's summarize this information in a list of "don'ts." Remember, it's worth the time it takes to choose a name carefully, because if your business becomes a success, your name will be one of your most valuable assets, and you won't want to have to change it.

- Do not use a name that uses words like "law," "legal services" or "paralegal." (See Section A for other words to avoid.)

- Do not use the same name as an existing business that operates in your area.

- Do not use a name that can be easily confused with that used by any business in your area. For example, if you call your business "How to Do Your Own Divorce Associates" and someone else in your city is using the term "Divorce Yourself Associates," you are asking for legal trouble because your name may mislead or confuse the public.

- Don't use a name other than your own (or, if you are incorporated, other than the name your corporation is registered under) without first filing a fictitious name statement (in most states). Contact your county clerk's office for information.

- If you plan to incorporate, don't use a name without first checking with your state's corporation commissioner or secretary of state. If the state finds your name is the same or confusingly similar to one already used by another corporation, you will probably be required to choose another.

- Do not use the name of a large national corporation, even if incorporated in another state.

- Do not use a name that could easily be confused with a service mark that you have reason to believe is federally registered (you can tell by the "®" that accompanies the mark) or registered in your state.

Chapter 6

Establishing an Office

*P*eople have successfully begun independent paralegal businesses from all sorts of places, including the kitchen table. When you are just starting out, your decision about where to carry on your business will probably be determined in large part by personal economic considerations. Although I believe on balance that it's usually easiest to rent a modest office as opposed to operating from your living space, this may simply not be practical. There is nothing inherently wrong with starting small, even if this means operating out of a spare bedroom or converted garage—unless you are in an area in which zoning laws prohibiting home-based businesses are strictly enforced or you can't get the motor oil off the floor of the garage.

A. Opening a Home-Based Business

There can be an advantage to operating a business from your home if you live in a state or city where organized lawyerdom is likely to try to put you out of business if it can find you. If you are able to attract enough customers via word of mouth or other semi-underground methods, you may be able to run a home-based paralegal business successfully for some time without organized lawyerdom even knowing you exist.

Operating from home is attractive to many people, especially those who have spent years battling their way to work at rush hour. It usually isn't. Take it from someone who has done it for years—the joy of being only one step from work can quickly turn into the anguish of never seeming to be able to get more than three steps away from it. In addition, anyone who runs a home-based business must deal with the fact that some potential customers are mistrustful of a business not located in a conventional office setting. You can, however, usually defuse this problem in advance. I ran both a small legal clinic and a publishing business from my home by taking most of the steps outlined below—but then, in fairness, I should point out that I had one big advantage. I was living in Berkeley, California, where to be a little bizarre was normal and to be conventional meant you had already moved away.

Here are a few suggestions based on my own experience that you may wish to implement if you plan to operate out of your home:

- Set up a defined work area separate from your living space. A good-sized room is best, but a corner of a larger room will do in a pinch if it is carefully screened or partitioned. Furnish your workspace like an office and, if possible, provide a small waiting area for customers should appointments overlap. You will need a desk, a couple of sturdy chairs for customers (so you don't have to bring one in from the kitchen), a file cabinet, word processor (or typewriter), and a supply of standard office supplies. It will help greatly if you can also afford a small photocopier and a FAX machine.

- If you live with others, absolutely insist that they respect this work area. This not only means that it's kept free of personal belongings, but that it's quiet and private when you are working with customers.

- See customers only by appointment. When you talk to them by phone to make an appointment, inform them you operate from a home environment so they won't be surprised when they arrive. Some home-based independent paralegals often add that they do this in order to keep overhead, and therefore prices, down.

- Establish a business phone with an answering machine—preferably one that lets a caller talk for as long as he wants. Having a separate line allows you to instantly distinguish between business and personal calls. Answer your office phone only during working hours and always state your business name.

- If your situation allows, establish a separate business entrance. I did this when I ran my home-based business and it worked extremely well. The people who came to see me on business never saw anything but the office.

- Have your office and waiting area reflect what you do. Displaying framed copies of newspaper articles about you and your business is one way to do this. For example, the waiting room of the Superior California Legal Clinic in Sacramento has several *Sacramento Union* newspaper articles about self-help law clinics mounted on the wall. Another effective means of doing this is to display a collection of self-help law materials. Also, as discussed in Chapter 3, you should provide customers with printed information making it clear that they are representing themselves and that you are not an attorney. A description of your basic self-help philosophy would also be helpful. Here is an edited version of one used by the Superior California Legal Clinic:

DIVORCE HELP

DO YOU NEED LEGAL ASSISTANCE OR A NONLAWYER TYPING SERVICE?

An alternative to hiring a lawyer to do your divorce is to "do it yourself." SUPERIOR CALIFORNIA LEGAL CLINIC'S trained nonlawyer personnel will help you prepare all forms necessary to do your own divorce.

■ You can handle your own legal form preparation needs with a little help from us.

■ Many people already know the basic information necessary to obtain their own divorce or accomplish other basic legal procedures. What they don't know is how to complete the necessary forms.

■ Our service is based on the idea that everyone should have the opportunity to handle their own case efficiently, simply and at an affordable price.

CAUTION!

Representing yourself can work well for routine uncontested actions. However, if you expect a legal battle, you should not do your own divorce without attorney representation or assistance.

- If you live with others, discuss your needs in detail and make sure they are supportive of your home business. If your family or housemates have doubts about your enterprise, don't embark on it until all their concerns have been positively resolved. For example, if your spouse is concerned about how you will cope with your customer's children or about customers who smoke, or perhaps about who will care for your own child while you are interviewing customers, don't brush these worries aside. Failure to do this risks having the efficient operation of your business negatively affected.

- Consider the needs of neighbors. In many areas where home-based businesses are technically illegal, municipal officials won't hassle you unless a complaint is filed. This usually occurs because neighbors are angered over losing their parking space or fearful because they don't know why so many people are coming and going. A little communication (e.g., "I type divorces, I don't deal drugs") and courtesy can work wonders. For example, if you have a driveway, keep your own car in the garage and ask customers to park in your driveway rather than in front of your neighbors' homes.

GOOD INFORMATION ABOUT RUNNING A HOME-BASED BUSINESS

For more information about running a business from your home, I recommend the following books:

- *Working From Home,* by Paul and Sarah Edwards (Jeremy Tarcher): This book offers a good overview and sound advice about living and working under the same roof. I particularly like the discussions on how to keep your personal and business lives separate and avoid loneliness.

- *The Home Office: How To Set Up and Use Efficient Personal Workspace in the Computer Age,* by Mark Alvar (Goodwood Press): As the subtitle indicates, this book focuses on the physical details of establishing a home office. Issues covered include choosing a suitable space, selecting furniture, and buying office equipment—including computer hardware and software.

Despite the advantages of a home-based business, all independent paralegals I know who started this way eventually moved to a formal office setting. Many, of course, were glad they started at home because it allowed them to test the financial waters of their new business without feeling that they were betting their whole economic future on its immediate success. Indeed, I know several who held on to their jobs until their independent paralegal business (operated from home mostly during evening hours and on weekends) started generating enough money to allow it to be a full-time occupation.

People's reasons for eventually moving their business to a commercial office space vary, but an important one is often the realization that the cost of office space is significantly less than that for living space. The fact that it was initially cheaper to start at home (you already own or rent it), becomes less important as your business expands and you require more room. Then it usually becomes cheaper to find commercial office space, as opposed to getting a bigger living/work space.

Wanting to get away from living with a business is another important reason why many home-based IPs eventually move to an office setting. In this context, several paralegals mentioned that it's one thing to share hearth and home with a little start-up business, but quite another—and much less desirable—to cohabit with a growing one.

Finally, some IPs report that the patience and support of family members, housemates and neighbors can eventually wear thin. The fact that they are willing to cooperate with your needs for a few months or years while you are getting started doesn't mean they will do it forever.

B. Running an IP Business From Commercial Space

If you do decide to operate from a business space, you have some choices to make. One is to simply rent an office and put your name on the door. Another is to share space with an established business. Doing this can be a sensible half-way measure between moving your business out of your living space and opening your own office. This can be particularly desirable if you are on a tight budget, since sharing a business space costs a lot less than opening your own office.

It's not hard to find space to share. All sorts of businesses, including real estate and insurance agencies, business consultants, financial planners, and tax preparers, commonly have extra room. For a modest monthly rental, you can often arrange to put your desk and typewriter in a partitioned off corner of a big office, or better yet, a small separate room. A big advantage to this sort of arrangement is that you gain the respectability an existing business provides without either the trouble or expense of renting your own place.

Another space-sharing alternative is to work out a cooperative arrangement with a nonprofit or other group that works in the same field that you do. For example, in exchange for free or low-cost space at a local women's organization, you might, in addition to typing divorces for a reasonable fee, agree to help low-income women prepare the paperwork for restraining orders for free. Similarly, if you want to do work for landlords, you might discuss your space needs with the county apartment house owners' association. In exchange for your offering members your services at a discounted fee, the association might be willing to provide you with free or low-rent space. (I discuss how IPs can work with nonprofits in more detail in Chapter 14.)

Sooner or later, however, you'll probably want to rent your own office space. There are loads of different types of office settings available, many of which are discussed in my interviews with Glynda Mathewson, Robin Smith and Jolene Jacobs in the Appendix. Here are some considerations about locating an IP business:

- You don't need or want a fancy office in a posh location, so it' fine to keep your rent budget relatively low.

- Location is important but not nearly as critical as it can be to a retail store or restaurant. Most of your customers will be referred to you by others, so any easy-to-reach location will work. There is no need to locate in a high rent district or an area with lots of pedestrian traffic.

- Access is important. Always ask yourself where customers will park. Also, check out public transit routes. Yours is not an affluent clientele and you'll do better if you're near a bus stop.

- Safety is important. Don't locate in an area people will think twice about coming to. Your customers will be working folks, many of whom will want to come by in the evening. If your neighborhood is scary after dark, a good number won't come.

- Older but still respectable business buildings like those recently abandoned by lawyers and doctors for fancy new office complexes are often a good choice, especially if they're located near courts and other city services. (See Glynda Mathewson's interview.)

- Older shopping centers and strip malls often have offices upstairs, over the shops, which are available at very reasonable rates. Since these areas are usually located on busy streets, have parking lots and are near public transportation, they can be a good choice.

In addition to location, you will need to think about how much space you'll need. It's my experience that working out of one room is difficult. Customers who are being interviewed or filling out paperwork appreciate a private area away from your reception space, which will often necessarily double as a child's play area. So rent at least two small offices, or a room big enough to be divided. If you can afford it, renting three work areas is even better: one for reception, one for customer interviews and one for form preparation. I recommend a separate area for form preparation, not only because your computer, typewriter, photocopy and FAX machines take up space, but because you will want easy access to them at all times, something that may be difficult if you are conducting interviews in the same location.

C. Negotiating a Good Lease or Rental Agreement

When you rent an office, you not only must worry about the amount of rent and the location and size of the space, you also must negotiate a lease or month-to-month rental agreement. Do you want to try and lock in a space for years or choose the shortest time period possible? There are no right answers—it depends on how established your business is, how fast it is growing and whether you are likely to be challenged by organized lawyerdom, among a host of other factors. Here are some general, and at times conflicting, factors you will want to consider:

- Renting moderate-priced office space is usually easy in most areas because the market is glutted. This means there is little need to lease a particular space for a long time. In the unlikely event you are asked by the landlord to move, there will be a wide choice of other available locations.

- When you first open, you'll be doing many things to get your business known in the community. One of these will be to inform people where you are. It follows, then, that assuming you have picked a good location, you will want to stay put for a while.

- If your business prospers, you'll probably want more (or perhaps better-located) space. Unless it's likely to be available at your first location, this means you won't want a long lease that will make it difficult or expensive for you to move.

Fortunately, there is a way to at least partially resolve the conflicts raised by these considerations. This involves renting an office space for a relatively short period with an option to renew for a longer period. For example, you might lease two rooms in a business building for six months or a year, with an option to renew at the end of the tenth month for an additional year or two at a pre-established rental amount. This allows you to see how things work out and make your decision accordingly. Because granting you an option potentially ties up a landlord's property, she may ask you for an extra payment in exchange. As long as the amount is modest, this request is reasonable and you may want to go along.

But suppose a landlord refuses to consider a short lease period with an option to renew and demands a lease for two or three years? Unless your business is well-established and you are absolutely sure you will stay there for that period, just say "no." Again, as I emphasized earlier, most communities have a glut of small- and moderate-priced offices in older buildings, and you should have no trouble finding one, with a landlord who will accommodate your needs.

D. Good Information on Small Business Operations

This book is primarily about how to run an independent paralegal business, not about small business skills generally. Just the same, when your thoughts turn to establishing an office, it's a good time to consider lots of other details of running a quality small business. Some of these are fairly mundane, such as getting a business license, buying appropriate equipment and establishing a good bookkeeping system. Others are more complicated, such as creating realistic financial projections and a sound marketing plan. In this regard, the National Association for Independent Paralegals, based in Sonoma, California (see interview with Catherine Jermany in the Appendix), offers excellent training seminars that address all of these areas. They even deal with such common business needs as establishing Mastercard and Visa accounts and buying cost-effective liability insurance.

In addition, there are several excellent books on how to accomplish these (and many more) small business tasks. I highly recommend the following:

- *Small Time Operator,* by Bernard Kamoroff (Bell Springs Publishing). This handy guide, which is updated yearly, has been popular for over twenty years for excellent reasons. It gives you essential information about the paperwork you'll have to deal with, including keeping books, paying taxes, becoming an employer, etc. The book also contains excellent information on how to efficiently use computers and other electric equipment in your business. In fact, it is so detailed, it even tells you the type of calculator to buy. If you never buy another business book, buy this one.

- *How to Write a Business Plan,* by Mike McKeever (Nolo Press). This easy to use guide shows you how to raise money for your new business, including tips on how to arrange loans from both family members and conventional lenders. As part of doing this, it helps you prepare a detailed financial plan for your proposed business. In my experience, doing this may demonstrate that even using your best case assumptions, your proposed business won't produce the financial rewards you expect. In short, this book not only will help you prepare to borrow money to get a business started, it gives you the financial tools necessary to realistically assess your business idea.

- *Honest Business,* by Michael Phillips and Salli Rasberry (Random House). This book might as well be entitled, Zen and the Art of Small Business Success. Although it's now a few years old, this remarkable book fills a niche occupied by no other in its focus on the personal and psychological qualities it takes to succeed in a small business. Much of Phillips' and Rasberry's advice stands conventional small business wisdom on its head. For example, they explain why having plenty of capital is usually much worse for a new business person than not having enough.

- *Marketing Without Advertising,* by Michael Phillips and Salli Rasberry (Nolo Press). The same authors demolish the myth of advertising effectiveness and outline practical alternate ways for a small business to market its products and services. As I further develop in Chapter 10, "Marketing Your Services," creating a marketing plan that does not rely on expensive advertising is usually a key to success as an independent paralegal.

Chapter 7

How to Establish a Good Relationship With Lawyers, Mediators and Judges

*T*here is no need to elaborate on the fact that organized lawyerdom has done a miserable job of providing routine legal services at a reasonable price to the American public, and that this is one reason for widespread public anger towards the profession. Indeed, many paralegals enter the legal form preparation business at least in part because of their own hostile feelings toward lawyers. However, even though antipathy to the legal profession by IPs is reasonable, especially when you consider you must compete with a group that commonly wants to put you in jail, paradoxically, it is often to the advantage of both you and your customers that you work closely with one or more lawyers.

A. Working With Lawyers

Think of it this way—should you ever need to ask for help or advice, wouldn't it be nice to have access to a sympathetic legal expert supportive of the idea of self-help law and your role in it? And wouldn't it be great to be able to refer customers who need legal expertise you can't safely provide to a lawyer who is both reasonably-priced and competent. And, while we are playing a fantasy game, wouldn't it also be terrific to know one or more lawyers willing to go to bat for you and your business should their less flexible brethren accuse you of unauthorized practice?

If your answer to any one of these questions is "yes," you're ready for the big question: "How do you find supportive lawyers, or at least one of them?"

Before I suggest ways to do this, a few more words about lawyers are appropriate. Throughout most of this book, I have pictured organized lawyerdom as a monolithic group almost universally hostile to the idea of nonlawyer competition. While viewing the legal profession as a monolith is necessary to focus your attention on necessary survival techniques—it is also an oversimplification.

If instead of looking at the entire legal profession with what amounts to a wide angle camera lens, you instead employ a zoom lens to focus on individuals, you will immediately see that lawyers don't have a monolithic view of anything—even their own divine right to dominate the delivery of legal services. Or, put another way, many individual lawyers understand that their profession is out of touch with the legal needs of millions of ordinary Americans and are embarrassed by it. While the traditional view that lawyers should preserve their monopoly at all costs still dominates most state and local bar associations and county courthouses, even in these places, the notion that independent paralegals should be squelched under all circumstances is slowly receding. And once you get away from lawyers associated with the delivery of personal legal services and instead canvass those who work for big firms and public agencies, you'll find a good number who are actually supportive of efforts to make high quality, low-cost legal form preparation services widely available. The fact that not all lawyers buy into the traditional views of organized lawyerdom should not be surprising when you consider that one-third of American lawyers have been admitted to practice in the last decade.

If you doubt that fair-minded lawyers exist, consider the views of Bob Anderson, an attorney in Berkeley, California who operated a divorce typing service as a paralegal prior to becoming an attorney:

> *While running the Divorce Center, I developed a list of friendly attorneys for advice and referral (whenever I made a referral I attempted to name at least two attorneys, so that the customer could make a choice). A number of positive effects flowed from this relationship as far as I was concerned. First, by referring questions to attorneys I greatly reduced the risk of my practicing law without a license. Second, I provided a better service to the customer in that s/he had questions answered that were beyond my knowledge. And third, I was able to refer people who called but could not use a self-help service for one reason or another to attorneys who were less likely to rip them off, but who would provide the required service. Now, as an attorney, I refer qualified cases to self-help typing centers. I get satisfaction from seeing that the self-help movement is continuing because (especially in California divorces) there is increasing recognition among us (attorneys) that we cannot properly service the typical self-help case because of the dollars involved versus the fees we have to charge.*

> *On the other hand, there are some negatives to the self-help center operator/attorney relationship. The first is that it is hard to find attorneys who will be willing to take on this responsibility, at least partly because of fear of malpractice suits (this is to be read as difficult, not impossible. My experience was that there were and are such attorneys). The second is that one takes a risk of losing the customer every time you send him/her to an attorney. This is warranted if the situation is too difficult to be handled by a self-help operation, but there may be times where the lawyer wrongly convinces the customer that the case is too difficult and takes the case away. I ran into this problem; but by following up on referrals*

and by constantly looking for sympathetic attorneys to add to the list, I minimized the problem.

B. How To Find Supportive Lawyers

Locating a lawyer or lawyers who will support what you are doing can be a huge help when it comes to dealing with (or fending off) those who don't. Remarkably, if even one or two lawyers in your community know what you are about and approve your work, you are less likely to be prosecuted. Indeed, one friendly lawyer may even be able to stop a prosecution that is in the works. I have seen this happen on at least three occasions. In each instance, after either one or several local attorneys quietly let it be known that they would go to bat for a particular independent paralegal who was threatened with an unauthorized practice charge, the planned prosecution was dropped. How can one, two, or even a small group of lawyers stop organized lawyerdom so easily? Because prosecutors know they are less likely to win the battle for public opinion if local lawyers are willing to take the witness stand or make public statements saying that the particular independent paralegal is not practicing law and is an asset to the community.

In addition to making contact with sympathetic lawyers for self-preservation reasons, you will also benefit from an alliance with at least one lawyer familiar with the legal subject or subjects you deal with for at least two reasons. First, if you pick a truly experienced lawyer, this person will probably know more than you do about the legal paperwork you are preparing. If you can occasionally call this person for advice when you face a difficult problem, it will be a big help.

Second, and at least as important, a relationship with a local lawyer will mean you have someone to whom you can refer customers who need formal legal advice, or whose problem changes from uncontested to contested before your horrified eyes. If you don't have the ability to do this, you may be tempted to try to help your customer solve a problem that you are not equipped or trained to deal with. Aside from the risk of being charged with the unauthorized practice of law inherent in giving any legal advice, you also assume the risk (to your customers, at least) of giving bad or incomplete advice.

But, suppose you are just starting your business in a section of America where most lawyers are still maniacal about defending their monopoly. How do you find lawyer allies without making yourself so visible to organized lawyerdom that you do more harm than good? There is no one right way to do this, but here are some hints. Please realize that like most general rules, each of these has its exceptions, and it will be up to you to creatively apply them to your situation:

- Avoid attorneys closely-associated with local bar associations and bar referral panels. They tend to attract just the sort of small office traditionalists who will feel most threatened by your business and will want to close you down.

- Attorneys with strong pro-consumer records are good people to feel out. Also, lawyers who work in the emerging field of mediation often tend to be predisposed to helping people help themselves.

- Lawyers in private practice who have worked for federally-funded legal services (often called "legal aid") programs can also be good bets, as they have already worked in a clinic-like context where the same sorts of legal tasks you handle are accomplished by paralegals. In addition, many lawyers who are attracted by legal aid work in the first place are sympathetic to the needs of the legally underserved. Current legal services intake workers, secretaries, and paralegals should be able to suggest some likely former legal services lawyers.

- Do not assume that a progressive political stance on social issues, such as the environment, women's rights, minority hiring, or disarmament means a lawyer will be sympathetic with what you are doing. To the contrary, in my experience, it is often people who are fairly conservative politically who are the most pro-self-help law. This isn't so surprising when you realize that many conservatives take seriously the traditional right of every American to have good access to the legal system at a reasonable cost. Paradoxically, many personal injury, criminal defense and other lawyers who often favor all sorts of reforms for society typically oppose long-needed legal reforms such as adopting no-fault automobile insurance, abolishing probate and licensing independent paralegals. They fear change in these areas because it will negatively affect their monopoly over the legal system and, as a result, the girth of their wallets. Again, the point is, do not bare your soul to a lawyer just because you respect the stance that person took on an unrelated social issue.

• Personal friends and acquaintances (or, if necessary, friends of friends) can be a good source of possibly helpful lawyers. If you worked previously at a court clerk's office, or a local law firm, you probably know at least a few lawyers you respect. If you don't have these contacts, think about whether you know anyone whose judgment you trust who can suggest lawyers who are likely to be sympathetic.

In an effort to create a network of lawyer supporters, start by locating one lawyer to whom you can refer customers with problems more complicated than you can handle. As a significant percentage of almost 800,000 lawyers in the U.S. are under-employed, there are plenty of likely candidates. Some of these lawyers are likely to be interested in (and often threatened by) the growth of heavily advertised chain law clinics such as Jacoby and Myers and Hyatt and want to get in on the low-cost legal clinic action without giving up their independent practices. One way for a lawyer to do this is to set up a paralegal division within their own office; another is to work closely with one or more legal typing services.

When you locate someone who you think is a potential supporter, approach her carefully. Start by soliciting their general views on the desirability of opening up the legal system to more participation by nonlawyers. If they are hostile or extremely worried, back off. If they express an openness to the independent paralegal movement, but seem tentative, go slow and don't presume too much at the start. Always remember that all lawyers, even your friends, have undergone a remarkably homogeneous educational experience which has repeatedly emphasized the fact that only lawyers are competent to practice law. This is a hard burden for even the most enlightened lawyer to completely put down and you are likely to find that even a genuinely supportive lawyer will experience moments when he doubts whether your profession should exist. Try to anticipate this and help your lawyer friend come to terms with and conquer these occasional attacks of professional paranoia. No matter how highly she was recommended, or how much you respect her for other reasons, go slowly when it comes to disclosing what you are doing or plan to do. Again, if you are greeted with hostility, or even a lot of obvious nervousness, don't argue—back off quickly.

Assuming the lawyer seems genuinely open to working with you, ask if it will be okay if you occasionally refer customers who wish to handle their own legal affairs, but need some legal advice as part of doing so. If the lawyer wants to know more about your business, be prepared to demonstrate that you really run a self-help legal typing service and do not provide legal advice. (The best way to do this is to follow the techniques I discuss in Chapter 3.)

Again, assuming all signs are go, send over a few people. Check back with your customers to find out how they were treated. If you find they got good service at a fair price, you will want to try to gradually establish a closer relationship with the lawyer. The best way to do this is to make yourself valuable to the lawyer by continuing to refer appropriate customers to his office. As the lawyer comes to see that you are a responsible business producer, you can begin to discuss some of your needs. Over time, you will want to work out an informal understanding with the lawyer that in exchange for the business you produce, he will answer your occasional questions and go to bat for you if you are accused of practicing law without a license.

In Bakersfield, California, a group of local independent paralegals has taken this sort of relationship a step further. A local lawyer, who believes strongly that IPs should be trained to do an excellent job, volunteers his time to help train the independent paralegals on how to do a better job typing divorce and bankruptcy forms. (See Virginia Simons interview in the Appendix.)

C. Make a Lawyer Your Partner

So far, I have assumed that you want to open your own business and relate to lawyers only as you need them. I have also extensively discussed the fact that operating independently makes you vulnerable to the charge that you are practicing law without a license. For some readers, beginning a new business (which is never easy), at the same time that you may be attacked by hostile lawyers will be too much to cope with.

One way to reduce the fear that you will be prosecuted for unauthorized practice is to work directly for a lawyer as a freelance paralegal. (See Chapter 13.) Another is to have a lawyer work very closely with your business. In other words, instead of working for a lawyer, encourage a lawyer to work with you. Before you dismiss this idea as silly, consider the fact that bill collectors have used this approach for years, often working with one lawyer in a stable long-term relationship which in all but name amounts to a shared business. Major portions of the medical profession also seem to be heading in this direction with business people increasingly owning hospitals, clinics and emergency treatment facilities, and hiring doctors and other professional care providers to work for them.

More to the point, I know of several divorce and landlord eviction services run by independent paralegals who have a lawyer directly associated with their practice. In exchange for having the lawyer available to provide reasonably-priced legal advice to the paralegal's customers when necessary, the independent paralegal typically refers all customers with contested cases and legal questions to the lawyer. Again, the advantage to this sort of arrangement to the lawyer, the paralegal and the customer is obvious.

The desirability of establishing an independent paralegal business that works very closely with a lawyer must, of course, be weighed against the fact that having a lawyer closely associated with your business may negatively affect the way you work. Remember, one reason why independent paralegal services are so popular is that they allow customers the right to simplify their legal problem. Lawyers, of course, commonly do the opposite, burdening even the most routine legal tasks with layers of often unneeded complexity—a process which, in the eyes of many legal reformers, all too often seems to continue exactly as long as the client's money holds out. In short, if you have a lawyer associated with your operation, you want to be sure that her lawyerly tendency toward high-cost obfuscation doesn't end up emasculating your business.

Another potential problem for independent paralegals and lawyers who work closely together are state laws and state supreme court opinions which state that every business offering legal services to the public must be owned and controlled by lawyers. Specifically, these statutes make it illegal for nonlawyers to participate in the ownership of a law practice (Washington, D.C. and North Dakota are limited exceptions) or to split legal fees with lawyers.

In the long run, I suspect that many of these laws will be struck down as being illegal restraints of trade under the Sherman Anti-Trust Act, but as this edition goes to press, they are still firmly on the books. Fortunately, if you engage in a little creative business organization, they shouldn't prevent you from working closely with a lawyer. The key is to keep the two businesses structurally separate. This not only means you should not formally hire the lawyer or split fees, but that each business should be an independent legal entity (that is, if you occupy the same office, put both names on the door, get separate business licenses and don't treat the lawyer as an employee or independent contractor). If a customer uses the services of both you and the lawyer, she should pay with separate checks. Yes, when an IP and a lawyer work closely together on a regular basis, respecting this somewhat artificial business division can be cumbersome, but if you're investigated by organized lawyerdom, you'll both be glad you took the trouble.

D. Working With Mediators

In some legal areas, a certain percentage of an independent paralegal's customers are likely to have, or develop, a contested dispute about a factual issue with another party. Divorce is the most obvious, where arguments over property division, support, child custody and visitation are fairly common.

If you are typing a divorce or paperwork for another domestic action, such as a step-parent adoption, and your customer tells you that he and his former mate are having a serious dispute about a factual matter, your best bet is to encourage them to see a private or, if such a program exists in your area, a court or other publicly-run mediation service.

Mediation is a process by which a third party (the mediator) helps people with a dispute arrive at their own solutions. Precisely because it is non-coercive—the mediator, unlike a judge or arbitrator, has no power to impose a decision—mediation often works brilliantly to settle domestic disputes. The idea is normally for you to refer the disputing couple to the mediator, have them work out their dispute (and write down the agreed-upon compromise) and then have your customer return to your office to complete the other paperwork.

The question then arises, what type of mediator should you work with? Here are some thoughts:

- Most of your customers will be on a tight budget. You'll need to find a mediator who charges a reasonable fee (often in the range of $60 per hour) and is result-oriented. A mediator who expects to help customers probe their psyches for many hours, at $150 per hour, may be fine for the BMW set, but would not be a good choice for your customers.

- In many states, mediated agreements to divide property as part of a divorce can be submitted directly to a court as part of the divorce paperwork you type. If so, you will want to work with a mediator who knows how to prepare the necessary forms.

- This raises the question of whether the mediator should be a lawyer. My answer is not necessarily. Although lawyer mediators will normally be adept at preparing necessary paperwork, they often aren't able to shed their "lawyer in control" attitudes and truly let the parties arrive at their own solutions. In addition, many charge more than most of your customers will be able to afford. In my experience, nonlawyer mediators, whose fees are often more modest, are typically more open to allowing disputants find their own solutions.

E. Working With the Courts

In some parts of America, court clerks and judges are implacably opposed to the self-help law movement and, by logical extension, to IP's. However, in many states, including large portions of Florida, Texas and most of the West Coast, the legal profession's outright hostility is beginning to be replaced by grudging acceptance and, in some instances, guarded support for independent paralegals.

Whether judges and court clerks are hostile or friendly, you may as well get used to the idea that you'll have to work fairly closely with them. Even if you never set foot in the courthouse, they will quickly come to recognize your paperwork, even though your name appears nowhere on it. Given this, I recommend that you try to form as positive a relationship as possible with key people at the courthouse. Here are some suggestions:

- Court clerks are often burdened by nonlawyers (and more often than you would guess, lawyers) filing incorrect and incomplete paperwork. Assuming that you really do know what you are doing, the papers your customers file will likely come as a welcome relief. This may result in your getting positive feedback from a court clerk. If so, use this as an opportunity to better introduce yourself. Make it clear that you only type paperwork and don't practice law. Then ask the clerk if she can suggest ways your work can be improved. One opportunity for this type of contact to take place is at the filing window, assuming, of course, you occasionally file paperwork yourself. In fact, in many communities, contacts at the filing window have lead to such a positive independent paralegal-court clerk relationship, that the clerk actually starts referring customers to the IP.

- If possible, get to know one or more local judges, who often review your paperwork. Sometimes this can be done through a civic organization or, if the judge must run for re-election, as part of her campaign. In other instances, a judge who is genuinely concerned about legal access for a particular group, such a single mothers, older people or minorities, may be willing to counsel you on ways to improve your work. If you are a member of an IP association, consider asking the judge to meet with your group. (See Glynda Mathewson's and Rose Palmer's interviews in the Appendix.) Obviously, in all meetings with judges, it pays for IPs to go to great lengths to indicate that they do not give legal advice to customers.

Chapter 8

How to Run a Quality Business

*A*ll of the advice in this book about how to prosper as an independent paralegal assumes one crucial thing: that you do excellent work. It is appropriate, then, to take a minute to touch on some basic business practices and procedures.

Before you even open your doors, it is essential that you do at least three things. The first is to make sure that you are thoroughly familiar with how to prepare all the legal forms and, if relevant, with the agency procedures that you will handle. The second is to understand how to run your business without engaging in the unauthorized practice of law. (See Chapter 3 for a thorough discussion.) Third, it is essential that you establish a number of ordered business procedures to ensure that every customer in fact receives quality error-free help.

A. Training

Some readers, who have worked for lawyers for years, typing the same forms they plan to prepare as an independent paralegal, will already have the technical form-preparation expertise they need. However, many others will need basic training on how to prepare legal paperwork. How to get this is ably discussed by Catherine Jermany in the interview that appears in the Appendix.

Prospective independent paralegals typically need both skills training and practical experience. Let's use the preparation of probate forms as an example. Your first step is to study all available materials on the subject that are relevant to your state. In California, Nolo Press publishes *How To Probate an Estate,* by Julia Nissley, a very accessible and easy-to-use resource. However, in most states, you won't find how-to books written for nonlawyers and will have to rely on materials aimed at lawyers. To locate these, you must become familiar with the law library, and especially with the practice books designed to show lawyers and paralegals how to probate an estate. These are published for all populous states. To locate the probate materials for your state, your best bet is to visit a good-sized law library at a non-busy time and ask the reference librarian for a list of the materials she considers most helpful in the probate area.

Once you have studied these and are thoroughly up to speed on the basics of form preparation, you will need some real world experience before you market your services to the public. Here are several ways to get it:

- Find a lawyer (usually a sole practitioner or member of a small firm) who needs help preparing probate paperwork but doesn't have a lot of money. In exchange for your freelance help at a very reasonable hourly fee (or maybe even initially as a volunteer), she can supply you with the necessary paperwork to learn on, as well as the guidance to make sure you do the work correctly.

- Study probate files at your local courthouse. Court records are public and your courthouse will have a procedure to check out files. You'll want to closely examine a god-sized pile. Court clerks may be hostile if you explain exactly what your purpose is, so if anyone asks, it may be best to state that you're doing a research project and leave it at that. (Glynda Mathewson discusses how she used this learning technique as part of training herself to type California divorces in her interview in the Appendix.)

- Work with, or for, a freelance paralegal who already prepares probate forms for lawyers. As discussed in Chapter 13, in many states, freelance paralegals do a large percentage of lawyer form preparation work. Your county paralegal association may be able to supply a list of freelancers working in your area. Obviously, you'll have to convince any freelance paralegal you call that your plans to ultimately sell form preparation services to the public will be non-competitive.

- Take a paralegal course that deals with probate specifically. The problem with this approach is that many paralegal schools won't allow you to take just the courses you are interested in but will want you to enroll for their entire program. Don't take no for an answer. Visit schools that offer hands-on probate form preparation courses and explore different ways you can get the help you need. At a minimum, find out what books and other materials the teacher uses and purchase them directly from the publisher.

- If possible, join local paralegal organizations, especially those that offer hands-on training. Some paralegal groups may not let you join unless you have already worked in the field or had formal training, but others aren't so fussy. There is no universally-used definition of the term "paralegal," and in many areas, self-taught people are accepted.

- Investigate to see if computer programs exist in your state to facilitate probate form preparation. Increasingly, legal publishers are publishing these for lawyers and freelance paralegals. These programs are designed to complete forms, not as a teaching tool, but there is obviously a lot you can learn by working with such a program.

INDEPENDENT PARALEGAL TRAINING COURSES

A few community colleges, adult education schools and private business schools are beginning to offer legal form preparation courses geared to the needs of IPs. Check locally to see what is available in your area.

The National Association for Independent Paralegals (NAIP) based in Sonoma, California offers skills training in a number of legal areas. For example, people regularly come from all over the country for their two- and three-day bankruptcy workshops. For a list of NAIP training courses, call (707) 935-3598.

HOW TO GET TRAINING TO APPEAR BEFORE
ADMINISTRATIVE AGENCIES

As noted a number of times in this book, many independent paralegals are beginning to specialize in representing people before federal and state administrative agencies, such as the Social Security Administration, which does not require advocates to be lawyers. As a result, I am often asked how a prospective IP can learn to do this. To my knowledge, there are no available courses; most IPs who currently represent people before agencies have learned either by working for the particular agency or for organizations such as a Legal Services Program, which regularly represents people who appear before the agency.

B. Avoid Unauthorized Practice of Law

This subject is thoroughly discussed in Chapter 3.

C. Good Office Management

The third attribute of a good paralegal operation requires that you run a topnotch business operation. This involves doing at least the following things:

- Run a clean, well-organized office from a good location. (See Chapter 6.);

- Learn good telephone skills so you can screen out inappropriate customers;

- Provide your customers with accurate and thorough information necessary to make their own decisions about the legal task they are concerned with;

- Use a typewriter or computer to prepare all necessary forms promptly and accurately;

- Make sure your customers thoroughly check your work before it is submitted to a court to ensure it's accurate; and

• Document that you have done all of the above.

Let's now briefly look at how to do this by tracking a customer from her first contact with your business through the preparation of all the necessary forms.

Step 1: Initial Contact with a Potential Customer

Assume that you prepare the forms necessary for small businesses to incorporate. You receive a phone call from Alexis Elmore, who wishes to incorporate her business, which consists of two children's shoe stores. Your first job is to tell Elmore what you do, at the same time that you find out whether her situation is appropriate for your incorporation typing service. Accomplishing both of these tasks efficiently and quickly is a real skill, especially given the fact that you are solely in the business of typing legal forms, not of transferring legal expertise.

Specifically, you would want to ask if Elmore has a pretty good idea of what a corporation is, what's involved in preparing the paperwork, who's going to own it and how many shares of stock will be issued. In short, you need to be sure Elmore knows enough about incorporation to sensibly provide you with the information necessary to incorporate her business. If Elmore replies that her accountant recommended that she incorporate and she has discussed the tax advantages with him and has read a self-help book on the subject, she is probably ready to go ahead. However, if she seems confused about what a corporation is, or is unsure that her decision to incorporate is wise, she has more work to do before she uses your typing service. You might suggest she read several good books[1] on the subject and consult a tax or small business adviser before going ahead.

---

[1]At the risk of plugging Nolo Press too much, the best hands-on incorporation books I know of are *How To Form Your Own California (New York, Texas, or Florida) Corporation* by Anthony Mancuso. Nolo also publishes computer software to prepare incorporation paperwork in California, New York and Texas.

Assuming Elmore's answers make sense to you, or she takes your advice, learns more and then calls you back, you will want to briefly tell her how your form preparation service works and how much you charge. Assuming this sounds good to her, it's time to make an appointment.

Step 2: Initial Office Interview

When Elmore comes to your clean, well-organized office for her first appointment, she should first encounter a reception room or area that contains material about self-help law in general and your incorporation form preparation service in particular. A small library of good small business operations books is also valuable. If Elmore must wait a few minutes, she will be surrounded by material that tells her more about what you do. Not only will it make a good impression, but you'll have excellent materials close at hand should you want to refer Elmore to good sources of more information. And don't forget to keep a few toys on hand just in case Elmore brings little Barbara.

Step 3: Open a File

Your first task at the interview is to open a file. First, have Elmore read and sign a statement that describes your self-help form preparation service and clearly states that you are not a lawyer. (This is discussed in detail in Chapter 3.) Assuming you have a computer, you will probably want to enter Elmore's biographical information and instruct the computer to generate the intake sheet. If you have the proper software, this will allow you to simultaneously add the customer's name to your master list for later use in keeping track of her file and communicating with her by phone and mail. At this stage, it is also appropriate to again verify that your customer knows how much your service costs and to establish how she plans to pay. Many independent paralegals appropriately ask for a substantial portion of their fee at the first interview. As discussed in Chapter 3, I recommend setting your basic fee to cover the cost of necessary self-help law books or kits, rather than trying to sell them separately. If Elmore has purchased the necessary material separately, you can offer her a small discount.

Step 4: Gather the Necessary Information From the Customer

Assuming that, like most business people, Elmore has done her homework and has a pretty good idea of what incorporation entails, your next task is to gather the information necessary to prepare the paperwork. The best way to do this is to have Elmore fill out a detailed information form. Incidentally, because this form is probably the most important tool you will use in your business, care should be taken to ensure that it is complete, well-organized and attractive. Creating a good information sheet is so important that a short digression on how to create one is appropriate.

Think of it this way—forming a corporation, or for that matter, preparing any other routine legal paperwork, consists of properly arranging a number of "pieces" or "bits" of information. Despite what lawyers might wish you to believe, no magic and precious little art is necessary. You simply need to identify all the information necessary to prepare a particular form and then create the best possible questionnaire to gather it. Many form books written for attorneys contain useful questionnaires and checklists of information necessary to fill out routine incorporation forms. Or you may want to purchase questionnaire forms from an independent paralegal who already works in this area.

Start by identifying the many "pieces" of information that are standard to all small corporations (or divorces, bankruptcies or whatever else you handle). Most of these will have long since been reduced to formula language, called "boilerplate" in law biz slang. Often you will find that sample Articles of Incorporation forms containing this boilerplate are printed by your state's Secretary of State or Corporations Commissioner, along with filing instructions. In addition, in many states, incorporation forms are sold by private legal printers.[2] Some incorporation forms are also commonly published in legal form books and self-help law books.[3] You will want to buy all the available forms you will need for your particular operation or create your own. Obviously, if you design a form, you will want to be sure it is acceptable to the court or agency you will file it with.

Step 5: Help Your Customer Fill in the Information Sheet

Assuming now that your questionnaire is written and you know that it works, you are ready to work with Alexis Elmore. You'll want to get as much information as possible from Elmore in her own handwriting. This way, if you are ever investigated, it's easier to demonstrate that you were typing forms under her supervision, and not engaging in the practice of law. In addition, you will probably want to interview Elmore to be sure the information she has supplied is complete. For example, your form will probably ask whether Elmore wants to elect "S corp" tax status (which would allow her business to be taxed as a partnership for federal tax purposes) as opposed to conventional federal corporate tax status. If she

---

[2]Legal printers operate in all states. Many office supply stores carry these state specific forms. One of the largest and best of these national companies (especially strong for east coast states) is Julius Blumberg, Inc., 62 White St., New York, N.Y. Blumberg's also produces excellent bankruptcy forms.

[3]Form manufacturers and publishers take the position that copying their forms, especially in a business context, is a copyright violation. If you use a particular publisher's materials, you should buy (not photocopy) them.

hasn't considered this question or seems confused, you will want to guide her to good written information on the subject, and perhaps suggest that she discuss the issue with her tax advisor before continuing.

Step 6: Review the Information Form With Your Customer

After Alexis Elmore has carefully reviewed and completed the information sheet, have her sign a statement at the bottom of the form which says that it is complete, correct and reflects her desires. Keep a signed copy of this form for your files. It is essential that you do this for two reasons. First, you need to protect yourself should Elmore, or any other customer, later claim that she gave you information that you forgot to include on the forms. In the bankruptcy area, where all debts must be listed to be discharged and customers sometimes fail to provide a complete list, keeping a signed copy of the customer's worksheet or questionnaire is particularly important. Second, if a prosecutor or other attorney organization ever questions whether or not you are practicing law, you'll want to produce the worksheet, complete with the customer's signed statement that they (not you) provided the necessary information.

Step 7: Prepare the Legal Paperwork

Your next task is to prepare the necessary paperwork. For incorporation papers, which can run 60 or 70 pages, the only practical way to do this is by use of a computer or typewriter with considerable memory capacity. Since most needed language is standard legal boilerplate, it's a waste of time, and hence money, to type them from scratch. In other areas of the law, such as filling out preprinted divorce forms, it is practical to either use a typewriter, or in many states, to purchase a computer form-generation package designed for use in law offices. If you begin with the typewritten approach, there is no reason you must bang all the keys yourself. With a good information sheet keyed directly to necessary legal forms, any competent typist should be able to prepare the forms quickly. Especially after your business becomes established, your time will be better spent dealing with customers or marketing your business.

Step 8: Review the Legal Paperwork With Your Customer

Review the completed paperwork with Elmore carefully. This will normally be done at a second or third appointment. When your joint review is complete, have Elmore sign a brief statement such as this:

I have carefully reviewed all forms prepared by the Pacific Rim Self-Help Incorporation Service according to my instruction and find them to be accurate and complete.

_____   _____
Date   Signature

When paperwork is complete and ready for filing, it's appropriate to ask for final payment. Most typing services prefer to be paid the balance on the spot to save the trouble of billing and collecting from slow payers. I think this approach makes sense.

Step 9: Tell Your Customer What To Do Next

Finally, you need to either file the paperwork for Elmore or give her a detailed instruction sheet telling her how to accomplish this. There is no legal reason why you can't file the papers, either in person or by mail. (Filing forms is not considered to be the practice of law.) However, I think it often makes sense to have your customer do the filing, to emphasize that it's her legal action and your role is simply that of a form preparer. Also, if your customer will have to make a court appearance, it makes sense for her to visit the courthouse first, to check out where and how this will occur. In any case, be absolutely certain that any filing information (including fees) you provide is accurate, complete and up-to-date.

In legal areas such as divorce, where a court appearance is often required, many customers will want you to coach them as to what to say and when to say it. Doing anything more than explaining how the particular procedure is normally structured comes perilously close to practicing law. Your best bet is to refer them to the relevant parts of any self-help resource that discusses how to present a court case. Another good approach is to suggest that your customer stop by the court and watch how similar cases are presented.

Step 10: Maintain Accurate Records

Keep neat records of all work done. All information you get from Elmore or any other customer, particularly the signed statement that she recognizes you are not a lawyer, the signed customer information sheet, and the signed statement that she has read all completed paperwork and finds it to be accurate, should be kept indefinitely in a well-organized file system. In addition, all information maintained in your computer, such as mailing lists, agency referral sources and customer demographic information, should be both impeccably maintained and regularly backed up.

Chapter 9

How Much to Charge

*I*f you are planning to go into business to help nonlawyers prepare legal forms, you probably already have some idea as to how much is reasonable to charge in your community. This usually depends on a number of factors, including:

- How much lawyers charge to do the same task;

- How much other independent paralegals in your area charge for the task;

- How many hours it will take you on average to complete the legal paperwork;

- How much your overhead is, over and above paying yourself a reasonable salary. If you rent a nice office, hire an employee and buy equipment such as a computer, this will be a significant amount;

- How much your customers are willing to pay;

- Whether some or all of your motive to work as an independent paralegal is to further a cause you are personally involved in, such as men's, women's or tenants' rights. If so, you may be willing to charge less than the market value for your services. This is especially likely to be true if you get support in the form of a grant from a foundation or other non-profit source.

A. Establish How Much Money You and Your Business Need

One sensible approach to setting a price for typing a divorce or bankruptcy, or any other form preparation task is to work backwards—to first decide on the total amount you need to take in to run your business and pay yourself a decent wage, and then determine how much you must charge per form preparation job to meet this goal. As part of doing this, you will want to budget carefully, making sure to add in all your costs, from the telephone bill and office rent to computer paper, brochure printing, phone book ads and office supplies. Also remember that if you will need to buy office equipment from your savings to get your business started, you should include in your budget an item to cover gradually reimbursing yourself before the equipment wears out. And if you plan to hire part-time office help, don't forget to include these costs.

Once you arrive at a final overhead figure, I recommend that you increase it by at least 20% to cover things you haven't thought of. If you have never previously been in business for yourself, increase your estimate by 30%.

Your next step is to realistically decide how much you need to live on. Again, I would budget a little on the high side so that even if the business doesn't initially produce enough income to meet your goal, you won't starve.

TAKE TIME TO PREPARE A PROFIT AND LOSS FORECAST

To really see if your proposed business will make money given your assumptions as to your costs and the number of customers you can realistically expect, it's wise to prepare a detailed profit-and-loss statement and cash flow forecast. It is particularly important to accurately estimate cash flow to determine whether money coming in will be adequate to cover your expenses. Remember, most of your expenses will be immediate, but a least some of your income will be delayed, because customers will pay late. Fortunately, it is easy to create both a profit-and-loss forecast and a cash flow analysis following the detailed instructions in *How To Write a Business Plan,* by Mike McKeever (Nolo Press).

Now add the amount you'll need for personal living expense to your estimate of the amount needed to cover business overhead. This is the grand total you'll need in order to prosper. For example, you might conclude that you and your business can both get by comfortably on $6,500 a month.

Your next task is to estimate how many customers you can realistically hope to attract in a month. If, for example, you decide to type divorces, and decide that, given a little time to develop your business, you should be able to attract and handle 50 per month, you must charge an average of $130 per customer to meet your $6,500 goal.

B. Find Out What Competitors Charge

Let's continue to assume that, like most IPs, you plan to type divorces. If so, you'll want to determine what lawyers, including any large, heavily-advertised legal clinics, charge for preparing divorce forms. In doing this, however, don't necessarily believe the lowest price quoted in ads; this is often a price for a bare bones service that very few customers qualify for.

For example, if a customer asks a legal clinic for a widely-advertised $350 divorce, she is likely to be told that if she owns property or has children, she must pay extra. This sort of "bait and switch" approach is the reason why many customers find that heavily-advertised legal clinics usually end up being no cheaper than your typical run of the courthouse lawyer. In the divorce area, you will probably find that no matter what other legal clinics advertise, $500-$900 is the usual low-end lawyer rate for uncontested divorces. If so, you should be very competitive if you charge half of that or less.

You should also check what existing independent paralegals charge for the same services you plan to provide. For example, if there are already several independent paralegals in your city who type divorces for $175-$225, you can probably charge about the same, or perhaps a bit less, until you get established—say about $150. As you gain experience, you will want to adjust those amounts up or down based on the average amount of time it takes you to prepare a divorce.

C. Estimate How Long Form Preparation Will Take

If you're operating efficiently, you will probably find that a divorce takes you about two hours to prepare.[1] The time it takes to type other legal forms varies greatly, depending on state law and the particular fact situation. For example, a bankruptcy often takes one-and-one-half to two-and-one-half hours to prepare, including meeting with the customer. An uncontested guardianship petition involving custody of minor children might typically take two to three hours of independent paralegal time in most states. Small business incorporations can be done very quickly if you have all the repetitive boilerplate information stored on a computer, or a

---

[1] In some states, very simple divorces that qualify to be done by mail can often be prepared in about one hour.

typewriter with adequate memory. Preparing a living trust or a will using a form on a disk program, such as those available from the National Association for Independent Paralegals, should take no more than 90 minutes, including the time it takes to interview the customer and show her how to use the computer.

D. Draw Up a Price List

Once you have canvassed what the competition charges and considered this in light of how much you need to make and how many customers you believe you can attract, it's time to set your prices. To give you some idea of what one experienced paralegal charges for a variety of typing services, I asked Robin Smith, of People's Paralegal Service in Beaverton, Oregon, for permission to print her price list (exclusive of filing fees) as of mid-1991. Here it is:

- Divorce (co-petition)...$125
  with children 75
  with serving the other party 145

- Bankruptcy (up to 35 creditors)...145

- Custody, visitation and support (unmarried couple).......145

- Stepparent adoption (with consent) 175

- Incorporation 185

- Guardianship...95

Commonly, some types of form preparation involve extra paperwork (e.g., some divorces require a formal property settlement agreement), for which you will wish to charge extra. Doing this is fine, as long as you clearly state this in your ads and flyers. In addition, be sure you indicate that your fees do not include court filing fees, fees for service of papers, etc., unless, of course, they do. The point is to fully disclose all of your prices from the beginning. This honest business practice will be appreciated by your customers and will set you apart from other independent paralegal offices and especially lawyer-run legal clinics, which commonly use deceptive bait and switch advertising techniques.

In talking to a number of independent paralegals who face competition from other IP's, several have noted that they believe price is a major factor when customers choose one paralegal service over another. For example, Robin Smith notes that the existence of several competing independent paralegals who list prices in the paper makes her think twice before raising prices and can even mean that a price may occasionally have to be lowered. However, she adds that as long as an independent paralegal offers a good service at a fair price, and is known in the community, he or she doesn't have to meet the price of every low-end competitor. Perhaps even a better illustration of this point can be found in the San Francisco Bay Area, where the divorce form typing business has expanded to the extent that over 60% of divorces are now handled without a lawyer. This has meant that a constant stream of new independent paralegals has been attracted to the business, often advertising low prices in an effort to build up volume. Jolene Jacobs, of the Divorce Centers of California in San Francisco, has this to say about pricing:

> *A lot of people just starting out are able to set a low price because they have another job, or other means of support, and they operate out of a house or very inexpensive office. Eventually, as they build a clientele and move out of the house, they are likely to conclude that it makes sense to raise their prices somewhat. For the most part, established typing services with reasonably competitive prices do not have to lower prices to meet every lowballer. As in lots of other businesses, consumers choose a typing service based both on price and their perception of the quality of the service offered, which often comes down to preferring an experienced over an inexperienced provider. In short, establishing a competitive price will be a factor in a typing service's success, but if you have a good reputation and sound marketing, you don't have to offer the lowest price in town.*

(See Jolene Jacob's interview in the Appendix for more about how this pioneer independent paralegal operates her business.)

Once you establish your prices, you should include them in your printed material for all to see and rely on. Here is a sample flyer:

Hours: 9:00-6:00: Mon-Sat   Phone: (416) 527-1111
(evening appointments available)   Call for Appointmentt

QUALITY
SELF-HELP BANKRUPTCY CENTER

A   N o n l a w y e r   T y p i n g   S e r v i c e

We type:

- Bankruptcy forms for Chapter 7 bankruptcy

- Our fee is $150 (this does not include the court filing fee of $120)

- We provide all customers with a copy of *How To File For Bankruptcy* and *Money Troubles*, published by Nolo Press. These excellent books provide comprehensive information about debt problems generally and bankruptcy specifically.

- All bankruptcy forms are prepared under the customer's direct supervision—we provide no legal advice.

- Our services are unconditionally guaranteed. If you are not satisfied, we will return your money immediately, with no ifs, ands or buts.

950 Pelham Road (at 45th). Park at Racafrax Parking, Pelham and 44th

Parking validated

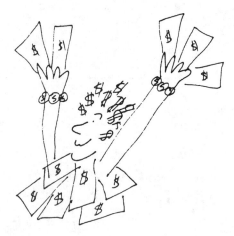

E. Fees For Preparing Bankruptcy Petitions

Unlike other legal areas, fees charged to help people file bankruptcy are subject to review by the bankruptcy judge. The original purpose of this review was to prevent attorneys from ripping off both the debtor and the unsecured creditors—who might otherwise be entitled to the money used to pay the fees. In practice, few bankruptcy courts care how much lawyers charge. But an increasing number of bankruptcy judges are using their authority over fees to push down the prices charged by independent paralegals who help people do their own bankruptcies.

Here is how this happens. Every bankruptcy filing includes a document, called a Statement of Affairs, that discloses the debtor's recent economic history. Among the items that must be disclosed is any money paid for help filing for bankruptcy. In addition, all attorneys must file a special form that discloses their fees, and most bankruptcy courts require IPs to complete this form as well. The bankruptcy trustee then reviews these forms and if it appears that a typing service is charging more than what the trustee thinks is acceptable for typing, the IP is sued for the balance. For instance, if the trustee thinks that the typing aspect of the bankruptcy would only cost $75 at a regular secretarial service, but the fees charged

An Excellent Resource for Independent Paralegals

Legal Research Made Easy:
A Roadmap Through the Law Library Maze

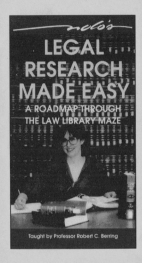

2½ hour video tape
with a 40-page booklet
by Nolo Press & Legal
Star Communications
$89.95

Legal research expert Robert Berring shows you how to find your way around the law library and get the answers you need quickly and easily. He explains all the basic research tools and shows you how to find and understand:

- federal, state and local statues
- court cases
- government agency regulations
- law review articles
- legal encyclopedias
- Shepard's case updates

Professor Berring is Professor of Law and Director of the Law Library at Boalt Hall School of Law at the University of California, Berkeley, and is known as an outstanding and humorous lecturer. He has spent 15 years working in the field of legal research and is co-author of several books on the subject.

To order your copy of *Legal Research Made Easy*:
Call us at 1-800-992-6656 or fill out and fax or mail us the order form in the back of this book.

Corrections for *The Independent Paralegal's Handbook*, Edition 2.2, April 1993

Note: Italicized text was originally missing from the latest printing

Corrections to p. 2/7, 3rd paragraph and p. 2/8, 1st paragraph:

1. Court Regulation of Independent Paralegals Who Appear Before State Administrative Hearings

Administrative agencies are created by statute and basically exist to facilitate some legislative purpose, such as administering health, labor or retirement programs. Many of these agencies have mechanisms to hear *and resolve disputes that somewhat resemble a court of law. For example, a person who is denied social security disability benefits has the right to an administrative hearing.*

Because, as we have seen, many courts assert inherent powers to regulate the entire legal system, nonlawyers who represent people before state agencies may be charged with unauthorized practice. This is true even though the state legislature or the agency itself allows nonlawyers to appear before it. And if this isn't confusing enough, consider that courts in some states acquiesce to this so-called unauthorized practice while others do not. With this in mind, let's look at a few cases.

Corrections to page 2/24, 1st paragraph:

*1990   In a Nevada Case, the court states that it is not UPL for a legal scrivener service to offer forms and procedures that induce self-*reliance by the customer. However, if the customer relies on the express or implied expertise of the IP form preparation service, it is unlawful practice. *State Bar of Nevada v. Johnson et al.,* No. CV89-5814 (Nev. 2nd Dist. Ct., April 12, 1990).

by the IP were $150, the trustee might sue the IP in bankruptcy court for $75.

If typing is all that is being done, this might be a reasonable approach by the trustee. But IP bankruptcy services often do a lot more than typing. Depending on the IP, additional activities and costs might include:

- conducting an extensive customer interview using a questionnaire;

- sorting debts into the proper categories;

- alphabetizing the customer's list of creditors;

- negotiating with creditors;

- providing the customer with adequate written materials to explain how to make their own legal decisions;

- helping the customer to use and understand whichever written materials are being used;

- preparing the customer to understand what will happen at the creditors' meeting;

- making photocopies and filing the forms with the court.

While many courts and trustees approve all of these activities by independent paralegals, others wrongly believe that any activity other than typing constitutes the unauthorized practice of law and that no fees can be charged for illegal services. Often, however, when IPs have carefully informed courts about how they conduct their business, pointing out that they offer a range of valuable services as part of helping people to help themselves, these courts are willing allow a reasonable fee.

If you are new to the bankruptcy typing area, start by finding out what your local bankruptcy court permits typing services to charge—many courts have reasonable limits—and stay within this limit. If there is no rule on fees, or you find the court has imposed a limit that is unfairly low, take the following steps:

- carefully itemize your activities (see above list) and costs;

- make these costs consistent with your overall business plan;

- restrict your activities to apparent clerical tasks;

- make sure that your customer gets all their basic bankruptcy legal expertise from publications or outside resources and not from you; and

- be prepared to present this information to any judge or trustee who inquires about how you set your fees.

For more information on setting up a bankruptcy form preparation service, consult the National Association for Independent Paralegals.

F. Grant Credit Conservatively

Another issue that always comes up when you run a small business is credit. Should you allow your customers to pay you in installments? Despite the fact that I know several IP's who manage to do this successfully, my advice is not to give credit. Assuming your prices are primarily in the rock bottom $80-$250 range, depending on the type of forms you type, it is reasonable to ask customers to pay your entire fee at your first meeting. Or, put another way, in business generally it usually makes sense to charge low prices and collect all your money right away, or higher ones and bill people, but not to attempt both.

By not advancing credit, you may lose a little business to the competition, but in my opinion, in the long run you will come out far ahead both economically and psychologically. Why? Because the fact that you will always be paid up front will mean minimal bookkeeping and no need to send bills. And of intangible, but no less real, value, your peace of mind will never be disturbed by all those folks who promise to pay you later for typing their divorce and then patronize another typing service to get a bankruptcy, listing you as a creditor. Of course, one good way to allow people to be served now and pay later is to take credit cards. A number of California IP's do this very successfully for all types of legal actions, except bankruptcies. If you have a good relationship with a bank, establishing a Master Card/Visa account should not be difficult.

In fairness, I should add that, in discussing my position on credit with a number of IP's, many, although generally agreeing, find it a bit too strict. As an alternative, a number ask for full payment up front but are willing to take half when the customer comes in for the initial interview and the other half when the papers are picked up for filing. If the second half isn't forthcoming, neither are the papers.

G. Establish a Money Back Guarantee

As noted in Chapter 12, "Customer Recourse," it is wise to establish a fast and generous recourse policy and to disclose it in advance. Obviously, you can't afford to include details in a small "penny saver" or phone book type listing, but you can and should put it in your general information sheet or brochure. This should be given to all customers, available in your waiting room, and generally circulated in your community as part of your marketing efforts.

Chapter 10

Marketing Your Services

*S*uppose now that you have done everything from getting skills training, to choosing a name, to printing disclaimers and have opened the doors on your own shiny new paralegal typing service. Congratulations—but what next? Well, if you wish to avoid quick starvation, you had better round up some customers. Let's look at the best, and a few of the worst, ways to do this.

A. Advertising Is Usually A Waste of Time

For a lot of people who are not experienced in small business economics, letting the general public know about your service means advertising. Indeed, if you are new to the independent paralegal business, you may have already considered getting as much money as you can together and running a series of splashy ads in local newspapers and perhaps even on radio or Cable TV.

If I do nothing else in this whole book but convince you of one thing, I hope it's that spending a lot of money on advertising your services in conventional ways such as these is unlikely to produce a profitable return. Or, put more directly, major advertising expenditures just plain will not work. There are two reasons for my dogmatism. The first is economic— the amount of business that conventional advertising will produce will not pay for its cost if you charge a reasonable amount for your services. How do I know this? The same way a jockey knows the ground is hard when he falls off a horse—I've tried it.

The second reason that a major advertising campaign isn't a good idea for the independent paralegal is that it is almost sure to produce a negative reaction from the bar. As mentioned throughout this book, especially when your business is new, you are far better off maintaining a reasonably low profile. Of course, this may change in the years to come (and indeed, has already done so in parts of California, Oregon and Arizona) but in most places, it's unwise to run a lot of ads that will remind the slightly tottering, but still powerful, legal establishment of your existence.

Before I discuss several cost-effective ways to market your paralegal services, here is a cogent excerpt from *Marketing Without Advertising*, by Michael Phillips and Salli Rasberry (Nolo Press):

> *A large and growing number of business people have become vividly aware that if they are to succeed in the long run, it is essential that they attract more loyal customers. Unfortunately, the mechanics of doing this are less obvious. After all, if you are al-*

ready working eleven hours a day, you have no time to join a self-improvement club for the self-employed, no money to compete with major advertisers and probably no desire to turn yourself into a super salesperson.

◆ ◆ ◆ ◆ ◆

And even if you can afford more advertising, many of you have probably begun to form the sneaking suspicion that despite conventional wisdom that dictates that advertising is essential, it is not cost effective in your business.

◆ ◆ ◆ ◆ ◆

The truth, of course, is that very few of the 1600 advertising messages we experience each day are effective in influencing our shopping or buying behavior and an even smaller amount of it is cost effective for the advertiser. When it comes to a small business trying to get its message heard against the babble of corporate America, the chances of people you want to reach really hearing or seeing your message is miniscule. And even worse than the cost involved, relying on advertising to improve your sales often stonewalls your imagination, keeping you from exploring the many superior methods available for promoting your business.

◆ ◆ ◆ ◆ ◆

In fact, the best and most economical way to attract and hold customers is through personal recommendation. A customer who is pre-screened and prepared for what you have to offer is far more likely to appreciate you and use your business than is someone responding to an ad offering a low price. The essence of marketing without advertising then is to encourage "personal recommendation." How do you do this? Lots of ways, all of which start with creating an atmosphere of trust. Central to doing this is to run an honest business."

B. Getting Recommendations And Referrals

Okay, assuming that positive personal recommendations of your business are better, and certainly cheaper, approach than advertising, how do you encourage them? There are two ways. The first is to provide an excellent service and to let your satisfied customers spread the word for you. This will work, but it will take time to build to a level that will support you. In the meantime, you should make your services widely known to the people who are most likely to refer you customers. Ask yourself, who are people who need the types of services you offer likely to be in contact with? For example, people in the armed services who need a divorce are likely to contact a military legal office (Judge Advocate General). Military lawyers don't handle divorce, but they can refer enlisted men and women to you if they know about your service. Similarly, lots of people who consider incorporating a small business talk to accountants or small business financial planners, both of whom are a good source of referrals if you prepare incorporation papers.

To tell referral sources about your business so they can tell others, you'll need good promotional material. Here is an sample:

Once you have designed a good packet of information, including listing your prices, location, general philosophy, disclaimer that you are not a lawyer, etc., make it available to as many referral sources as possible. Depending on the type of forms you prepare, you will want to communicate with some or all of the following:

- Legal services offices (legal aid)

- Battered women's shelters

- Immigrants' help organizations

- Public library reference librarians

- Law school "*pro per*" assistance centers

- Law librarians (at courthouses and law school libraries)

- Community services referral agencies and directories

- Drug treatment centers

- Marriage counselors and family therapists

- Social services

- University and college student assistance offices

- Grey Panthers and other senior advocacy organizations

- Local corporation personnel departments

- Parents Without Partners and other singles groups

- Law enforcement (including the Sheriff's Office, Probation Department, Parole Officers and the County Jail)

- Consumer organizations

- The State Employment Office

- Women's organizations

- Collection agencies

- Child care centers

- Military bases, including all Judge Advocate General military law offices

- Local media (send it to reporters who care about consumer, legal or family issues)

- Foreign language media and support groups (but only if you or an employee can speak the language)

- Any community group directly interested in your activity. (For example, if you do small business incorporations, you will want to contact a wide range of small business groups, accountants and bookkeepers who work in this area, as well as the reference librarian at any public library with a large collection of business materials. Similarly, if you do evictions, you should work as closely as you can with the local apartment house owners' association, as well as real estate management groups and any other community organizations of interest to landlords.)

Sample Cover Letter to Referral Agencies

Here is a cover letter appropriate for communicating with guidance counselors. Modified slightly, it will also work well as a cover letter when you send marketing material to other groups.

Date _____

Dear _____:

   As a guidance counselor, we know you deal with
difficult family concerns every day. Some of these
involve counseling people who need basic legal
services in areas such as divorce, child support
modification, bankruptcy, step-parent adoption and
guardianship.

   At Legal Form, Inc., we offer high quality,
low-cost legal form preparation in all these areas.
We strive to create a relaxed, non-adversarial
atmosphere in which our customers feel comfortable.

   We are not attorneys and cannot give legal
advice. But as part of our highly efficient legal
form typing service, we can, and do, stock a large
selection of quality self-help law materials
designed to help our customers inform themselves
about the legal issues they face. These materials
may be used free of charge at our office library
and are also available for purchase.

   As you can see from our enclosed pamphlet, we
also offer a fairly wide array of other legal form
preparation services, including conservatorships,
wills, living trusts and small business incorporations. If you have any questions, please feel
free to call me at any time.

                    Sincerely,

                    John Kennedy
                    Owner, Legal Forms, Inc.

Bob Mission of the Sacramento, California Superior California Legal Clinic, reports that about fifty percent of his total referrals come from community agencies such as these. Robin Smith, of Oregon's People's Paralegal Service puts her estimate slightly higher. Glenda Mathewson of the Divorce Center in Oakland, California emphasizes that you should not only just send groups a flyer, but if possible, "follow up personally to see that it got to the right person and to convince them that you know your business and aren't a dingbat." For example, she occasionally speaks at luncheon meetings of groups interested in family matters and keeps in close touch with a number of attorney mediators who work in the domestic law area, because she believes it's her responsibility to convince people who can refer customers that her office provides a really good service.

POST YOUR FLYER ON COMMUNITY BULLETIN BOARDS

Another cost-effective way to get the word out is by the use of flyers. Design an eye-catching informative one, clearly stating your services and prices. Post it at appropriate places around town. Good locations include laundromats, food stores (including natural food stores), factory, military and graduate school bulletin boards.

Especially in coastal states, such as New York, California and Texas, where there are significant concentrations of non-English speakers, targeting your services to people who speak a language such as Spanish, Chinese or Vietnamese can also make sense. To do this effectively, you will need to have all the promotional materials translated into the particular language. In addition, someone who is fluent in the particular language will need to be regularly available to handle your non-English speaking business. This will include telephone screening as well as customer interviews.

GETTING HELP DESIGNING ADS AND FLYERS

In twenty years of working with IP's, I have yet to see a truly well-written, well-designed ad or flyer. Some are mediocre; most are terrible. So here is the truth, whether you want to hear it or not. Unless you are a trained writer or graphic artist, you are not competent to write and paste-up a flyer that will make the best possible presentation of your business. To accomplish this, you need skilled, cost-efficient help. Here is how to find it:

- Contact a small, local, reasonably-priced ad agency or, better yet, an independent reporter, freelance writer, English teacher or someone else with truly excellent language skills. With their help, write, re-write and proofread every word of every flyer, pamphlet and other promotion piece you distribute at least five times;

- Find a reasonably-priced graphic artist. Usually you can get a referral from a local "instant printing" shop. Work with her, incorporating your written material into well-designed promotional material. And don't let her talk you into ultra-slick designs—instead, your materials should be a little on the conservative side, to reassure customers that your business is reliable and trustworthy.

C. Keep a Good Mailing List

As part of contacting likely referral sources and your satisfied customers, it is essential that you collect, maintain, and regularly use a good mailing list. Keeping in touch with former customers, supporters and others interested in your work provides these people with the necessary information to tell others about you. If you store your list on a microcomputer and request the post office to supply you with all address changes (there is a small fee), you can easily and cheaply maintain and expand this marvelously effective, relatively low-cost marketing tool.

You will want to use your mailing list in all sorts of contexts, including:

- To inform customers if you offer new services;

- To let people know about significant law changes that could affect them;

- To help organize potential supporters should you face a political fight, as will be the case if you introduce legislation (as discussed in Chapter 15) or are sued by organized lawyerdom;

- To remind customers to refer friends (a coupon offering a small discount often helps);

- To invite everyone to a party. Try this once a year or so—it allows you to market your services and have fun too.

D. Listing the Availability of Your Services

In addition to talking to community services organizations, it is essential to widely list the availability of your services in places where people are pre-disposed to look for them, such as the yellow pages. Some types of listings are free, such as those maintained by public service organizations and agencies. More typically, you must pay a small fee to list, as is the case for business directories and phone books. But even where a fee is involved, costs are usually very reasonable when compared to your likely return. This is because unlike display ads or electronic media spots, where you pay fairly large sums to aim your message at a very broad and mostly uninterested audience, listings are targeted at people who are looking for the service you offer. In addition, business listings have the advantage of being fairly inconspicuous and thus are far less likely to come to the attention of organized lawyerdom than is a real advertising campaign. Here are a number of good places to list:

- Phone book yellow pages—you can't list under "Attorneys," but probably can list under headings such as "Document Preparation," "Divorce," "Legal Form Preparation," "Typing Services," and so on. The phone company makes up the headings; the best you can do is pick the available one that comes closest to describing what you do;

- Local business and community service directories, such as those put out by the Better Business Bureau and local trade groups;

- Self-help law books—Several publishers of divorce, bankruptcy and other self-help law books charge IPs a modest fee to list right in the book. This, of course, is a great opportunity for IPs, as many book purchasers get disgusted in the middle of doing all their own paperwork and are likely to turn the whole thing over to an IP One book that does this is *How To Do Your Own Divorce in California,* by Charles Sherman;

- Classified ads in newspapers. Most newspapers place these ads under "Business Personals." You need to leave the ad in for a month or two to begin to see results;

- Classified or display ads which list your services in low cost "penny saver" or "classified flea market" type papers. This of course is advertising of a sort, but is far different in general approach and cost than are large display ads. People who pick up classified ads are often looking for a specific service at a reasonable price. Again, these ads work best if you keep them in the publication over a long period of time in the same place;

- Directories and business listings aimed at people who don't speak English. In many communities, there is a large and growing need for IPs who work with Spanish and Chinese speakers, as well as those who know Southeast Asian languages.

Here is a small ad—essentially a listing of services—that would be appropriate for a free classified ad paper:

OREGON DIVORCE TYPING, INC.
Since 1978

UNCONTESTED DIVORCE .... $85-$200

We help you prepare your own divorce without an attorney.

1113 Melrose Street, Pullman, Oregon   441-5157

Monday - Saturday 10-6

And here is an ad that appeared in a classified ad publication in Portland, Oregon, called "Nickel Ads":

PEOPLE'S PARALEGAL SERVICE, INC.

Legal Form Preparation Without a Lawyer

WILLS • NAME CHANGES • DIVORCE • BANKRUPTCY

PROBATE • INCORPORATION • STEP-PARENT ADOPTION

High quality/Low Cost

VISA   646-0990   MASTERCARD

E. Prepare Factual Information About the Areas You Specialize In

When telling people about the existence of your service, you usually want to keep your message short and to the point. After all, most people have more important things to think about than the details of your business. However, for those who ask for more information (and for helping agencies and others who are genuinely interested in your service) you'll want to develop material that goes into more detail. In Section B, above, I present a general flyer designed to accomplish this. In addition, you will want to prepare more in-depth material about each of the form typing areas you specialize in. Your goal in doing this is to simultaneously accomplish these few objectives:

- explain what you do in detail

- educate the potential customer or referral source about the particular legal task

- convince the reader that you offer a high quality, reliable service

- present your message in a way that does not give organized lawyerdom an opportunity to charge you with unauthorized practice of law

Here, by way of example, is a very informative flyer used by the Divorce Center of California Office in San Francisco:

CENTERS OF CALIFORNIA

870 Market Street #7
San Francisco, CA 94102

(415) 434-4485
(415) 956-5757

Information About Uncontested Divorce

There are now two kinds of uncontested divorce procedures in California. The first and most widely-used is the **"standard dissolution,"** which usually requires a court appearance and the preparation of a good-sized packet of forms. The second, for those who meet its requirements, is a "summary dissolution," which has fewer forms and no court appearance. Both divorces take 6-1/2 months to complete.

Who Qualifies for a "Summary Dissolution"

1. One spouse has lived in California for six months and in the county of filing for three months just before the date of filing.

2. The Petition for the divorce is filed before the fifth wedding anniversary.

3. There are no minor children of the marriage (or of this relationship), and the wife is not pregnant.

4. Neither spouse has any interest in real property (houses, land, etc.)

5. There is less than $4,000 in community obligations, not including car loans.

6. There is less than $25,000 in community property, not including cars.

7. Neither spouse owns more than $25,000 separately, not including cars.

8. Both spouses must sign the first papers.

9. Both spouses must read and understand the Summary Dissolution Booklet published by the State of California.

DIVORCE
CENTERS OF CALIFORNIA

870 Market Street #7   (415) 434-4485
San Francisco, CA 94102   (415) 956-5757

If for any reason you don't qualify for the Summary Dissolution, you must use the Standard Dissolution.

What Does it Cost?:

	Our Fee	Court Filing Fee
Summary Dissolution	$80	About $140 in many counties (it varies slightly)
Standard Dissolution	$180	About $170 in many counties (it varies slightly)

Please call for an appointment:
Monday-Friday, 9:00 a.m. to 5:30 p.m.
Telephone: 956-5757 or 434-4485

Thank you for your inquiry.

_____
Jolene Jacobs

F. Longer-Term Marketing Strategies

So far we have discussed several things you can do to get the word out about your business fairly quickly. This is crucial to the survival of a new business, of course. But taking a slightly longer view, it's also important that you plan now for the growth and expansion of your business in the years ahead. Again, to emphasize the point I made at the beginning of this chapter, the best way to do this is through the positive personal recommendations of satisfied customers. To encourage people to be enthusiastic about your business and tell others about you (and to report back favorably to referring agencies), it's essential that you do an excellent job. If your customers come to respect you and the service you offer, they will send others. If they don't, negative word will spread just as fast. To fully understand this point, ask yourself this: How often do you patronize a restaurant, service provider (carpenter, plumber, shoe repair shop) or buy a particular product or go to a movie because someone you know recommended it? Now ask yourself how often you engage in any of these transactions after a friend tells you the service or product is poor?

In *Marketing Without Advertising,* which I again heartily recommend (you can order it from Nolo—see ad pages at back of book), Phillips and Rasberry state that there are three essential elements to building the trust necessary to get the personal recommendation process going. They are:

- Providing a good service at a good price. (See Chapter 9 for a discussion on price.);

- Giving your customers a way to measure the quality of your service and reasonableness of your prices. Phillips and Rasberry discuss the general principles of how to do this. For independent paralegals, one good approach is to create office and waiting room displays and written material indicating exactly the services you perform, how much time it takes, how much the competition charges, etc.; and

- Providing your customers a money-back guarantee if they are unhappy with your service for any reason should be an essential part of your marketing strategy. Many public agencies and others may be reluctant to refer people to your somewhat controversial business unless they have confidence that any problems will be taken care of.

One good way to allow the community to see for itself that you are competent is to teach a course in your specialty. A number of legal typing service owners have done this. To reduce chances of being hassled for practicing law without a license, many charge no fee. Others charge a modest fee for the course but require students to own and read a good self-help law text and limit their oral presentation to the material in the book. The approach of reaching potential customers through courses works particularly well for typing service owners in specialized fields, such as those who prepare forms for landlords, nonprofit corporations or people who want living trusts—areas where customers typically want a good deal of information about the subject before committing themselves.

Another good approach is to occasionally publish and distribute good consumer information about the subject areas in which you work. For example, if your state changes any aspect of its divorce, adoption or landlord-tenant law and you type papers in any of these areas, you might prepare a flyer describing the details. Of course, the circular should also remind people of how your business works. Do a nice job on the graphics (again, it often it pays to work with a graphic artist) and make sure you proofread it three times to catch all errors in spelling and grammar. When you're satisfied, mail the flyer to all interested individuals, consumer groups, media organizations, former customers and referral agencies.

G. Where to Get Marketing Training

Throughout this book, I highly recommend the National Association for Independent Paralegals (NAIP). I do so again here. NAIP offers intensive training courses on marketing and market research techniques for independent paralegals. In addition, members receive a free copy of the informative booklet, *50 Ways to Leave Your Competition Behind,* written by

Catherine Jermany and published by NAIP. The booklet makes many of the same points I cover in this book, as well it should, since it's author, Catherine Jermany, is a good friend, and we often share information and ideas. However, NAIP's courses go into much more hands-on detail than anything you'll find here, or in 50 Ways, and are well worth the cost. For information, write to NAIP, 585 5th Street West, Sonoma, CA 95476 or call 1-800-542-0034.

H. Summing Up

To put the marketing suggestions made in this chapter in the context of the independent paralegal business, I recently discussed marketing strategy with Robin Smith, of People's Paralegal Service, in Beaverton, Oregon. Here is an excerpt of our discussion (see Appendix for a longer discussion with Robin):

Jake Warner: How important are referrals to People's Paralegal Service?

Robin Smith: Crucial. It takes time and patience to develop a positive reputation with lots of community agencies. But once you do, and they trust you, they can really make a big difference. The power of 50 to 100 groups all occasionally referring you customers is amazing.

JW: *How do you develop good contacts at places that are likely to send you customers?*

RS: Slowly. People at legal aid, or the Sheriff's Office, or the Army (which, incidentally, is a great source of referrals), aren't going to plug your business unless they truly believe in it. It's up to you to prove that you are worthy of their trust.

JW: *And how do you accomplish that?*

RS: As I've said, offering good service is essential, but you also have to make sure the key people who make the referrals know who you are. One excellent way to do that is to send good solid information to them on a regular basis. Your best bet is to adopt many of the strategies followed by non-profit consumer organizations. In other words, draft informative newsletters, contact the media when you have something to say, and generally tell the world what a truly good, innovative and cost-effective job you are doing.

JW: *What about talking to people at public agencies, courts and law libraries directly?*

RS: Yes, sure, but a hard sell won't work. Remember, these people are motivated to help the people they deal with on a daily basis, not to help your business. You have to convince them that when a person is referred to your typing service, you will really provide a great service. This takes time.

JW: *What about the media? Does People's Paralegal get much free coverage?*

RS: Definitely. The lack of access the average person has to the legal system is a story of continuing media interest, which means our business is newsworthy. I've been providing consumer help and information for over ten years now, which means I know a number of local news, feature and consumer reporters.

JW: *How often are they interested in hearing from you?*

RS: It's a fine line. If you self-promote too much, too often, you'll turn people off. Reporters are interested when there is something new, as would be the case if your business changes significantly.

JW: *What about the bar association? Does their hostility to the self-help law movement help you?*

RS: Absolutely. Whenever the bar makes a negative statement about non-lawyer legal form preparation, two things happen. First, the press needs to get the other side of the story, which means they are likely to call an IP they know and trust. Once the article is printed, many people who need help with legal paperwork and can't afford a lawyer will find out that alternatives exist and are likely to call the IP who is quoted in the article.

JW: *What else does an IP need to know to deal with the media effectively?*

RS: Tell the truth, and if you make any promises, keep them. For example, if you send out a press release about a protest event that doesn't happen, or promise exciting news you can't deliver, your credibility will be shot. Finally, let me make one more point. No matter how clever your promotional efforts, they will avail you little in the long run unless your business really delivers what it says it will. In this age in which all sorts of mediocre products and services are vastly over-hyped, people are looking for performance, not promises.

Chapter 11

Computers and the Independent Paralegal

*B*efore I discuss how independent paralegals can best work with computers, a few introductory words are in order. Computers have come to the law relatively late. More than most groups, lawyers have resisted storing and massaging information electronically. More recently, however, there has been an explosion in the availability of legal software. Some is designed to help manage law office tasks, such as word processing, billing and case management. Others provide "expert systems" that help lawyers do research and make choices in complicated legal areas. And increasingly, legal applications software is becoming available—software designed to accomplish a particular legal task, such as preparing the paperwork necessary to probate an estate, file for bankruptcy or divorce, compute child support levels or incorporate a business.

While most of this task-oriented software is designed for use by lawyers, some, such as *WillMaker, Partnership Maker, Nolo's Living Trust* and *California Incorporator,* all published by Nolo Press, *and* Bloc Publishing's *Personal Lawyer* and Mecca Ventures' *Home Lawyer,* are designed to be used directly by the consumer. Indeed, consumer legal software has become such a good-sized business that in the 1990's, it's likely that more wills will be prepared on a self-help basis using a personal computer than will be written by lawyers. Against this background, it's appropriate to ask why legal software is so attractive to nonlawyers. After all, printed self-help law materials designed to help people accomplish uncontested actions in a number of fields, such as divorce and bankruptcy, have been available for a number of years and have never achieved the same level of popularity.

The answer is that computers do three things better than books. First, computers are well-suited to printing out a fresh copy of legal forms such as wills, living trusts and small business incorporations after the user has entered the necessary data. By contrast, with a book you must tear-out a form and try to print or type necessary data in the designated spaces.

Second, unlike a book, which is an excellent tool to provide access to a broad spectrum of information, computers can be programmed to be directly responsive to a particular need. Thus, a book may be the most efficient way to review the broad field of landlord-tenant law, but a good software program offers a far more efficient way to custom-tailor a lease form to fit a particular need. This is because the computer can store all common lease variables, allow the user to examine, edit and change them and then to print out the final product. To accomplish this using a self-help law book would commonly involve hours with scissors and a glue pot.

Finally, computers are better at guiding the user to the desired result than are printed materials. Correctly programmed, software can present the user many options, all of which have been error-checked in advance to almost guarantee a legally accurate result. Thus, in relying on good legal software, the user gains a justifiable sense that she is receiving guidance from an expert.

COMPUTER TERMS DEFINED

Before we go further, let's briefly define several basic computer buzz words.

Hardware: The computer itself, consisting usually of an input device such as a keyboard, a memory and processing component which stores and, at your command, regurgitates the data in a usable form (hopefully), and an output device such as a printer (or communications modem), which allows you to reduce the fruits of your interaction with the machine to paper (or other "hard copy," such as magnetic tape).

Software: Broadly defined, this is the information that tells the computer what you want it to do. Initially stored on small floppy disks that are inserted into a slot in the computer, software, which can then be transferred to and stored on the computer's hard disk, can allow to you do everything from word processing, to financial projections, to game playing, to writing a will. When software is task-oriented (e.g., tells you how to cook an egg or form a corporation), it is called "applications" software. This type of software should be distinguished from "systems" software, which is designed to tell the computer what to do (turn on, turn off, etc.), or "operations" software, which allows you to accomplish very general tasks, such as word processing, accounting, or financial forecasting.

Database: A database can be analogized to a file cabinet full of information on a particular subject (e.g., "all antique cars in San Francisco" or "landlord-tenant laws in New York City"). Access to the data is provided though a system of electronic indexes, usually called "menus." For example, if, as a tenant, you use a landlord/tenant law database to determine your legal rights to get your roof fixed, you would first look at a general index (menu) for the program and select a topic, such as "habitability problems." You would then be presented with a more specific index that would list a number of habitability problems, including "leaky roofs." At this point you would be in a position to ask the computer to print all the relevant legal information on the subject.

A. The Independent Paralegal and Legal Software

The fact that legal applications software is increasingly available on both the home and lawyer market raises an obvious question. How can the IP use it as part of his legal form preparation business?

Because of unauthorized practice laws, the answer is more complicated than you might guess. As I will develop further below, the problem is that using legal software necessarily involves making legal choices. If the IP makes these choices, she risks being charged with unauthorized practice. So the problem becomes how can the IP make sure the customer makes the legal decisions at the same time the computer is used efficiently?

One approach is for the IP to rent the computer and software to the customer, letting the customer make her own choices. In my experience, this doesn't work. Most people who come to typing services simply aren't familiar with computers. Another method is to provide the user with a self-help manual and questionnaire keyed to the program. If the user reads the manual and then completes the questionnaire, she, not the IP, makes the legal choices. Now, entering the information into the computer becomes a "word processing" as opposed to a "legal" function.

 In Chapters 2 and 3, I thoroughly discuss UPL and how an IP who types legal paperwork can avoid it. This involves making sure the customer has the legal information necessary to make her own choices. The best way to insure this happens is to require the customer to purchase a good self-help law book. If you do not thoroughly understand this point, please go back and reread this material.

1. Forms on Disk

A number of programs are now available for lawyers that automate the process of filling out legal forms. For example, in California, where pre-

printed state-mandated forms are in use for most routine actions, purchasers have a choice of competing programs for both IBM and Apple
Macintosh computers. Bankruptcy forms on disk are also available from
several publishers in both software formats. And Nolo Press publishes
forms-on-disk software to incorporate small businesses in California, New
York and Texas. To repeat the important point I discussed above, as long
as the customer has access to a good self-help law book and completes a
questionnaire based on the information provided in the book, use of this
type of program is also pretty safe as far as UPL charges are concerned.
After all, the IP is simply using this software as a sophisticated typewriter.

2. Clauses on Disk

Programs are also available both to lawyers and the general public that
allow the user to assemble a document by selecting appropriate clauses
from a large library of clauses. This approach is particularly useful in
drafting documents such as leases and contracts, which do not readily
lend themselves to the form-on-disk approach discussed above. Nolo
Press publishes *Nolo's Partnership Maker,* which fits the "clauses-on-disk"

category, since it allow the user to choose and assemble partnership clauses from a pre-selected menu.

3. Stand-Alone Programs

A number of stand-alone legal programs are now available. This software typically accomplishes one or more legal tasks by asking the user a series of questions and using the answers to create the necessary legal paperwork.

As an example, let's briefly examine *WillMaker* (Nolo Press), the all-time most successful self-help law program. *WillMaker,* a computer program designed to help the average nonlawyer make a will, operates by asking the user a number of questions. Depending on the answers, the program asks, or bypasses, other questions. It's a bit like climbing a tree. Based on your choice as to which way to proceed at the first major fork, you have an option to climb certain higher branches but not others. For example, *WillMaker* asks the user if she is married. If the "No" answer is entered, *WillMaker* skips to another area entirely. If the answer is "Yes," *WillMaker* provides the user with certain information about marital property rules as they affect wills and asks for the name of the spouse. A little later, *WillMaker* asks the user if she has any children. If the user responds in the affirmative, *WillMaker* first asks for the children's names and then if any of the children are under 18 years of age. If the user answers "Yes" (meaning one or more children are minors), *WillMaker* asks if she wants to appoint a guardian to take over should the user and the other parent, if there is one, both die simultaneously. However, if the user responds that there are no minor children, *WillMaker* skips all questions about appointing a guardian.

Now, suppose a computer user becomes confused as to how to answer a question because he doesn't know the meaning of a technical word. How does *WillMaker* deal with this, or with a user's need for answers to general background questions of the type a lawyer would handle routinely? For example, suppose a user is faced with the question as to whether a child from a former marriage, or a child born while the user wasn't married, should be considered a "child" for purposes of the will. First, *WillMaker* contains an information screen that backs up every operations screen. In this instance, the back-up screen tells the questioning user that it's best to list all possible children, including those born out of wedlock or in a former marriage. Second, as part of the *WillMaker* package, the user receives a manual that contains a thorough discussion of all major issues involving children and wills.

What do programs designed for home use offer to the IP? As mentioned, if an independent paralegal simply asks a customer a series of questions and then plugs the answers into a program, she risks being charged with the unauthorized practice of law. What's needed to avoid UPL is for the customer to have a copy of a self-help law manual that explains all of the legal decisions included in the program and then to complete a detailed questionnaire to supply the information to the IP for entry in the computer. Foreseeing this type use, Nolo licenses *WillMaker* and all of its other software to IPs for commercial use. (See back of the book for commercial license information.) In addition, Nolo sells extra copies of their manual for distribution to IP customers at a very reasonable price.

CALIFORNIA INCORPORATOR:
A STAND-ALONE PROGRAM THAT AVOIDS UPL

California Incorporator is a stand-alone program that allows the user to form a privately-held California corporation. It comes with a comprehensive manual that contains detailed information necessary for the user to supply the relatively few bits of information necessary to incorporate. As long as every user has a copy of the manual and the IP follows the general approach to avoiding UPL discussed in Chapter 3 of this book, I believe using this package is relatively safe.

At this point, you may be wondering why publishers of all legal software programs sold for home use don't include more comprehensive legal help. The real reason is that most don't understand the needs of the

IP market. As the legal typing service movement grows, this will surely change.

B. Software Designed or Customized by IPs

To solve the software shortage problem, some computer savvy paralegals have begun to design their own, based on the increasingly sophisticated word-processing technology now on the market. For example, one Oregon paralegal service has entered the language necessary to write a basic will, living trust or incorporation into its computer. Then, following the customers' instructions taken from the information sheet, they are able to use the program Wordstar 5.0 to create the finished document. While this process may sound difficult, it often isn't, because many common legal forms mostly consist of standard language, with a few blanks and boxes to complete. If the information sheet is well-designed, it should provide the information necessary to quickly complete the paperwork.

Three warnings are in order. First, the layout and design of legal forms such as leases, powers of attorney and wills published by commercial printers and publishers are protected by copyright. If you wish to enter these forms in your computer and use them as part of your business, you must get permission. Some form publishers won't license their forms to paralegals at all, while others, such as Nolo Press, do so if you pay a license fee.

Another alternative is to create your own form and enter it into your word processing package. For example, there are dozens of lease forms in print, and most of the language is fairly standard. It shouldn't be hard to study these and rewrite the language and reorganize the presentation with the result that you create a form of your own that doesn't violate anyone's copyright. If you follow this approach, however, be sure that you really do create a new lease and that you have your work checked by a knowledgeable expert in your state to be sure it's accurate and up-to-date.

Second, if the finished form must be filed with a court or agency, it must be acceptable in both content and lay-out. This means you will need to pay close attention to all relevant rules before you design your own form.

The third, and more serious, problem of following this approach is UPL. As discussed above, unless your customers have access to the information necessary to make their own legal choices, you risk being charged with supplying it, which is the same thing as saying you are practicing law without a license. Specifically, the customer would need a manual or other published legal information containing a thorough discussion of the legal forms and documents to be completed. And the independent paralegal would need a well-designed questionnaire to record the user's legal choices for later entry into the computer. So, once again, the IP's objective must be to supply customers with enough self-help information that they, not the IP or the computer, is calling the legal shots.

C. Computer Databases

As discussed near the beginning of this chapter, a computer database typically consists of a great deal of information on a particular subject available to the user according to a broad range of selections or indexing criteria. A computer programmed to contain fairly comprehensive information dealing with the legal concerns of the average person (debt problems, divorce, landlord-tenant, real property ownership, wills) could be operational now. Housed at the same location with a small printed library of good self-help law books and other resources, and staffed by knowledgeable paralegals, this would allow a great deal of legal information to be brought to the street corner at a very reasonable price.

TELE-LAWYER: A FIRST STEP TOWARDS A PEOPLE-FRIENDLY LEGAL DATABASE

In Chapter 3, I mention Tele-lawyer, a service that allows nonlawyers to pay a small per-minute charge to get legal questions answered by phone. It is interesting to note that while callers talk to a lawyer, these people in turn can pull needed information from a computer database. Growing all the time, this specialized information retrieval system allows Tele-lawyer lawyers to have an incredible array of consumer legal information at their fingertips.

Are such interactive people's law databases likely to be operational soon? I doubt it. Why? Because despite the great need, no one is likely to spend the time and money necessary to see that it happens. Expect little help from lawyers, who currently monopolize legal information and have seen to it that publicly-available forms and instructions are rare, even for the simplest task. Eventually, when self-help law information systems are seen to offer a good profit potential, private businesses will surely develop them.

Legal databases have been developed for lawyers. Some, such as Westlaw and Lexis, are sophisticated and expensive on-line legal research tools used by both lawyers and paralegals, including freelancers who establish their own legal research business. Others, such as Dialog's TRADEMARKSCAN, are very specialized databases used for a particular purpose, in this case to check business and product names to see if they have already been reserved for use. Few independent paralegals currently use these tools. Expect that to change as creative people figure out how to develop profitable businesses based on providing the information databases directly to the public.

D. Computers As Office Efficiency Tools

Up to this point, I have stressed how computers can help independent paralegals generate legal forms. However, computers are also wonderful office automation tools, and the reasons most businesses eventually decide to computerize are also applicable to independent paralegals. Here is a brief review of some of these:

Word Processing: Good word processing software, and a knowledgeable person to use it, is essential in any modern office. Whether you are creating a form, writing a letter or customizing a document, the power of this type of software to quickly and efficiently create the format you want is wonderful. Because much legal software is designed to work with it, WordPerfect on the IBM (DOS) style personal computer is probably the software program of choice for legal applications.

Accounting: There are many good office accounting programs which, especially if set up at the beginning, can make basic business accounting chores a lot more efficient. You will want a program that does accounts payable, accounts receivable and maintains a general ledger. If you're a novice, one good way to choose one is with the advice of an experienced small business accountant or tax preparer. You will want the system you choose to generate the information you'll need for your tax return without much additional labor. *Small Time Operator,* by Bernard Kamoroff, is a good introductory source of information about small business accounting.

Pricing: Spreadsheet programs can be very useful for predicting the effect that changes in such variables as fees, costs, and client volume will have on your bottom line. For example, if you're trying to figure out whether you'll gross more income by charging $150, $160, $170 or $180 to prepare a bankruptcy, assuming customer volume drops 5% with each incrementally higher price, a spreadsheet will accomplish it in a wink.

There are a number of excellent ones on the market, such as Lotus 1, 2, 3 and Excel.

Office Management: There are a number of programs designed to help law offices manage their cases. These keep client information, list crucial filing and notice dates, organize follow-up tasks, and generally act as a storehouse for other data related to individual cases. They then can produce daily, weekly and monthly reports showing what activity is required on all open cases. The degree to which this type of information is useful to independent paralegals clearly depends on the scope and variety of services being offered. If you have a significant volume of customers, or type forms in several legal areas, or have several offices, a management program can be a big help.

Mailing Lists: As I discuss in Chapter 10, "Marketing Your Services," it's essential that you maintain an up-to-date lists of all former customers, agency people who make referrals to you, media contacts, etc. Names on your list should be easily recoverable by category. For example, if you want to send a flyer to reporters but not former customers, your mailing list should be coded to allow you to do this. A computer is the only sensible way to maintain this information. Mailing list programs are available for all microcomputers. Make sure you buy a printer that will print on mailing labels at high speed.

Database: Finally, a number of popular database-management programs can be used to collect and store information in an organized form about the unique characteristics of each customer. It thus becomes possible to build an intra-office database which allows quick retrieval of materials from an earlier case that can help solve a current problem. For example, if a question comes up about how to serve a divorce complaint on someone living in Canada, it would help to be able to punch up a list of any previous customers who had the same problem.

E. Getting Started With Computers

Of course, all the wonderful uses of computers discussed here may seem like a distant dream to a person with no computer experience who is new to the independent paralegal business and worried about how to afford a good secondhand typewriter. Indeed, even those readers who own a personal computer may not have the experience necessary to effectively use it in the ways suggested here. If you are one of them, it's past time you bootstrapped yourself into the computer age.

If you have no computer experience at all, your first step is to become at least somewhat computer literate. When you set out to explore which hardware and software are most appropriate to your needs, this sort of basic understanding will be absolutely essential if you don't wish to waste a small fortune. Many community colleges and adult education programs have beginning computer courses. Take one of these and read a few introductory self-help books, which are available in virtually all bookstores.

Once you can tell a hard disk from a floppy, and don't hide the cheese every time someone mentions a mouse, your next step is to figure out which type of computer and software you require for your tasks. Your choice is basically between the Apple Macintosh and a personal computer using a DOS operating system. The latter are made by IBM, Tandy, Compac and dozens of other companies who manufacture IBM clones.

The Macintosh is easier to learn and more fun to use. In my opinion, it's the best choice if you plan to use your computer as an office efficiency tool, not to run legal applications programs. However, if you want to experiment with legal document and form completion programs such as those discussed above, you will probably want to buy an IBM (DOS) type computer, because a good deal of law office-oriented software is available in this format only. And as mentioned above, when you check out word processing software, take a close look at WordPerfect.

Chapter 12

Customer Recourse

his is one of the shortest and most important chapters in this book. It deals with what to do if a customer is not satisfied with your work. I refer to this process as providing customer recourse.

A. The Importance of Satisfying Unhappy Customers

The willingness to provide the dissatisfied customer with an efficient way to gain recourse is important to all businesses. Huge and successful companies, such as the mail order high flyers Land's End and L.L. Bean, have been built to a substantial degree on their commitment to promptly taking care of all customer complaints. In the retail area, Nordstrom's bases much of its marketing effort on convincing customers that it provides excellent recourse should any of its merchandise fail to live up to a customer's expectations.

Providing a quick, fair way to resolve customer complaints is even more crucial to small business success, because it's an essential element of establishing a good "word-of-mouth" marketing plan. (I discussed how to do this in Chapter 10.) If you doubt the strong link between taking care of the occasional customer complaint and generating positive recommendations about a business, ask yourself this: If you hear about a skilled carpenter who does spectacular work, but also hear that he is temperamental and has a reputation for not taking care of problems, would you hire him? And if you did, and were upset by his refusal to take care of several loose ends as part of an otherwise competent job, would you recommend him to your friends? Despite his skill, probably not.

And it isn't only carpenters whose business will suffer if they don't satisfy customer complaints. The same is true of a dentist, plumber, computer programmer and, as you have no doubt guessed, an independent paralegal. If word gets out that you aren't reliable and don't take care of complaints, your business will not grow.

And don't think it's adequate to simply work out solutions to the occasional customer complaint as they come up. This is a rotten business practice for several reasons. First, you are likely to be emotionally involved with the particular complaint and thus may not be objective enough to look at the situation from your customer's perspective.

Second, and more important, your failure to establish a complaint resolution procedure in advance and announce it early and often means that your customers, and the agencies and other people who refer your customers, won't know what to expect if something goes wrong and therefore may not patronize you in the first place. Think about how many times you have patronized one store or service provider (again, L.L. Bean, Land's End and Nordstrom's are excellent examples) instead of another because you know you'll be in good hands if a problem develops.

Third, if you fail to reassure all customers that you will promptly take care of any problems, you risk a dissatisfied customer complaining to the Bar or a public agency such as the district attorney or State Department of Consumer Affairs instead of to you. This reason for adopting a good recourse policy deserves emphasis. Never forget that you are working under the always mistrustful, and often hostile, eye of organized lawyer-dom and that the majority of prosecutions for unauthorized practice that are not initiated by lawyers or judges themselves, result from complaints from members of the public who feel ripped off by an independent para-legal.

Here are the key elements of any good customer recourse policy:

- The customer should be encouraged to tell you about any pro-blems;

- The customer should know her rights (and responsibilities) from the beginning;

- The customer should be able to ask for her money back at any time, with no need to give a reason;

- The customer—not you—should feel in control. Again, it's far better to provide a full refund if the customer is dissatisfied with your service for any reason than it is to demand that the customer come up with a "good reason" why she is dissatisfied;

- The customer should know exactly what to do to take advantage of her rights;

- Once a customer asks for her money back (or any other recourse you offer), it should be provided promptly.

One more important point. When you're deciding whether it's worth the trouble to develop a bullet proof recourse policy, consider and learn from the current plight of lawyers. Because bar associations and other law-yer-controlled professional regulatory groups provide such a poor system to handle and resolve complaints about lawyers who are corrupt, incom-petent and price-gouging, the entire legal profession's reputation isn't much higher than the Moscow subway. This is evidenced by the fact that in many states we are now witnessing a groundswell of public demands to take away the bar's historical power to police its own members and, instead, give this responsibility to nonlawyer-controlled public agencies.

The reason I belabor the point that establishing a good recourse policy in advance is essential is based on my finding that many independent paralegals haven't done so. A few have even told me proudly that they never give a refund. Clearly, no matter how good a legal form typing service some of these independent paralegals offer, they have not learned the basics of running a successful small business. It's as if Macy's advertised "The customer is always wrong."

I have found the intransigence of a number of paralegals on this issue to be particularly surprising in light of the fact that many do excellent work and, as a result, receive only a couple of complaints a year. The idea that these IPs are willing to fight with customers (even if the customer is being unreasonable) over the return of a few hundred dollars at the risk of having these people badmouth them to the public at large, or to the bar in particular, is appalling.

B. The No "Ifs, Ands or Buts Recourse" Policy

I recommend that you establish a "no ifs, ands or buts" money-back recourse policy. Not only is doing this a good deal for your customers, it is also a good deal for you. Why? Because assuming you sensibly screen your customers in the first place to eliminate inappropriate people, and you do a good form preparation job, experience indicates that less than 5% of your customers will be dissatisfied. (This percentage may be a little higher for divorces and lower in many other types of form preparation, such as small business incorporations.) The reason divorce seekers are more likely to complain is explained by the fact that these people are often under consider emotional stress, and occasionally some of this is bound to spill over to their relationship with you.

Here is a recourse policy that I believe makes sense:

The ABC Typing Service is dedicated to providing quality legal typing services under the direction of its consumers for a fair price.

If at any time you believe we have not fully met this goal, please ask for your money back. It will be provided promptly, no questions asked.

And here is some language you may wish to include in your printed material to deal with two of the common problem areas discussed above:

Any uncontested legal action has the potential to become contested, often resulting in both parties hiring a lawyer. If this occurs during the course of a legal action for which ABC typing service is helping a consumer prepare paperwork, all fees and charges will promptly be refunded.

As part of preparing your legal paperwork, you may need to obtain legal advice or information from a lawyer or legal information telephone service. It is understood that you are responsible for paying for this legal advice separately and that it is not included in the fee paid the ABC Typing Service to prepare your legal paperwork.

C. How To Deal With Predictable Customer Complaints

Enough lecturing! Let's assume you are convinced that it is wise to make sure that you don't have unsatisfied former customers wandering about maligning your reputation and have adopted the policies listed above.

Let's now look at how to handle several predictable situations in which at least a few customers are likely to be unhappy. The first involves what to do when the customer simply changes his mind about pursuing the legal action and asks for his money back after you have competently completed the work. (IP's who type marriage dissolution forms call this "divorce remorse.") Some independent paralegals provide no refund, or only a partial one, reasoning that since their work was done before the customer changed his mind, it's the customer's problem. While this policy is logically defensible, I believe it's nevertheless mistaken. As mentioned above, it's far, far easier, and therefore, in the long run far less trouble, to simply state a policy that if a customer is dissatisfied for any reason, you'll give a full refund—no "ifs, ands or buts."

Another fairly common refund situation can occur when a legal action that starts out to be uncontested becomes contested while you are typing paperwork. If, as is likely, a lawyer ends up taking over the case, and you do not complete the paperwork, your customer may feel ripped off by having to pay an attorney in addition to having already paid you. Again, the best way to deal with this problem, which probably won't happen more than a few times a year, is to simply refund all, or at least a substantial part, of the customer's money.

Customer unhappiness can also occasionally develop if, as part of working with your typing service, the customer needs legal information or advice not available from a self-help law book. As discussed above, it's best to cover this possibility in your original information sheet, indicating that the fee for your service does not cover any necessary lawyers' consultation fees. Assuming your customer simply confers with a lawyer (or calls a legal information phone service) who charges a reasonable fee, and comes back to you to complete the paperwork, there should be no problem, since the customer will almost surely understand that your typing fee has been fairly earned.

D. What To Do If You Make a Serious Mistake

Finally, we come to the sticky question of what to do if a customer feels that your negligence or lack of knowledge resulted in loss of a substantial right and is not satisfied with a refund. Many IPs I have talked to state that, over the many years of preparing legal forms, this has never occurred. Others say that they have made mistakes that have caused consumers problems, but it's always been possible to fix them at a reasonable cost, usually by redoing the paperwork.

Fortunately, in most situations, the economic harm that an IP's mistake causes is fairly modest. For example, one IP who has been in business for a decade can remember a situation in which she filed a final decree of divorce before the end of the year, forgetting that the customer had asked her to wait until January 2, for tax reasons. The IP immediately asked a trusted tax preparer to compute the extra tax liability and reimbursed the customer. The amount was only a few hundred dollars.

Even though IPs who know their field and keep good records don't often experience customers who claim that their lack of care resulted in a substantial loss, it can happen. For example, let's say you type divorce papers for Mary C. A year later, she claims you neglected to include several valuable assets that she told you about and blames you for the fact that she wasn't awarded this property in the court divorce decree. Assuming you did all the things I discussed in Chapter 3 to establish that you are only a typing service, do not provide legal advice, and it's up to your customers to understand the laws that affect the particular legal area, you are off to a pretty good start. In addition, however, it's essential that you keep a written record of all information provided by your customer (preferably in her own handwriting), and have her sign a clear statement that the information provided is accurate and complete. (I discuss this in detail in Chapter 8.) In addition, after you type the necessary court or agency forms, your customer should read them carefully (or if necessary, have them read to her) and again sign a statement that they are complete.

Assuming your divorce customer did all this, and the missing property wasn't listed, you are in an excellent legal position. Assuming property existed in the first place, it's your customer's responsibility, not yours.

BUY INSURANCE TO COVER NORMAL BUSINESS RISKS

In addition to providing recourse to customers who complain about your service for any reason, you should purchase normal types of business insurance to protect your business and, especially if you are not incorporated, your personal assets, should customers be hurt in or outside your premises. This liability insurance is often sold as part of a package with fire and theft coverage, which is also a good idea to cover your business equipment. In addition, if your car, or a car of any employee, is ever used to do errands for the business, be sure your auto insurance policy covers you for any liability incurred. (This usually involves paying extra for business coverage.) If an accident occurs while you or an employee is on a business errand, even if the employee is driving his or her own car, your business is likely to be sued.

But suppose now that you are faced with a large financial claim by a customer in a situation where you may be at fault (e.g., you didn't include property your customer listed). After you recover from the urge to run and hide, what should you do? Instead of arguing with the customer over who is at fault, your first job is to see if anything can be done to salvage the situation. Because lawyers themselves make a great many mistakes, the legal system as a whole is very forgiving of errors, especially if prompt action is taken to fix them. In this context, you may want to check with a friendly lawyer to see if corrective action can be taken. Be ready to move fast and be willing to pay for the lawyer's services, even if you still aren't convinced you caused the problem.

Now suppose you establish that it's too late to take corrective action, but you believe your work didn't cause the problem (e.g., your customer signed off on a property list that didn't include the disputed property). Your best bet is to suggest mediation. This involves both of you sitting down with a trained mediator to try and work out your own settlement of the dispute. Since the mediator has no power to impose a decision that you don't agree to, there is no risk that the process will result in financial liability on your part, unless, of course, you voluntarily accept it. One of the best aspects of mediation is that it allows your customers (and you, too, for that matter) to air all grievances, not just the one that directly caused the dispute. Once everything is out in the open, a surprising number of supposedly intractable disputes are settled.

Finally, a note on malpractice insurance. One good reason to work with a lawyer is to gain the coverage provided by the lawyer's malpractice insurance. At this point, I know of no insurance company that writes insurance coverage for errors and mistakes made by IPs. Given the fact that I have rarely heard of a substantial monetary claim being made against an IP, I don't think that gaining insurance coverage is so important that it mandates that you work with a lawyer, but it is something to consider.

Chapter 13

Working for Lawyers:
The Freelance Paralegal

*T*he fastest growing area of business opportunity for paralegals isn't helping nonlawyers prepare legal forms. Instead, it's doing work for lawyers as an independent contractor. This takes many forms. In some instances, this means establishing an independent business to prepare legal documents that have traditionally been prepared in-house by a legal secretary. Other times, it means collecting evidence, preparing exhibits (often involving visuals), and lining up witnesses for personal injury cases. In still others, it means helping lawyers manage the information that must be gathered as part of any major case.

In this age of specialization, many lawyers have learned that by contracting with freelance paralegals to handle specialized work in a particular legal area, such as divorce, personal injury, probate, or incorporation, the work is accomplished faster, more accurately and, best of all, substantially more cheaply than they could do it in their own offices. A few lawyers have taken this principle so far, they don't really have an office in the traditional sense. Instead, they rent an "executive suite" which comes with a receptionist, and contract out all their form preparation.

A. The Pros and Cons of Being a Freelance Paralegal

The juxtaposition of lawyer need and lawyer greed has created a unique opportunity for freelance paralegals with an entrepreneurial bent to sell their services to a number of different lawyers and make a good living doing it. In addition to being able to run their own business, however, there is another big advantage enjoyed by paralegals who work for lawyers on a contract basis. Since lawyers profit from the relationship, you rarely hear organized lawyerdom complain that freelance paralegals are guilty of unauthorized practice.

The state of New Jersey is the one major exception to this generalization. The Committee on the Unauthorized Practice of Law appointed by the New Jersey Supreme Court has issued an opinion that freelance paralegals who work for lawyers as independent contractors are guilty of the unauthorized practice of law.[1] In an odd way, this opinion is as insightful as it is doomed. It is insightful in that it recognizes that the trend towards freelance paralegals establishing independent businesses to prepare legal forms outside the lawyer's office greatly weakens the intellectual premise that justifies the lawyer monopoly over legal services—that only lawyers are skilled enough to competently cope with legal matters.

It is doomed because the trend toward freelance paralegals contracting with lawyers is so advanced that it can't be stopped. The reason is simple: Many lawyers no longer have the necessary skills to do many

---

[1]N.J. Committee on the Unauthorized Practice of Law, Opinion #24, November 1990.

types of legal paperwork themselves and can't, or don't want to, hire skilled employees to bring form preparation back into their offices.

THE FREELANCE PARALEGAL: EMPLOYEE OR INDEPENDENT CONTRACTOR?

The Internal Revenue Service and other federal and state agencies have established criteria to decide if a business person is truly an independent contractor or has the legal status of part-time employee. This is a crucial distinction for both you and the lawyers you work with, as tax withholding and employee contribution rules are far different for employees than they are for independent business people. Very generally speaking, an employer/employee relationship exists when the business for whom the services are performed has the right to control and direct the person who carries out the services—both as to the result of the work and to the detail of how it is carried out.

If you only work for one or two lawyers, do much of your form preparation in their offices, and operate under their direct supervision, your legal status is that of a temporary employee.

If you work with lots of lawyers, spend most of your time in your own office, have a local business license, establish your own hours and working conditions, join professional associations, own your own sophisticated equipment, occasionally hire people to work for you (don't forget to get Federal tax I.D.numbers) and make many of the decisions necessary to accomplish your work, chances are you are a legitimate independent contractor.

So while the New Jersey bar and Supreme Court may posture and bluster about this issue, very little is likely to change, except perhaps that New Jersey freelance paralegals may have to be called temporary employees for a few years. This will be a record keeping problem both for law offices and freelancers, but lawyers who generally have poor computer skills will undoubtedly solve it by pushing their extra bookkeeping work onto the paralegals and extra costs onto their clients.

For a few readers of this book, the idea of working with lawyers, even as an independent businessperson, will be an anathema. After all, if a significant part of the reason you want to be an independent paralegal in the first place is your conviction that the self-help law movement is a wholesome development as compared to lawyers' monopolistic approach to legal information, you probably won't want to work with lawyers at all.

For other freelancers, working with lawyers and their clients is a positive experience. In fact, many freelance paralegals report that once they establish their own businesses and contract to provide specialized services to lawyers, they do interesting and challenging work and are treated with far more collegial respect than they were when they worked as law firm employees. For example, freelance paralegal Afroditi Price states:

> *I never work for lawyers who treat me in a condescending manner. In most cases, they respect me more than their in-house staff, because they know I am not a "yes person." In fact, because I walk in with a contract and act like a businessperson, like their own clients, they have a lot of respect for me.*

There are some other good reasons why an independent paralegal might consider working for lawyers rather than the public:

- As opposed to preparing paperwork for nonlawyer customers, you need relatively fewer lawyer customers, because they will often supply repeat business. This doesn't free you from the need to market your services, but it does allow you to concentrate on a much smaller group of potential customers;

- Your income will often be better, at least at the beginning, as it's commonly easier to line up a few lawyers than it is to become known to the general public;

- The work you handle will usually be more complicated and challenging than if you were working directly for consumers;

- As an independent business person providing valuable, cost-effective service, you may be accorded more respect than you would be if you were an employee of a law firm;

- There is no paranoia that you will be arrested for practicing law without a license (except maybe in New Jersey). As I mentioned above, as long as you are economically benefitting lawyers, few will challenge your right to do legal work;

- You will have the opportunity to work with new and sophisticated technology. For many, this will mean using computers and specialized software to produce legal documents, create databases or do legal research. For others, it may mean supervising the creation of visual presentations for use at settlement conferences or trials.

B. What Services Do Freelance Paralegals Offer?

Okay, suppose now that you are interested in setting up your own independent business to do subcontracting work for attorneys. How do you begin? First, it helps if you have a specialty.

An independent paralegal who works directly for an attorney usually makes herself extremely knowledgeable about a particular, often narrow, legal area that requires the preparation of routine, labor-intensive paperwork. Probate is a good example. Security regulation filings necessary to establish a public corporation, preparing evidence and witnesses for personal injury cases, tax form preparation, bankruptcy, evictions, and family law are other good examples. As a general rule, the more you specialize in a narrow area, such as doing trademark searches or preparing patent applications, the more you will end up dealing with the relatively few lawyers in your area who handle that speciality.

LAWSUIT MANAGEMENT

Today, major court cases quickly produce massive amounts of information. This means sophisticated information and paper tracking systems must be implemented to catalogue, store and retrieve it. To accomplish this, lawyers often hire freelance paralegals who specialize in case management to work with in-house staff. In most urban areas, groups of freelance paralegals have set up small businesses to provide these services.

Don't assume that because I have not mentioned a particular area here that it isn't a suitable one. Freelance paralegals are currently working with lawyers on a freelance basis in dozens of form preparation areas. The trick to analyzing whether a particular legal field is a good one for an independent paralegal to work in is to ask yourself the following: Does the particular legal area involve picky, time-consuming, repetitive form or evidence preparation work? If so, lawyers are likely to want to farm it out to a freelancer, who, in turn, can apply efficient computer techniques to accurately accomplish the necessary work in a minimum amount of time.

By contrast, legal areas that principally rely on the personalized advice or skills of a lawyer, such as negotiating contracts or settlement agreements, are not good candidates for freelance paralegals. Remember, since freelancers don't have a law license, they risk being charged with unauthorized practice if they transfer legal information or expertise directly to a customer.

In the probate area, particularly, where in many states fees are set by statute or court custom as a percentage of the gross value of the estate, freelance paralegal/lawyer relationships often work beautifully. In part, this is because attorney fees are high enough that the lawyer can afford to pay the freelance paralegal well for processing the paperwork and still make a bundle himself. For example, in many states, a $12,000 - $15,000 attorney fee is typical to probate an uncomplicated estate with a gross value of $500,000.[2] Incidentally, when you realize that most of the work involves completing 10-25 pages of routine (but picky) paperwork and filing it with the probate clerk, it's easy to see why lawyers, who often need not even make a court appearance, are so opposed to reformers' proposals to eliminate probate.

In more populous states, one way to get an indication of whether a particular legal specialty will work for a freelance paralegal is by checking out whether form preparation computer software is available. If the answer is yes, it means that a legal publisher has done market research that indicates that the particular form preparation niche is large enough to be profitable. For example, in several states, you can purchase one of several legal form packages designed to produce family law forms or incorporations on a personal computer.

It is also important to recognize that the existence of state specific computer packages designed for, and marketed to, lawyers, presents the freelance paralegal with a great business opportunity. Because these programs are relatively expensive (often $500 or more), it means that many small general practice law offices do not find that purchasing them is cost-effective. However, a freelance paralegal who works with a number of law firms, will often have the volume to justify the purchase. And once she does, the fact that she has the state-of-the-art software will be a good selling point as part of recruiting new lawyer customers. To learn about software packages available in your community, read the ads in your state bar publication and in local newspapers. Also, Julius Blumberg, Inc. publishes and distributes useful software. You can get their catalogue by writing them at 62 White St., New York, NY 10013.

---

[2]If the lawyer is both the executor and the lawyer for the estate (a practice known as "double dipping"), the lawyer will get twice as much for the same work.

C. How To Get the Necessary Skills

There are two principal routes to gain the skills necessary to open your own freelance business that are often used in tandem. One is to work in a law firm or court clerk's office. In a sense, the paralegal serves an apprenticeship to learn how to perform particular tasks.

The other main approach is to attend a paralegal school where the relevant skills are taught. But if you consider the school route, be sure you pick one that emphasizes hands-on training as opposed to lots of legal theory. It is beyond the scope of this book to discuss paralegal schools in detail; your best bet will be to talk to local freelancers and get their recommendation.

Once you are established as a freelancer, you'll want to further develop your skills. One way to do this is to join a paralegal organization, most of which sponsor training sessions and/or work with bar associations to allow paralegal members to attend lawyer training sessions. In California, the California Association of Freelance Paralegals, Inc. sponsors excellent training sessions by and for freelancers.[3]

D. How to Get Freelance Work

Once a freelance paralegal develops the skills to handle legal paperwork in a particular legal area, she often gets her business started by quietly and privately letting local lawyers know about her specialty. For example, many lawyers, especially those who only have part-time secretarial help or who employ a typist with little legal form preparation experience, have a need for help in specialized areas such as probate, non-profit corporations, guardianships or adoptions, especially if they only handle a few per year. In this situation, working with a highly skilled freelance paralegal is very attractive. After all, the lawyer only contracts with the paralegal service in a situation when he is assured of collecting a much greater fee. For

---

[3]CAFP can be reached at P.O. Box 3267, Berkeley, CA 94703.

example, Nancy Baird, an extremely successful paralegal whose office is in Alameda, California, works with about 25 lawyers and has 40 to 50 open probate files at one time.

Larger firms also work with freelancers, although here the freelancer is likely to function as a small cog in a big law machine. Big firms are especially likely to look for freelance help as a part of collecting, storing and managing evidence for complex major litigation, such as copyright and patent infringement, asbestos and toxic waste cases, construction defects, and all types of class actions. Freelancers also often work in personal injury cases, where their job is usually to work up a case (find expert witnesses, manage discovery, organize evidence and supervise videotaped testimony) as part of making a settlement offer.

Most freelance paralegals who set up a business to work with lawyers already have lawyer contacts. Typically, these are developed while working in a law office, for a court clerk, or in some other way that has brought them into close contact with lawyers.

If you don't choose to make your contacts via this traditional route, you will not only need to develop the necessary skills on your own, but you'll have to convince at least one lawyer to give you a chance. If you do well, and the lawyer is willing to put in a good word with others in your community, before long, lawyers will be calling you.

Another way freelancers find work is through employment agencies specializing in legal secretary and paralegal placement. Many of these businesses that started out as traditional employment agencies have more recently broadened their scope and also act as employment brokers for freelance paralegals.

Still another way to get the word out about your freelance paralegal business is to join a local paralegal association. These associations often promote the services of their members by circulating lists of freelancers and specialties to lawyers and other in-house paralegals. In California, freelancers have established their own membership organization, the California Association of Freelance Paralegals, Inc. (CAFP), which helps freelancers develop focused marketing efforts. In an effort to better understand how the freelance paralegal movement is developing, I asked Afroditi Price, President of CAFP, a few questions:

Jake Warner: Paralegals selling their services to lawyers on a contract basis is a recent development, is it not?

Afroditi Price: Not really. Some freelance paralegal specialists, such as those working in the probate area, have been running their own businesses for more than 15 years.

JW: *If that's true, why was it 1989 before CAFP was founded?*

AP: It was largely a question of critical mass. Until a few years ago, there were not enough freelancers in one geographical area to justify a separate paralegal group.

JW: *What changed?*

AP: Suddenly freelancers were being hired by law firms to do all sorts of things beyond the original freelance paralegal standby's probate, deposition summary work and computer litigation support. Let me back up a little. Over the years, law firms trained in-house paralegals to do all sorts of specialized tasks in areas such as worker's comp, family law, personal injury, environmental law, corporate securities litigation and regulation and ERISA, to mention a few. Once they had these valuable and highly specialized skills, paralegals began to leave the law firms and start their own businesses which, for the most part, consisted of selling their skills back to their former employers and other law firms on a contract basis. In a sense, it was the birth of new service industry.

JW: *So most CAFP members have a high level of skill. Do your membership rules require a lot of paralegal experience or training?*

AP: Yes, to be a regular CAFP member, paralegals must provide services exclusively to attorneys on a freelance basis, and must have had two years experience as a paralegal providing services to attorneys.

JW: *That amounts to saying a new CAFP member has to work for a lawyer to meet your experience rule.*

AP: Right. The reason for this requirement is CAFP does not want a recent paralegal school graduate with no real world experience claiming CAFP membership as part of marketing their services to law firms. Very few businesses hire other professionals who have zero year's experience.

JW: *You obviously believe freelancers should have a track record?*

AP: You bet. A paralegal school gives exposure to what a job may be like—but until the job is successfully completed, you will never understand what is really involved. And I don't just mean skills—you need to learn about taking responsibility to get a job done, have a good handle on practical legal ethics, and manage deadlines and stress.

JW: *CAFP doesn't accept members who also sell their services to both lawyers and directly to the public. How come?*

AP: Because our job is primarily to help members with marketing. To do that in a focused way, we want to concentrate on the attorney/law firm market.

JW: *Is there some other reason? Do you look down on people who market their services both to lawyers and directly to the consumers?*

AP: No. My parents taught me the value of an honest day's work, regardless of the type of work. If individuals have the chutzpah to sell information directly to nonlawyers without giving legal advice, more power to them.

JW: *Over the long term, do you see a trend towards paralegals selling legal information directly to the end user, bypassing lawyers?*

AP: I don't advocate violating current unauthorized practice of law rules, but taking a longer view, information is just that—information. If a legal tech steers clear of giving legal advice, there should be no barrier preventing marketing it to anyone. And yes, this probably qualifies as a trend. Lawyers will not be able to artificially restrict the flow of information just because they find it profitable to do so. And as I said earlier, legal advice and information are two different things.

E. Combining Freelance and Independent Paralegal Work

It's possible to combine doing work for lawyers with providing services for the general public. I know several paralegals who do this successfully. Obviously, however, this can be a difficult career path if the lawyers you work with are hostile to the self-help law movement. However, if they are supportive of your efforts to help nonlawyers, combining both types of customers can have several advantages. The most obvious of these is that you get referrals from two different sources. Another is that from a self-protection point of view, it will be much harder for organized lawyerdom to attempt to have you prosecuted for unauthorized practice if you are doing much the same form preparation work for both lawyers and the public.

Evelyn Rinzler of Oakland, California is a good example of a freelance paralegal who works directly for lawyers as an employee, freelances for other lawyers, and runs her own independent paralegal business. Evelyn's expertise is in the field of Medicare and Medi-Cal (California's medical plan for low-income people) appeals—a legal area which is not prohibited to nonlawyers by UPL rules. She does this work at her part-time job at a local legal aid program. In addition, one day a week she handles the same tasks on a freelance basis for a legal aid program in another county. And recently, she has begun to offer her services directly to individuals as an independent paralegal.

One way she recruits customers for her independent business is to contact lawyers to tell them about her cost-efficient service. Because the amounts of money involved are usually in the range of $500-$2,500 (rarely more than $5,000), lawyers can't handle these appeals in a cost-effective way. In addition, most don't have the specialized expertise necessary to do a good job. The result is that many are happy to send business to Evelyn.

Chapter 14

Working for Volunteer, Community or Social Change Organizations

*T*he Pittsburg, Pennsylvania bar association charged "Legal Advocacy for Women," a nonprofit center which helps mothers get child support they are legally entitled to, with unauthorized practice of law. (See interview with Rose Palmer in Appendix.) In Lackawanna, N.Y, the Erie County Bar association called Judy Lamb on the carpet for similar activities. (See interview with Judy Lamb in the Appendix.) In other areas of the country, similar types of bar harassment have occasionally been directed against nonprofit groups involved in environmental, consumer and tenants' rights activities. So the question arises, if you work with a good cause and, as part of doing so, help people understand their legal rights and formally deal with the legal system by filing papers and appearing in court, are you likely to become the target of organized lawyerdom's official ire?

The answer is a qualified "probably not," although, as the Pennsylvania and New York examples illustrate, this is not always the case. Why do I say that volunteer groups normally have less to fear? Because by definition these groups work in areas where people traditionally don't have the money to hire a lawyer. And despite lip service to the contrary, the American legal profession has traditionally had little interest in representing people who can't pay their stiff fees. What about all the free (pro bono) work lawyers claim they do? It's mostly public relations hooey designed to frustrate any serious reform of the legal system.

Put more directly, when all the professional hype is stripped away, the legal profession defines the practice of law to involve only legal disputes and procedures where there is money to be made. It follows then that since lawyers profit handsomely from business formation, probate, personal injury, domestic disputes (especially between affluent people), and estate planning, to name just a few, they are extremely interested in defending their monopoly power in these areas. This means they are quick to charge nonlawyer interlopers with the unauthorized practice of law.

In many other legal areas, however, lawyers have never found a way to collect what they view as decent fees. These include small consumer disputes, the collection of child support, arguments among neighbors, the right of a poor person to die with dignity, domestic violence, and dozens of other everyday hassles. So, even though working in these areas involves giving advice about legal procedures, completing legal forms, etc., lawyers are often willing to look the other way if nonlawyers do it.

You surely get the point. Because many nonprofit organizations work in areas of little or no lawyerly profit, lawyers normally do not initiate charges of unauthorized practice of law against them. This is true even though paralegals who work for these nonprofits often get far more involved in giving legal advice than do independent paralegals who sell form preparation services directly to the public. And once a particular nonprofit legal self-help group exists for several years (say an AIDS support group, where nonlawyers help dying people complete a living will or durable power of attorney), the very fact that lawyers haven't harassed it in the past often results in a politically convenient and widely-accepted fabrication that the organization in question doesn't really engage in the practice of law.

A good example of how this process works is the establishment of tenants' rights groups in the 1960s in many areas of the country. At first, there was a great deal of nervousness about the reaction of organized lawyerdom. The fear was that since in most tenants' rights groups nonlawyers routinely counseled tenants as to their legal rights and helped them fill out court forms, such as answers to eviction suits, organized lawyerdom was sure to file unauthorized practice charges. Instead, of course, the bar's response in most places was to do nothing. Apparently, this was for two reasons. First, because lawyers never made much money defending tenants in the first place, no one cared enough to get involved in trying to suppress these activities. Second, lawyers were afraid if they put nonlawyer tenant-advocacy services out of business, they would have to do the work themselves, often on a pro bono (free) basis.

By contrast, organized lawyerdom has gone after a number of independent paralegals who offer services to landlords, most recently in several locations in Orange County, California.[1] These for-profit landlord paralegal typing services are often charged with unauthorized practice, even though the work they do is the mirror image of what tenants groups do. There is, of course, one crucial difference between the two: When it comes to landlords, who have traditionally hired lawyers, an independent paralegal eviction service is seen as taking money out of lawyers' pockets rather than providing a community service.

A. Appearing In Court

There is one legal area, besides representing paying clients, over which lawyers are extremely protective of their monopoly. This involves appearing in court on behalf of a client. As you'll see when you read Rose

---

[1]One of the leading cases in this field, which incidentally establishes rules for California IPs who wish to operate in this field, is *The People v. Landlords Professional Services*, 215 Cal.App.3d 1599 (4th Dist.,1989).

Palmer's interview in the Appendix, this is one of the things that got Legal Advocacy for Women in trouble in Pittsburgh, PA. Indeed, the first formal complaint against the group was filed by a lawyer who objected to volunteers from the group attending court sessions and whispering instructions to women trying to petition for adequate amounts of child support. And later, when Pittsburg lawyers accepted a settlement allowing nonlawyers to come to court to provide moral and legal support to women, one of the stipulations was that nonlawyer advisors not be allowed to touch, or put their belongings on, the lawyers' (counsel) table. Yes, it's sad that the once proud legal profession should stoop to measure its prerogatives in such petty ways, but petty or not, it's a good illustration of the overt lawyer hostility nonlawyers who try to help people who appear in court are sure to encounter.

No matter what the dispute, or how much or how little money is at stake, lawyers are absolutely bent upon defending their right to be the only people who can speak for others in court. The reasons for this probably have as much to do with concerns about loss of status as they do with economics, but it is also true that, traditionally, enforcement of this rule has done much to fatten lawyers' wallets. When faced with the need to file or defend a court action, even perennially cash-starved public interest groups such as environmentalists, advocates for the disabled, friends of animals and supporters of the homeless have often been able to raise money, often significant amounts of it, to pay a lawyer.

Lawyers, of course, argue that greed has nothing to do with their position that only they can speak on behalf of clients in court. They contend that only they are trained in, and tested on, courtroom skills and it would risk doing great consumer harm to allow others to represent people in court. Without boring you with many pages as to why this argument is a largely self-interested sophistry, let me simply point out that in the vast majority of American law schools, courtroom advocacy is not a required course, and that bar examinations do not test this skill. In short, lawyers normally pick up courtroom skills by working with more experienced colleagues and by practicing (literally) on clients. The fact that nonlawyer advocates who work in non-profit organizations gain their skills in much the same way is, of course, ignored by lawyers.

 In Chapter 2, Section C, I discuss how judges use the "inherent powers" doctrine to protect the legal profession's monopoly over the courtroom and in some instances even the preparation of routine legal paperwork.

B. Defending Yourself From Lawyer Attacks

But suppose you plan to work with a volunteer group in a situation where you will be routinely dispensing legal information and, despite my advice that you are unlikely to experience trouble with the bar, you are worried. After all, like the people who worked with Pittsburg's Legal Advocacy for Women, you might be the exception that proves the rule that lawyers usually don't go after non-profits. Certainly it is appropriate to ask what is likely to happen to you personally if organized lawyerdom tries to suppress your group?

As long as you are working in the broad public interest sector, the answer is "little or nothing." I know of no current criminal prosecutions in this area. Instead, even when a complaint by organized lawyerdom is initiated, what almost always occurs is something like this:

1. The bar, district attorney, or state supreme court threatens to charge your group (let's assume you work at a center which helps with the legal problems of students) with unauthorized practice. Incidentally, this threat is almost always initiated because a local lawyer handles a dispute against someone who gets legal help from your organization, not because a consumer of your services complains;

2. The media gets involved on the side of your group, asking where else penniless students (or in other situations, mothers without child support, tenants, immigrants, etc.) can get affordable legal help;

3. Organized lawyerdom comes under general attack for not offering free *"pro bono"* help in the particular area, and for generally over-charging and not providing reasonable access to the legal system for the average student (and by extension, most Americans);

4. Meetings are held between the advocacy group and organized lawyerdom and a compromise is worked out. It typically allows organized lawyerdom to save face by getting the nonprofit group to agree to slightly modify its activities to avoid a charge of UPL (or, if a UPL action has already been filed, to have it dropped). Sometimes this "slap on the wrist" takes the form of limiting some inconsequential aspect of the non-profit's activities; other times it is accomplished by the nonprofit agreeing to token supervision by a lawyer who is personally interested in the particular activity or cause. Almost always, when you look beyond the surface, the advocacy group is allowed to keep operating much as before.

As Rose Palmer discusses in her interview, the Legal Advocacy for Women situation well illustrates how this usually works. The Bar and Legal Advocacy for Women settled their dispute as follows: In exchange for organized lawyerdom backing off, the organization agreed to change its name to "Support, Inc." and clarify a few of its procedures. This consisted of informing all clients that their paralegal helpers are not lawyers (something they knew already), agreeing not to whisper to clients in court and, as mentioned, agreeing not to touch the counsel table. In short, whispering excepted, Support, Inc. is free to do exactly the same work as Legal Advocacy for Women did. And while the group refused to accept any official supervision by a lawyer or bar association, they were canny enough to partially mollify the local legal establishment by 1) putting a few lawyers on their Board of Directors, 2) working closely with several local sympathetic lawyers and supportive judges, and 3) beginning a law student intern program under which students from two local law schools help out with Support, Inc. programs.

C. Paying the Bills

Unfortunately, paralegals who work with non-profits often face a larger problem than the threat of lawyer harassment. Their problem is economic. Most nonprofit groups, whether organized to help AIDS sufferers, artists, alcoholics, or animals, or any of thousands of other worthy endeavors, are severely under-funded. All too often they try to survive from one inadequate grant to the next, existing in large measure because of the personal economic sacrifices made by their own staff. Or put more bluntly, a paralegal who works in this setting is typically either unpaid or underpaid. For the rare persons with plenty of money in the bank, this may not be a problem. For everyone else, it is a severe one.

The result is that many nonprofit organizations that try to help their members, or the public generally, with legal problems usually experience rapid staff turnover. Often it seems that as soon as a competent paralegal is trained, she has moved on. Commonly, this isn't because the person wants to leave, but because the hard rock of their altruism has been ground into dust by the even harder economic reality of being poor in America. Obviously the consequences of this rapid turnover in terms of the quality of legal service delivered to the group, as well as to the paralegals involved, are not good.

In my view, many of the problems non-profits have paying paralegals to deliver good legal services could be avoided. The key to doing this is understanding one of the great lessons of the independent paralegal movement—people are willing and able to pay for competent, reasonably-priced legal help if charged for it at paralegal, not lawyer, rates. In other words, the seeming conclusion of many nonprofit groups that there are only two alternatives to the delivery of legal services—hire a lawyer and pay the market rate, or provide free services—is often wrong.

PARALEGAL SERVICES AND NONPROFIT TAX LAW

Most nonprofit organizations are exempt from income taxation under Section 501(c)(3) of the Internal Revenue Code as educational or charitable organizations. Since education is defined by IRS regulations to include "instruction of the public on subjects useful to individuals and beneficial to the community," and since "charitable" generally means "promotion of the public good," non-profits that provide paralegal services should fall well within the guidelines of their tax exemption requirements.

Can tax-exempt non-profits charge hourly fees for paralegal services? Yes they can. (Just think of the substantial service fees collected by other nonprofit organizations, such as nonprofit colleges, trade schools, hospitals, medical clinics and the like.) As long as the services charged are reasonable, the IRS should not object. In fact, in Ruling 78-428, the IRS decided that a nonprofit group that operated a legal services clinic could charge a fee based upon the income of the client.

This is not the place for a detailed discussion about the mechanics of setting up an economically self-sufficient paralegal office as part of a nonprofit organization. However, it is appropriate to look at one example of how an independent paralegal could provide low-cost legal help at the same time he charges enough to support himself.

Artists of all stripes and spots (dancers, painters, sculptors, jugglers, to mention but a few) often form nonprofit corporations when they want to come together to further their activities, whether it be to establish a performance space, publish educational materials, or sponsor a performance or display. Like the rest of us, most can't afford to hire a lawyer to do this at $150 an hour. As a result, unless they know a lawyer interested in the arts who will volunteer her time, most end up either doing it themselves or knocking on the door of a local nonprofit artists' support group with the hope that someone there can provide free legal help. Because artists' groups are chronically underfunded, they are often unable to do this.

Now, as an alternative, let me propose a different solution. Have the arts support organization work with an independent paralegal, or a paralegal on its own staff, to provide low-cost nonprofit incorporation services to local artists. To establish a fair fee, the first step would be to determine exactly how long it takes to prepare the paperwork to establish a nonprofit corporation and apply for a federal tax exemption. *How To Form a Non-Profit Corporation,* by Anthony Mancuso (Nolo Press), provides instructions on how to do this in every state and contains the step-by-step instructions necessary to apply for a Section 501(c)(3) federal tax exemption. After reading this book and examining the specific forms and procedures necessary in your state, you are likely to conclude the answer is about four to five hours, assuming someone in the nonprofit group has read Mancuso's book and worked with other members to gather necessary information and make practical choices.

The next step is to figure out a fair hourly return for the person doing this work. Assume after taking overhead into consideration you decide this is $50 per hour. This means you will probably find that a paralegal can prepare a nonprofit corporation for $200. Most arts groups, no matter how struggling, can scrape together this amount, especially if they have already checked prices with local lawyers, which are likely to range from $1,000-$2,000.

Chapter 15

Political Organizing for Change

 L et's start this chapter by reviewing several points that have been discussed throughout this book.

1. The American civil legal system is slow, expensive and inaccessible. Too often, it's also unjust and corrupt. As a result, the monopoly power of lawyers to deliver legal services in the U.S. is under attack as, increasingly, people see that lawyers are primarily interested in protecting themselves, not the public.

2. The self-help legal movement (and public support for it), has grown immensely in the last twenty years. For example, in several

states, including California and Arizona, almost two-thirds of divorces are now done without a lawyer.

3. The number of people who are running independent paralegal businesses has grown dramatically in the last decade, especially in Florida, Texas, Arizona, California, Oregon, Washington, and Nevada which, taken together, now have thousands of independent paralegals.

4. Several studies,[1] as well as a good deal of practical experience with independent paralegal offices, supports the proposition that nonlawyers are competent to handle routine legal paperwork.

5. Self-help law software such as *WillMaker* have sold hundreds of thousands of copies. Ten years ago, these materials didn't exist.

6. The types of legal tasks that the general public is successfully accomplishing on its own using self-help law books and software (and often the help of independent paralegals), are expanding rapidly. In 1980, when people thought of self-help law, they thought primarily of divorce; today, nonlawyers routinely prepare a wide variety of basic legal forms, including those for step-parent adoption, incorporation, probate and wills, living trusts and house purchases.

7. Consumers are increasingly objecting to organized lawyerdom's monopoly power over the legal system, and it is beginning to be reflected in judicial decisions. Specifically, several recent court decisions (see Chapter 2) more narrowly define what constitutes the practice of law and allow the role of independent paralegals to expand.

---

[1] One of the best is Rhode, "Policing the Professional Monopoly: A Constitutional and Empirical Analysis of Unauthorized Practice Prohibitions," 34 Stanford Law Rev. 1 (1981).

This laundry list of trends adds up to the fact that America is in the midst of a period of fundamental and powerful change in the ways routine legal services are delivered to the middle class. This switch, which is of truly historic proportions, is clearly towards low-cost alternatives to the traditional ways lawyers deliver legal services. As one of these alternatives, the independent paralegal movement is in an excellent position to both help this trend along and to profit from it.

The fact that independent paralegals have made significant strides towards public acceptance in the last few years is not the same thing as saying this new profession is bound to succeed. As noted throughout this book, independent paralegals still face serious political and legal problems because of the hostility of organized lawyerdom. This brings me to the central question of this chapter—how can IPs best protect the advances their occupation has already made and take sensible steps to further expand their role in delivering routine legal services.

A. Paralegal Political Organizing

The best way to accomplish both of these goals is to organize politically. As long as the independent paralegal movement consists of isolated individuals and lawyers are organized through bar associations and judges' associations, the trend toward acceptance of paralegals can be slowed, if not contained, by lawyers. Once organized and politically active, however, independent paralegals obviously have a much better opportunity to get the message across to the public that they represent a low-cost, high-quality alternative to lawyers. (If you doubt this, see Virginia Simons' interview in the Appendix.)

There are several important elements to any successful political organizing effort. One of these involves establishing an efficient way for IPs to communicate with each other at both the state and national level. It is particularly essential that IPs in the same state be in close touch, as unauthorized practice is regulated at the state level. It's important to realize that while IPs may all be competing with each other to some degree, the organized bar, with its dedication to putting everyone out of business, is the real adversary. Or, put more directly, it is essential that IPs avoid squabbles with each other at least long enough to present a united front to the bar. If you doubt this, think back to what it cost the Native American tribes to continue their inter-tribal spats after the Europeans arrived.

Jolene Jacobs, one of the first successful independent paralegals, advises:

> *Develop, if possible, good relationships with your competitors. Try to have a friendly, positive relationship with them rather than an adversarial one. It can not only make life and your business environment more pleasant, you will build relationships that will help all independent paralegals if the bar gets aggressive.*

Once all the IPs in your state are talking to each other, your next job is to establish a solid state-wide organization. There are a number of ways to do this, no one of which is the best in all circumstances. With this caution in mind, let me tell you some of the things Charles (Ed) Sherman and I did in the early 1970s as part of establishing California's pioneering Wave Project:

- Established a central office which, for a small fee, coordinated state-wide efforts of project members, and was available for counseling when the bar threatened any Wave Project member.

- Produced a quarterly newsletter to serve as a training vehicle and to give Wave Project members a forum in which to share good ideas and good gossip.

- Held regular meetings and training sessions. After an initial training course for new counselors, which lasted about four days, we periodically (three to four times a year) held follow-up two-day training sessions in different parts of the state. Incidentally, if you conduct this sort of training, keep things interesting by bringing in outside speakers who are expert in the area of the law you are working in. Also, leave plenty of time for your own political strategy sessions. Keep costs to a minimum, but be ready to chip in whatever it takes.

- Established the idea of centralized legal defense help for the 15-20 independent paralegals in the Wave Project. To accomplish this, the Wave Project assessed members a couple of dollars from every fee charged customers. The idea was to have each member independent paralegal know that he could get quick, effective legal help and counseling by picking up the phone. I strongly recommend that all paralegal organizations do this. If organized lawyerdom tries to put you in a small room with bars on the windows, it should go almost without saying that your ability to deal with your inevitable feelings of fear and paranoia will be greatly enhanced if you have set up a defense fund in advance.

One state that has a good organization is Oregon, where a membership group, Oregon Legal Technicians (OLT), represents many of the state's independent paralegals. The group meets fairly regularly, providing a great opportunity for members to communicate about common business and legal concerns. OLT also lobbies actively for legislation to break down the legal monopoly—including efforts to simplify legal forms—and is a sponsor of legislation to allow IPs to operate free of the fear of UPL prosecution. The organization also makes an effort to see that individual IPs follow honest business principles. Thus, if a new IP enters the field and engages in bait-and-switch advertising, or seems inadequately prepared, an OLT member is likely to offer counseling on how to improve his or her business. In California, the much larger California Association of Independent Paralegals (CAIP) plays a similar role.

In her interview in the Appendix, Catherine Jermany discusses the efforts of the National Association for Independent Paralegals to establish state organizations.

B. Independent Paralegals in California and Florida

Because Florida and California are the two states where the modern independent paralegal movement was born, and which currently have the most practicing independent paralegals, let's briefly look at the history and current political situation in each.

Florida

In the 1970s and early 1980s, Rosemary Furman, a former court clerk, began to help nonlawyers prepare legal paperwork. Along with the original Wave Project members, who did the same thing in California, Furman was an authentic pioneer. (See interview in the Appendix.) When the Florida bar mounted a campaign to close down her office in Jacksonville, Florida, culminating in a 30-day jail sentence from the Florida Supreme Court in 1984 (it was later commuted), Furman fought back. When she appeared on TV shows such as "60 Minutes," she did much to convince American consumers that the lawyer monopoly over legal services was so fraught with self-interest that it had to be broken.

In addition to Rosemary Furman's brave determination, the battle to allow IPs to operate in Florida was aided by several law suits prepared by the Washington-based consumer rights group, Public Citizen. Filed on behalf of Florida citizens who could not afford to hire lawyers, these suits argued that low-income people were being denied reasonable access to justice. Eventually, the activities of Furman and Public Citizen embarrassed the Florida courts into taking some first steps to provide better citizen access to the law. Specifically, the Florida Supreme Court approved a series of simplified legal forms designed to be used without a lawyer, including those necessary to obtain a divorce, collect child support, obtain a restraining order against domestic violence, as well as a number of land lord-tenant forms.[2] As this book goes to press, other forms are in the works.

Of great interest to Florida IPs is that, in adopting this simplified form approach, Florida has also changed its UPL rules as they concern the use of these forms. Specifically, the Supreme Court of Florida amended Chapter 10 of the Rules Regulating the Florida Bar to state:

> ...*For purposes of this chapter, it shall not constitute the unlicensed practice of law for nonlawyers to engage in limited oral communications to assist individuals in the completion of [approved] legal forms...Oral communications by nonlawyers are restricted to those communications reasonably necessary to elicit factual information to complete the form(s) and inform the individual how to file them...*

Also of interest is the fact that the Florida Bar has set up a legal technicians study committee to look at the feasibility of authorizing legal technicians to provide certain legal services directly to the public, and has recently stated that it's UPL for nonlawyers to prepare living trust forms. (See Chapter 2, Section C.)

California

The Golden State tends to be a trend setter. Certainly this is true when it comes to the independent paralegal movement. Thanks, in part, to the self-help law books published by Nolo Press and the organization of the Wave Project self-help divorce centers by Charles Sherman and myself in 1972-73, California has always had more independent paralegals than any other state.

---

[2]These forms are available from the Florida Bar, 650 Apalachee Parkway, Tallahasse, Florida 32399.

In the mid-1980s, this rapidly growing new service industry was attacked by the Los Angeles County bar. It urged the California State bar to vigorously police the unauthorized practice of law, especially in the fields of domestic relations (divorce), bankruptcy, immigration and landlord/tenant law, all of which the Los Angeles attorney group claimed were rapidly being taken over by independent paralegals.

In response, the State bar appointed the Public Protection Committee to look into the L.A. bar's claims. The Committee was made up of a majority of lawyers and paralegals who worked for lawyers. In what is surely the most surprising event in recent California bar history, instead of proposing a crackdown on IPs, the Public Protection Committee unanimously recommended, in April 1988, that the California legislature completely abolish the state's UPL laws. It further concluded that independent paralegals should be allowed to provide all types of legal services as long as they are registered with a state agency and disclose their nonlawyer status to all customers.

Even though a sub-committee of Bar Governors largely supported the conclusions of the Public Protection Committee, its recommendations were rejected by the State bar in August 1989, after many local bar associations reacted in horror to the threatened loss of their traditional monopoly power. The California Bar then appointed a third group (The Commission on Legal Technicians) to restudy the issue. This Committee largely agreed with the conclusions of its predecessors and recommended that non-lawyers be authorized by the California Supreme Court to deliver legal services in several major areas (bankruptcy, family, immigration and landlord-tenant), under the terms of a licensing scheme that would be supervised by an independent state agency. However, after being repeatedly scaled back, the state Bar again refused to adopt their own committee's recommendations.[3] In the meantime, a much more ambitious proposal sponsored by Nolo and HALT, the Washington, D.C.-based

---

[3]To obtain a copy of the Public Protection Committee's report (April 1988) or the Legal Technician Commission's report (July 1990), contact the California State Bar at 415-561-8200.

public interest organization that lobbies for better consumer access to the American legal system, has been introduced in the California legislature. Called the Affordable Legal Access bill, this legislation, which originally called for testing and regulating independent paralegals, stalled in 1992 in large part because of California's budgetary crisis, which all but procluded any new programs. As of this writing, in early 1993, the bill has been reintroduced in less ambitious form, which basically calls for registration of existing IPs, suspension of any UPL enforcement against registrants and a three-year study of whether or not more regulation is needed.

 See Section C, "Legislation to Legalize IPs," below, and the interview with HALT Legislative Director Debbie Chalfie in the Appendix.

C. Legislation to Legalize IPs

In 1989-1990, Glen Nishimura and Debbie Chalfie, of HALT—An Organization of Americans for Legal Reform—led an effort to draft model legislation to allow independent paralegals to render certain types of legal services directly to the public free of the fear of prosecution for unauthorized practice of law. The legislation, which was developed during a series of meetings between independent paralegals and consumer advocates, has served as a jumping off place for many pro-IP bills introduced in state legislatures.

The legislative purpose portion of the model bill states in part:

a. Indigent persons and persons of moderate income are generally unable to afford to hire lawyers to provide needed legal assistance. Studies have shown that roughly 80 percent of the legal needs of low-income Americans go unmet, and 130 million middle-income Americans are unable to get help with civil legal problems when they need it, because they cannot afford it. This has resulted in a two-tiered system of justice, with only the very rich able to afford legal services and the vast majority being shut out of the legal system.

b. The factors chiefly to blame for the high cost of legal services are the high cost involved in becoming a lawyer and the profession's monopoly over delivery of services. The time and money necessary to enter the [legal] field [college, law school, bar exam passage] involve high costs which, unless mitigated by a presence of competition, are inevitably passed on to the consumer.

c. New and innovative approaches to meet this overwhelming need are required because traditional solutions, such as government-funded legal aid and voluntary efforts by the bar to provide free legal services, even when obtained optimally, can accommodate only a very small fraction of that need. Permitting nonlawyer "legal technicians" to provide services directly to the public for out-of-court legal matters is just such an approach, and its advocates include consumer representatives, bar groups and legal scholars.

In brief outline here is what HALT's Legal Technician (Independent Paralegal) bill proposes:

- Legal technicians prepare paperwork and supply information in a long list of areas, including, but not limited to, the following:

   (A) Immigration

   (B) Family law

   (C) Housing law

   (D) Public benefit law

   (E) Litigation support law

   (F) Conservatorship and guardianship law

   (G) Real estate law

   (H) Liability law

   (I) Estate administration law

   (J) Consumer law

   (K) Corporate/business law

   (L) Intellectual property law

(M) Estate planning law

(N) Bankruptcy law

(O) Employment law

- Legal Technicians would operate under the general supervision and control of a Board of Legal Technicians, which would be under the general jurisdiction not of the state bar or Supreme Court but a public agency such as the Department of Consumer Affairs.

- People who run legal typing services limited to preparing legal paperwork following a customer's instructions would not be covered by the bill, so would not have to register with the Legal Technicians Board or meet any licensing requirements.

- All legal technicians would have to register with the Legal Technician Board and disclose to the public that they were not lawyers.

- Legal technicians who prepare certain types of forms must be licensed. It's up to the Board to decide which areas require licensure and which require registration only. In making this determination, "The Board shall balance consumer's interest in affordable costs with consumer's interest in receiving competent services...The Board shall require licensure only for those substantive areas or tasks in which it finds there is a substantial likelihood of irreparable harm to consumers, the ability of consumers to evaluate the quality of legal technicians' work is low, and mistakes cannot be easily corrected or remedied."

- In areas where legal technicians must be licensed, a license shall be granted upon completion of a "practice-oriented examination" on the law and procedures of the relevant specialty areas of no more than four hours.

- The bill also proposes a comprehensive system to handle consumer complaints, including quick investigation of claimed problems, and efforts to conciliate consumer claims. If this fails, the dispute would be promptly arbitrated. A compensation fund, paid for by legal technician registration fees, shall be available to compensate consumers who win arbitration awards against insolvent legal technicians.

In fairness, however, it should be noted that the approach taken by the HALT legislation, which essentially proposes a system of paralegal registration and, for some legal tasks, licensure in exchange for the right to operate, isn't universally favored. Some independent paralegals and many paralegals who work for lawyers are reluctant to let go of the present freedom to operate in a completely unregulated environment. After all, some independent paralegals argue, if much of the problem with the delivery of legal services can be traced to the monopoly power of a legal profession that depends on licensing to suppress competition, why should we go the same route? In addition, many people are concerned that regulation will be unfairly extended to typing services that do little but prepare legal forms under direct supervision of customers and do not provide legal information or advice.

I believe that while pure typing services should not be regulated, IPs who wish to provide legal information and expertise should be willing to accept a reasonable level of state supervision. This might appropriately include registration, skills testing and a recourse system to help customers who have received inadequate services. Why? Because the main argument that lawyers have always used when they attempt to suppress independent paralegals is that they are not competent and, therefore, allowing them to operate constitutes a serious risk to the public. An IP's having passed a test on the specific skills needed to prepare legal paperwork in the field in which the IP operates is an excellent way to refute this argument.

D. Introducing Legislation as a Technique to Build Political Support

Introducing legislation, such as has occurred in California, Oregon, Hawaii, Washington, Wisconsin and several other states, gives IPs a wonderful opportunity to build public support. Assuming the bill's reasonably energetic in pushing it, hearings will be held. This will not only give IPs a chance to organize people to testify, and get sympathetic political interest groups to take a supportive stand, it will provide them with a legitimate opportunity to approach the media.

Before arranging for a sympathetic legislator to introduce legislation, try to get all the independent paralegals within your state to chip in and hire a part-time lobbyist to represent your group's interests in the state capitol. Obviously, if you already have a state-wide association (which, incidentally, should be organized as a nonprofit corporation), this is the appropriate entity to use to do the hiring. Fortunately, working with a lobbyist need not be prohibitively expensive. Many consumer-oriented lobbyists represent a number of small consumer, environmental, and other groups supporting themselves with a modest annual fee from each. Here again, the National Association for Independent Paralegals and HALT should be sources of good advice.

Why do you need a part-time lobbyist? Both to teach you the legislative ropes and be your knowledgeable friend when it comes to advising you on how to deal with the governor and the legislature. You will want to lobby and testify on your own, too, but you will benefit greatly from someone who knows what it takes to get a bill passed.

E. Dangers of Licensing IPs

So far, I have primarily focused on the advantages of licensing independent paralegals. There are also some dangers. One that IPs who introduce legislation should be prepared to deal with is that the IP regulation they propose may be amended by lawyer interests in the legislature. If this is done, it will almost surely be to give lawyers control of the IP regulatory body. If this occurs, you can bet that lawyers will use their power to frustrate the growth of the independent paralegal movement. To prevent this, it's essential that independent paralegals do their homework before legislation is introduced so they know they have enough votes to insure that the IP regulatory board will not be controlled by lawyers or the courts.

In addition to the threat that lawyers will control any IP licensing effort, there is another danger inherent in any independent paralegal licensing effort. This is that licensing will be used primarily to create a monopoly for those who have the licenses, but will not really guarantee the public good and honest paralegal service. To see how this occurs, and a negative public image results, you need look no further than the legal profession, where lawyers need only take one very general examination (and in many states, do not have to participate in continuing education or be subjected to any ongoing skills testing), in exchange for their lifetime right to practice.[3]

So, the question becomes how can IPs create an honest licensing system that is not controlled by lawyers and isn't so self-serving that it's sure to backfire on them in the long run? In "The Case Against Credentialism" (*The Atlantic,* December 1985), James Fallows points out that at least one American groups of workers has managed to develop a system of competence certification that really works. These are airline pilots who, according to Fallows, have a system that operates like this:

> *The pilot licensing system was built on the premise that competence was divisible: people can be good at one thing without being good at others, and they should be allowed to do only what they have mastered. As opposed to receiving a blanket license, the way members of other professions do, pilots must work their way up through four certificate levels, from student to air-transport pilot, and be specifically qualified on each kind of aircraft they want to fly. What's more, a pilot must demonstrate at regular intervals that he is still competent. To keep his license, a pilot must take a review flight with an instructor every two years, and the pilots for commercial airlines must pass a battery of requalification tests every*

---

[3]Indeed, precisely because many consumers now understand that license to practice law means little when it comes to guaranteeing that a particular practitioner is competent, they are more likely to consider a paralegal or other self-help alternative.

six months. "A small but regular percentage is washed out each time," John Mazor, of the Air Line Pilots Association, says. It is reassuring to know they are gone, but what about their tenured counterparts in the other professions? The results of this licensing scheme are a high level of proficiency and a profession more open socially than the rest.

What can IPs learn from this? First, that the public respects a licensing system in which the person licensed has really mastered the particular job. Thus an IP who wants to type divorce and bankruptcy forms should be separately licensed and tested in each field. Second, that licensing is of little value to the public (and therefore worthy of little respect) unless the licensees are regularly retested to be sure their skills are still sharp.

At this point, it's also necessary to remind you that most paralegals in the United States do not work independently but are employed by lawyers. Traditionally, these employed paralegals oppose licensure and certification, arguing that since they do not deal with the public directly, it isn't necessary. Some also oppose it because they are insecure about their own legal training and fear that they might have to go back to school to qualify or because they fear that any board established to regulate paralegals would be controlled by lawyers. I mention this not to deal with these arguments in detail, but to point out that because independent paralegals and lawyer-employed paralegals will not always agree on the licensure issue, it is essential that lines of communication be opened between the two groups so that they can hash out their differences in private.

One advantage of communicating with paralegals who work for lawyers is, of course, to present a united front to the bar. Another is to take advantage of the organizational skills employed paralegals have developed. There is a paralegal association in every good-sized city. In California, there are separate groups to represent the interests of paralegals who are employed by lawyers and those who work as freelancers. Most have regular meetings, newsletters, and sponsor training sessions. And while the long-term interests of employed, freelance and independent paralegals aren't the same, they do overlap to a considerable degree.

F. Lawsuits as a Paralegal Organizing Device

Another way to focus paralegal organizing efforts is around litigation. This happened to some extent in California in the 1970s, when the State Bar of California tried to pull the law licenses of Wave Project pioneers Charles Sherman and Phyllis Eliasberg. In the early 1980s, the Florida Bar's efforts to persecute nonlawyer Rosemary Furman through a lawyer-controlled kangaroo court civil contempt proceeding resulted in national publicity and helped convince the public that the legal profession often abused its monopoly power over the legal system. More recently, the prosecution of Louisiana bankruptcy IP, Jerome Papania was widely reported, included being the centerpiece of an ABC "20-20" show focusing on how the average American is denied access to the legal system.

One alternative to waiting for the bar to prosecute independent paralegals one-by-one is for IPs to get together and sue them. This can be done based upon any one of a number of legal theories, all of which come down to the fact that the bar is improperly using its monopoly power to prevent public access to the courts. This approach has been tried in Federal Court in Florida (*Dunn v. Florida Bar*), where Alan Morrison and David Vladeck of the Ralph Nader-affiliated Public Citizen Litigation Group in Washington D.C., argued a number of legal theories, including the fact that the bar's monopolistic practices deny citizens the right to access to the courts. Although this suit did not result in a court victory, it was, as noted in Section B, above, an important factor in the Florida Supreme Court's decision to require easy-to-use court forms and allow independent paralegals to prepare them without fear of being charged with unauthorized practice.

If you are interested in filing suit against the bar, however, be sure you know what's going on in this legal area in other parts of the country. Test case litigation is best coordinated so that the right case is fought on the right legal theories in the right court. In this context, HALT (again, at 1319 F Street, NW, Suite 300, Washington, DC 20004, (202) 347-9600), is an excellent source of up-to-date information. Several HALT staffers work full-time in this area, and they produce a high quality quarterly publication entitled "Legal Reformer," which regularly carries helpful material on pending court cases which raise significant UPL issues.

Appendix

Interviews

Jolene Jacobs Interview

Jolene Jacobs, a long-time friend, is one of the first successful, modern independent paralegals. She has operated a divorce form typing business since 1973.

Ralph Warner: *How did you first become involved in paralegal work?*

Jolene Jacobs: In 1972, when I was just finishing my undergraduate degree, I was interested in doing some kind of consumer advocacy or public service work. I admired Ralph Nader and his Raiders and other individuals who battled large corporations for consumer rights and protection. In December of 1972, I met you and Ed Sherman. I heard about the Wave Project from a family friend who told me you were looking for people to train to type divorces based on the information in Ed's book, *How To Do Your Own Divorce in California.* I remember coming over to your old, brown-shingle house in Berkeley with several other recruits. You had samples of divorce forms taped to the dining room walls and we all sat around while you showed us how to fill them out, process them through the clerk's office and talked about how people could best represent themselves in court. What attracted me to the Wave Project was that although the divorce book worked well for lots of people, many others obviously needed more personal help than any book could provide—both of a secretarial nature and personal support. I signed on, along with a dozen or so others, to train as divorce counselors.

RW: *Come on, you must have been somewhat scared embarking on an illegal business fresh out of college.*

JJ: You warned us that there would be problems, possibly serious problems, with the bar, and that we might even face criminal charges. Oddly, I wasn't scared at that point. I believed the bar's monopoly control over access to legal information and legal assistance was a bad thing. My perspective on the work was that it was a consumer advocacy project rather than a career as a "paralegal." I was so excited that I didn't really worry about it. The prospect of helping people with very little money, and sometimes without much education, put their own decisions on paper, file their papers at court and represent themselves before a judge was truly exciting. While people may not have been happy about the outcome of their marriage, they could at least feel good about having done their own divorce.

RW: *When the Wave Project training was over, where did you start working?*

JJ: I opened an office in San Jose in 1973. I stayed there until 1978 and then moved to San Francisco, where I have been since.

RW: *Was it hard to get your business going?*

JJ: It was both simple and hard. I had never been self-employed and had no family history of self-employment as a model. I had just graduated from college with no debts, no responsibilities and a lot of enthusiasm, but not much else. Of course, I needed very little money to get by at that point. Incidentally, now I might not take that economic risk, so it was good that the chance to do something new crossed my path then.

I ended up in San Jose because you and Ed suggested that San Jose was a good place to start because there were no other Wave Project counselors in that area. It was somewhat difficult to move to a new town, look for a place to live and start a business in an area where I didn't know a soul.

The mechanics to set up an office weren't hard: get an office, telephone, typewriter, etc. The furniture and office equipment were particularly simple. I started with two wooden apple boxes and a typewriter. One apple box was for the customer to sit on and the other was for the typewriter. If I only had a picture!

It was harder to learn how to get the word out that this new self-help service was available. In addition to the fact that I knew nothing about marketing, I faced an old California law, passed in the 1890s but still on the books, which made it illegal to "aid or encourage birth control, abortion or divorce." These were all legal activities, yet, at least according to California law, it was illegal to give out information about them. This prevented me from advertising, so I took brochures around to public agencies such as social services and legal aid and to a local newspaper, which wrote a story about my service. Now and then, I was able to get a classified ad into the paper, but then a lawyer or the DA would see it and call the paper and get them to take it out, based on the 1890 law. Of course, I believed this law was unconstitutional, but it was upheld a few years later, I believe, in a case in Southern California. I think it is still on the books, but was forgotten as soon as lawyers wanted to advertise their own divorce services. At any rate, this old law and the determination of lawyers to enforce it was a serious obstacle to the growth of my business.

RW: *What about the local bar association? What was their position on your typing service?*

JJ: The bar association claimed at every opportunity that the Wave Project was a "fly by night" business, a rip-off, "here today and gone tomorrow," etc. It was difficult for me as an individual, and the Wave Project as a small group, to combat this. While people didn't particularly trust or like the bar association even then, they had no idea who we were and what our credentials or intentions were. In other words, typing divorce forms was a new field and there was no positive history of such a service to make people feel confident. So, if the bar said it was bad, some people, at least, were hesitant to take a risk. In fairness, I should say, however, that there were individual lawyers who supported me.

To face the bar alone would have been impossible for me. Being a part of a group backed up by you and Ed made me feel more confident, and help was just a phone call away. Later, the Wave Project counselors began a legal defense fund that we contributed to monthly. This made most of us feel more secure that we could weather a prosecution financially by pooling our money. And we did use money in the fund several times. But the risk of being put out of business, or being arrested, was always there.

RW: *How long were you in business before the bar figured out what you were doing?*

JJ: They noticed me almost immediately. The bar association had already criticized Nolo Press in general, and *How To Do Your Own Divorce in California* specifically, so they were watching everything you and Ed did, especially the Wave Project. Also, remember, there was an article about my new business in the newspaper and classified ads I placed, so my business wasn't a secret. I can think of five instances when I was investigated that I know about. There may have been others.

RW: *Can you tell me a little about the five?*

JJ: One involved an investigation by the district attorney. The Wave Project responded by hiring one of the best constitutional lawyers in the state. The DA was so impressed with the quality of the lawyer's work, and the apparent seriousness of the Wave Project in fighting prosecution, that the case was dropped "for the time being." The DA did successfully prosecute another paralegal who worked in the area, however. This person worked independently and had no support.

Another time an investigation/prosecution was nipped in the bud because my roommate happened to be a law school classmate of a staff member in the DA's office who was supposed to write a memorandum recommending prosecution. Both my roommate and the classmate had actually done their own divorces using Ed Sherman's divorce book. This meant I had a friend to argue to the DA that while she had no trouble with a total self-help approach because she had the benefit of a legal education, the average consumer needed, and should be able to get, reasonably priced help preparing their papers.

RW: *That was a lucky coincidence, your roommate knowing the person who was to investigate you.*

JJ: Yes, but maybe it wasn't as important as I thought at the time, because a little later there was another investigation by the DA's office. This one I didn't know about until it was over. The investigator who recommended that I not be prosecuted called up to say how impressed he was with the quality of my work. Later, when he left the DA's office, he called and asked for a job at the Wave Project.

The next incident was scarier. A judge who usually worked in criminal court, but was hearing domestic cases and was unfamiliar with the new trend of petitioners appearing in pro per—that is, representing themselves—told one of my customers that he would have me arrested if I didn't appear in his courtroom the next morning. I wasn't sure that he could legally pull off this King of England routine, but I went over. My customer was also ordered to be there. She was terrified. It didn't help that she had a heart problem.

The clerk read me my rights, the stenographer took down every word, and so on. The judge assured me I would be prosecuted for all sorts of heinous, but not very specific, crimes if I didn't shut down my business. Afterwards, I raced back to my office and called a criminal lawyer, who called the judge. Also, again by coincidence, I knew the judge's former clerk. This person also happened to have worked as a divorce consultant. So, I called the former clerk, who also called the judge on my behalf. After talking to these two people, the judge decided to "put it on the back burner." I think he still would have pursued the matter with the DA to get me prosecuted, but he died suddenly.

RW: *Your experience really underlines the fact that the legal establishment isn't monolithic. At almost every level, from lawyer to law clerk, you found allies when you needed them. But don't let me interrupt a great story. What happened next?*

JJ: Several times a number of divorce typing offices in the Bay Area were investigated on the phone, with no resulting action. We never knew who was doing the investigating, but it was easy to tell something was going on, because the callers kept asking questions that required legal opinions. You can spot this technique because the questions are usually inappropriate—not what most people ask. I think somehow related to these calls was an incident where an undercover investigator posing as a customer walked in and asked some questions, which I answered. Since my responses were not the incriminating answers she expected, or hoped for, she left the office somewhat curtly.

There may have been investigations other than these. I expect there have been. Sometimes the investigator stands out like a sore thumb, or more like a pain in the neck. But there may have been times when I wasn't able to detect them. The point is, of course, to try to be careful all of the time.

RW: *Do you have any other advice for people just starting out about how to avoid unauthorized practice of law charges?*

JJ: I think the more friends and contacts someone has in the local legal world, the easier it is to find out what is going on, and to deal with problems that come up. Also, I would say it is important to have a good lawyer lined up in advance. This is one context in which lawyers have really done a good job for me. I wouldn't have expected it, but it's true. It's ironic, of course, that I need lawyers to save me from lawyers, but that's the American legal system in a nutshell. Also, you need to have friends in the media who will go to bat for you should things get rough. I certainly would have been prosecuted were it not for the realization that if lawyers go after paralegals who do good work and have access to the press, the public will see the lawyers as trying to unfairly suppress a person who is offering a reasonable alternative to their over-priced monopoly. In other words, you need to know how to play David to the bar's Goliath. This isn't hard, because the legal profession can't really deny that they are a monopoly, that their services are expensive and many people can't pay their fees. They claim that the public does not get competent help when they use paralegals, but this is increasingly being recognized as a diversion from the truth that lawyers go after paralegals because they don't want competition. The public has really come to understand as a result of the many recent revelations that lawyers don't regulate their own profession very well, and that hiring a lawyer is no guarantee of competent legal care.

RW: *Do you still fear bar harassment by the bar?*

JJ: Sure, remember, I have only related my personal experience. I have friends in the business who have been arrested and had their offices closed down and their livelihood lost. Certain areas of California seem to be safer than others to work in. But still, this is one job where a little paranoia is healthy. Even to be the subject of an investigation is no fun. A long prosecution is horrible. I admire the steadfastness and courage of Rosemary Furman of Florida in standing up to the bar. Because she was so vocal in her anger and her belief in the importance of what she was doing, the bar association came down very hard on her. It would have been so much easier to give up. We have all gained something from her fight and from the national publicity her case received. She went through a great deal, and I think that paralegals around the country should have provided more emotional and financial support—myself included.

RW: *Let's leave the unauthorized practice issue for a bit and come back to some of the practical problems of being an independent paralegal. What price did you first charge for a divorce? What do you charge now? Can you make a good living?*

JJ: Our first price was $55 for typing an uncontested divorce. This covered overhead and provided a small income. It wasn't really adequate, so we raised the price to $65, then $75. In California there are now two forms of divorce; my office charges $80 for the very simple variety and $180 for the more complicated standard form (and up to $210 if support is involved). Other paralegal offices charge slightly different fees for divorce. I think the two primary factors that affect price are the cost of office overhead and the price charged by competition. Initially, I think our services were underpriced. I know I was so into consumerism that I felt uncomfortable about charging very much at all. I had never had the experience of setting a fair market value on my own labor. In addition, I had no idea how much it cost just to run an office. Of course, now I am much more sympathetic to people who are self-employed and who have substantial overhead. I know it is certainly not all profit. The idea of charging a fair fee to cover good work and support oneself decently is comfortable to me now.

RW: *Can you make a good living now as an independent paralegal?*

JJ: My income is good, but my work is stressful and it doesn't always seem enough for the number of years of experience I have, or for the volume of work required and the level of stress that accompanies helping people do divorces. It goes beyond typing forms (that's the first layer). I end up being a social worker, family counselor, helping people find jobs and providing emotional support. Also, with the unresolved status of independent paralegals, the job never feels secure.

RW: *Why did you move to San Francisco from San Jose?*

JJ: I was in San Jose from 1973 until 1978. At that time, my friends who ran the San Francisco office of what by this time had changed in name from the Wave Project to Divorce Center, were completing law school and wanted to sell their office. I was ready for a change and I missed the central Bay Area (San Jose is 50 miles south), so I decided to sell my San Jose office and buy the San Francisco office.

As it turned out, though, working in suburban San Jose was much easier than working in urban S.F. In San Jose, people were much more easygoing and trusting that I would do my best job for them. In San Francisco, people were fearful of being ripped off, more hostile, more angry, more demanding—all of the things I myself have started to become since I moved back to San Francisco. Also, in San Francisco I work with people from a number of countries, who speak many languages. The language barrier slows things down and makes the work harder. But I have learned so much about other cultures and have enjoyed these relationships to such a degree that I find this to be one of the most rewarding aspects of working in San Francisco.

RW: *Tell me a little about how your current office works.*

JJ: There are two rooms; one is a reception and secretarial area and the second is the area I work in. Sometimes the secretary and I share the same room, depending on the configuration of the office. Over the years, the office has moved several times within the same large building.

We try to get everyone to call before coming in or to make an appointment. I do all of the initial interviews, pre-hearing interviews, preparation of certain sets of papers. The secretary-receptionist types the other sets of forms and mails them out. The office is bilingual in Spanish.

Normally people come in between one and five times, depending on the complexity and how much people want to visit. For the simple form of divorce, some people come in once to give us all necessary information, pay the fee and ask that all papers be mailed.

We review all files at least three times a year and send out notes to customers we have not heard from in some time to make sure there hasn't been some misunderstanding about the status of the divorce. But we only send out one note. We want to let them know that their divorce is not final, but we don't want to push them into completing a divorce that they would just as well drop or delay.

The office is open five days a week, 9-6, with later, or earlier appointments possible. The customer who qualifies for the basic $80 divorce usually pays the entire fee at the first visit. For the more expensive divorces, we accept the fee paid in two payments. I've had some problem with bad checks. In addition to our fee, the customer will also have to pay a filing fee to the court, unless they are low income.

Often people need to get a consultation with an attorney about some unresolved legal issue, such as dividing an expensive asset, like a house or pension plan. Sometimes, the spouse is hiding assets, or the person who wants to file is so emotionally drained that they need someone to do all the work for them. I have a list of attorneys available to refer customers to who want or need to see someone.

Sometimes it's hard to get people to go to a lawyer, even when they should. They fear it. As a society, we're trained to go to the dentist and doctor, but we're not told that probably sometime in our lives we will need to see a lawyer. People feel very insecure in relating to lawyers. They don't know what the parameters of the relationship are, and what rights they have, that they are hiring the lawyer to do work for them. They fear, often with good reason, that once they get involved with a lawyer they will lose all control of their case and will end up with a $10,000 bill. In fact, I have had a number of customers who started with lawyers, spent thousands of dollars, and then felt the lawyer would not respect their decisions. As a result, these people fired the lawyer and decided to do it themselves.

RW: *What happens when you interview a customer?*

JJ: Usually only one person comes in, but sometimes they come with the spouse they are getting divorced from, which I prefer. Occasionally, of course, they come with children, friends or family. Sometimes, the parent wants to leave the child unattended in the waiting room, which I will not allow. (There is a window with a five-story drop.) I have toys for the children. Friends of course are no problem. In fact, sometimes they will speak up and offer information that the customer may not have brought up, and they will give a lot of support to the customer. My least favorite situation is where the parent comes in with the married daughter or son, and it is the parent who does all of the talking. Occasionally, there will be the married couple and representatives of both sides of the family. So, a good rule for any divorce typing office is to have plenty of chairs.

In most instances, it has been determined on the telephone which type of divorce they need, and they have been told what information they will need to bring. I give them a copy of the book *How To Do Your Own Divorce in California* and review the basic information it contains. I then have them sign a disclaimer which states that I am not a lawyer and they are responsible for all of their decisions. If they don't have any further questions, they can begin filling out the worksheets. If they want to think about it, they can take the book and the worksheets home and make another appointment. If the worksheets are completed right then, I immediately prepare the first set of papers. The customer then reviews the papers, signs and dates them, and they are ready to be filed by the customer. The customer is also responsible for serving the divorce papers on the spouse. In the simple form of divorce, called the "Summary Dissolution," there is no formal service of papers, since both the wife and husband sign the first set of forms.

The first interview can take anywhere from one to two hours, although two hours is unusual. The visits after that are shorter, maybe one-half hour.

I feel strongly that in addition to processing enormous amounts of paperwork, the job entails providing a lot of emotional support, information, and often referrals. People who are going through a divorce are usually going through changes in other parts of their lives as well. They may be changing jobs, looking for child care, having trouble finding affordable housing, having credit problems, car hassles, etc. They may not have family in the area, or even in this country, and sometimes don't even have friends they feel comfortable sharing this part of their lives with, so they really need to find an appropriate support group or get emotional help from another source. The point is that often people need more than just getting their papers typed.

RW: *What about marketing your services? How do people know how to find you?*

JJ: Primarily from referrals from previous customers. Positive recommendation by satisfied customers is a very powerful marketing device. I also get a lot of agency referrals. I also get referrals from the court clerk's office, even sometimes from lawyers and other unexpected sources. Advertising in the phone book and other lists where people look for information is also important. I don't do too much new marketing because I'm operating at maximum capacity—that's 60 to 70 new cases per month. I've given some thought to expanding my business, but haven't figured out how to do it in a high quality way.

RW: *What do you do if a customer says you did a poor job?*

JJ: Out of thousands of divorces, I only remember one time when I didn't do something correctly. This occurred in the first few months; the judge pointed out the problem and I was able to fix it. Generally, my high success rate is because I was carefully trained and give every customer a copy of *How To Do Your Own Divorce in California,* which we go through carefully. I encourage people to see an attorney if they have any questions that are not answered in the book, or if they need more information. The customers make all of the decisions about their divorces.

However, I can think of a few instances where I provided good service but the customer thought I did a poor job. For example, I typed the papers as directed in the divorce book, but a particular court clerk or judge would want them done a slightly different way and a nervous customer might wonder if I initially did them correctly or not. Of course, whenever there is any problem, I redo the papers at no extra cost. It is also the case (and anyone who serves the public will know this) that even though you try to provide excellent service to every single person, there are going to be a few who will find some problem, no matter how hard you try. Remember, for most people, going to a nonlawyer for help with a divorce is a new experience, and a number are unsure. But generally I have had very little trouble with this. By the end of almost every divorce I've typed, people feel that they have had excellent help, and usually refer their friends. Lawyers, of course, make a hue and cry about the "terrible" and "incompetent" work done by by divorce consultants/independent paralegals like myself, but I know of hundreds of thousands of divorces typed by IPs and I know of very few problems. Compare this to the number of complaints and lawsuits filed against lawyers!

RW: *How do you relate to lawyers in an organized sense?*

JJ: Not well. I see the California Bar Association, indeed, all bar associations, as monoliths with basically conservative memberships antagonistic to change that might erode their traditional paternalistic role and monopoly control. They represent an enormous concentration of power, money and legislative influence, and almost always use it to block constructive change.

I don't see individual lawyers as necessarily being part of the monolith, but put them in three general groupings. First, lawyers who may feel the adversarial system is not the best way to solve family problems and who support the development of reasonable alternative for the delivery of legal services. In other words, they are at least somewhat critical of the legal monopoly the bar association is trying to protect. Second, lawyers who are honestly opposed to "divorce consultants," as we are currently called in California, as not being in the public interest because there are no standards for training, licensing and we are not monitored in any way. Third, I would guess the majority of lawyers, who constantly and cynically cry "consumer protection" as an excuse to suppress alternatives and maintain their control.

Remember, divorce and family law used to be considered the "bread and butter" of law, and the most common reason the average person sought out a lawyer. Now, close to 60% of California divorces are done without lawyers, which is a loss of many millions of dollars of lawyers' income. And remember, this has all happened since 1971. Wouldn't you be threatened if you lost almost half of your business?

RW: *Do you think some lawyers who want to put you out of business are honestly motivated?*

JJ: Sure, I think that some lawyers actually believe that people want and need lawyers to make decisions for them. I once went to a bar association luncheon in Palo Alto, California, an upper-middle to upper-class area. At the luncheon, a lawyer told me that he thought people were "too stupid to make their own decisions" and that they needed lawyers' "firm guidance." Well, fortunately, a lot of people aren't too stupid to see this sort of arrogance for what it is.

I am also appalled at lawyers' lack of concern about the unavailability of legal services to poor and low-income people who can't pay lawyers' fees. This sort of attitude makes me think of all the people I have worked with who had very little money, and what a severe hardship it would have been for some of them to come up with the money to pay a lawyer. In fact, many of them couldn't come up with the money and weren't able to file for a divorce until they heard about the Wave Project/Divorce Center. So, I feel angry when I have any contact with lawyers who think like that. They live in a different world than I do.

RW: *Do you think there is any validity to the attorney charge that many independent paralegals are not sufficiently trained, and therefore may not be competent?*

JJ: Since lawyers have fought all legislation supporting training and licensure of independent paralegals, I question their right to make that charge. How can they work to keep us ignorant and then attack us for being ignorant? I support reasonable requirements for licensing and training and some kind of regulation done by an independent state agency—absolutely not by bar.

RW: *Do you think lawyers will eventually accept the presence of paralegals?*

JJ: They already have when it suits their convenience. They hire paralegals instead of lawyers and assign them the same type of work I do. So the consumer should have that same right. The way it is now, consumers have to pay lawyers' rates for paralegal work, which of course is the idea, from the lawyers' point of view. I think the future for IPs is bright because the public wants alternatives to lawyers. And, hopefully, through some evolutionary process, lawyers will learn to accept the right of the public to use independent paralegals. They may even find a way to work cooperatively with independent paralegals as they realize that IPs take the pressure off them to provide services to millions of low- and moderate-income people.

RW: *What would be your advice to someone starting out?*

JJ: Do you want me to give you a few bits of general advice, or a laundry list of helpful suggestions?

RW: *How about the whole list.*

JJ: You asked for it. I'd say the following:

- Read books, or attend workshops on starting a small business, but don't let them scare you off.

- Have adequate savings to carry you for a while.

- Get good initial training and periodic updates.

- Be willing to take a risk or start part-time and keep the security you have until you see if your paralegal business is going to fly or not. It's hard to tell. Sometimes it seems best to get your feet wet a toe at a time, and sometimes a new business will only work if you make a full-time commitment.

- Have lawyers quickly available to ask questions, and be happy to pay for the help.

- It is not necessary to spend a lot of money furnishing the office at least to start. Save your money for more important things.

- Select a convenient location, with easy access to public transportation. And, hopefully, an area without much competition.

- Cultivate the attitude that what is best for the customer will be best for your business.

- Give financial breaks to the deserving.

- You do not have to accept every customer. Screen out those not appropriate for a fill-in-the boxes clinic approach.

- Develop a fair refund policy.

- Build a network of supportive lawyers to refer your customers to.

- Build good relationships with the landlord, printer and other business people you deal with.

- Get known in your community. Dozens of groups will refer customers to you if they know about your service.

- Keep good records—every case in its own file, every disclaimer signed, every worksheet saved, etc.

- If you don't know a bookkeeping system, find a bookkeeper or accountant that specializes in small businesses and have them set up a simple system for you.

- Develop, if possible, good relationships with your competitors. Try to have a friendly, positive relationship with them rather than a cut-throat one. It can make life, and your business environment, more pleasant. You can help each other. In our group, we have shared advertising, even in cases where we were sharing the same area.

- Consider sharing office space, possibly with someone whose business or service complements yours, like a tax preparer.

- Be willing to spend money to improve your service. One way to do this is by using a small computer.

- Get insurance—liability and theft—if you have anything of value.

- Look for safety hazards in your office, especially if there will be children. For example, coffee pots with cords hanging down where the child can pull the pot over.

- Watch for changes or trends in your field by reading a local legal newspaper as well as specialized legal materials relevant to your work.

- Diversify beyond divorce and bankruptcy.

RW: *What's about the future? What are your plans?*

JJ: I have an interest in organizing paralegals and I do work to help make more types of paralegal assistance available to the public. There is a lot to be done to establish paralegal work as a "safe occupation." I have organized some community workshops and volunteer work around the subject of people doing their own divorce. I think I have a lot to teach others. And of course, I need to learn new things, too. I have taken some courses that I felt would improve my service: Spanish, business applications of computers, a one-year legal secretarial course and so on. I've also had to update my legal skills.

After 18 years of this work, I have considered a career change, but I think I am faced with the same thoughts that many who are considering trying to be an independent paralegal face: What should I do? Will I make more money? Do I need to be retrained? How much in debt do I want to go to be retrained? Do I want to move? Should I expand this business? Will I like my new career more, as much as, or less than the career I am leaving? Can I successfully work for someone else, or do I want to only consider careers that will allow me to continue to be self-employed?

Basically I feel that I have invested a great deal of energy in the work I am now doing, and find that hard to give up. So, I have turned a lot of my thinking to considering how the independent paralegal field will develop in the next few years and how to best facilitate and participate in that growth and change.

Robert Mission Interview

Robert Mission has been an independent paralegal for close to 20 years. One of the true pioneers in this business, Bob currently coordinates the Superior California Legal Clinic in Sacramento, California.

Ralph Warner: *Bob, tell me about your background. How did you get into the independent paralegal business?*

Robert Mission: In the late 1960s, I was a process server. I did gofer work for a lawyer and also worked with a private detective.

RW: *What does the "creep and peep" business have to do with helping nonlawyers prepare legal forms?*

RM: Well, in about 1971, I developed a package of divorce forms complete with simple instructions. I called it "Divorce Economically," and sold the packets for $35. I also helped people type the forms if they needed it. Then, in 1973, I ran into Charlie Bloodgood, a University of California law student who was running a divorce typing service in Sacramento that was affiliated with the Wave Project. As you know, the Wave Project system was based on Ed Sherman's book *How To Do Your Own Divorce in California,* published by Nolo Press. I immediately recognized that the Wave Project, which had training sessions, continuing education meetings, as well as the divorce book, embodied a more sophisticated approach than mine, so I got in touch with Charlie, met Ed and you, and joined up.

RW: *How did you and Charlie do?*

RM: Great, at least for awhile. We made contact with all sorts of community organizations, listed our service in the classifieds, and the people rolled in. After all, at about $75 to type a divorce, the price was right.

RW: *And then?*

RM: We had heard rumbles that the bar association was very unhappy about the so-called "do it yourself" movement, and was investigating our project. However, nothing direct was ever said until one afternoon in 1974, when a Sacramento County Deputy DA swooped into my office, identified himself, read me my rights and handcuffed me in front of a client.

RW: *Were you scared?*

RM: I didn't have time to figure out how I felt, I was so busy demanding to make a phone call. They finally let me call my attorney, the man I had worked for for years as a gofer. I was confident he would help me, but was told by his secretary that he had just had a heart attack and was in intensive care.

RW: *Oops!*

RM: Oops, nothing! I was so upset I demanded to talk to him—tubes and all.

RW: *What happened?*

RM: By the time I got downtown, my attorney's secretary had made some calls and I was released on my own recognizance, charged with the crime of unauthorized practice. My next step was to call Phyllis Eliasberg, a Southern California consumer advocate and lawyer who had taken over the Wave Project from you and Ed when you guys decided to concentrate on Nolo Press. Phyllis eventually referred me to a Sacramento County attorney, Jim Reed, to defend me.

RW: *Tell me a little about the defense.*

RM: It was based mostly on constitutional grounds, utilizing Ed Sherman's book and the Wave Project method. I maintained that I was only a typing service offering scrivener services, using as my guidelines *How To Do Your Own Divorce in California*. I pointed out that all my clients received a copy of the book, read it carefully, and made their own decisions. I argued that I clearly had a First Amendment right to refer my clients to Ed's book generally and, if they had a specific question, to the particular chapter that dealt with that procedure.

RW: *Did this defense work?*

RM: Beautifully! When the bar counsel took my deposition, he asked me questions related to complicated matters of contested divorce procedure. I replied, "I'm sorry, I can't answer that question." The bar counsel would ask me, "Why can't you answer?" I replied, "Because that information is not covered in *How To Do Your Own Divorce in California* and so to do so would constitute my giving legal advice."

RW: *What did you say when they asked you something that was covered in Ed's book?*

RM: Since I had directed clients to all the key passages so many times, I didn't even have to open the book. I just quoted the relevant passages verbatim.

RW: *What happened in court?*

RM: The criminal procedures simply stopped. Instead, the bar attorneys suggested to my attorney that we enter a broad stipulation as to how I could and couldn't operate. Their proposal was so strict that it would have effectively stopped our operation. I refused to go along, on my attorney, Jim Reed's, advice. Fortunately the judge agreed with Jim that what the bar wanted to force us to do was unconstitutional. I personally feel that in making this decision the judge was heavily influenced by the fact that I received referrals from dozens of public and private agencies, especially those designed to help low-income persons.

RW: *Could you give me several examples?*

RM: Well, agencies such as the State Department of Justice, County Welfare, McGeorge Law School, the Battered Women's Shelter, various community service organizations and, believe it or not, even the DA's office. In fact, the funniest thing about the whole thing was that the day the deputy DA arrested me, someone in the DA's office had referred me a client.

RW: *Was that the end of your troubles with the bar?*

RM: Not exactly. To the best of my remembrance, the judge suggested that the guidelines proposed by the bar be amended to allow me to still operate as a scrivener. Since these guidelines were basically the same as the Wave Project rules, I accepted them. I could see that to survive in Sacramento in the long run, I had to go along with some of what the bar wanted.

RW: *How did your new guidelines work out?*

RM: Well, in a sense I never used them as part of my service because by this time my partner, Charlie Bloodgood, had been threatened with reprisals by McGeorge Law School if he didn't quit the independent paralegal business. Incidentally, Charlie is now a prominent lawyer in the area, who recently ran for judge.

RW: *What did you do?*

RM: My attorney and I worked out a new way of operating. I bought out the Wave Project and reorganized operations completely, utilizing secretaries, independent paralegals and attorneys working together. We call it Superior California Legal Clinics, Inc. Charlie Bloodgood was president of our organization until 1984, supervising the operation of the clinic.

RW: *Who owns Superior California Legal Clinic?*

RM: It's a nonprofit corporation with a Board of Directors. Our mandate is to help low- and moderate-income people educate themselves to deal with the legal system.

RW: *Then, legally, you work for the nonprofit corporation?*

RM: Right. I'm an officer, on the Board of Directors and an employee.

RW: *Let me change the subject a little and ask what you really do, day by day.*

RM: In 19 years, I've personally (with secretarial assistance, of course) assisted in preparing about 15,000 uncontested divorces. In addition, I've counseled a great many individuals and couples who were going through changes in their lives. I also schedule the attorneys on their appointments for the actions that the Clinic doesn't do on a paralegal basis. In addition, I supervise the many procedures necessary to provide these services as reasonably and effectively as possible, following the prescribed guidelines of the Clinic.

RW: *Have you figured out what your average charge for typing a divorce has been over the years?*

RM: Well, it's gone from $35 in the beginning to close to $150 today for a fairly basic divorce. I guess the average would be about $90, with the exception of a simple Summary Dissolution, which has gone from $40 to $75 today.

RW: *What do you think the same people would have had to pay if they went to an individual attorney or legal clinic and both were represented?*

RM: On the average, with children and little property, probably about $1,000 using a heavily advertised clinic and a minimum of $1,500 for the same thing using a conventional private attorney.

RW: *So, even figuring that some people might have represented themselves or simply gotten along without a divorce, you saved people several million dollars over a period of 14 years.*

RM: Yes, in the divorce area, but Superior does lots of other things now, still at a very economical rate, using a sliding scale, so that all of our low-income clients receive service very economically.

RW: *Give me an example of the work you do.*

RM: We specialize in family law matters, including uncontested divorces, wills, bankruptcies, child support modifications, nonmarried custody actions, name changes and the like, but we also handle guardianships, paternity actions, adoptions, restraining orders and, by use of our attorney-referral procedure, some criminal and personal injury cases.

RW: *How does the Clinic work?*

RM: We use a paralegal approach on divorces, separations, annulments, etc. On the others, we refer to one of five attorneys who work with us, according to our sliding-fee schedule, which we make clear to everyone in advance.

RW: *What are your charges?*

RM: We have set charges for many actions. For example, a bankruptcy is currently $125-$150, a name change is $100, and so on. If a particular problem doesn't fit into a predictable category, we charge by the hour on a sliding scale based on our clients' income. This is basically $40 for low-income and $60 for middle-income people.

RW: *How does this compare to local attorney rates?*

RM: The going rate in Sacramento is $125 to $175 dollars per hour. The heavily-advertised legal clinics charge at least $150 per hour.

RW: *When you changed your method of operating to include attorneys, did the bar's attitude change?*

RM: It was a whole new ballgame from the moment we changed the name and included lawyers. I guess you could say it allowed me to become almost respectable.

RW: *But when it comes down to typing divorces, you are doing pretty much the same thing you always did?*

RM: Right, my approach is identical, only under supervision.

RW: *Does that make you smile?*

RM: Chuckle, somewhat, might be a better way to describe it.

RW: *In 19 years, you must have seen a lot of big changes. What's the biggest?*

RM: Attitude. These days the courts, the district attorney, social services and law schools all refer cases to us. That would have been unheard of 10 years ago. Now, when a person picks up a divorce form package at the court clerk's office, they get an information sheet with our name on it. And that's not only happening in Sacramento. We prepare forms for people in 26 counties, and in most of them, one or another county agency sends us referrals.

RW: *How do you prepare paperwork for people at a distance?*

RM: They call us and we do a little initial screening. If our service is appropriate for the customer, we send out an information package. The customer fills it out and sends in a money order. If we have more questions, we handle them by phone. Otherwise, we type the paper to send them out.

RW: *What do you think about the future of the independent paralegal business?*

RM: The surface hasn't even been scratched. There are certain to be more clinics with paralegals and attorneys working together on a more-or-less equal footing, because the economics of delivering legal services to low- and middle-income people don't allow for anything else. How can a person who makes $8 to $10 an hour afford to pay a lawyer $150 or more per hour? It doesn't make sense. There have been a lot of changes in our legal system over the past 19 years, and you know what?

RW: *I'll bite.*

RM: The changes in how legal services are delivered to people, whether by phone, computer, lawyer or independent paralegal, in the next 20 years are going to make what we have accomplished so far look small.

Virginia Simons Interview

Virginia Simons is an independent paralegal in Bakersfield, California. With over ten years in the business, she has much valuable experience in how to cope with bar association attacks, work with other paralegals and develop a paralegal business.

Ralph Warner:: *Let's start with your personal history as an independent paralegal.*

Virginia Simons: I've been in the business since 1981. In the beginning, I only typed divorces and bankruptcies. Now I also do restraining orders in domestic violence situations, family law restraining orders, harassment orders, child support and custody orders, responses, guardianships, terminations of guardianship, stepparent adoptions, paternity orders, name changes and joinders on pension plans.

RW: *When did you first run into trouble with the local bar?*

VS: Not until 1988, when two other local typing service owners and I were sued by a bankruptcy court trustee.

RW: *I'm interested in why it took the bar eight years to go after you. In a metropolitan area with a population of about 360,000, your business can't have been a secret. Do you know why it took them so long?*

VS: I'm not sure. I tired to keep a very low profile at first. I figured that if I was a good little girl, no one would bother me.

RW: *But in 1988, they did sue you. Had you done something to be perceived as a bad little girl?*

VS: I wasn't doing anything different. It may have been that over the years, as there were more IPs in Bakersfield, lawyers felt they were losing so much business that they decided to crack down. Remember, I wasn't the only target—Marilyn Marvin and Bobbe Powers were also charged with unauthorized practice of law for bankruptcy form preparation.

RW: *What were your feelings when you learned of the suit?*

VS: I panicked. I really thought I would end up in jail. If you had heard the horrible stories about Kern County Jail that I have, you would have some idea of how scared I felt.

RW: *What did you do?*

VS: The hardest part was telling my husband. When I did, his first re-action was to tell me to quit the business and get a job.

RW: *Obviously, you didn't do that. What did you say to your husband to change his mind?*

VS: I said, "You've never backed away from a fight that you couldn't avoid with dignity. You've always told me there are times when you have to stand up and be ready to fight back."

RW: *What was his response?*

VS: He thought about what I said and replied, "Go for it. I'll back you, even if it means losing our house and savings"; and then he said, "You're right."

RW: *Once you had your domestic ducks in a row, what did you, Bobbe and Marilyn do?*

VS: First, we needed legal help. We had been sued in federal court and we had to respond. The first lawyer we approached turned us down flat. He refused to go against the local legal establishment.

RW: *Whoa. You mean this was so political, a local criminal lawyer who represents all sorts of unpopular people was afraid to take your money?*

VS: Yes. We finally got an attorney who made no bones about the fact that he thought we were guilty of UPL, but said that he was such a good lawyer he could get us off. I'm sorry I can't mention his name, but we had to promise that we wouldn't publicly associate his name with ours.

RW: *Was this because he feared the reaction of his lawyer colleagues?*

VS: Yes. At this point, local lawyers were determined to do away with our competition. Anyone who represented us was in danger of being seen as a traitor by their colleagues.

RW: *What next?*

VS: Even with a lawyer, we felt terribly lonely and isolated. Finally, we called Steve Elias, who works with both Nolo Press and the National Association for Independent Paralegals (NAIP). Steve normally limits his advice to independent paralegals to NAIP Seminars in Sonoma, CA, but he got interested in the details of our case and came to Bakersfield. He really gave us the strength to go on. Catherine Jermany, the Executive Director of NAIP, and Glynda Mathewson of the California Association of Independent Paralegals (CAPE) also helped spread the word about our plight and rallied crucial support. But it was really Steve who turned us around when he looked right at us and said "You have a basic personal choice to make. Either stop crying and moaning and enjoy the fight, or quit right now." We decided to put fear behind us and take the offensive.

RW: *What did you do?*

VS: Lots of things. We told each of our customers that we had been sued by a bankruptcy trustee in federal court in an effort to put us out of business, and got them to sign petitions on our behalf. We went to the bankruptcy court once a month when it was in session and took notes as to any unequal treatment given to nonlawyers representing themselves. We testified at public hearings at the state level, where the subject of whether IPs should be certified or licensed was being considered. In short, we started to have fun.

RW: *What happened at the trial?*

VS: The best thing was that 25 people came from all over California to be there to support us. Then, all of a sudden, it was over and we won. Patrick Kavanaugh, the bankruptcy trustee who sued us, thought it was a violation of UPL to simply type bankruptcy forms and didn't present any evidence as to how we were guilty of UPL. The judge, who would have loved to convict us, had to disagree, based on other court decisions that held that simply typing forms wasn't unauthorized practice. In short, he demanded that Kavanaugh produce evidence that we had given customers legal information. Since he wasn't prepared to do that, the judge reluctantly dismissed the case.

RW: *Great, you won. How did you celebrate?*

VS: We organized a public forum at a conference room at the Red Lion Inn on the subject of whether typing services should exist. A couple of lawyers showed up to speak on our side of the issue and several more who opposed us. The press covered it and began to get interested in our story.

RW: *Was this a continuation of your offensive?*

VS: Yes, we had decided to affirmatively contact and engage our opponents. We wanted to convince individual lawyers that many people who couldn't afford lawyer fees really needed our services. In addition, we wanted our adversaries to know that, personally, we weren't monsters. For example, we contacted each of the lawyers who spoke against typing services at the Red Lion Inn.

RW: *Did you apply the same strategy to Patrick Kavanaugh and Gary O'Neil, the two lawyers who had been your principal adversaries?*

VS: Yes, we did, but first we contacted the Kern County DA, because we heard he was thinking of filing criminal UPL charges against us. We asked for an appointment and discussed all the issues. In fact, there was no plan to go after us, but it was good to clear the air. We also contacted a local judge who was rumored to believe that we were keeping filing fees customers paid to us when we filed fee waivers based on the customer's poverty. Interestingly, the judge wasn't worried about that, but did say that, in his opinion, we were practicing law. He then added that given the difficulty in defining UPL, we were okay as long as we stuck to the types of form preparation we were doing.

RW: *In short, the judge presented you with a sort of horseback deal—you can violate the law a little bit, but don't go too far.*

VS: Something like that. But to get back to Kavanaugh and O'Neil, we tried to open up lines of communication. Initially, this happened at public meetings. For example, Kavanaugh and I were both on a bankruptcy subcommittee of the State Bar's committee looking into the possibility of licensing typing services. Of the two trustees and one bankruptcy judge on this subcommittee, Kavanaugh was the only one who provided unbiased opinions on how typing services could operate within the bankruptcy field. At a seminar where Gary O'Neil and I both sat on the panel, he claimed Kern County was unique because they had "all those sleaze-bag typing services." When it was my turn to speak, I introduced myself by saying I was one of the "sleaze-bags," and invited Gary to come to one of our local CAIP (California Association of Independent Paralegals) chapter meetings.

RW: *Did he come?*

VS: Yes, he did. First we invited him to lunch with the five of us who ran the main typing services in town. (Incidentally, to show solidarity, we always went together to meetings with the bar, judges or lawyers.) We worked out a plan for him to speak at our meeting and he invited us, in turn, to speak to a bar association lunch on the issue of whether legal typing services should be licensed.

RW: *Sounds great. Did the communication lead to anything positive?*

VS: Very much so. We had said to Gary that if he thought we were doing a bad job, why didn't he teach us to do better?

RW: *Did you learn anything?*

VS: Yes. It was extremely valuable, and we plan to repeat it on a monthly basis.

RW: *Why do you think you were suddenly beginning to be accepted?*

VS: It's complicated, of course, but I think, at bottom, lawyers are beginning to realize that the independent paralegal licensing issue isn't going away. The fact that IPs are organized at the state and local level, that legislation to legalize IPs has been introduced in Sacramento and that even state bar committees have made some positive recommendations all helps us. Why, we have even been invited to attend bar lunches.

RW: *Hey, that a big change. Are paralegals who work for lawyers also invited?*

VS: Yes, and I guess you could say we are being included in a somewhat similar way.

RW: *What about your competitors? The fact that you and many other typing services in town have worked so closely together tells me that you value cooperation.*

VS: Very much so. Solidarity in this business is essential. The bar is really impressed by the fact that we stick together and can't be picked off one by one.

RW: *Does this strategy extend to new typing services? After all, they are your competitors, much as you compete with lawyers.*

VS: Our strategy is to train the new people to do a good job. Sure I have mixed emotions at times, but by and large I think we all will prosper if the legal form typing business expands. Also, it just feels good to cooperate. It brings me lots of friends. Also, because I can get help from another knowledgeable IP if I need it, I can serve my customers better. And if I don't do a particular type of legal form typing, I can refer the customers to someone who does, either locally or elsewhere in the state.

Glynda Mathewson Interview

Glynda Mathewson is an independent paralegal based in Oakland, California. She types a number of family law forms, including divorce, guardianship, name change, child support modifications, probates, stepparent adoptions and wills. She has been in business since 1984 and is a past president of the California Association of Independent Paralegals and a volunteer arbitrator with Oakland Better Business Bureau.

Ralph Warner: *How did you start in the independent paralegal business?*

Glynda Mathewson: I prefer the term "public paralegal" or "legal technician," but to answer your question, my training is as a career counselor. In 1984, I became my own client in that I was looking for a career change for myself. A person I knew told me she was getting a divorce with the help of a nonlawyer divorce typing service in Oakland. I was fascinated that this occupation existed. To make a long story short, I investigated and learned that the divorce typing office was run by Sandra Edwards, who also had another, larger office in Walnut Creek, California. I also learned that Sandra followed a system originally taught by you and Ed Sherman as part of the Wave Project. It allows nonlawyers to prepare routine legal forms with little risk that they will be accused or practicing law without a license. I worked for Sandra for months—typing divorce forms as sort of a paid apprentice, and then I bought the Oakland office.

RW: *What other training did you have?*

GM: I read all the Nolo divorce materials many times, which, by this time, had been used by thousands of people to do their own divorces without help from lawyers. Also, remember, I was typing divorce forms every day under the supervision of a person who had been doing it for years. Under her training, I learned the appropriate work standards and ethical behavior that later helped build my reputation as a reliable service. In addition, I checked out lots of divorce files at the county clerk's office. Court files are public records, so I just checked dozens of random divorces and studied them. I do this with any new procedure I want to learn.

RW: *Where did you operate your first office?*

GM: On a neighborhood shopping street in a middle-class area, about a half-mile from Oakland's downtown area. At that point I was cautious and didn't want to be too close to the downtown legal establishment.

RW: *How did you build up your business?*

GM: It was slow at first. I didn't have much money for promotion, and anyway, I was worried that advertising might bring me trouble with the bar or the district attorney. As a result, I concentrated on building a personal referral network. I contacted the personnel offices of big businesses, social services agencies, child and family counselors, and even some lawyers, to tell them who I was and what I did.

RW: *Weren't you afraid of lawyers?*

GM: As I said, I was afraid of the bar association and the district attorney, but not necessarily of individual lawyers. I concentrated on lawyers I knew, or friends knew, and yes, some of them did refer me customers.

RW: *What advertising did you do?*

GM: I tried a few small classified ads in weekly shoppers and penny saver type papers. That didn't produce much, so finally I tried the big city paper, the *Oakland Tribune,* under the "legal services" classifieds heading. It didn't bring in much business at first, but I kept it in, and before long, the phone began ringing. It taught me a valuable lesson. In this business, you need to have an ad in the same place very day. When you do, lots of people eventually figure out its there and tell others.

RW: *Okay, you started in 1984, how would you describe your business two years later.*

GM: I was having fun, but the business was in poor economic shape. I took in about $45,000 dollars that year and spent almost all of it on overhead and promotion.

RW: *How did you survive?*

GM: Fortunately, my husband doesn't own a business—he has a "regular" job with a "regular" paycheck—otherwise, I would not have been able to stick with it.

RW: *What did you do to improve things?*

GM: I got frustrated enough to see that I needed help on how to run a good small business and found an excellent small business consultant, Roger Pritchard, in Berkeley. He helped me focus on improving my business in a number of ways. The most important was making a marketing plan to produce more customers and sticking to it.

RW: *Can you give me some specifics?*

GM: For the first time, I kept track of where l my customers came from. Once I knew that, I concentrated my marketing efforts on the best referral sources. Before I developed a plan, I was often spending as much time on promotional activities that produced 5% of my business as I was on those that produced 25%.

RW: *What else did Pritchard help you with?*

GM: He talked me out of borrowing money to expand the business. He got me to see that the additional money would be wasted until I had a better plan, and better day-to-day control. I was so frustrated, I cried, but he was right. Lack of money wasn't my problem; it was a symptom of running my business.

RW: *Insights are cheap. What did you do to change things?*

GM: As I said, I focused my marketing money and energy where it would do the most good. In addition, I began to offer more services, including typing name changes, child support modifications and guardianships. I also made an effort to stay in touch with former customers and others I had worked with to encourage word-of-mouth referrals. Suddenly, after three years or so, people began to see me as established and trustworthy. Individual lawyers, employees at the public law library, people at court offices dealing with child support, even the local bar's legal help service, began sending me people who couldn't afford a lawyer and weren't eligible for legal aid.

RW: *So you found your market niche?*

GM: Exactly. Whether or not they always want to admit it, in the high-cost Bay Area, lawyers can't afford to provide services to working people who have a family income of $50,000 or less. At the same time, they hate to admit that the American legal system is closed to the average person, so they refer these people to me.

RW: *Okay, your business improved; what next?*

GM: I got excited about running an excellent small business and began to see ways to improve it more. My biggest step was to move to an older professional building in downtown Oakland. Now I am near the courts, county offices, such as social services, and the DA's child support collection offices. I am also in the same neighborhood as the majority of Oakland's law firms.

RW: *Were you worried to become more visible to the legal establishment?*

GM: Not in the least. I had been threatened by a few lawyers and investigated by the DA for unauthorized practice when I first started, but I was confident that I knew how to type forms without giving legal information. In short, I felt my business could stand scrutiny and there was no need to hide it. Also, by now, most of the people who might investigate me were sending me customers. I believed that if someone in the legal establishment tried to close me down, a number of conscientious lawyers who respected and trusted my work and knew I didn't practice law would stand up for me.

RW: *How did the move work out?*

GM: Business increased substantially right away. I began to get referrals from lawyers in my building, and when the feedback was good, from others in the downtown area.

RW: *Which leads me to ask whether lawyers, who have been enemies of the Independent Paralegal movement, are turning out to be friends.*

GM: Surprisingly, to some extent, some are. It's like a dual reality. At the state level, bar association types want to put IP's out of business, or to so limit what they can do that it amounts to the same thing. But at the local, day-to-day level, dozens of individual public and private lawyers, and even establishment legal agencies, which I won't name so as to not embarrass them, absolutely depend on the fact that legal typing services such as mine exist. They know something bar associations don't know or won't admit; despite all the hoopla about providing legal access to ordinary Americans, the legal profession is economically completely unable to do it. In the S.F. Bay Area, lawyers claim they need a minimum of $150 an hour or more to get by; how in the world can they get that from people who make $10 an hour?

RW: *Are you pussyfooting around, saying that you have had referrals from court clerks, judges, the local bar associations and even the district attorney's office?*

GM: I'd better not comment.

RW: *Okay, let me change gears a little. Rose Palmer, who runs a service in Pittsburg, Pennsylvania to help women with divorces and child support, has reported that while the organized bar has been hostile to her organization's efforts to help women deal with issues of divorce, support, custody and domestic violence, she has gotten support from some judges, who see clearly that many of the people who need help can't afford lawyers. Have you had encouragement from the bench?*

GM: Yes, to a limited but very welcome degree. Some judges never grow up—they keep their narrow lawyer attitudes forever. But its a mistake to see the judiciary as a monolith. A few judges have helped me refine my paperwork technologies and generally supported my efforts. Also, since I've become established, several court clerks have become very supportive.

RW: *Have you done anything to encourage or institutionalize your relationship with judges or the courthouse personnel generally?*

GM: I often file papers in person so that I can speak to the clerks, and I drop by the law library often. Our local Independent Paralegal Association invited one of our area's most prominent family law judges to give us a training session. He did, and has generally let it be known that he supports IPs who do top quality form preparation and stay away from complicated areas of the law, where they don't have expertise. When he told me "Glynda, I recognize your paperwork because it's of such high quality," it made my month—or, more so, it made my year!

RW: *You raised the issue of how careful you are to avoid practicing law. Let me follow up on that. What do you do when people ask a question that requires legal expertise?*

GM: I don't answer it. All my customers sign a statement saying they know I am not a lawyer and I don't give legal advice, so I am very clear on this point from the start. In addition, there is a prominent sign in my office that says, "We are not attorneys. We do not give legal advice."

RW: *Sure, but that won't stop them from asking.*

GM: First, you must realize that most questions on the preprinted forms I type aren't legal—it's the same sort of name, address and age type of information that any other government form requests. When questions on a form depend on a customer having some legal knowledge, it's typically fairly routine and accessible. For example, someone might ask if a certain type of property is community property and therefore owned by both spouses 50-50. I simply refer them to the relevant discussion in *California Marriage and Divorce Law,* or *How To Do Your Own Divorce in California,* both of which are available on my desk or in any bookstore in the state. If the answers aren't there, the person probably does need more in-depth information. An example might be a divorce where one person has a job which will provide a pension, or there's a lot of property involved and the couple is unclear about how to divide it.

RW: *So what do you do then?*

GM: Most legal information or help my customers need can be efficiently provided by one of three sources. The first is lawyers who know me and are willing to see a customer for a modest fee, provide the necessary information and perhaps do a property agreement before sending the customer back so I can finish typing the divorce. In many cases, though, the lawyer doesn't really need to do any form preparation. There is a sample property settlement agreement in *How To Do Your Own Divorce,* which I can prepare under the customer's supervision once they have the legal information they need.

The second is mediation. Suppose spouses haven't decided important issues, such as property division; in that case, I recommend mediation. Usually, after two or three mediation sessions, which might cost $200, the couple works out their own compromise and the mediator writes it down in a form that I can include with the papers I type and submit to the court. You might be surprised, but people are more savvy and knowledgeable than most lawyers want to admit, and given the sort of positive framework mediation offers, they will usually work out a mutually satisfactory and reasonably fair solution, whether it involves property division, custody, visitation or whatever.

Finally, there is a Divorce Helpline in Santa Cruz, California. This is a phone-in service where lawyers provide legal advice about self-help divorce for a reasonable fee. They even provide a service to compute the value of pensions, which can be complicated, especially if the person covered by the pension hasn't retired yet. Assuming the customer talks to the lawyers at Divorce Helpline for 15 or 20 minutes, they can get the legal help they need for $30 or $40, and I can finish typing their paperwork.

RW: *Sounds good. What do you see for the future?*

GM: Well, I'm interested in broadening my business to type other types of routine forms. I need to grow in what I do so I'll stay fresh and interested. In addition, I see a need for public paralegals to get together on a number of important issues, including skills training, legal defense and political organization. Bills are before the California legislature to say typing services are not subject to laws which prohibit the unauthorized practice of law, but which, in exchange, would tightly regulate them. Several proposals, such as the one drafted with the help of HALT, aren't too bad; others put forward by the bar are much worse. I think we need to be careful before we implement an expensive, complicated licensing board. Any licensing scheme would inevitably be costly to the service provider, which means costs would be passed on to the consumer. Licensing could also overly restrict the freedom of typing services to provide a wide variety of services, meaning that some might close. In short, we need to unite to be sure that the legal profession doesn't push through a bill that pretends to legalize our work but, in fact, regulates it out of existence.

And one more point I want to make. Traditional paralegals, many of whom work for lawyers, have been debating the licensing issue nationwide for at least the past 10 years. It's naive of us independent business owners to see this as an issue that only affects us. It is a paralegal issue—public, freelance or traditional. We all need to come together and form a powerful lobbying group to stand up to the legal profession.

Rosemary Furman Interview

Rosemary Furman began typing legal forms for low-income residents of Jacksonville, Florida in the early 1970s. Her inspired one-woman fight against the monopolistic practices of the Florida bar took her to the threshold of a Florida jail cell.

Ralph Warner: *Lots of people know at least a little bit about what's happened to you in the last few years, including the fact that the Florida Bar Association tried to jail you for providing high quality, low-cost legal help to nonlawyers, so I'd like to start a little earlier. I'm curious—how did a respectable middle-aged woman, and mother of three, with no credentials as a radical, get to become Public Enemy Number One to American lawyerdom? What's your background? Were you born feisty, or is it something you just grew into?*

Rosemary Furman: I was born in Alexandria, Virginia, where my grandmother owned a bakery and made a little bootleg beer in the back room. I spoke German as my first language until I was eight. I went to public school, first in Virginia and later in New York State, south of Albany, after being orphaned.

RW: *How did you get involved in the legal system?*

RF: Court reporting. I took classes to become a court reporter. It seemed like a very good income for the hours expended.

RW: *You mean you learned how to key punch one of those little transcribing machines?*

RF: Never! I learned Gregg shorthand, a far more accurate system, and one I keep up with today.

RW: *Where did you work as a court reporter?*

RF: Where didn't I work? I married a military man, and when he was transferred, I packed up the kids and went along. When I'd get to a new city I would put my name on the court reporter list and eventually I'd have a job. At one time or another, I worked in Trenton, New Jersey, Nassau County, Long Island, Boston, Washington, D.C., and Jacksonville, Florida.

RW: *So, it was as a court reporter that you first started seeing the legal system as being flawed?*

RF: If that's a polite way to say that I began to see lawyers as barracudas, preying on the public, you're right. You see, a court reporter quickly becomes part of the furniture, and lawyers and judges would often carry on their self-serving schemes in front of me, almost as if I weren't there. I mean, it isn't hard to understand what's going on if you literally see the money changing hands. How many times can you sit in a judge's office and watch the lawyers and judges bargain and sell clients for the highest fee and then go out into the public courtroom and put on a charade for the benefit of the public before you realize that our American justice system is run by a bunch of self-interested charlatans who call themselves officers of the court?

RW: *You just made some pretty strong statements. How about some specifics to back it up.*

RF: Okay, sure, but first, let me just say I'm an old-fashioned constitutionalist. I really believe in fundamental American values like the Bill of Rights, the right of every man and woman to vote, a court system where the average taxpaying citizen can get a fair shake and so on. You want an example of what turned me off? I could give you dozens, hundreds, but first let me say that any of the bailiffs, marshals, clerks and other personnel who work at the courthouse could tell you the same sort of thing. What goes on in the so-called halls of justice is closer to a Persian market, with the buying and selling of cases among lawyers, bargaining for probated sentences, cooling down clients whose conviction is a foregone conclusion to avoid violence in the...

RW: *Sorry to interrupt, but how about the example?*

RF: I was a court reporter in Jacksonville, Florida. I was sitting in the judge's office one morning listening to the local lawyers back door the judge when one lawyer said he represented Alfredo Fernandez (that's not the real name) and wanted to know how the judge was planning to handle Alfredo's case. The judge checked the file and determined that Alfredo was barely 18 and had been charged with possession of a controlled substance. I can't remember if it was speed or marijuana or what. As it was the kid's first offense, his parents were solid working people in the community and so on, the judge said he would sentence Alfredo to six months in jail, and then, when the parents were done fainting, suspend the sentence and send him home. Then he would withhold adjudication and if after six months Alfredo didn't get into more trouble, he would expunge the record upon Alfredo's petition.

RW: *That doesn't sound so bad.*

RF: Let me finish, please. The lawyer thanked the judge and walked over to the bookcase and selected the book containing the code section that applied to Alfredo. As it happened, the lawbooks were my responsibility as a chambers clerk, so I followed the lawyer into the court room, which was full of people waiting for the law and motion calendar. To make a long story short, the lawyer opened the book to the relevant page, put on a long face, and told the Fernandez parents that it looked like five years—the maximum penalty under the law in question—unless they could come up with $5,000 that morning, in which case he was almost sure he could get Alfredo off. The stunned parents left the courtroom, and the lawyer said "not ready" every time the case was called. An hour later the parents came back with an envelope full of money. The lawyer counted it quickly, answered "ready" when the case was called, and made a brief argument about what a good kid Alfredo was. The judge then gave Alfredo the six-month suspended sentence that he had planned to all along.

RW: *You have convinced me that there was one dishonest lawyer, but not that the judge knew about what was going on.*

RF: Come on. I saw a version of this same story no less than three times a week. Whenever lawyers spot a worried parent in the courtroom or the hall, they move in for the kill. And as to the judge knowing about it, who do you think judges are but lawyers in black dresses? In many states, you have to pay two-years' salary to the local politicos to get to be a judge. Where do you think the money comes from? To be specific, I can't tell you how many times I've seen lawyers (the DA and the defense lawyer) work out what was going to happen to a defendant with the judge in his office and then have the defense lawyer say that since he had gotten a good fee he had to put on a bit of a performance when they got into the courtroom. The other DA and the judge would laugh and someone would say, "Great, but don't go on so long we miss our starting time."

RW: *You're saying that lawyers and judges are buying and selling justice for their own ends?*

RF: You're damn right, I am. The lawyers that make their phony speeches to try and justify those big fees turn right around and make hefty contributions to the judge's next election campaign. Who do you think finances most judicial election campaigns? The lawyers who appear before those very judges, that's who. And the judges know darn well who contributes. And I might add, the recent scandals in Chicago, New York and Tampa involving judges taking bribes are just the tip of the iceberg. Ninety-nine percent of all judicial offenders go merrily on their way, playing the system for all it's worth.

RW: *Okay, let's get back to you. How did you break free of working at the courthouse and set up your own business?*

RF: Well, in 1972, I was involved in setting up a shelter for battered women in Jacksonville, Florida. On at least four occasions frustrated, battering husbands set fire to the shelter in an attempt to get at their wives. When we sought police protection, we learned that it was a crime to deny a man access to his wife in Florida. What to do? We concluded the only way we could get police protection was for the woman to file for divorce, so they would no longer be treated as some man's property. The problem was that most of the women who came to us had low incomes and couldn't afford a lawyer, and legal aid had a two-year backlog of divorce cases. If you're getting beaten all the time, two years can be a death sentence.

RW: *What happened?*

RF: As you can probably guess, since I had worked at the courthouse, I was elected to type the divorces. From there, one thing led to another and before long, I was doing a thriving legal typing business, which I called the Northside Secretarial Service.

RW: *What sorts of papers did you prepare?*

RF: Divorces, name changes, adoptions, bankruptcies, etc. I did the typing and my customers made their own decisions which, before lawyers captured the legal system and called it a crime, was an American tradition. Of course, everyone who came into my office signed a disclaimer stating that they knew I wasn't a lawyer.

RW: *Tell me about a couple of them.*

RF: Well, the ones I cared most about were situations in which people's lives were being negatively affected by the fact that they couldn't afford to hire a lawyer. For example, I helped grandparents prepare simple adoption papers to adopt their grandchild so that they could qualify for Navy benefits to repair the child's serious spinal problem. Local lawyers wanted $650, which the grandparents (he was retired) didn't have. Another time, I helped a high school graduate from a very poor family change his name officially to the name he had used all his life and which appeared on his school records. The name on his birth certificate was different, which confused things when it came to his getting a scholarship, loans and grants.

RW: *How did the bar close you down?*

RF: It's a long story, but part of it involved their hiring a former FBI
agent to track down my clients. They found over 100. And even
though none would testify against me and there was no proof that I
did bad work, I was hauled into court on contempt of court charges
for giving people legal advice. As far as the bar was concerned, if I
told a person how to find the courthouse that constituted giving legal
advice, so you can see the charge was a sick joke.

RW: *You mean, you weren't charged with a crime? I thought you ended up
with a jail sentence.*

RF: Both are true. When you challenge lawyers, you have to be prepared
for anything. They have usurped the power to simply lock you up,
even though there is absolutely no legal justification for their action.

RW: *You're exaggerating.*

RF: The bar association complained about me. I was hauled before a
contempt of court proceeding—a sort of kangaroo court where I had
no right to a jury trial because I was charged with no crime. I was
found guilty of competing with lawyers and sentenced to four
months in jail by a judge, A.C. Soud, who said, and I am quoting
him, "Only her imprisonment will provide the sting necessary to preserve the integrity of the court."

RW: *Are you serious?*

RF: Sure, and another judge, John Santora, chief circuit judge in Jacksonville, said publicly that people like me who ran public services as
legal stenographers are "a cancer on society."

RW: *Did you go to jail?*

RF: I'm almost sixty years old, and the idea of doing hard time to
appease a bunch of lawyers who were mad because I charged less
than they did didn't appeal to me. I appealed and was eventually
turned down by everyone, including the U.S. Supreme Court in the
fall of 1984. Incidentally, in the whole process, everyone who passed

on the question of my freedom was a lawyer. I was never charged with a crime, and never had a jury trial.

RW: *So, how come I'm not visiting you in jail right now?*

RF: A day before my sentence was to start, in November 1984, the Governor of Florida commuted my sentence in exchange for my promise not to run my business any longer.

RW: *What made him commute the sentence?*

RF: Tens of thousands of ordinary people wrote, called and telegraphed to support me. The interesting thing is that the governor, who as you can probably guess is also a lawyer, had no power to commute my sentence because I had never been charged with or found guilty of a crime. Remember, I was held in contempt of court, so only the original judge could have relieved me of the contempt citation.

RW: *Did the governor know he was acting illegally?*

RF: Sure, he went to Harvard Law School, but that isn't the point. When it comes to protecting their own, lawyers are perfectly willing to act illegally, and the public outcry produced by "60 Minutes" and other TV shows had made me a huge embarrassment to the Florida bar. In a way, it was funny. They became desperate to keep me out of the very jail they had conspired so hard to put me in.

RW: *What are you doing now?*

RF: Rabble rousing in what I consider to be the best tradition of men like Tom Paine, Tom Jefferson and Patrick Henry. I travel around the country talking to paralegal groups and others in the legal system who do the real work to tell them to challenge the bar by opening their own offices. I am particularly interested in pushing for a basic change in how our courthouses work. Instead of telling people they can't practice law, court clerks should actively help people prepare forms in most routine uncontested actions. After all, the public pays the salaries of these people. Why shouldn't they get help filling in the blanks on forms which are contained in the codes of civil procedure of the various states? We must break the monopoly of the lawyers over the delivery of legal services. The practice of law in the U.S. is a confidence game, nothing more.

When I'm home in Jacksonville, I train others to help the underserved Florida people of low and moderate incomes who have been abandoned by the bar association and who are suffering from economic hardship.

RW: *Do you expect the Florida bar to leave you in peace now?*

RF: Absolutely. They never dreamed that by attacking me they would bring the whole county down on themselves. But if they do come after me again, I'm ready to fight.

Robin Smith Interview

Robin Smith provides independent paralegal services at People's Paralegal, in Beaverton, Oregon. She has been involved in the consumer movement for over ten years and has been an independent paralegal since 1985.

Ralph Warner: *Robin, why don't you start by telling me who works at People's Paralegal.*

Robin Smith: We have a staff of three, counting me. Angela Vaillancourt is our receptionist. She screens new customers on the phone, makes appointments and when a customer comes in she helps them fill out our intake form. Cathy Welch, our office manager, helps customers complete the necessary substantive questionnaire based on the type of legal procedures they want. Incidentally, we used to ask customers to complete these questionnaires themselves, but doing so sometimes intimidated them, or they provided incorrect information which slowed things down.

RW: Can you give me an example?

RS: Sure. A divorce that involves minor children requires information about visitation. Seeing a question on a form that asks what type of visitation they want often confuses people. By contrast, in an interview setting, Cathy can tell people that as long as both spouses agree, they can settle on any visitation terms they wish, or simply provide for reasonable and seasonable visitation under Oregon law. If they still have questions, Cathy can then give them written information on the subject. For example, we often provide people with a copy of an Oregon court case in which the judge clearly explained the options and defines what reasonable and seasonable means.

RW: Great. But let's get back to staffing. What do you handle?

RS: Cathy does most of the form preparation, which often involves inserting customers' information into a computerized form preparation system. Incidentally, our basic word processing program is Wordstar 5.0. We also use a document generation program called OverDrive. A few forms still must be prepared using a typewriter. I handle interviews and form preparation in several areas, including living trust, incorporation and divorce modifications where the former spouses agree. I also handle the business side of our operation, which involves marketing, dealing with the media, supervising bookkeeping and so on.

RW: *What does your office look like?*

RS: People's Paralegal operates out of an upstairs, two-room office on a commercial street with older office buildings and store fronts. One room, which is very large, is divided by partitions into three spaces. One space functions as a reception-intake area with a play space for small children. It also houses Angela's desk and our computer. A second, more private space has two work tables where Cathy or I work with customers to fill out the questionnaires. Cathy's office is in the third space. It also functions as our lunch/meeting area. My office, which serves as a file room as well, is just down the hall.

RW: *What sorts of legal actions do you handle?*

RS: Quite a range—divorce, bankruptcy, wills, living trusts, probate, stepparent adoption and small business incorporations make up most of it.

RW: *That's a lot. How do you get enough information to customers so they can sensibly tell you what to type?*

RS: In a remarkably high number of areas, people have a good grasp of what they want. For example, a customer might read about a probate-avoiding living trust and then go to a lawyer's "free" seminar at which the lawyer will provide a lot of basic information and then try to get a $1,500 fee. Similarly, a small businessperson who wants to incorporate is usually pretty savvy. In these situations, the customer doesn't need more information. Of course, in other types of form preparation, such as probate or adoption, they are more likely to. We give them procedural information, such as what forms are necessary to accomplish a particular task. Under Oregon law, we don't believe doing this is the unauthorized practice of law. When it comes to substantive questions, we have a whole library of information we've gathered from a number of sources, including Nolo Press publications, and we put the customers' hands on the information they need. Once they have educated themselves, we can go forward. For more complicated questions, we advise people to see a lawyer.

RW: *Have you been hassled by the bar around unauthorized practice issues?*

RS: We have been contacted several times, mostly based on our typing of probates. To do a probate, you need the original will. Sometimes this is in a lawyer's safe and that lawyer is hoping for a nice fat probate fee. When the executor asks the lawyer for the will and says she plans to handle the probate pro per with our help, the lawyer may complain to the bar, which then results in our being called.

RW: *How do you respond?*

RS: That we use the forms provided by the same legal printer that Oregon lawyers use, and that we type and file them in the order required by the court. All information is supplied by the executor, who often has a copy of the will. So far, that seems to satisfy the bar.

RW: *Do you make a good living?*

RS: Charging $125-$145 for a divorce , $175 for a stepparent adoption and $225-$275 for a living trust (which includes transferring real estate deeds in the name of the trust) and so on, you don't get rich. But we make a decent living and, even though I work very hard, I love what I do. I really feel I provide services people need at a fair price.

RW: *What's your attitude about companies who advertise kits, training packages and franchises to get people started as IP's and charge huge fees?*

RS: It's often customer fraud, especially when people are conned into spending lots of money based on a promise of big dollar returns. In fact, many of these promoters act like they are selling a franchise but don't comply with state franchise laws. But even more basically, the IP business is not one where huge returns are possible. We are not mass-producing anything—if an office does lots of form preparation, they must hire people and buy equipment to do the intakes and process the forms. In short, the overhead increases with the growth of the business. At the prices we charge, there isn't a big profit margin and that isn't likely to change. If IP's try to raise prices too much, someone new will open an office and undercut them.

RW: *Let's shift gears a little. How do you do your marketing?*

RS: Our biggest source of customers is the positive recommendations from people we have worked with before. Every day we get calls from new customers who have heard about us from someone we worked with previously. To help this along, we keep a mailing list of all our customers and once a year send them a letter reminding them of our services and telling them about anything new we offer. We include a discount coupon that they can use or give a friend.

RW: *What about public agencies and community organizations? Do you market to them?*

RS: Definitely. It's our second largest source of referrals. We contact all sorts of agencies—from the military to battered women's shelters to sheriff's victims' rights office to senior organizations. We have a large list that we regularly update and add to. We make every effort to stay in touch with people who are in a position to refer others.

RW: *What else do you do?*

RS: Lots of community activities. For example, the Chamber of Commerce to which I belong has an event called "Good Neighbor Days," a sort of local fair to raise money for area nonprofits. It's fun—you know, baby races, pie throwing, chili cook off, crafts booths and so on. Along with a lot of other small business, we take a booth. We also do some advertising—our yellow pages ads under "divorce" and "paralegals" produces the most. We also have a classified ad in the big Portland daily and also in the local free classified paper called "The Nickel," and in a paper for seniors. In each, we target our message to our audience. For example, in the senior paper we list wills and trust.

RW: *Finally, if you were going to give someone contemplating going into the paralegal business some advice, what would it be?*

RS: To be successful as in Independent Paralegal, you must have a tough side. Or maybe a better way to put it is that you must be a little bit of a renegade, willing to be controversial and unafraid of the Bar Association. I am not suggesting belligerence, but if you are easily pushed around or intimidated, this isn't the business for you.

For example, suppose someone calls your from the state bar and says: "This is Investigator Smith from the Unauthorized Practice of Law Committee. We have received a complaint that you are practicing law without a license. Did you do Ms. Neededhelp's Probate?"

Your answer: "Yes, we typed the papers."

Investigator Smith: "Did you select the documents?"

Your answer: "We prepared the papers in the order in which the court requires."

Investigator Smith: "The committee will bring this up at our next meeting. Thank you for your time."

If having someone call and question you like this would be overwhelming, then this business is not for you, at least until the laws are changed and the legal system reformed to allow for licensing of this profession. I say this because every IP runs the daily risk of the next call or visit being from a prosecutor or bar official. It just goes with the territory of trying to stand up to a powerful self-interest monopoly. However, if you enjoy (or don't mind) controversy, and you like hard work, enjoy a challenge and can manage a business, being an IP is a great business to be in. Personally, I've always enjoyed controversy.

Rose Palmer Interview

Rose Palmer is Executive Director of Support, Inc., a Pittsburgh, Pennsylvania-based organization that informs, counsels and provides advocacy assistance for women on issues of child support, custody, visitation and domestic violence.

Ralph Warner: *Rose, take me back a few years and explain how you got involved in helping women with support issues.*

Rose Palmer: It all began in the late 1970s with my own personal struggles as a single parent. I was literally depriving my kids of necessities to pay lawyer fees to try and collect support I desperately needed. And to add insult to injury, I wasn't getting any results.

RW: *You were in the same situation as millions of others. What was the catalyst that led to your decision to make a career out of helping other women learn how to cope with the legal system?*

RP: At one point during my case, when we were in court, I saw that a legal mistake was being made. I interrupted and pointed it out. Even though I was correct and the error had the potential to jeopardize my rights, the Allegheny County hearing officer (in the role of a judge) told me to "shut up." She stated, "You have an attorney; he will speak for you. You do not talk unless I ask you to." Her attitude made me furious. It was as if I had no right to speak, even when the lawyers were messing up. It was a real turning point for me. I went home determined to learn how to do my own legal research and to take charge of my own legal destiny. Soon after, I got in touch with other women who were in the same situation, and Legal Advocacy for Women was born.

RW: *Where did you start your new work?*

RP: At the Pittsburgh YWCA. They gave us space in December of 1979. We stayed there for more than a year, but eventually left and ran our program out of a spare bedroom, because we were simply too controversial for the Y. They had a conservative board, and challenging the legal power structure worried them.

RW: *When did you come out of the bedroom and really get established in Pittsburgh?*

RP: October 1983, and like so many things in life, the story of how we got our first grant has an odd twist. The wife of a city councilman came to us for help with a long story of how she was being victimized by her husband. We were doing consciousness-raising activities at the time—marches, picketing and other events—to focus attention on how divorced, separated and single women with children were being discriminated against, and we saw her situation as a chance to further dramatize the issue.

RW: *So you took it public?*

RP: In a big way. And, of course, we got lots of publicity. There was only one problem. The heroine of our little drama was lying.

RW: *Oops. You mean the city councilman hadn't mistreated your client?*

RP: Nope. James O'Malley was a nice guy—such a good man, in fact, that despite our part in unfairly attacking him, he took an interest in what we were doing, applauded our goals and counseled us to form a formal nonprofit corporation. He then used his influence to get us our first grant.

RW: *What a wonderful story, but don't stop. What happened next?*

RP: With a real office and a few dollars to pay staff, we were much more visible. In fact, in 1985 we saw 700 clients in person and counseled another 2,000 by phone. There was only one problem—all of this activity got us in hot water with the county bar association.

RW: *How exactly did it occur?*

RP: We helped a women with minor children involved in a divorce, whose husband was represented by a prominent local lawyer. Our client was awarded everything she asked for—child support, day care and medical care. The same day the judge made the award, the lawyer filed charges with the Unauthorized Practice of Law (UPL) Committee of the Allegheny County bar association, charging us with practicing law without a license.

RW: *So that started a brouhaha about what you could do and not infringe on lawyer turf?*

RP: You bet. They challenged everything, right down to our right to use our name, which at that time was Legal Advocacy for Women. They questioned our right to go into court with women and counsel them as part of court proceedings, as well as helping women prepare budget sheets and other court forms.

RW: *I know you are doing all these things and lots more today, so you must have prevailed.*

RP: We are, and you're right, we eventually did, but it was a real struggle. Fortunately, the media was very sympathetic. Lawyers, after all, do not and can not provide affordable legal services to the average person, so if we were put out of business, it was obvious that no one was going to help a lot of desperate mothers. Also, we had (and still do, I should add) some brave people on our board of directors. Several local lawyers, judges and other prominent people who spoke out on our behalf. The result was compromise in the form of a consent order. We agreed to change our name from "Legal Advocacy for Women" to "Support, Inc.," not to whisper to our clients in court and not to use or touch the counsel table when we sat next to our clients in court. We could talk to our clients in a normal voice in court and ask for a recess at any time to confer privately in the hall, all of which was fine with us and, of course, made whispering unnecessary.

RW: *No, you can't be serious! The lawyers actually claimed that someone using their tables made you guilty of unauthorized practice of law?*

RP: Funny isn't it? But they were so desperate to draw a bright line between us and them that they drew it along the edge of the table. Since our clients can sit at the table, we had to be able to be there too in order to provide counseling and support. But since it's called the counsel table, and lawyers see this as a synonym for lawyer, we can't touch it or put our papers or research materials on it.

RW: *Lawyers go to law school for three years to make distinctions like that.*

RP: Apparently.

RW: *But otherwise, you carried on the same services as before? You still taught women how to use the legal system and helped them prepare paperwork and accompanied them to court?*

RP: Yes. In a way, it was as if the bar backed down but declared victory.

RW: *Does the Gilbert & Sullivan aspect of this story continue?*

RP: You bet. The next year, Councilman O'Malley helped sponsor an art show/benefit at the main city-county building, with all proceeds going to our organization. The opening was great—fancy dress and so on. Even the mayor presided at the opening ceremonies. There was only one hitch: the invitation went out saying the benefit was for "Support, Inc. (Legal Advocacy for Women)." There was no AKA before Legal Advocacy for Women, or other explanation that this was our former name. Even though we had nothing to do with printing or paying for the invitations (the city did that), attorney James Victor Voss, the same person who had gone after us before, filed another UPL complaint. Fortunately, this one died quickly when we showed that we weren't really using the old name.

RW: *What's new? What are you are you doing now that you didn't used to do?*

RP: For one thing, we have grown. We now see over 1,000 people in person each year and help 4,000 more by phone. In addition, since there are now more types of pre-printed forms available for the confirmation of child custody, visitation and so on, it means we help clients with more paperwork. We also have worked with courts to set up a court-approved visitation room so fathers can visit their children during the time when allegations of violence that form the basis for temporary protective (restraining) orders are being investigated. Incidentally, this gives us status as a public service with the courts. Also, I should mention our clinical program. Working with the two local law schools, third-year students are assigned to work with us as part of a family law clinical program, for which the students get credit. Since they are bar-certified to appear in court and supervised by Lesley Grey, a practicing lawyer who works with our program, it's a real plus.

RW: *Has the bar caused further trouble?*

RP: We have been investigated more than once. You can often tell when you get an inappropriate telephone call or visit, but officially we have been left alone.

RW: *Perhaps you have convinced them that you are too determined an opponent.*

RP: I don't know, but we do have allies. The media, particularly, gives us fair treatment. We are well into our second decade of service, so we have built a reputation as being a trustworthy news source. When you are under attack, it's terribly important to have access to the media to get your story out. To achieve this, you must make yourselves available, tell the truth and be ready to substantiate your statements.

RW: *Support, Inc. has obviously grown in lots of ways. Personally, what have you been doing to stay excited and not get stale?*

RP: I have done general mediation training at the college level and then followed up with specific courses in family mediation. I also host a TV show on our local city cable station which allows me to teach large numbers of women how to deal with the support problem. In a sense, I do self-help law on TV. It's exciting. I've even had family court judges appear in mock courtroom scenes to teach women how to handle the court process.

RW: *Didn't I also hear that you ran for public office?*

RP: Yes, for the state legislature, against a prominent and very entrenched opponent who had heavy financial backing and had been in office 20 years. I had no chance, but I had a great time and got plenty of opportunity to talk about consumer justice issues. The fact that the average person has no access to law is beginning to be important to voters. People know that our present system—which provides access to our legal system only for those who can afford high lawyer fees—is unfair.

RW: *Let me ask you one final thing. What about fathers? Aren't they victimized by the legal system, too? Who helps them?*

RP: The answer to your first question is yes, absolutely. The legal system treats everyone shabbily. For example, if a father loses his job or suffers a loss of income and can't afford to pay as much child support, he needs to get his support order reduced. But most fathers don't know how to do this, and if they can't afford to pay their normal bills, including child support, how can they afford a lawyer? The result is that the father, who may be doing his best, becomes a statistic for violating his child support order. In fact, the real statistic should indicate that one more person was denied access to the law. In short, the father who couldn't afford to petition the court to reduce his support order because of changed circumstances now is likely to be prosecuted because the system made it impossible for him to take advantage of his legal rights. Although I don't always agree with the positions fathers' groups take, I certainly support their efforts to teach men how to use the legal system and develop better ways for fathers to get affordable legal access. For example, I often invite fathers' groups to participate in my TV show, and Support, Inc. has dealt with both genders on issues of child support since 1989. Men and women will only achieve real structural reform when they realize that law in America is administered primarily for the benefit of lawyers and victimizes both groups. Men and women must work to-gether to achieve a more democratic justice system, as well as to cooperate to raise good kids.

Judy Lamb Interview

Judy Lamb is the Director of the Court Advocacy Program, a nonprofit service organization located in Weibern, New York, which provides legal information and emotional support to women dealing with domestic problems, including child custody and support, divorce, paternity and physical abuse.

Ralph Warner: *Judy, tell me a little about what you do.*

Judy Lamb: I'm the director of the Court Advocacy Program here in the Buffalo, N.Y. area. We provide information, referral and support to women concerned with being physically abused (battered) as well as those who need information about and/or assistance with divorce, custody, child support and paternity. Our services focus primarily on promoting personal growth, self-esteem and self-sufficiency. For the past four years, we have received approximately 6,000 phone calls and have provided a supportive presence in over 800 court appearances.

RW: *You operate as a nonprofit?*

JL: Yes, the Court Advocacy Program is a joint, state-funded program sponsored by the Western New York Coalition of Women for Child Support and Friendship House, a local umbrella organization which provides help for low-income citizens in a number of ways.

RW: *What do you do?*

JL: We distribute pamphlets about women's legal rights, hold occasional public information meetings and provide individual and group counseling designed to empower women to make their own decisions. Unlike lawyers, we never tell people what to do. It's a fundamental part of our approach that women, especially battered and abused women, have to decide for themselves to change their lives. If and when they do, we provide basic legal and practical information to assist them to do it.

RW: *Does this mean you go to court with women?*

JL: Often we do, if we're asked to. For example, a woman who has been battered might go to court to ask for a protective order, or a woman who has separated from her husband might request support. We would accompany them to court and sit in the back of the courtroom. The woman would present her own case if she didn't have a lawyer, or her lawyer would present it. We don't speak in court except in the very rare circumstances of being asked to participate by the referee or judge.

RW: *What if a woman is confused and wants your help in the middle of the proceeding?*

JL: It has happened, and we can provide counseling if the referee or judge temporarily delays the proceeding so we can confer. But remember, we only provide social work-type personal support and basic legal and practical information. We don't tell a woman what choice to make. Our job is to help people find the power to make their own choices. On the whole, judges and hearing examiners have been quite sensitive in allowing court advocates to support their clients. Unfortunately, on occasion, our clients did not receive that same sensitivity from lawyers.

RW: *All of this sounds pretty non-controversial.*

JL: That's what I thought, until I got a letter from the Erie County Bar Association asking me to appear before their Unlawful Practice Committee.

RW: *When was this?*

JL: Spring, 1989.

RW: *What reason did they give you?*

JL: That's it. The letter was quite vague, just stating that they wanted to discuss the activities of my program. It wasn't until the last sentence that I realized we were in trouble.

RW: *What was that sentence?*

JL: Well, the whole context of the letter appeared as if it was an invitation to a social function, but the last sentence said that when I appear before the Committee, I could be represented by a lawyer if I chose.

RW: *I see. The iron fist in the velvet glove approach. So what did you do?*

JL: I got on the phone to talk to the couple of local lawyers who were friendly to our program to find out what was going on.

RW: *And?*

JL: And it turned out that the bar was acting because they had received a letter of complaint about the program from a local lawyer who had recently lost a case. She represented the batterer and we provided support and information to the victim.

RW: *You mean a lawyer with a bad case of sour grapes wanted to put you out of business?*

JL: Essentially.

RW: *So what happened?*

JL: Even though the bar is, in my view, just a private trade group and shouldn't have the power to order me to do anything, I concluded that our program would be best served if I cooperated, so I went to the Unauthorized Practice Committee meeting. It consisted of ten lawyers (nine of them men) grilling me about everything Court Advocacy did.

RW: *Such as?*

JL: Oh, they objected to our use of the word "Advocacy" because only lawyers should be able to use that word. I pointed out that all of our materials say clearly that we are not lawyers and don't give legal advice, and that all sorts of groups advocate things, but they weren't convinced. They also wanted to know about the public education program we run to educate people about New York's new child support guidelines and the basic procedures of divorce. In fact, the public education program focused primarily on assertiveness in the legal system.

RW: *What was the objection?*

JL: To this day, I'm not really sure, but I think it came down to the fact that, in their view, lawyers own the law and have the right to sell it to the public. Anyone else who gets involved in public education about legal issues is trespassing on their turf. At the bar meeting, they were concerned about the fact that we charged a small fee for one of the pubic meetings. Their comment was I might be talking clients from attorneys. They were also concerned about my education. They claimed I wasn't qualified. They weren't interested in whether I knew and understood the new child support guidelines I had discussed at the meeting (in fact, I did, but many of them didn't). It was simple; if I wasn't an attorney, I wasn't qualified.

RW: *Even assuming, for purposes of argument, that lawyers are right when they claim they are the best qualified to provide legal information about physical abuse and child support, the next question is are lawyers doing this for low-income women.*

JL: That's it, they aren't. In fact, many laugh at the entire issue, believing that the problems of battered woman don't exist or are greatly exaggerated. Some even think our written materials telling woman their rights are hilarious. Just the same, some local lawyers do make a little money from representing desperate women who somehow scrape a legal fee together. They don't want to lose the business.

RW: *So, back to the story, what happened at the meeting?*

JL: Well, the funny thing is that so much of this sounds trivial when you explain it. One of their big objections had to do with the fact that the local Supreme (trial) Court clerk would occasionally notify me that a case had been dropped from the calender and reset for a different day.

RW: *What does that have to do with UPL?*

JL: What does any of this have to do with UPL? According to them, knowing in advance when a case would be heard was a lawyer privilege and, incidentally, one they often used to exert power over clients ("only I know when the court will proceed"). They just hated the fact that a nonlawyer had this information and could pass it on to their clients before they got around to it. I guess it is all part of their feeling that the legal system is set up for lawyers rather than the public.

RW: *What happened after the meeting?*

JL: Well, the funny thing is that even though there was a formal complaint against us, I never saw it or had a chance to directly respond. I heard via the grapevine that it was withdrawn. Part of the reason may have been that I did get the word out as to what was happening to our program. The UPL committee definitely knew that if they tried to close us down, we would fight back, including challenging their right to harass us on both anti-trust and constitutional grounds.

RW: *Could you explain that more?*

JL: Well, I was hardly being given a fair hearing, was I? My accusers were my judges. Also, where does the bar get the legal authority to establish a monopoly cartel and then claim the right to put competitors out of business? The whole thing smells bad.

RW: *Did the bar issue a formal statement?*

JL: No. I received some suspicious phone calls and visits from men posing as people needing help in child support matters, but that was it for eight months. Of course, despite our best efforts not to be intimidated, we all felt pressure. Finally, I received a call from the president of the UPL committee, who asked for a meeting and to review all of our material (handouts). At first, he wanted me to again appear before the UPL committee, but I refused. I let them know through my advising attorney that I would meet with the president of the committee alone, one-to-one, and that he could review materials but not copy them. After some fencing about time and location, I went to this office, but refused to allow him to make copies.

RW: *Weren't they widely available to the public?*

JL: Sure, but I wasn't going to submit them to an official inspection. I wasn't going to play willing victim to their kangaroo court approach.

RW: *So what happened at the meeting?*

JL: Essentially, the bar president kept politely trying to tell me that only lawyers could deal with legal affairs and I kept politely saying I didn't agree. I was obviously very angry about this continued intimidation process. He couldn't understand why. When I raised objections to the way I had been treated before the UPL Committee, he told me that lawyers and judges are brought in before committees all of the time. I replied that it wasn't quite the same—lawyers and judges were judged by their peers, but I wasn't. I suggested that my peers or the community should also judge my services through a public hearing. I went on to suggest the holding of a public hearing on the quality and availability of legal services to citizens of low and moderate incomes.

RW: *In short, the meeting was part of a continuing bar effort to put you in your place—intimidate you—and you politely tried to turn the tables, right?*

JL: Right—but I really believe what I said. The legal system must better serve the average citizen. The idea that lawyers own the law is absurd and produces bad results, especially in domestic disputes. It's appalling that our society countenances a system in which lawyers routinely fan the flames of domestic disputes because, by doing so, they profit.

RW: *Do they catch themselves playing such a negative role?*

JL: A good question. Normally I think they pretend that no conflict exists between their interests and those of their clients. But deep down, they must know there often is. I think trying to suppress this knowledge accounts for much of their anger when the conflicts are pointed out.

RW: *But since you are one of the people doing the pointing out, doesn't it mean you will probably stay on the hot spot?*

JL: Yes, but I see that as an opportunity. Our program really is based on a different model than lawyers—we don't tell people what to do. Or, to put it in lawyer terms, we don't give advice—either personal or legal. So again, in lawyer terms, we don't practice law.

RW: *I don't follow your point.*

JL: Well, if the practice of law consists of doing what lawyers do, or acting like a lawyer, we don't. We do something different and I think it needs to be better understood. We give people access to the law itself, and basic consumer information about the law.

RW: *It sounds a little bit like Alcoholics Anonymous approach. People can be given information about the problems concerning liquor, but whether to drink or not must be their own choice. If they want to die in the gutter—fine.*

JL: Well, that's the extreme, but in a way, yes. If a battered woman decides to stay in an abusive situation, that's her choice. We can only provide emotional support. However, if she wants to change her circumstances, we provide the information and referrals necessary for her to change her life.

RW: *What's next for your program? How would you like to grow and expand?*

JL: It is really unfortunate, but our court advocacy program right now is on hold. Our four-year grant ended in October 1990, and due to the devastating state budget cuts, public funding for non-residential domestic violence programs is nil. We hope to secure funding privately or through another public agency in Western New York. Our staff of three has always utilized student interns and volunteers, and hopefully we could increase this. Victims of either physical, emotional, verbal or economic abuse need help, and we plan to survive to provide it.

Catherine Jermany Interview

Catherine Jermany is currently Director of the National Association for Independent Paralegals, a nonprofit support and training group for independent paralegals based in Sonoma, California. For more than 20 years she has conducted paralegal training for a number of organizations, including the Legal Services Corporation, where she served as Director of Paralegal Training and Career Development, the National Paralegal Institute, as their training director, and the Children's Defense Fund, as their Community Legal Education Specialist.

Ralph Warner: *How did you get involved in a legal career?*

Catherine Jermany: If I really go back to the roots of it, it's because of my grandmother Callie Jackson, who started her own legal-help service, The Listening Post, in 1929. She was a grand old lady who died at the age of 105 in 1978. She lived in the big house of a courtway and was the informal lawyer for everyone around. My memories date from my own childhood in the late 1940s and early 1950s. She ran her business from her home and handled leases, burial rights advocacy (black people even had trouble getting equal rights after they were dead it those days), employment claims, you name it. Remember, in those days few people had access to the formal legal system, except perhaps for the very few who had money. People like my grandmother filled in the void—serving as legal advocates to unserved people. Today we would call her a "paralegal," a term which, incidentally, she would have hated.

RW: *Why is that?*

CJ: Because she was a proud, effective person. She wasn't para-anything or sub-anything. It wasn't in her nature to kowtow to anyone.

RW: *Somehow your being around Callie as a child inspired you?*

CJ: It sure did. For example, she built a library full of notebooks about people's legal rights which she kept on a shelf beside the sugar bowl. I keep similar types of notebooks today, although in the last ten years, lots of my information has been transferred to computer disks.

The other big influence was my father, who absolutely insisted on perfection. If you didn't get something right the first time, you could just keep doing it over until you did.

RW: *When did you first get involved in law?*

CJ: When I was fourteen, it was obvious to me that some elderly friends who used to live down the street, and had subsequently gone into a nursing home, were being mistreated. This was before all the modern nursing home regulations, so there were no obvious legal handles to use to help them. To make a long story short, I succeeded in going before the L.A. County Board of Supervisors and getting my friends reinstated in another nursing home (they had been kicked out of the first one when we complained), and having the first home closed down. The whole experience taught me that there was a process to deal with everything. This was a powerful lesson—to get things done you simply had to learn the process and then go step by step.

RW: *Today you're the Director of the National Organization for Independent Paralegals. How did you get involved with paralegals?*

CJ: I was involved with the Southern Christian Leadership Conference before Martin Luther King, Jr. was murdered. I organized in the South and West, and was also deeply involved in the Welfare Rights Movement. In 1968, there was a poor people's campaign in Washington D.C. I handled the parade permits, contracts, and even carried the money. In a sense, I was bag lady for the campaign.

RW: *Where does the paralegal work come in?*

CJ: In 1969, I was back in Los Angeles and I started an organization called the "Dependency Prevention Center," or DPC, to teach poor people how to stand on their own feet. We did welfare, health, housing, and education rights training. I was also still very involved with the local welfare rights organization. Both organizations were doing all sorts of things that were basically legal advocacy. In short, we were doing work that the Legal Aid Society of Los Angeles was unable to do because they didn't always understand the needs of the community. At any rate, a series of confrontations with Legal Service resulted in a number of community people who were trained by DPC being included on the Legal Services Board.

The next step, of course, was to get community people into the Legal Services offices themselves. We did this by doing welfare rights advocacy on a volunteer basis right at the Legal Aid office, throughout California and other states. Then, when openings for interviewers, receptionists and eventually case advocates happened, our people got the jobs. Of course, these new employees were short on traditional legal skills. They had plenty of fire to change things, but most had never worked in an office before. Through DPC, we provided the training.

RW: *What next?*

CJ: Because of all these activities, I ended up on the Board of Directors of the National Paralegal Institute in 1971 and I worked as a paralegal for the Children's Defense Fund.

RW: *You sure got around.*

CJ: I'm only telling you half of it.

RW: *What is the National Paralegal Institute and when did you start to work there?*

CJ: In 1973, the National Paralegal Institute, which is still in operation today, was founded to determine and define the role of paralegals. It conducted numerous studies and was the first to design and implement training for the nonlawyer staff of Legal Services Offices. Then, in 1976, when Legal Services brought all its training in-house, I did the same work for the federally funded Legal Services Corporation, as Director of Training.

RW: *What exactly did you do?*

CJ: Our job was to figure out what the various types of people who had stumbled into paralegal jobs in Legal Services offices needed to know to do their jobs better. For example, since lawyers don't like to interview people, or attend welfare or unemployment hearings, we taught laypeople how to do it. I trained people from Mississippi to Maine to Micronesia. Eventually we even trained lawyers how to run their offices better by the effective use of paralegals.

RW: *Looking back, how do you feel about the work you did in the early- and mid-1970s?*

CJ: On balance, great. We taught people lots of good things, but maybe in retrospect some not so good ones, too. For example, we trained paralegals to make lawyers more efficient. You know, things like tickler systems, efficient filing, doing their client interviews, etc.

RW: *And you see that as a mistake now?*

CJ: Well, in the sense that we taught paralegals to be somewhat dependent, yes. We supported the traditional lawyer-dominated system of delivering services that I now see is often a mistake. Let's get rid of the label "para" and call them legal specialists. Let's get specialists thinking and acting like entrepreneurs. The age of the deregulation of lawyers' monopoly is at hand. People need to be ready.

RW: *So you see paralegals escaping from lawyers?*

CJ: Sure, legal specialists should be able to work with or without lawyer supervisors as they choose. And they will be able to very soon now. The age of legal entrepreneurs providing routine legal services is already upon us because the public demands it. People are sick of our inefficient, over-priced, uncaring legal delivery system. It's got to change. And you know it's funny—in many ways people in low-income communities are open to change because they have had such minimal access to lawyers that their tradition of legal self-reliance is stronger.

RW: *And they have less to lose.*

CJ: That too.

RW: *If you wanted to open your own independent business to help non-lawyers deal with the legal system, would you go to a two- or three-year paralegal school?*

CJ: Personally, no. The reason is simple. Paralegal education is almost always general in nature. It's very weak on usable skills. Or, to say that another way, they don't teach you to do specific tasks independently.

RW: *What does an independent paralegal or legal specialist—someone who is working with nonlawyers around specific form filling-out tasks —need to know?*

CJ: Three things. First, they have to be able to deal with real people in the (often frustrating) course of real-life, legal problem solving. That is, they need to have good interviewing, counseling, data management and hand-holding skills. And don't underestimate the value of hand holding. People very often are unable to tell you what they really want or need—it's up to you to be able to help them find out not only what they need, but be able to guide them through the self-help law materials that are appropriate to their situation. Second, the independent paralegal must know how to do the mechanics of the particular task. Third, they must have enough general background or breadth in the particular subject area to be able to help the customer avoid the obvious pitfalls and get legal advice when needed.

RW: *How do people who have never done interviewing in a legal context, kept files or run an office learn to do this well?*

CJ: For starters, they need at least some structured interviewing, fact gathering, management and analysis training skills. There are definite techniques in conducting a customer visit and being able to assist the customer use the information properly. Through the National Association for Independent Paralegals, we provide this type of training for independent paralegals.

RW: *Which brings us to what you are doing now. Just what is the National Association for Independent Paralegals?*

CJ: The goal of the association is to provide timely training, information and business services and support to independent paralegals. These include statewide national training events, skills clinics, seminars and on-site evaluations for new and ongoing IP businesses. The Association also provides help and information on solving office problems, getting credit, hiring staff, getting insurance, etc. Publications include special alerts on unauthorized practice of law issues and legislative activity that affects independent paralegals.

RW: *How can one get more information about the NAIP?*

CJ: Just call us in Sonoma, California, at 1-800-542-0034.

RW: *You think about the independent paralegal movement every day. Tell me what's going on.*

CJ: The growth is unbelievable—that's first. Here at NAIP, we expected about 200 members in 1990, our first full year. Instead, we got over 1,400.

RW: *Where do all these people come from?*

CJ: All over the U.S. We now have members in every state. The largest percentage are in California, of course. You would expect that, since the IP movement was born here and it's also the most populous state.

RW: *What sorts of backgrounds do your members have?*

CJ: A wide variety. Former teachers, business people, social workers, you name it. About one-third are graduates of a formal paralegal school who often work in law firms now or have done so until recently. The goal of many of these people is to combine freelancing for lawyers with working directly for the public. In fact, we have so many members in this category, we have had to initiate some new programs. One is Legal Research Associate Training. It's designed for people who already have good legal research skills and want to learn how to do freelance legal research for lawyers at the same time they beginning offering legal form typing services directly to consumers.

RW: *What about the other two-thirds? You said they came from a wide variety of backgrounds. Can you be a little more specific?*

CJ: The largest group are business people who already deal directly with the public, such as tax preparers, public stenographers, people who run telephone answering services and so on. They see learning legal form preparation skills as a way to expand the services they already offer to the public.

RW: *Give me an example.*

CJ: We have members who run credit repair and counseling services, not the sleazy variety, but honest business. We teach them how to type bankruptcy forms as well as to better counsel people on how to avoid bankruptcy but not lose their wages and property through garnishments and repossessions. It's a great combination because credit counseling is generally recognized as a nonlawyer function. This means, in the credit context, nonlawyers can actually transfer legal information and expertise without falling victim to UPL charges. Then, if necessary, they can simply transfer over to the typing service model to prepare bankruptcy forms.

RW: *I gather bankruptcy form preparation is a fast-growing Independent Paralegal area. What are some others?*

CJ: Well, bankruptcy is the second, only after the demand for wills. With hard economic times, there is an unfulfilled need in virtually every community. Also living trusts, immigration form preparation, guardianships and support modifications are all rapidly growing areas.

RW: *What about the traditional bread and butter area—divorce?*

CJ: About 75% of all IPs already do divorces. In some states, such as California, Arizona and Oregon, the business is pretty well saturated. There are really not enough divorces to go around when you figure that there are lots of low-cost alternatives to IPs—for example, self-help lawbooks, battered woman's shelters and legal services for the poor all take chunks of the divorce business. And then, of course, lawyers have held on to most of the most affluent 25% of the market. In other states, where the IP movement is really just getting going, there is still plenty of opportunity to type divorces. But remember, as the U.S. population ages, divorce won't be the fast-growing field it was from the mid-1960s to the mid-1980s.

RW: *Let me pick one of the legal areas you mentioned—living trusts. Tell me what's going on generally first, and then what the NAIP is doing.*

CJ: As you know, lots of lawyers and have begun to advertise living trust seminars. These are typically designed to sell living trusts for $1,500-$2,500 each, a vastly inflated price given the amount of work involved. It didn't take IPs and financial planners long to see that they could make a good living doing the same thing for $250-$300.

RW: *Are you saying that IPs are engaging in guerrilla marketing by playing off the lawyers' seminar ads?*

CJ: Sure, many list their services in the same senior papers and newsletters that the lawyers advertise in.

RW: *How does the National Association for Independent Paralegals work with people who want to type living trusts or wills?*

CJ: To oversimplify, first we teach them a business development approach. One aspect of this is to go to all the lawyer-sponsored seminars in their area to find out what's being said and to count heads. Some of our trainees stand right up at the seminar and explain that they help people do much the same thing for much less money using a self-help typing approach.

RW: *Don't the lawyers have a cow?*

CJ: Well, a calf anyway, but there isn't much they can do. Remember it's a public meeting in a hotel conference room, so they can't call the cops. Often they try and retaliate in other ways. They might complain to the bar association or write a letter to a local newspaper attempting to put down nonlawyer services.

RW: *How do you prepare people for this?*

CJ: Remember, we teach IPs how to help people help themselves in a way that doesn't violate UPL laws. In this case, we use Denis Clifford's *Plan Your Estate With a Living Trust,* which has sold over 150,000 copies direct to the public. As long as the customer has the book and the IP follows the customer's instructions, there is no UPL problem.

RW: *Isn't this approach hard for some consumers, especially those that aren't experienced in the use of a fairly sophisticated book?*

CJ: Not if the IP is trained properly to act as a coach or guide to help the person extract relevant information from the self-help resource. To go back to bankruptcy for a second, it's important for the customer to locate the exempt property information for the state where he or she lives. For the IP to simply tell the customer this information has been held to be unauthorized practice. This is a ridiculous, lawyer-centric, legal rule, of course, but for now we are stuck with it. At any rate, to circumvent it, a well-trained IP can simply direct the consumer to the part of the book where this information is clearly spelled out.

RW: *Do you see this typing service model in which the consumer is educated to make their own decisions primarily as a cover-your-behind device for the IP.*

CJ:. No. It's an affirmative way to do business. The concept of self-reliance is buried deep in the American psyche. When functioning properly, the IP acts as a helper to the self-helper. When you see it that way, it's an exciting business niche. And best of all, approached this way, the consumer doesn't see the IP as a second-class lawyer and feel cheated because he or she can't afford a "real" lawyer. Instead, customers see the IP as a positive adjunct to their own learning process.

RW: *If we make an analogy to adding on a deck to a house, would it be fair to say that the IP should play the role of a teacher to a self-help builder rather than that of a cheap unlicensed contractor?*

CJ: Yes, and the best part is that whether it's a deck or a divorce, once a person really learns to do the particular task, they are empowered to attack other, larger problems. In the legal area, it really builds better citizens.

RW: *Enough theory. Now tell me some of the specifics of what NAIP does.*

CJ: We are based in Sonoma County, where we have a small training and development center. One of our major functions is to provide IPs with business development skills. In addition, we do skills training in particular areas, such as bankruptcy, estate planning, probate, family law (divorce, guardianship, restraining orders) and housing. For example, in bankruptcy, we periodically hold one- and two-day seminars. People (24 maximum at one time) come from all over America and become totally immersed in how to operate a top quality bankruptcy typing service with a minimum of risk of being charged with UPL.

RW: *Who teaches the substantive skills portion of your trainings?*

CJ: Usually the author or editor of the self-help book we recommend to the public as part of the do-it-yourself model. For example, Steve Elias, co-author of *How to File for Bankruptcy,* teaches the bankruptcy course.

RW: *Aren't there other places that IPs can get bankruptcy training?*

CJ: In theory yes, but in practice it's more difficult than you might imagine. For example, of the many NAIP members who graduated from an ABA-approved paralegal school, none took a bankruptcy course or was taught how to guide a customer through self-help law materials. Bankruptcy is not taught in law school either. Regrettably, we may be the only formal source for learning how to operate a self-help law service. Let me say a word about paralegal schools. The goal of a paralegal school is to prepare individuals to work for, and be supervised by, lawyers They are very good at this. Even students who enter paralegal school determined to have a lawyer-free career are soon convinced that working for lawyers is the only way to go. In other words, if you want to be an independent legal worker, don't become a full-time student at a school whose sole purpose is to turn out dependent ones.

RW: *What about paralegal groups? Don't they sponsor training?*

CJ: Yes, many paralegal organizations sponsor lectures and workshops on all sorts of legal tasks, including bankruptcy. However, to actually fill out the forms, you would be better off starting with a good self-help book, such as Nolo's *How to File for Bankruptcy,* hanging around the bankruptcy court and then volunteering in an office where a lot of bankruptcies are typed, such as a consumer legal services office. Remember, rule number one of learning any skill is to carefully observe the correct practice of that skill and then to correctly practice the skill yourself. This can best be done by volunteering and finding a mentor, or taking a course such as those which NAIP offers which adopts this approach.

RW: *Can you be a little more specific about the content of independent paralegal training? How do you teach the forest as well as the trees?*

CJ: Any legal area can be broken down into a finite number of discrete variables. These variables are interrelated. Understanding the forest is not only knowing what the main variables are but how they relate to each other. To impart this type of information to independent paralegals necessarily requires the use of outlines, charts, lists of steps and some basic rules. Of course, there is no substitute for real-life experience.

RW: *How, specifically, do you teach this information?*

CJ: Basically, I've always used an extended and detailed hypothetical case that covers an entire range of variables in the field. In working through the hypothetical, NAIP teaches each of the three skills I mentioned earlier and emphasizes the relationships between the various factors that will be present in each individual case.

RW: *Okay, can you tell me why it is so important to have a broad base of background information on a particular subject area. After all, don't most self-help typing services just type forms?*

CJ: If they do, they may find themselves in trouble in a hurry. For example, suppose someone gives you a set of facts and asks for a particular result. You need to know whether their fact situation entitles them to the remedy they want under current laws, and you also need to know whether the remedy they want is appropriate under the circumstances. What's more, you must know the self-help law material better than the customer in order to point out any mistakes they may have made and direct them to the part of the book or other resource that contains the correct information.

RW: *Can you be specific?*

CJ: Let's stick with bankruptcy. Suppose someone lists a whole bunch of bank credit card accounts and you see the dates involved indicate that the person was borrowing money from one bank, then opening another account, paying back the first and so on until they got a very high credit limit. They then borrow a lot of money and declare bankruptcy to avoid getting involved. You need to know what an illegal credit and kiting scheme is so you can decline to type the papers in this sort of situation.

RW: *Is this sort of thing a big danger to an independent legal worker?*

CJ: In addition, in any field, 15% or 20% of the people who walk in will be asking for help you can't provide, or there will be some other reason why you should not handle their business, like avoiding the occasional crook. You absolutely need to know enough to spot all the issues that may affect the case. As I've said, you have to live the particular areas of the law you are working in before you open your business. Remember, as with any professional, you have to be extremely careful not to get in over your head.

RW: *I know your organization also works with IPs all over the country who are trying to survive in an often hostile, lawyer-dominated legal environment. Tell me about the specifics of that.*

CJ: The key is to know your limitations. Everywhere throughout the U.S., the UPL laws are interpreted the same. Nonlawyers cannot do what lawyers do. This simply means that to minimize your risk of UPL, you must operate as a self-help law specialist, guiding your customers through published materials, without personally providing legal advice and preparing the paperwork under their direction. Secondly, to get a strong statewide organization in place to help IPs with organizing, training and fighting back against lawyer harassment. In many of the Western states, especially California, Oregon and Arizona, IP organizations already exist and we work them fairly closely. In states where the movement is newer, we try to identify a strong person as the initial state coordinator. They then try to pull the others together. It's really not too difficult, since a strong organization offers obvious protection against UPL charges. It's not hard to see that it's a lot easier for the bar to pick off an isolated IP than it is to go up against a well-organized group.

RW: *The main purpose of the state groups is to protect members from unauthorized practice charges?*

CJ: No, that's only one function. Once the group is in place, it can start training members in the right ways to do business—good skills development, good consumer recourse and other honest business practices. A consumer needs to know he or she will get good services from an IP If they do, they will use more services, tell their friends and won't complain to the bar. It's a virtuous circle.

RW: *How many states currently have formal independent paralegal organizations?*

CJ:　Sixteen have organizations that meet on a regular basis and do the things I just mentioned. In another 20 or so, organizations are at a formative stage. In some areas—North and South Dakota, Wyoming, Utah and Nebraska, for example—we emphasize a regional approach to organization, because it will be a long time before there are enough IPs to organize on a state-by-state basis.

RW:　*How else do you help the state organizations?*

CJ:　We travel to various states to attend their meetings, provide training, etc.

RW:　*What about for people outside of California who are in need of paralegal services?*

CJ:　We provide a structured referral service. It really got started by accident, when we got a write-up in *U.S. News and World Report*. It generated 7,000 calls and we began referring consumers to local IPs. It also made us realize that NAIP's approach to increasing access to the legal system is newsworthy, so we decided to make a concerted effort to market the IP movement nationally. When calls come in, we screen them and look for an IP who handles the type of need the consumer has in the same geographical area.

RW:　*What do you see for the legal movement in the years just ahead?*

CJ:　Right now, the movement is consumer driven—consumers want and need better legal access at a reasonable cost. Unfortunately, some IPs don't see that—they believe they are prospering because of something they are doing as individuals. So the answer is that IPs will do well individually and as a group as long as they see that their continued success depends on their doing an excellent job to meet consumer needs. People are fed up with lawyers—not only because of ridiculous fees but because lawyers deny them control over their own lives. As long as IPs deliver good services that empower people at a reasonable cost, all will be well. If they begin to act like junior lawyers, they will be in trouble.

Stephen Elias Interview

Stephen Elias is an author of a number of self-help law books, including *How To File for Bankruptcy,* and *Legal Research: How to Find and Understand the Law.* A senior legal editor at Nolo Press, he was a member of the California bar's eight-person Public Protection Committee, which unanimously recommended, in 1988, that the California legislature repeal the state's Unauthorized Practice of Law statutes. In his capacity as General Counsel to the National Association for Independent Paralegals, Steve teaches paralegals how to avoid engaging in the unauthorized practice of law.

Ralph Warner: Let's plunge right in at the deep end. How do you currently see the question of whether independent paralegals are vulnerable to being fined or jailed for the unauthorized practice of law?

Stephen Elias: I'm quite optimistic that properly trained legal form preparers can almost completely avoid the risk of being charged with UPL, and in the unlikely event they are charged, be able to successfully fend them off.

RW: *Let's talk a little about UPL. You seem to think it can be defined—so it can be avoided. But when you were a member of the California bar's Public Protection Committee in 1987-1988, you said that the phrase "practice of law"—and therefore the "unauthorized practice of law"—could not be intelligibly defined.*

SE: Logically it can't be. Although some states have tried to give the "practice of law" a very specific definition, the definitions end up circular in nature—using words and phrases like "legal advice or counselling," "preparation of legal instruments and contracts" and "activity requiring the services of a legally trained and skilled individual." Clearly, this type of language can apply to virtually any law-related activity and is therefore far too broad to inform nonlawyers what they can and cannot do. Most states, like California, don't even try to define UPL. Instead, they rely on the Alice-in-Wonderland world of the courts, where judges, serving as lackeys for the legal monopoly, decide on a case-by-case basis whether UPL has occurred. In this world—which is absurd but real—UPL is all too easy to define. Here it is: "If anyone other than a lawyer acts in a way that induces a customer to rely on their expertise in matters that are customarily handled by a lawyer, it's UPL."

RW: *Aren't you being overly pessimistic in your definition? I mean, as legal information becomes more and more accessible to the public, doesn't it pass beyond the purview of the UPL laws?*

SE: Sure. And my definition recognizes that when lawyers stop becoming involved in a particular area, it opens up to others. But until the lawyers fully acknowledge that they have given it up, it remains squarely under the UPL laws. To get an idea of how the courts define UPL, take a look at how the judge instructed the jury in a 1990 Wisconsin UPL prosecution. He stated that UPL "is the giving of professional legal advice and instruction to clients to inform them of their rights and obligations, or the preparation for clients of documents requiring knowledge of legal principle not possessed by ordinary laymen." Kind of hard to wriggle out of that.

RW: *Given this hopelessly broad definition of UPL, how can you be so optimistic about the future of independent paralegals? Are you saying that the concept of UPL has become irrelevant to an independent paralegal's day-to-day work life?*

SE: Yes and no. As long as the IP limits himself or herself to distributing self-help law materials and preparing paperwork under their customer's direction and doesn't directly transfer legal expertise, he or she is pretty safe. And this legal typing service model has an additional benefit. It does a much better job of empowering and informing customers than the old lawyer model of taking over responsibility for getting the task accomplished.

RW: *Whoa! Slow that down. When you start talking about models, I start thinking about cars or computers. Explain what you mean by model in the context of providing legal services to the public.*

SE: Okay. The lawyer or professional model of legal services presumes that the provider of the service has a special or professional competence on which the seeker of the service can and should rely on to get the service accomplished. The simplest form of law office has two people—the lawyer, who is the legal expert, and the legal secretary, who knows all the court rules about typing, filing and serving legal documents. Under this model, the client typically gains little understanding about either the underlying laws that affect his or her case or the procedures, and is forced to depend almost completely upon the law office having the requisite knowledge and skill.

The legal typing service model stands the lawyer/professional model on its head. The typing service makes sure that the customer uses a book or other constitutionally protected information source to inform himself or herself about the laws and procedures involved in the particular task, and limits its role to the same typing, filing, serving and other clerical tasks that legal secretaries routinely carry out in law offices under the attorney's direction. In a very real sense, the customer, aided by the legal information source, takes the place of the lawyer, and the independent paralegal serves as the customer's legal secretary.

RW: *The difference between these models seems clear enough when you explain it. But will the the state bar associations know the difference? Won't the bar still use the UPL laws to harass businesses operating under the legal typing service model?*

SE: They may try, but the typing services have legal authority on their side. Even before the original California Wave Project in the early 1970s, that you and Ed Sherman pioneered, public stenographers or scriveners were allowed to type forms of any kind for the general public, including such legal forms as wills and divorce petitions, as long as the customers ran the show. And the courts have ruled for over twenty years that the First Amendment to the U.S. Constitution allows nonlawyers to prepare and distribute written legal information addressed to the general public rather than to an individual customer. All the legal typing service does is combine these two protected functions, a combination that the courts have specifically approved in a number of reported decisions. In short, the typing service does have the law on its side as long as it doesn't try to augment the published information with legal expertise of its own.

RW: *But isn't the typing service model of transferring information by referring customers to self-help law books artificial and worky, as opposed to an IP just telling a customer what the legal rules and procedures are and kind of taking charge of the case?*

SE: Perhaps, but in addition to avoiding UPL charges, the typing service model also produces a better result. The customer may have to work harder than if someone did all the work, but the rewards for this extra effort include large dollar savings, control over the case and enormous satisfaction at successfully completing a legal task. Look at the health professions. The alternative health movement has taught us the same lesson—doctors aren't god, and better health decisions are made when patients fully inform themselves with accurate, up-to-date information and make their own decisions based on that information.

RW: *What about the real world of real customers who need a divorce, bankruptcy or adoption but have language or reading problems? Not everyone can or will master a 300-page self-help law manual in enough detail to tell a legal typing service operator what to do.*

SE: There are all sorts of ways to empower people with language or reading difficulties—a good translation, video and audio tape presentations and group seminars are obvious ones. But push this back a step. I can't accept the prevalent social worker/lawyer view that poor people, immigrants and minorities are too dumb or incapacitated to help themselves. It's not only silly and insulting, but often borders on racism. Low-income and minority communities have lots of help networks—families, churches, schools and government agencies. For instance, I know of a recently arrived Vietnamese family that relies on their 15-year old son—whose English language skills are the best in the family—to interpret the IRS tax brochure and help prepare the family's tax returns. The idea that the poor and minorities need professionals—almost always white professionals—to take over their problem and solve it for them is mostly a fantasy of our professional classes, who depend upon dependent people for their livelihoods.

RW: *But aren't there many legal tasks that are just flat out too complicated for people with little education or reading skills to undertake?*

SE: Of course—there are plenty of legal tasks that challenge or exceed the skills of most lawyers. But most routine legal tasks can be broken down into a series of small, straightforward steps. This fact has resulted in upwards of 70 Nolo self-help law books that allow non-lawyers to successfully undertake 70 different legal tasks—by themselves. Although an entire legal task might be viewed as complicated, each step in the process is seldom difficult. So it's simply a matter of following the steps in the book, one step at a time. This does not require a higher education or sophisticated reading skills. It just takes a little confidence and the willingness to persevere—human attributes the successful legal typing service operator, acting as a kind of cheerleader, should be able to engender in its customers.

RW: *Let's return to unauthorized practice. You seem to advocate an approach to operating an IP service that makes UPL irrelevant. But isn't the concept becoming irrelevant anyway? In some areas, aren't IPs supplementing the legal typing service method by occasionally answering customers' questions about basic legal issues free from lawyer harassment?*

SE: Sure. During any given year, 99 out of 100 IPs who directly provide customers with legal expertise will do so without a peep from the bar or district attorney. And don't get me wrong. The fact that I prefer the legal typing service model doesn't mean I approve of the UPL laws. If it were up to me, these laws would be off the books and out of the courts—yesterday. Despite the lawyer refrain that UPL laws are there to protect the public from charlatans, their real function is to protect the lawyer monopoly—which results in a law access gap for millions of people.

RW: *But getting back to the point, do independent paralegals really have to worry much about the UPL laws if they aren't enforced?*

SE: Unfortunately, it only takes that one-out-of-a-hundred UPL prosecution to accomplish the bar's objective. Although enforcement of the UPL laws is uneven and sporadic, the potential for harassment is still always present. The bar well knows that several prosecutions spaced out over a five-to-ten year period will put the fear of god into anyone thinking about crossing the UPL line. And such prosecutions do exist—I know of at least a dozen in the last year or two in a number of states, including Nevada, Florida, Louisiana, Oregon and Wisconsin, in addition to California.

RW: *What about the West Coast? Depending on who's counting, there are over 1,000 nonlawyer typing services in operation. Clearly, the fear of the bar association doesn't seem to be overwhelming in that part of the country.*

SE: Good point. Lots of the West Coast IPs follow the typing service model I discussed earlier and feel well protected from UPL charges. But those who don't are still subject to feelings of extreme insecurity when a UPL prosecution—no matter how infrequent—occurs. And many more who might have become IPs are probably scared off. Anybody who doubts the repressive power of the California UPL laws should consider the case of Mershan Shaddy, an IP in San Diego. In 1989 Shaddy was convicted of UPL and sentenced to jail for providing a prospective customer (really an investigator wearing a wire) with basic information about what she might expect if she filed for divorce. Throughout the interview, Shaddy reminded the customer/investigator that he was giving her a legal "orientation"— for which he charged the more than fair price of $35—and that she would have to consult with a lawyer before he would type her papers. The judge informed the jury that providing this type of basic information constitutes the giving of legal advice, and the jury convicted on the basis of the judge's instruction. The case has been appealed, and hopefully will be reversed. But since the appeals court is staffed by lawyer-judges, Shaddy's ability to have a fair appeal is obviously in doubt.

RW: *But come on Steve, isn't pointing to one UPL prosecution and using it to paint a picture of extreme legal jeopardy for IPs who offer legal expertise to the public the same as saying that DAs still actively prosecute the crime of adultery because every year there are a couple of oddball prosecutions?*

SE: As long as the widespread potential exists for jerk DAs to jail, fine or shut down IPs who in reality are only providing basic legal information, we haven't made real progress, at least on the UPL front. The real progress is in the number of IPs who are adopting the legal typing service model to avoid confrontation with UPL altogether.

RW: *I get your point, but I've recently talked to a number of IPs who are verbally providing some legal information and are doing just fine. They communicate regularly with the local judges, get referrals from local attorneys and, in some cases, even are trained by court clerks and local lawyers. Some are even so much an integral part of the legal community that they are invited to bar association social functions. Isn't this a sign that the lawyer-driven UPL monolith is breaking down, and that IPs may find allies in unexpected places?*

SE: Yes and no. It's like some of the European Jews in the Middle Ages. The commercial power structure needed them to do the banking that Christians couldn't do because their religion prohibited them from charging interest. But this important function didn't always translate to official protection when the public's mood turned ugly, and Jews were rounded up to be deported, burned at the stake or moved into ghettos. Maybe I'm being too pessimistic, but I've seen too many examples of "friendly" lawyers who suddenly drop out of sight when an IP gets some heat from the local DA. The unfortunate truth is that only lawyers are licensed to practice law, and until the laws against unauthorized practice of law go away, the only truly safe way to operate is to use the legal typing service model and avoid the professional model. It's not the way I want it to be, but I think that's the way it is.

RW: *What about computers? I've talked with a number of independent paralegals who are successfully using software written for lawyers to crank out all kinds of paperwork. Doesn't software eliminate most of your UPL concerns?*

SE: Not really. When an IP uses a questionnaire to get the customer's information in a form that can be put into the computer, they are doing the same thing that attorneys do. Although the software may have some built-in expertise, the user still has to decide which forms to use and what information to put in these forms, and these are functions that have classically been considered to be the practice of law. Only if the customer has direct access to the information necessary to intelligently complete the questionnaire and make the decisions that the task requires would the IP be safe from UPL charges.

RW: *Suppose the questionnaire is published as part of the software package sold to consumers, as an aid to their use of the computer?*

SE: That's an interesting question. A questionnaire that is closely keyed to a self-help resource, such as a computer manual, could collect information for the customer while giving the customer the means to provide it on an informed basis. Same with the choices that the task involves. This approach would let IPs use computer software to efficiently produce legal documents, but under the customer's informed direction, which avoids the UPL laws the same as the legal typing service model I mentioned earlier.

Debbie Chalfie Interview

Debbie Chalfie is the former Legislative Director of HALT—An Organization of Americans for Legal Reform. She is a leader in the effort to provide the average American better and fairer access to law and has spearheaded HALT's efforts to pass legislation allowing nonlawyers to deliver legal services to the public.

Ralph Warner: Debbie, can you begin by telling me a little about who you are and what you do.

Debbie Chalfie: I've been at HALT since 1985. Incidentally, for the uninitiated, HALT is the only national public interest group representing consumers of legal services—the average American who needs access to the legal system.

RW: *Before we get into what you do at HALT, fill me in on your background.*

DC: In college, in the mid-1970s I was actively involved in the women's movement and civil rights issues, mostly on anti-rape and anti-violence concerns. I graduated in 1979 and went on to law school.

RW: *You didn't come out a typical lawyer, or for that matter, even a typical public interest lawyer. Most lawyers, no matter what side of an issue they are on, look and sound, even smell like lawyers; you don't.*

DC: Thanks. I'm sure a little lawyer must have rubbed off, but I was protected to some extent by the fact that I didn't go to law school with the intention of becoming a practicing lawyer. I wanted to learn what lawyers knew, not to be one. I wanted the information and skills lawyers had to help me work on issues I believed in.

RW: *I have heard thousands of law students say much the same thing when they entered law school, but by the time they left, they looked exactly like lawyer clones.*

DC: Maybe the difference is that many of those people really wanted to be lawyers—lawyers for good causes, perhaps, but lawyers just the same. I really didn't want to be a lawyer, so I was never on the same track.

RW: *How did you end up working with HALT?*

DC: HALT was my second job out of law school. After graduating, my first job was at a public interest law firm, where I worked on civil rights and consumer protection issues. It was there that I began to see accountability of lawyers to clients as a key problem within our legal system.

RW: *Slow that down for me.*

DC: This public interest law firm was also a teaching clinic for law students. Each week, we conducted a seminar for the students on the practicalities of public interest law. One of those seminars was about the dilemma public interest lawyers face when their clients' needs and desires conflict with their own agenda and goals. I respected the dedication and work of public interest lawyers, but I was disturbed that very few of them wanted to face the fact that it was the lawyers, not the clients, who were calling the shots.

RW: *This connects pretty directly to issues HALT worries about, doesn't it— the American legal system primarily serves lawyers' interests, and the concerns of the average American have been forgotten?*

DC: Absolutely. Consumers of legal services have almost no rights. It's really the last frontier of consumer advocacy. Led by lawyers, consumers have won reforms in loads of areas, such as product safety, fair credit, the environment, even health care and the quality and availability of services provided by doctors. But lawyers have a huge blind spot when it comes to consumer rights—themselves. Even most public interest lawyers don't see that the American legal system is run in large measure to benefit the legal elite, not the public.

RW: *Let's get down to the bare bones; do you mean that ordinary citizens are denied reasonable access to the laws and legal procedures that affect their lives?*

DC: Sure. And that's why the work HALT does is so necessary. The legal system is structured in such a way that most people can't vindicate their rights. The legal system is expensive, slow, unduly antagonistic and often inequitable. This means most people are shut out and ill served. HALT seeks to make the legal system more affordable and accessible, and the legal profession more responsive and account-able, to the public. We educate the public about their options and we also lobby for legal reform.

RW: *Today you are in California, trying to get the California legislature to adopt HALT-sponsored legislation designed to cut back the lawyers' monopoly on providing legal services. Under the HALT bill, legal tech-nicians (independent paralegals) could legally deliver services to the public.*

DC: Yes. Unauthorized practice of law statutes (UPL laws) are used by lawyers to kill competition. Doing away with them, or at last sharply curtailing them, is at the heart of HALT's agenda to provide con-sumers better legal access.

RW: *Can you explain why in a bit more detail?*

DC: UPL laws, which ensure lawyers a monopoly over the delivery of legal services, have the direct effect of keeping prices for legal ser-vices beyond the reach of millions. By being able to jail their com-petitors, lawyers are free to charge more. Since there is no place else to get legal information or help with filing legal paperwork, you either pay a lawyer or go without.

RW: *Without UPL laws, all sorts of people would be able to sell legal infor-mation and form-preparation assistance and advice, and consumers would be free to decide who to buy it from and how much to pay.*

DC: Exactly. They could choose to purchase services from a lawyer and pay a relatively high price or shop around for other providers. It's what we already do in hundreds of areas of our lives. For example, when we need to fix our car, we can go to a dealer, an independent garage that specializes in our particular make of car, or a corner gas station. It's up to us as consumers to make the choice—and for the most part, we make it well.

RW: *Bar associations, judges and other lawyer interest groups say that non-lawyers aren't competent to render legal services.*

DC: They may say that, but the facts don't back them up. Lawyers claim that only they, because of their training, are competent to perform divorces, bankruptcies, name changes and other routine legal tasks. Yet lawyers are not trained in law school or tested on bar examinations to deliver these basic consumer services. Also, all the studies show that consumers who've used paralegals have few complaints, while nearly 100,000 complaints are filed against lawyers every year. In short, the lawyers' monopoly is no guarantee of competence or consumer protection, and there is no intellectual basis to justify restricting competition by nonlawyers. But even if lawyers cleaned up their acts and delivered a better quality service to consumers, it would make no difference—what good is a monopoly, even a high quality one, which sets prices so high the vast majority of people can't afford their services? It's a question of balance. Sure, consumers want competent service, but they also want affordable access. A better setup would address both interests.

RW: *What specifically is HALT doing to cut back or eliminate UPL laws?*

DC: Ever since its founding in the late 1970s, HALT has been a strong proponent of busting the lawyer monopoly. For example, in the early 1980s, we supported Rosemary Furman, the Florida legal secretary who typed low-cost divorces and provided other legal paperwork services for very low fees, and, as a result, was hounded by the Florida bar. We organized the public awareness and letter-writing campaign that kept her from going to jail. We have also won legislation to allow court clerks to give consumers over-the-counter legal information and form-processing help.

RW: *Great, but what about legislation that will really change things?*

DC: In California, HALT is spearheading a bill to allow nonlawyer legal technicians (or Independent Paralegals—call them by whatever name you like) to provide legal services directly to the public without lawyer supervision.

RW: *In all areas?*

DC: For starters, in at least 16 areas of law—divorce, bankruptcy, real estate transactions, immigration, small business incorporation, probate, wills, consumer complaints and other everyday legal matters.

RW: *You mean the HALT bill would suspend UPL in these areas to let non-lawyers freely compete?*

DC: Yes, but they would have to meet some sensible requirements. For example, a legal tech would have to register with a state agency, be at least 18, have no prior convictions for consumer fraud and could not be a disbarred lawyer. In addition, for services where a consumer could be irreparably harmed if the services were not done right, paralegals would have to pass a practice-related test.

RW: *You mean these nonlawyers would have to take a mini-bar examination?*

DC: No, the exam they would take would be directly related to the particular task to be performed. Unlike the bar exam, it wouldn't test theoretical knowledge, but whether a provider knew the rules and procedures to competently do the work.

RW: *So someone working in the immigration area would not be tested about probate, right? But what exactly would they be tested on?*

DC: The details of each test would be up to a board under the jurisdiction of the Department of Consumer Affairs. But the point would be to test on one's actual competence to do the work. For example, in the immigration field, a candidate might be asked, "If a person with permanent resident status wanted to bring a family member to the U.S., what procedures are available and how should the necessary applications be completed?"

RW: *Once a person registered or passed this exam, they could open a street corner office on the order of an H & R Block tax preparation office?*

DC: Yes. And remember, the test would only be required in relatively complex areas, or where consumers need an up-front assurance of competence. If a legal tech wanted to do a basic uncontested divorce or probate, he or she would need to register with the state, but not pass an exam. And typing services wouldn't have to do anything, as long as they limit their services to just typing.

RW: *Don't nonlawyer legal services like you describe already exist in most California cities?*

DC: Yes, so in some ways the HALT-sponsored bill legislates the status quo.

RW: *If that's true, why do we need it?*

DC: Today, nonlawyer providers exist under a cloud of possible illegality. They're always open to selective prosecution, which usually happens when they get a complaint from a lawyer stung by the competition. The HALT bill would remove this daily threat, allowing the existing ones to flourish and encourage many more people to enter the field. When this happens, consumers will have much better access to affordable legal help.

RW: *How would doing away with UPL change the way typing services work?*

DC: Today, many typing service operators are afraid to answer even the simplest legal question for fear of being charged with UPL. They have to refer all customers to other information sources, which can be cumbersome. In the 16 areas covered by our bill, this would no longer be necessary.

RW: *You mean the so-called model I talk about in this book of always referring a customer who asks for legal information to a protected source of legal information, such as books, videos or lawyers, could be bypassed?*

DC: Right, but remember the HALT bill wouldn't restrict or regulate self-help typing services in any way. No one would have to take an exam or register to be a public stenographer. The HALT bill would legalize everyone, but it would only regulate those who wanted to do more than type.

RW: *What about the rest of the country? So far, your bill has only been introduced in California?*

DC: It's also been introduced in Oregon, and we are in touch with legislators in other states who are interested in introducing it. We are excited about that, and expect that by the time these words are published, it will be introduced in at least two more states.

NOLO PRESS

ACCESS TO LAW

CATALOG

ESTATE PLANNING & PROBATE

Plan Your Estate With a Living Trust
Attorney Denis Clifford • National 2nd ed.
Covers every significant aspect of estate planning and gives detailed, specific instructions for preparing a living trust to avoiding expensive and lengthy probate court. Includes all the forms and instructions to let you prepare an estate plan designed for your special needs.
$19.95/NEST

Make Your Own Living Trust
Attorney Denis Clifford • National 1st ed.
Find out how a living trust works, how to create one, and how to determine what kind of trust is right for you. Contains all the forms and instructions you need to prepare a: basic living trust to avoid probate, a marital life estate trust (A-B trust) to avoid probate and estate taxes, and a back-up will.
$19.95/LITR

Nolo's Simple Will Book
Attorney Denis Clifford • National 2nd ed.
It's easy to write a legally valid will using this book. The instructions and forms enable you to draft a will for all needs, including naming a personal guardian for children, leaving property to minor children or young adults and updating a will when necessary. Good in all states except Louisiana.
$17.95/SWIL

How to Probate an Estate
Julia Nissley • California 7th ed.
If you are responsible for winding up the legal and financial affairs of a deceased family member or friend, you can save costly attorney's fees by handling the probate process yourself. This book also explains how to settle an estate and how to transfer assets that don't require probate, including property held in joint tenancy or living trusts or as community property.
$34.95/PAE

The Conservatorship Book
Lisa Goldoftas & Attorney Carolyn Farren • California 1st ed.
When someone becomes incapacitated due to illness or age, a conservator may need to take charge of their medical and financial affairs. This book comes with all the forms and instructions necessary to file conservatorship documents, appear in court, be appointed conservator and end a conservatorship.
$24.95/CNSV

Who Will Handle Your Finances If You Can't?
Attorneys Denis Clifford and Mary Randolph • National 1st ed.
Contains all the forms and instructions necessary to create a durable power of attorney for finances. Creating this document means that you, not courts and lawyers, decide who will handle your financial affairs if illness or old age makes it impossible for you to handle them yourself.
$19.95/FINA

law form kits

Nolo's Law Form Kit: Wills
Attorney Denis Clifford and Lisa Goldoftas • National 1st ed.
Create a legally valid will, quickly and easily. You can draft a will that distributes your property according to your wishes, select beneficiaries, choose a guardian for your children, set up a children's trust and appoint an executor. Good in all states except Louisiana.
$14.95/KWL

audio cassette tapes

Write Your Will
Attorney Ralph Warner with Joanne Greene • National 1st ed. • 50 minutes
This tape answers the most frequently asked questions about writing a will and covers all key issues: What provisions the will must contain, how to provide for children and grandchildren, how to appoint a guardian, how to assign an executor, how to have the will signed and witnessed, when a living trust is useful and when a lawyer might be needed.
$14.95/TWYW

software

WillMaker
Nolo Press • Version 4.0
Prepare and update a legal will—safely, privately and without the expense of a lawyer. Leading you step-by-step in a question-and-answer format, *WillMaker* builds a will around your answers, taking into account your state of residence. Comes with a 200-page manual which provides the legal background necessary to make sound choices. Good in all states except Louisiana.
IBM PC $69.95/WI4
MACINTOSH $69.95/WM4

Nolo's Personal RecordKeeper
Carol Pladsen & Attorney Ralph Warner • Version 3.0
Lets you record the location of personal, financial and legal information in over 200 categories and subcategories. It also allows you to create lists of insured property, compute net worth, consolidate emergency information into one place and export to *Quicken®* home inventory and net worth reports. Includes a 320-page manual filled with practical and legal advice.
IBM PC $49.95/FRI3
MACINTOSH $49.95/FRM3

Nolo's Living Trust
Attorney Mary Randolph • Version 1.0
By putting certain assets into a trust, you save your heirs the headache, time and expense of probate. *Nolo's Living Trust* lets you set up an individual or shared marital trust, make your trust document legal, transfer your property to the trust, and change or revoke the trust at any time. The manual guides you through the process, and help screens and an on-line glossary explain key legal terms and concepts. Good in all states except Louisiana.
MACINTOSH $79.95/LTM1

GOING TO COURT

Everybody's Guide to Municipal Court
Judge Roderic Duncan • California 1st ed.
Explains how to prepare and defend the most common types of contract and personal injury law suits in California Municipal Court. Provides step-by-step instructions for preparing and filing all forms, gathering evidence and appearing in court.
$29.95/MUNI

Everybody's Guide to Small Claims Court
Attorney Ralph Warner • National 5th ed. • California 11th ed.
These books will help you decide if you should sue in Small Claims Court, show you how to file and serve papers, tell you

what to bring to court and how to collect a judgment.
NATIONAL $15.95/NSCC
CALIFORNIA $16.95/ CSCC

How to Win Your Personal Injury Claim

Attorney Joseph Matthews • National 1st ed.
Armed with the right information anyone can handle a personal injury claim. This book shows you how to avoid insurance company run-arounds, evaluate what your claim is worth and obtain a full and fair settlement —without a lawyer.
$24.95/PICL

Fight Your Ticket

Attorney David Brown • California 5th ed.
Shows you how to fight an unfair traffic ticket—when you're stopped, at arraignment, at trial and on appeal.
$18.95/FYT

Collect Your Court Judgment

Gini Graham Scott, Attorney Stephen Elias & Lisa Goldoftas • California 2nd ed.
Step-by-step instructions and all the forms you need to collect a court judgment from a debtor's bank accounts, wages, business receipts, real estate or other assets.
$19.95/JUDG

How to Change Your Name

Attorneys David Loeb & David Brown • California 5th ed.
Explains how to change your name legally and provides all the forms with detailed instructions on how to fill them out.
$19.95/NAME

The Criminal Records Book

Attorney Warren Siegel • California 3rd ed.
Shows you step-by-step how to seal criminal records, dismiss convictions, destroy marijuana records and reduce felony convictions.
$19.95/CRIM

Legal Breakdown: 40 Ways to Fix Our Legal System

Nolo Press Editors and Staff • National 1st ed.
40 common-sense proposals to make our legal system fairer, faster, cheaper and more accessible.
$8.95/LEG

The Legal Guide for Starting & Running a Small Business

Attorney Fred S. Steingold • National 1st ed.
An essential resource for every small business owner. Learn how to form a sole proprietorship, partnership or corporation, negotiate a lease, hire and fire employees, write contracts and resolve disputes.
$19.95/RUNS

Sexual Harassment on the Job

Attorneys William Petrocelli & Barbara Kate Repa • National 1st ed.
Describes what harassment is, what the laws are that make it illegal and how to put a stop to it. Invaluable for employees experiencing harassment and for employers interested in creating a policy against harassment and a procedure for handling complaints.
$14.95/HARS

Your Rights in the Workplace

Dan Lacey • National 1st ed.
A comprehensive guide to workplace rights— from hiring to firing. Learn the rules about wages and overtime, maternity and parental leave, unemployment and disability insurance, worker's compensation, job safety, discrimination and illegal firings and layoffs.
$15.95/YRW

How to Write a Business Plan

Mike McKeever • National 4th ed.
If you're thinking of starting a business or raising money to expand an existing one, this book will show you how to write the business plan and loan package necessary to finance your business and make it work.
$19.95/SBS

Marketing Without Advertising

Michael Phillips & Salli Rasberry • National 1st ed.
Outlines practical steps for building and expanding a small business without spending a lot of money on advertising.
$14.00/MWAD

The Partnership Book

Attorneys Denis Clifford & Ralph Warner • National 4th ed.
Shows you step-by-step how to write a solid partnership agreement that meets your needs. It covers initial contributions to the business, wages, profit-sharing, buy-outs, death or retirement of a partner and disputes.
$24.95/PART

How to Form A Nonprofit Corporation

Attorney Anthony Mancuso • National 1st ed.
Explains the legal formalities involved and provides detailed information on the differences in the law among all 50 states. It also contains forms for the Articles, Bylaws and Minutes you need, along with complete instructions for obtaining federal 501 (c) (3) tax exemptions and qualifying for public charity status.
$24.95/NNP

The California Nonprofit Corporation Handbook

Attorney Anthony Mancuso • California 6th ed.
Shows you step-by-step how to form and operate a nonprofit corporation in California. It includes the latest corporate and tax law changes, and the forms for the Articles, Bylaws and Minutes.
$29.95/NON

How to Form Your Own Corporation

Attorney Anthony Mancuso • California 7th ed. • New York 2nd ed. • Texas 4th ed.
These books contain the forms, instructions and tax information you need to incorporate a small business yourself and save hundreds of dollars in lawyers' fees.
CALIFORNIA $29.95/CCOR
NEW YORK $24.95/NYCO
TEXAS $29.95/TCOR

The California Professional Corporation Handbook

Attorney Anthony Mancuso • California 4th ed.
Health care professionals, lawyers, accountants and members of certain other professions must fulfill special requirements when forming a corporation in California. This book contains information plus all the forms and instructions necessary to form a California professional corporation.
$34.95/PROF

The Independent Paralegal's Handbook

Attorney Ralph Warner • National 2nd ed.
Provides legal and business guidelines for those who want to take routine legal work out of the law office and offer it for

a reasonable fee in an independent business.
$24.95/ PARA

Getting Started as an Independent Paralegal
Attorney Ralph Warner • National 2nd ed. • Two tapes, approximately 2 hours
If you are interested in going into business as an Independent Paralegal—helping consumers prepare their own legal paperwork—you'll want to listen to these tapes. They will tell you everything you need to know about what legal tasks to handle, how much to charge and how to run a profitable business.
$44.95/GSIP

How to Start Your Own Business: Small Business Law
Attorney Ralph Warner with Joanne Greene • National 1st ed. • 50 minutes
This tape covers the basic issues facing the small business start-up: whether to organize as a sole proprietorship, partnership or corporation, how to protect the business name, what legal pitfalls to look out for when renting space, hiring employees and paying taxes.
$14.95/TBUS

Nolo's Partnership Maker
Attorney Anthony Mancuso & Mickael Radke • Version 1.0
Prepares a legal partnership agreement for doing business in any state. You can select and assemble the standard partnership clauses provided or create your own customized agreement. And the agreement can be updated at any time. Includes on-line legal help screens, glossary and tutorial, and a manual that takes you through the process step-by-step.
IBM PC $129.95/PAGI1

California Incorporator
Attorney Anthony Mancuso • Version 1.0 (good only in CA)
Answer the questions on the screen and this program will print out the 35-40 pages of documents you need to make your California corporation legal. Comes with a 200-page manual which explains the incorporation process.
IBM PC $129.00/INCI

The California Nonprofit Corporation Handbook
Attorney Anthony Mancuso • Version 1.0
Shows you step-by-step how to form and operate a nonprofit corporation in California. Included on disk are the forms for the Articles, Bylaws and Minutes.
IBM $69.95/ NPI
MACINTOSH $69.95/ NPM

How to Form Your Own Corporation
Attorney Anthony Mancuso
All the instructions and tax information, forms you need to incorporate a small business and save hundreds of dollars in lawyers' fees. All organizational forms are on disk. All come with a 250-page manual.
NEW YORK 1ST ED.
IBM PC 5-1/4 $69.95/ NYCI
IBM PC 3-1/2 $69.95/ NYC3I
MACINTOSH $69.95/ NYCM

TEXAS 1ST ED.
IBM PC 5-1/4 $69.95/ TCI
IBM PC 3-1/2 $69.95/ TC3I
MACINTOSH $69.95/ TCM

FLORIDA 3RD ED.
IBM PC 3-1/2 $39.95/FLCO

Neighbor Law: Fences, Trees, Boundaries & Noise
Attorney Cora Jordan • National 1st ed.
Answers common questions about the subjects that most often trigger disputes between neighbors: fences, trees, boundaries and noise. It explains how to find the law and resolve disputes without a nasty lawsuit.
$14.95/NEI

Dog Law
Attorney Mary Randolph • National 1st ed.
A practical guide to the laws that affect dog owners and their neighbors. Answers common questions about biting, barking, veterinarians and more.
$12.95/DOG

Stand Up to the IRS
Attorney Fred Daily • National 1st ed.
Gives detailed stategies on surviving an audit with the minimum amount of damage, appealing an audit decision, going to Tax Court and dealing with IRS collectors. It also discusses filing tax returns when you haven't done so in a while, tax crimes, concerns of small business people and getting help from the IRS ombudsman.
$19.95 / SIRS

Money Troubles: Legal Strategies to Cope With Your Debts
Attorney Robin Leonard • National 1st ed.
Essential for anyone who is behind on bills or loan payments. It covers everything from knowing what your rights are, and asserting them, to helping you evaluate your individual situation. This practical, straightforward book is for anyone who needs help understanding and dealing with the complex and often scary topic of debts.
$16.95/MT

How to File for Bankruptcy
Attorneys Stephen Elias, Albin Renauer & Robin Leonard • National 4th ed.
Trying to decide whether or not filing for bankruptcy makes sense? This book contains an overview of the process and all the forms plus step-by-step instructions on the procedures to follow.
$25.95/HFB

Simple Contracts for Personal Use
Attorney Stephen Elias & Marcia Stewart • National 2nd ed.
Clearly written legal form contracts to buy and sell property, borrow and lend money, store and lend personal property, release others from personal liability, or pay a contractor to do home repairs. Includes agreements to arrange childcare and other household help.
$16.95/CONT

Nolo's Law Form Kit: Personal Bankruptcy
Attorneys Steve Elias, Albin Renauer & Robin Leonard and Lisa Goldoftas • National 1st ed.
All the forms and instructions you need to file for Chapter 7 bankruptcy. Shows you how to fill out and file all forms, cancel and reschedule debts, keep creditors at bay, keep the most property through the bankruptcy process and appear in court.
$14.95/KBNK

Nolo's Law Form Kit: Power of Attorney
Attorneys Denis Clifford & Mary Randolph and Lisa Goldoftas • National 1st ed.
Assign someone you trust to take of your finances, business, real estate or children when you are away or unavailable. Easy,

step-by step instructions show you how to fill out all forms, make all documents legal and binding and revoke a power of attorney when it is no longer necessary.
$14.95/KPA

Nolo's Law Forms Kit: Rebuild Your Credit

Attorney Robin Leonard • National 1st ed.
Provides strategies for dealing with debts and rebuilding your credit. Shows you how to negotiate with creditors and collection agencies, clean up your credit file, devise a spending plan and get credit in your name.
$14.95/KCRD

Nolo's Law Form Kit: Loan Agreements

Attorney Stephen Elias, Marcia Stewart & Lisa Goldoftas • National 1st ed.
Provides all the forms and instructions necessary to create a legal and effective promissory note. Shows how to decide on an interest rate , set a payment schedule (amortization schedules provided) and keep track of payments.
$14.95/KLOAN

Nolo's Law Form Kit: Buy and Sell Contracts

Attorney Stephen Elias, Marcia Stewart & Lisa Goldoftas • National 1st ed.
Bills of sale for cars, boats, computers, electronic equipment, household appliances and other personal property. Helps you clearly record the condition of the goods changing hands to avoid later disputes over defects, liens etc., and provides step-by-step instructions for creating a bill of sale.
$9.95/KCONT

FAMILY MATTERS

Divorce & Money

Violet Woodhouse & Victoria Felton-Collins with M.C. Blakeman • National 1st ed.
Explains how to evaluate such major assets as family homes and businesses, investments, pensions, and how to arrive at a division of property that is fair to both sides.
$19.95/DIMO

The Living Together Kit

Attorneys Toni Ihara & Ralph Warner • National 6th ed.
A detailed guide designed to help the increasing number of unmarried couples living together understand the laws that affect them. Sample agreements and instructions are included.
$17.95/LTK

How to Raise or Lower Child Support in California

Judge Roderic Duncan and Attorney Warren Siegal • California 1st ed.
Appropriate for parents on either side of the support issue. Because of recent law changes, many parents are entitled to a large increase. And those who have support obligations and have suffered a decrease in income are entitled to have their payments adjusted downwards. This book contains all the forms and instructions necessary to modify an existing child support order.
$16.95/CHLD

The Guardianship Book

Lisa Goldoftas & Attorney David Brown • California 1st ed.
Provides all the forms and instructions needed to obtain a legal guardianship without a lawyer.
$19.95/GB

A Legal Guide for Lesbian and Gay Couples

Attorneys Hayden Curry & Denis Clifford • National 7th ed.
Laws designed to regulate and protect married couples don't apply to lesbian and gay couples. This book shows you how to write a living-together contract, plan for medical emergencies, and plan your estates. Includes forms, sample agreements and lists of both national lesbian and gay legal organizations and AIDS organizations.
$21.95/LG

How to Do Your Own Divorce

Attorney Charles Sherman (Texas ed. by Sherman & Simons) • California 18th ed. & Texas 4th ed.
These books contain all the forms and instructions you need to do your own uncontested divorce without a lawyer.
CALIFORNIA $18.95/CDIV
TEXAS $17.95/TDIV

Practical Divorce Solutions

Attorney Charles Sherman • California 2nd ed.
A valuable guide to the emotional aspects of divorce as well as an overview of the legal and financial decisions that must be made.
$12.95/PDS

California Marriage & Divorce Law

Attorneys Ralph Warner, Toni Ihara & Stephen Elias • California 11th ed.
Explains community property, prenuptial contracts, foreign marriages,

buying a house, divorce, dividing property, and more.
$19.95/MARR

How to Adopt Your Stepchild in California

Frank Zagone & Attorney Mary Randolph • California 3rd ed.
Provides sample forms and step-by-step instructions for completing a simple uncontested stepparent adoption in California.
$19.95/ADOP

JUST FOR FUN

Devil's Advocates: The Unnatural History of Lawyers

by Andrew & Jonathan Roth • National 1st ed.
Find out about the world's worst lawyers, most preposterous cases and most ludicrous courtroom strategies.
$12.95/DA

29 Reasons Not to Go to Law School

Attorneys Ralph Warner & Toni Ihara • National 3rd ed.
Filled with humor and piercing observations, this book can save you three years, $70,000 and your sanity.
$9.95/29R

Poetic Justice: The Funniest, Meanest Things Ever Said About Lawyers

Edited by Jonathan & Andrew Roth • National 1st ed.
A great gift for anyone in the legal profession who has managed to maintain a sense of humor.
$8.95/PJ

PATENT, COPYRIGHT & TRADEMARK

Trademark: How to Name Your Business & Product

Attorneys Kate McGrath and Stephen Elias, With Trademark Attorney Sarah Shena • National 1st ed.
Every business owner needs to know how to protect names used to market services and products. This book shows how to: choose a name or logo others can't copy, conduct a trademark search, register a trademark and protect and maintain the trademark.
$29.95 / TRD

Patent It Yourself

Attorney David Pressman • National 3rd ed.
From the patent search to the actual application, this book covers everything

including the use and licensing of patents, successful marketing and how to deal with infringement.
$34.95/PAT

The Inventor's Notebook
Fred Grissom & Attorney David Pressman •
National 1st ed.
Helps you document the process of successful independent inventing by providing forms, instructions, references to relevant areas of patent law, a bibliography of legal and non-legal aids and more.
$19.95/INOT

How to Copyright Software
Attorney M.J. Salone • National 3rd ed.
This book tells you how to register your copyright for maximum protection and discusses who owns a copyright on software developed by more than one person.
$39.95/COPY

The Copyright Handbook
Attorney Stephen Fishman • National 1st ed.
Provides forms and instructions for protecting all types of written expression under U.S. and international copyright law. Detailed reference chapters explain copyright infringement, fair use, works for hire and transfers of copyright ownership.
$24.95/COHA

LANDLORDS & TENANTS

The Landlord's Law Book, Vol. 1: Rights & Responsibilities
Attorneys David Brown & Ralph Warner •
California 3rd ed.
Covers deposits, leases and rental agreements, inspections (tenants' privacy rights), habitability (rent withholding), ending a tenancy, liability and rent control.
$29.95/LBRT

The Landlord's Law Book, Vol. 2: Evictions
Attorney David Brown • California 4th ed.
Shows you step-by-step how to go to court and evict a tenant. Contains all the tear-out forms and necessary instructions.
$32.95/LBEV

Tenants' Rights
Attorneys Myron Moskovitz & Ralph Warner •
California 11th ed.
Explains how to handle your relationship with your landlord and understand

your legal rights when you find yourself in disagreement. A special section on rent control cities is included.
$15.95/CTEN

HOMEOWNERS

How to Buy a House in California
Attorney Ralph Warner, Ira Serkes &
George Devine • California 2nd ed.
Shows you how to find a house, work with a real estate agent, make an offer and negotiate intelligently. Includes information on all types of mortgages as well as private financing options.
$19.95/BHCA

For Sale By Owner
George Devine • California 2nd ed.
Provides essential information about pricing your house, marketing it, writing a contract and going through escrow.
$24.95/FSBO

Homestead Your House
Attorneys Ralph Warner, Charles Sherman &
Toni Ihara • California 8th ed.
Shows you how to file a Declaration of Homestead and includes complete instructions and forms.
$9.95/HOME

The Deeds Book
Attorney Mary Randolph • California 2nd ed.
If you own real estate, you'll need to sign a new deed when you transfer the property or put it in trust as part of your estate planning. This book shows you how to find the right kind of deed, complete the tear-out forms and record them in the county recorder's public records.
$15.95/DEED

OLDER AMERICANS

Elder Care: Choosing & Financing Long Term Care
Attorney Joseph Matthews • National 1st ed.
Guides you in choosing and paying for long-term care, highlights practical concerns and explain laws that may affect your decisions.
$16.95/ELD

Social Security, Medicare & Pensions
Attorney Joseph Matthews with Dorothy
Matthews Berman • National 5th ed.
Contains invaluable guidance through the current maze of rights and benefits for those 55 and over, including Medi-

care, Medicaid and Social Security retirement and disability benefits and age discrimination protections.
$15.95/SOA

REFERENCE

Legal Research: How to Find and Understand the Law
Attorneys Stephen Elias & Susan Levinkind •
National 3rd ed.
A valuable tool on its own or as a companion to just about every other Nolo book. Gives easy-to-use, step-by-step instructions on how to find legal information.
$19.95/LRES

Family Law Dictionary
Attorneys Robin Leonard & Stephen Elias •
National 2nd ed.
Here's help for anyone who has a question or problem involving family law—marriage, divorce, adoption or living together.
$13.95/FLD

Legal Research Made Easy: A Roadmap Through the Law Library Maze
2-1/2 hr. videotape and 40-page booklet •
Nolo Press/Legal Star Communications •
National 1st ed.
University of California law professor Bob Berring explains how to use all the basic legal research tools in law library with an easy-to-follow six-step research plan and a sense of humor.
$89.95/LRME

CONSUMER/REFERENCE

Nolo's Pocket Guide to California Law
Attorney Lisa Guerin and Nolo Press Editors •
California 1st ed.
Get quick, clear answers to questions about child support, custody, consumer rights, employee rights, government benefits, divorce, bankruptcy, adoption, wills and much more.
$10.95/CLAW

Barbara Kaufman's Consumer Action Guide
Barbara Kaufman • California 1st ed.
Filled with information on hundreds of consumer topics. Gives consumers access to their legal rights, providing addresses and phone numbers of where to complain when things go wrong, and providing resources if more help is necessary.
$14.95/CAG

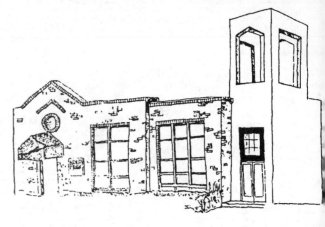
O R D E R   F O R M

Name

Address (UPS to street address, Priority Mail to P.O. boxes)

Catalog Code	Quantity	Item	Unit price	Total
		Subtotal		
		Sales tax (California residents only)		
		Shipping & handling		
		2nd day UPS		
		TOTAL		

in the light of you

in the light of you

NATHAN SINGER

BLEAK HOUSE BOOKS

MADISON | WISCONSIN

Published by Bleak House Books
a division of Big Earth Publishing
923 Williamson St.
Madison, WI 53703
www.bleakhousebooks.com

ISBN 13: 978-1-932557-82-4 (Trade Cloth)
ISBN 13: 978-1-932557-84-8 (Evidence Collection)

Library of Congress Cataloging-in-Publication Data has been applied for.

Printed in the United States of America

11 10 09 08 07   1 2 3 4 5 6 7 8 9 10

Set in Times New Roman

Interior by Von Bliss Design
www.vonbliss.com

1.

IT'S hard to know how to feel when your best friend blows out a man's stomach with a shotgun. Self-defense, you understand. The guy had a knife. Picture it: my friend is sitting in his trailer one evening making moves on his lady *du jour*, when there comes a banging on the window. The girl's ex stumbles in drunk waving a butterfly knife, screaming, "Bitch! You broke my heart! Can't you see I love you, you fucking cunt!?!" because he's a smooth operator, see, with lyrics to spare. My friend says, "Get the fuck out!" Guy goes to stab, triggers are pulled, messes are made. Hands are cuffed. Courts are adjourned. Not guilty. Like I said, it's hard to know how to feel.

"Congratulations."

"I had to," he said.

"I understand completely."

"It was him or me, Mikey."

"No doubt."

"I'm eighteen this month. I coulda gotten death."

"Dodged that bullet."

"It's not like I'm not sorry it happened."

"Hey man, I'm here for you."

But I wasn't. We moved away from Louisville not long after that. Not because my friend decorated a double-wide with a dude's intestines. Dad just thought there'd be better work in Ohio. He was right ... more or less. This was 1994. I was fourteen. It was nearly three years before I had another friend. That's just the way it is.

People often ask me, "What was it that made you decide to dedicate your life to hate?" They want an answer that starts with, "Well, you see, I was hurt this one time ..." And when people ask me, "What was it that turned you around?" They want an answer like, "Jesus." Or, "Jail really opened my eyes." Or, "Soandso taught me the meaning of love / peace / tolerance / *inserthippieshitbuzzwordhere*." But none of that is right. My answer to both is "Nothing."

My dad is a boiler operator. Or rather, he was until the accident. Mom is a tele-marketer. At least fifty times on an average day my mother is invited to go fuck herself, get cancer, die a fiery death, or suck any number of anatomical bits and pieces. If she works after 9:00 PM she gets an extra two dollars an hour. Good times.

Let's get one thing straight: my parents are not stupid people. But it's safe to say that academia was never in their cards. I mean, my name is Mikal. M-I-K-A-L. Because the "chae" in "Michael" made them nervous. When we moved up north a piece in 1994 they were both thirty years old. You do the math.

I'm glad the plan to move to Ohio did not include hopes of leaving the manslaughter behind, because that would've been mighty disappointing. Finances being what they were, we ended up in a little pocket of the world called Blackchurch. Although that name is shorthand for the whole eastern side of the neighborhood, the area that can rightfully be called Blackchurch is really just one intersection where Blackstone Street crosses Desmond Road (or even just one of the four actual churches that occupy the adjacent corners). And you see, a million years before Christ was born Desmond Road was called Churchwalk, and everyone in the neighborhood still calls it that. Get that wrong and you expose yourself as a Blackchurch virgin. Not a good thing to be. Another thing not to be in Blackchurch is white.

You go to sleep there every night to the sound of gunfire. To this day I toss and turn in fits of restless slumber without the melodious sounds of the *ratta-tat-tat bop pop tagow.* We hadn't been there but two months when I watched a boy get shot in the face at midday. I'm out by the basketball courts by the old, abandoned YMCA building, delusional enough to think that I might get in on a game, when this young homeboy makes the scene, pulls a 9mm out of his shorts, and blasts this other young cat right in the forehead. I duck behind a big yellow LTD. Folks are screaming, running for cover. And glacier-cool, the boy caps the poor son of a bitch once more in the thigh, walks up to a girl who's curled up on the sidewalk screeching and bawling and goes, "How ya like me, huh?" And then he just strolls away. (When I think about that now, I hear the funky bassline of his theme song kick in just then. Sort of a Curtis Mayfield / Isaac Hayes kinda joint.) The boy he shot lay on the sidewalk crying, "I need uh amboolass! I NEED UH AMBOOLASS!!!" the blood from his temple spilling into his mouth, spraying out with every wail.

Sirens sang in the distance, advancing. Paramedics pulled up, tossed him on a stretcher, slapped a mask on him. They peeled his shorts off the bullet wound with *shhhhhhhlt,* his thigh shredded and burnt like barbecue gone wrong. I didn't see the exit wound, but it was enough to make one of the paramedics gasp, "Motheragod on a pogo stick!" So they loaded the boy into the wagon, rolled away, and that was that. That was that. I never heard what happened to him.

I sat on the curb leaning against the LTD, locked up so tight you could bounce a quarter off of me. This baller from the court came walking over, shirtless and sweaty, hair half-fro'd / half cornrowed.

"How 'boutcha, whiteboy?"

"How about me what?"

"Welcome to Niggatown," he said, and headed on back to his game. He hadn't really even looked at me. His name was D'antre Philips. And I would grow to hate him.

Blackchurch is fifteen minutes from downtown proper as the Metro rolls. Twenty to University Village, but it may as well be a million. Blackchurch is an island. It is its own nation with its own language and law. The rule for non-blacks around those parts was simple: act black or suffer. And the Catch-22 addendum to the first part of the rule is "quit tryin' ta perp." If you wanted to at least attempt to play their game, the uniform was set and not to be altered: XXL white T-shirt / XXXL blue jeans. It is to date the most startling example of voluntary conformity in all of recorded history, and I should know. Don't get me wrong, I understood the concept behind it perfectly. Like many young men I always dreamed of being a soldier. The idea of being part of a perfectly oiled, perfectly regimented fighting machine … *damn* … that's pure power. A wall of strength. One mind. Charge in, search and destroy. So boys make armies in the streets. But I knew I'd never make rank there.

D'antre Philips was one of the many low-rent thugs to populate our little hamlet. He sold a bit of dope, drove a car far out of his price range, played "da hoes" like it was his job, and spent his money on big, ugly, gold jewelry as he continued to live off his mother well into his twenties. As he was a little older, he acted as the *de facto* leader of a small group of local players: Arnold Lincoln, Arnold's older brother Tremaine, Ezekial Johnson, Rakeem Hollis, the Willis twins, and token white nigger Jack Curry. Of all the people in the neighborhood for whom I had no love, I hated Jack Curry most of all. I'm not going to tap dance around the fact: I was terrified of him. A lot of people were. "There go that crazy white muh-fucka Jack," folks would say, "so jus' keep yo' distance." And believe me, the fear was justified. I know that better than most. Myriad rumors about him echoed in hushed tones throughout the neighborhood, and after what I've seen I have no reason to doubt a single one of them.

At first it seemed Jack Curry rolled with D'antre Philips and that crowd completely on his own terms. He gained respect by bringing every ass-thumping he received back on his attackers tenfold. He didn't wear the uniform. He didn't play the game. In fact, he didn't look like anything else in town. He wore his hair down to his belt, knotted into dreadlocks that he dyed black and oxblood red. He wore shirts by bands like EYEHATEGOD that read "Kill Your Boss." He was coated in tattoos like something out of a nineteenth century circus sideshow. (I'm fond of tattoos myself and have a number of them, as do most of the people I know. But that fucker was more colored paint than man.)

This is the only conversation I ever had with Jack Curry:

"Hey dude," I said. "Your ink work is bad ass."

"Just trying to cover the white up," he growled, and kept walking. Never even looked me in the eye.

Just trying to cover the white up. That was why I detested him. His seething, undying contempt for white people made me shudder. Curry grew up right there on Blackstone Street, and his response to a childhood spent abused for his skin color was to hate *us*, his own kind. I wasn't particularly up on racial ideology at that time, but it seemed to me even then that self-loathing of that magnitude could only lead to horrible things. I definitely hold to that belief today.

From 1994 to 1996 I kept completely to myself. I had no friends. I didn't speak to one single girl. Either at school or at "home" I dealt with no one I wasn't forced to. I was beaten, threatened, robbed, ridiculed, and run down as a matter of habit. By the time my dad had destroyed his hand on the job and his drinking had gotten so out of control that he had to be taken away, there wasn't an eight-by-eight stretch of this earth where I felt all right. I was an alien in every space. I couldn't even wrap myself in some fake nostalgia for my own friends in Louisville. I just didn't feel it.

The one slice of joy I had during that period came as a bit of *shadenfreude* when D'antre Philips's little gang disintegrated. In the tireless pursuit of absolute insufferability it seems the well of ideas had all but run dry, and some time in '95 D'antre Philips discovered politics. Needless to say, shortly thereafter the rest of them did likewise. Philips, reinventing himself as a boho MC called Daddy Molotov, started some "conscious" rap group and began seriously pursuing the craft of writing—which did exactly nothing to keep him out of prison. (Life being the baffling mess that it is, he recently published a book for children, which he wrote in jail. It's called *Princess Africa Jones*. There's just no telling.) Arnold Lincoln, taking "black awareness" to new heights, changed his name to Senbe Shabazz and cut all ties to white people ... Jack Curry in particular. The two had a frighteningly heated public falling out where the police had to be called and property was damaged (little did I know then, but I would come to play a part in reuniting these two men ... a role about which I'm conflicted, to say the least). Jack Curry, in some capacity, took up with

Ezekial Johnson's sister Lisa, who by that time had changed her name to Niani Shange (nee-AH-nee SHON-gay). They enrolled in University and—strap yourself in because it's just so shocking—became lefty cause-heads. I doubt they realized at the time what an explosive decision that would turn out to be.

None of this meant much of anything to me at the time. I was busy struggling through high school where, thanks to God and his cruel sense of humor, I was once again one of few whites. I wore my hair in a crew cut at that time and was decked out in camo every day, taking the whole "army of one" concept to heart. I had big plans to enroll in the Air Force. On the rare occasion that I actually showed up for school I was attacked and tormented without fail. That's just the way it was.

I was a sophomore, sixteen, one quarter from expulsion, when I met Joe and Phil. They were both eighteen and had been shuffled through pretty much every public school in the system. This was their last chance at state-enforced education. I'd seen them once before about a week prior, likely when they first arrived, but didn't think much of it at the time.

I was sitting in third bell, Algebra I, and these two girls behind me were having a bit of fun at my expense: ruminating at length about the size and quality of my dick, which, by their estimation, probably didn't amount to much. *Where's the fucking teacher?*, I thought, trying to ignore them, torching up inside, but keeping still and quiet on the surface. I'd been down this road plenty, and I never seemed to know the right way to turn. Finally,

"Pssssssst! White boy! Yo, white boy!"

And it just came out ...

"What the hell do you want, black girl?"

Fuck.

"OOOOOoooooh, no no no no no no no no no no no no NO! NO you di'en't! You did NOT jus' call me 'blackgirl.' Uh uh."

People started to laugh and taunt me. I'm catching erasers to the head and all sorts of slurs about my family tree and the color of my neck (which had to have been mighty red by that point).

"You called me 'whiteboy,'" I said, trying to remain cool. "I called you 'blackgirl.' Adds up real nice the way I see it. Stop me if I'm going too fast for you."

"Fool! You betta rekuhnize!"

"I recognize that you ain't got much manners," I continued digging my own grave. "Didn't your mother and father teach you nothing? But then, you probably ain't got a father, do you?"

"Awwwwwwwwwwwwwww SHIT!"

"Did you just insult this here fine sista, punk?" some homeboy said, getting right in my face. "I know you wouldn't dare use 'at tone with a BLACK woman. Original woman. Mother of da Earf."

"He sho NUFF did! Fuck 'im up!"

This is how I figured I would die, I thought to myself ... when out of the blue one of the new transfers, silent to this point, decided to chime in.

"Just punch the fucking chimp, kid," he said to me. "Just jack him in the mouth. Look at them gi-normous lips. It won't even hurt your fist." We all turned around to see this thick, shaven-headed Caucasian side of beef, smiling like a sunny afternoon. Phil Reider by name. Seated next to him was a fellow named Joe Briggan. They were dressed in identical gear down to the white laces in their black books: bowling jackets, red suspenders, neck tats that each read "white power." They both leaned in with a cocksure arrogance that I had never seen on white people. Ever.

"You just say somethin' to me, peckawood?" the homeboy asked, hissing, his cheek twitching furiously as everyone braced for the inevitable.

"No, Rochester, I didn't," Phil answered casually. "I said something about you. When you hear the words, 'Go fetch my slippers, Darkie,' THEN you'll know I'm talking to you."

And then, the mayhem.

The entire class spilled out into the hallway on a wave of flying fists. Unbeknownst to anyone, Phil and Joe were packing an arsenal's worth of weapons: black jacks, chains, brass knuckles, which almost, but not quite, leveled the playing field. I got in my licks and took a few as well, but strangely enough, I wasn't really all that scared. One of my brand new lifelong friends handed me a retracting baton, which I flipped to its full extension and swung as widely as my arm would reach. Aiming for legs, I built a comfortable little force field all about me. It took a good half of the faculty plus all of the assistant football coaches to subdue the melee and separate the offending parties. We were all expelled. Surprise.

My parents didn't care that I was no longer in school. And even if they had it wouldn't have made any difference to me, for I saw very little of them after that. I've seen very little of them since.

Phil and Joe took me to meet their crew.

"This here's Mikal Fanon, y'all. He's a bad mamma jamma and he don't take no guff."

Phil and Joe were the youngest of the group. At least of the guys. The rest were all in their early to mid-twenties. Top dog was a fellow named Richard Lovecraft.

Richard's got a way about him, everyone would say. *That Richard's just got a special something.*

"Welcome to the revolution, Mike," Richard said, shaking my hand and chucking my shoulder as if he'd been patiently awaiting my arrival, and now that I was here all could rock 'n' roll as scheduled. Within minutes of meeting this guy I couldn't help but notice how he could dictate the mood of the room with a look or a joke or the tone of his voice. (In all the time I would spend with Richard from that day on I'd see him work that same energy over and over again, with groups as small as two or crowds of hundreds, and always with the same ease.) You could have told me he was a rock star or the middleweight champion or the Prime fucking Minister and I wouldn't have bat an eye or thought it at all dubious. And if you had told me right at that moment, *You will follow that man off the edge of the earth,* I would have told you to go fuck yourself ... but you'd have been right.

"You proud to be white, kid?" Somebody asked me.

"Oh, yeah, sure," I stuttered. "I mean not so much proud as grateful, you know?"

Silence. Not even so much as a shrug. Feeling the need to qualify, I continued, "I mean, my mom, you know, got it on with my dad. He's white, she's white, here I am reflecting sunlight. Worked out well. Should pay off at job interviews and shit. So big thanks to Mom for her discriminating tastes. Coulda gone some other way maybe. I guess ole Mom coulda fucked a Samoan, or one of them Ugandan tribesmen who wear dinner plates as lip jewelry. But she didn't. I think that showed real class."

Seven and a half miles away an old woman dropped a thimble on her kitchen floor. I know that because I heard it plain as day. Then, all at once, everyone fell about the place roaring with laughter. Richard most of all.

"That," Richard said, wiping a tear from his eye, "is the single best answer I've ever heard. I hope you people are taking notes. Somebody get this boy a beer." And somebody did.

2.

FROM that day forth Richard's pad became my hangout. I never officially "joined" the Fifth Reich in any ceremonial way. There was no initiation, no memorizing philosophies or swearing allegiance to anything. We just all hung out there drinking brew, talking about chicks, listening to tunes, playing cards. Before too long I started crashing there. Not long after that I pretty much became Richard's roommate.

Late at night after everyone else had left or cashed out, Richard and I would stay up shooting the shit until sunrise. Not about anything specific, just whatever came to mind. He gave me books to read, mostly detective thrillers and true crime stories, occasionally historical non-fiction. He'd warn me ahead of time what was a fun read and what was "a little dry," and said it was up to me if I wanted to read the shit or not. I devoured everything he gave me.

It was all badass and brand new ... but it all felt familiar as well. Lived in. It felt *right* to me.

I remember my first warehouse rally like it's the only memory worth having. I remember the fear and the anticipation as we drove for what seemed like hours through cracked out ghettoes, farms and fields, and miles upon miles of industrial wasteland. I remember the mob of bald heads and liberty spikes filing into the most bombed-out-looking structure I had ever seen.

The stage was set with amps and a drum kit. Behind it hung a banner, which read "The Hangmen." The walls were lined with kegs every which way. The smell of impending ruckus hung in the air in rippling sheets. There weren't a lot of girls there that night, but the ones who were present were all gorgeous: blondes and goths and fine pixie punk babies. Some older roughneck was on stage screaming about "taking out the trash," but people were cheering and "sieg heiling" so loudly I could barely make it out. I wasn't really interested anyway because I had designs on a little punk rock girl named Suzi who had driven with us and was friends with Joe and Phil's current squeezes Anne and Reeba. (I've heard other skins lament the overall lack of women in the movement, but I can honestly say that in Richard's gang we never wanted for tail. Call it luck.) Suzi was sixteen like me, and had only been with the Fifth Reich for a couple of weeks. I grabbed us both a beer and we tried to find a place where we could talk, which was pretty much impossible. Over the cacophony I picked up that Suzi had a fairly rotten home life. Her mother beat her and tormented her. She had a bandage on her brow over her left eye that night because her mother had smacked her in the face with a broom handle. Her eye was bruised maroon, with just a shade of emerald. She loved her father, though, and hoped that he would divorce her mother and she could go off to live with him. I was as interested as I needed to be.

I was just about to ask her if she'd like to step outside for a bit of air when we heard the roughneck holler, "... And it's my pleasure to invite to this stage ... y'all know you love him ... RICHARD FUCKING LOVECRAFT!!!"

The roar of the crowd was so intense just then that you would have thought Sid Vicious had risen from the grave and walked through the door. Suzi and I wedged up as close to the stage as we could. I knew he was cool, but I hadn't realized until right then just how important Richard was to the movement. He was *the star*. The bright shining light.

"So hot ...," Suzi whispered to herself as she watched Richard take to the mic. To look at the rest of the women in the crowd, the sentiment was universal.

"I'm not going to waste your time with a lot of blah blah blah, cuz we all know who we're really here for ...," Richard said, and everyone cheered, throwing up their hands in salute. From there he talked about taking the country back from the mud people and sending the liberals back to Woodstock and it was all very funny and sharp. But truth be told, he could have stood there and read from *Goodnight Moon* and he would have still had those people in the palm of his tattooed hand. *Richard's got a special something about him. Richard's just got a way.*

"... So are you just about ready?!" Richard yelled. The crowd cheered. "What, are you fuckers asleep out there?!?! I said ARE YOU FUCKING READY TO GO FUCKING BATSHIT?!?!?!"

ROOOOOOOOOOOOOOOOOOOOOOOOOOOOOOOOOAAA AAAAARRRRR!!!!!

"Then bash your fucking skulls together for THE HANGMEN!!!"

The crowd erupted, and Richard dove in, riding the wave of hands all the way to the back wall of the warehouse. Four gruesome looking mutants who looked like they just crawled out of a sewer somewhere took to the stage, grabbed their instruments and let loose with a ferocious, "WHITE POWWWWWWEEEER!"

Four chords, four beats per measure, and a cluster bomb of unbridled rage:

One two three four

We want our Racial Holy War!

Five six seven eight

Let the monkeys feel our hate!

Nine ten eleven twelve

Send the faggots straight to Hell!

Here it is the final hour

Dirty Jew, time for your shower!

RAHOWA!!!!!!!!!

Bodies collided with bodies. People dove from the window ledges down into the swarming mass. Blistering hardcore bludgeoned us back from the stage and we charged back in screaming for more. And everyone knew the words:

One two three four

This is how we settle the score!

Five six seven eight

The White Man reigns, it is our fate!

Nine ten eleven twelve

Every mud fuck for himself!

The time has come for true White Power

C'mon, Jew, it's just a shower!

RAHOWA!!!!!!!!!!!!!!

I didn't know the lyrics yet, but I was damn sure I'd know them all word for word before next time. As Suzi pogo'd in place I hurled myself into the throng. Tearing off my shirt I let my skinny arms flail. *I am a tornado.* RAHOWA!!!!!!! *What does it mean?* RAHOWA!!!!!!! *I'll figure it out.* RAHOWA!!!!!!!!!! *It's the only thing that matters to me now.* RAHOWA!!!!!! I screamed it at the top of my lungs.

We slammed and skanked and punched and drank and bled away the hours. Every song just like the one before it, yet somehow better. Pride. Strength. Unified. Power. *An army.*

The drive back home seemed to take no time at all. The van was packed to its splitting point, as we appeared to have twice the crew we had on the ride there. Suzi and I rode in the far back—the perfect place to be.

"Yup yup," she said. "I'm so happy right now."

"How come?"

"Because you have your arm around me."

And I did and I didn't even realize. We stayed that way the whole ride.

Everyone else was asleep except for Richard, who drove, and a girl Richard had picked up at the rally. I don't remember her name. We all called her Special Olympics. Special Olympics was Barbie-doll hot, but nowhere near as smart. This girl had it all: tight, acid washed jeans, white high top tennis shoes, hot pink halter top, fried blonde Jersey girl coral reef hair. The whole package. I mention her only because she hung around for about a month and a half. Richard grew weary of her after a couple of days and passed her along to Brian. At one point she and Brian had a tiff and he threw her out of the house completely bare-ass naked. Somehow, without any money or a stitch of clothing on, she made it back to Kentucky. She was only mad at him for a day or so. Last I heard she's a hair stylist at some high-end boutique and she strips on the weekends. And she's pregnant by some Mexican with a tattoo of Jesus on his cheek. The most memorable thing about Special Olympics was that you could hear her having an orgasm from out in the driveway. Like guinea pigs in a blender.

We made it home from the rally at about three AM. Richard's apartment was actually half of a house, just southeast of downtown, right outside the Metroline. No one occupied the other half of the building so we pretty much infiltrated that as well. People grabbed space to crash wherever they could. Suzi and I staked out prime real estate on the screened-in back porch. I dragged a couple of sleeping bags out from the closet and pulled some cushions off of a beat up old sofa. Suzi stripped down to her panties. I peeled off my sweat-soaked jeans and lay next to her. She ran her fingers over my neck, my face, and through my short, bristly hair.

"So what's the style here exactly," she asked, "crew cut or fade?"

"Huh?"

"I mean," she giggled, "are you tryin' to look like a jarhead or a nigger?"

"Well, I ain't trying to look like no nigger."

"Okay, that's a start."

Not the most romantic repartee you're likely to hear, *but fuck it*. After we ran out of dumb shit to talk about we got rest-of-the-way naked and down to business. Still pumped up from the rally, I thought I did pretty well and was mighty pleased with myself. But afterward Suzi patted me on the back and said, "That's okay. It happens sometimes. No need to be embarrassed." That's just the way it is.

Suzi fell asleep shortly thereafter, but I was wide awake. I yanked my jeans back on and went into the house to scrounge up some vittles. I found Richard in the kitchen rummaging through the fridge, and finding naught but a sack of geriatric French fries and what was hopefully a kiwi. Boots and boxer shorts was all he wore, his multitude of tattoos glistening with perspiration. Clearly he and Special Olympics had had a far more vigorous workout than Suzi and I.

"Some night, eh Mikey?"

"You're telling me."

"I just want to say, I'm really glad you're with us, man. I can tell you're a thinker. It's good to have another thinking man around."

"Cool. Thanks."

"You do drugs?"

"Nope."

"Not even weed?"

"No way."

"Good. Glad to hear it. Fuck that hippie shit. I don't allow it in my house. Makes your mind slow." He cracked two cans of Fosters and handed one to me. We toasted. I hadn't realized it, but I was humming that Hangmen song. "One, two, three, four ..."

"You like that tune?" Richard asked.

"Shit yeah. It rocks like holy hell."

"You wanna learn how to play it?"

"I can't play guitar."

"Dude, it's punk rock. Anybody can play it."

Richard went and fetched a beat up old Larrivée. He handed it to me and wrapped his hand around mine to show me the fingering.

"Now see this? This is a G power chord. Three fingers: the root note, the fifth, and the octave. You use this same shape for all the chords up and down the neck. Give it a shot."

I gave it a shot. It sounded like hog balls. Richard laughed and ruffled my hair.

"Keep practicing. You'll get it."

So I did. And he was right. If any of you were wondering how to play "Count Them Off" by The Hangmen, it goes like this:

```
===============================================
The Hangmen - Count Them Off
-----------------------------------------------
G
One two three four
C                         D
We want our Racial / Holy War!
G
Five six seven eight
C                       D
Let the monkeys / feel our hate!
G
Nine ten eleven twelve
C                       D
Send the faggots / straight to Hell!
G
Here it is the final hour
C                       D
Dirty Jew, time / for your shower!
E
RAHOWA!!!!!!!!!
C
RAHOWA!!!!!!!!!
E
RAHOWA!!!!!!!!! OI!
C         G
RAHOWAAAAAAAAAAAAAAAAA!!!!!!!!!
```

"So, Mike. Tell me. You have an issue. One that really matters to you. What is it?"

"I ain't political, Rich. I don't have no issues really."

"You're not in high school now," he said, looking me straight in the eyes. "It's just you and me talking in the kitchen at four-thirty in the morning with no shirts on. I hear those wheels in your head turning from out here. Tell me what's going on in there."

"Well ...," I said, and it dawned on me that what I was about to tell him I had never told anyone before, "I'm kind of concerned about, you know, things about the environment and whatnot." I expected him to scoff and roll his eyes, but he just nodded. I had his full attention. So I continued, "You know, like global warming and pollution and all."

"Go on," he said.

"My family is, well, I guess, kind of poor."

"Yeah."

"And we've lived in lots of different low income areas, like by the river, okay. In the fucking flood plain of course. And it seems to me that big corporations get away with dumping their waste near poor neighborhoods and in creeks that run by more ... impoverished areas, you know, and I'm thinking that's fucked up. I mean, no wonder so many people, kids and all, in like West Virginia and shit, are sick. Right? I don't know. I guess I sound like some fucking, whooooo! Peace and love queer-ass right now."

"Hell no you don't," Richard said emphatically, then looking around to see if he had awakened anyone. "You are absolutely right, Mike. Absolutely. Our planet is being ravaged by poison and people don't give a rat's ass about it. You think that fat fuck Clinton or his bosses care? Yeah, sure. But ... you know who was actively working for the environment way back before the tie-dyes hugged their first tree? *Hitler*."

"Zat right?"

"Hitler. The great bogeyman of history. The Third Reich were promoting and enacting ecological initiatives since day one."

"I didn't know that."

"How could you? You're not gonna learn it in the public schools, that's for damn sure. It doesn't fit within the framework of their propaganda. If it doesn't conform to the dogma of multiculturalism, then snip, snip, out it goes. The truth just doesn't suit their agenda. And that's why we have to fight."

I didn't know what to think. I didn't want to think right then. Not about ecology or school or the president or world history or any of it. I just wanted in. I wanted boots and white laces. I wanted red braces for my pants. I wanted my uniform. I wanted in the army. This army.

Richard must have sensed it, and he crooked his finger and headed off down the hall. I followed him There I stood in the doorway of the bathroom looking at myself in the full mirror.

"You mentioned your family," he said, rummaging around in a small cabinet filled with odds and ends, "Are you close with them?" I shrugged. "You have any brothers or sisters?" I didn't answer, for I was busy mapping out where all my tattoos would go. An eagle on my left shoulder. A swastika over my heart. "RAHOWA" across my stomach. And, of course, "white power" on my neck. White power. *WHITE POWER*. White man. *I'm a WHITE man*. White Power.

"Well, it doesn't matter," he said. "You've got brothers now. A shit ton of them."

Without another word Richard clicked on his electric razor and ran it across my scalp. My hair sprinkled down to my shoulders and across the bathroom tiles. I watched in the mirror and saw the person I used to be, whomever he was, disappearing. Then gone. *Goodbye and good riddance to me.*

3.

I'M often asked how True Aryan Warriors spend their time day in and day out. Let me tell you, there is a lot of *Tetris* involved. And the importance of *Sonic the Hedgehog* to the struggle for total ethnic supremacy simply cannot be overstated. Speaking just for my chapter, we also spent an inordinate number of afternoons at vinyl record swap meets, Richard being the most dedicated vinyl fetishist I'd ever met before or since. If I had a halfpence for every time I heard him say, "Ahhh vinyl ... why listen to anything else?" I could self-publish this book, believe me. My assertion that digital recording was far and away superior to analog fell on deaf ears, to say the very least. ("It fell upon hostile ears" would be an odd thing to say, but not altogether inaccurate.)

That's not to say that we weren't active. There were parties most nights of the week, and a rally at least once a month. And, of course, the fights. Up until the time I joined I had been in my share of scraps and street scuffles. But in the Reich we would have battles like other people had neighborhood get-togethers. Most were planned, few were fair. Even if the rest of us were clueless about the where, when, who, and why of any rumble, Richard knew and he knew just how to win. And if it got hotter than he had thought it would he always knew the way out (well … almost always). After SHARPs (Skin Heads Against Racial Prejudice), Richard's favorite targets were military folk. Marines especially. Richard held that marines were nothing but the Government's sheep, and "his army" could take out "theirs" any time. He batted a thousand as far as that went, but I'd be lying if I said that there was anything fair about it. This would usually take place in a bar, most often our favorite haunt Eldon's Tavern, which was run by an old guard racialist whom Richard had known since he was preteen. El was with our cause, so he never gave us static about me or the girls being underage, and he always covered for us when the police were called. It would start when one of us would insult some soldier boy's wench. This was particularly effective if said wench was non-white. Richard would then walk over extending an olive branch, pretending to be the voice of reason, then he would smash the biggest guy over the head with a bottle or a beer mug. We would then swarm the rest of them, their ladies included, with pool sticks, chairs, what have you. That's just the way it was.

Rumbling with SHARPs was even more ludicrous. These showdowns were actually scheduled ahead of time. "We'll meet you on the floor at the Agnostic Front show …" Idiocy. SHARPs were so easy to beat because invariably at least a couple of their guys would be racialist undercover. Call it the COINTELPRO of the white underground. The only time that backfired was at the Kreator concert when the lead singer stopped in the middle of the song "Betrayer," pointed us out, and admonished the rest of the crowd to, "Kill zoze fucking racist pigs!" We made a break for it out the back of the venue and escaped unscathed. Everyone else thought it was hilarious, but I was pissed off because I really liked Kreator, and I still do.

Within the group I was seen as something of an "intellectual." There's just no telling. I suppose because I actually read the books Richard recommended. Although I was the youngest, there was a sense that at least some of the guys deferred to me. Some even jokingly referred to me as the Minister of Information. (That's indeed a joke because we did not have ranks. Technically Richard was not even "the leader" in any official way. But he was. And everybody knew it. That's just the way it was.) The fact that Richard appeared to value my input and respect my intelligence carried all the weight. Who was I to protest?

I imagine that there is a moment in everyone's life that is THE moment. *That was the crossroads*, you'll say to yourself, *and if I'd taken a different path everything would have worked out differently.* You only spot it after the fact, of course, and it has to seem innocuous at the time. The biggest of the Big Stuff doesn't hinge on *Sophie's Choice*, it hides behind, "Hey, what do y'all wanna do tonight?" Maybe other people have more than one THE moment in their lives. Maybe I will too someday. But as for right now I have just the one night. It was my seventeenth birthday.

Everything, I feel, that had happened in my life leading up to that night, as rough as it may have been, had pretty well gone as scheduled. And everything since has followed the course set that night. On the evening of my seventeenth birthday I had no idea that I would be making a flip o' the coin decision that would ultimately mean the difference between life and death. I could have just as easily chosen something else. We could have gone out for burgers. We could have gone to the movies. We could have burned down some old abandoned apartment complex. But that's all *the other*. There is only *what we did* and *the other*. I have no idea where the other path would have lead. Maybe to the same place in the end. But I doubt it.

Like I said, it was my seventeenth birthday. Richard's pad was packed with crazed hooligans. Final Solution on the stereo, beer was flowing, people were dancing and skanking this way and that. Richard was smart enough to have nothing of value in what passed for the living room, as bedlam and mayhem were the norm around his place. The TV had been stuffed in the closet along with the stereo console. There were a couple of already-broken couches that ended up completely demolished that night, and a recliner that never really had a prayer. Everything worth anything was kept in Richard's bedroom, which no one but he and invited guests could enter. He even took down his beloved Nazi flag that night and rehung it in the bedroom, where it pretty well stayed from then on.

Within our little circle of friends the notion began to float about that we should ditch the party for a while, head out on our own, and come back later ready to rage the night away. We could have stayed right there, of course. We could have gone for a walk or hitchhiked to Detroit. Somebody said, "It's up to the birthday boy." To which I replied, "Sure. Fuck it. Let's head downtown for a drink or two." And that's what we did.

Suzi was with me, Reeba with Phil, Anne with Joe, and another couple, Jennie and Geoff, came along. Richard and Brian were as yet unattached to anyone. We ended up at this trendy, collegey place called The Stable. All the little students were scrubbed and squeaky-clean drinking fruity cocktails, dancing to whatever slug vomit pop radio told them to love that week, and hoping to maybe acquire a little company for the evening. The crowd was a fairly liberal mix of types ... all in their designated uniforms. And there we were strolling in: six cue-balled knuckle heads in red braces and black bowling jackets wearing four fine and dandy punk rock girls on our arms like it's a grand gala affair. We were not the folks with whom to fuck, the whole club knew it, and good on them for the sharp eye. But although we were in enemy territory that night, we were there on a mission of peace. More or less.

"Hey Mikey," Richard whispered, "What do you think. Worth my time?"

He indicated toward the bar at these two pitiful little skirts sitting overwhelmed and unsure. Neither looked old enough to be there, even to my seventeen-year-old eyes. I wasn't sure which had caught Richard's attention: the knobby-kneed four-eyes who looked like Peppermint Patty's girl toy in the Peanuts cartoon, or the wispy little puff of nothing next to her. No sooner did I see them when a raver-boy in outlandishly large blue jeans came up to "Marci" and whisked her away to the dance floor.

"Which one, Rich, the geek or the leftover?"

"The fucking 'leftover,' jackass," He said irritated. "She's the one I meant from the get-go."

"She's all right. Go for it."

"Meh … we'll see."

Joe ordered us each a pint and we muscled a group of trust-fundies away from the table we decided was ours. The tragic comedy surrounding us on all sides was almost too much to bear. Big Pants and Nerd Girl on the dance floor alone, slobbering on each other like two spastics sharing a mutual fit, was enough to make you bust a gut either laughing or puking.

"Fags over there," Brian said pointing. "Dykes over there. Mutts of every stripe, shade, and stench. Somebody just say the word, I'm ready to stomp this trash."

"Richard," Reeba said, "that baby blonde at the bar is staring at you."

Well, of course she was. Most of the chicks there had their eyes on Richard, even the dark-skinned ones who should know better. Richard looked over at her, raised his glass and smiled. She smiled back all bashful-like, and looked intently at her parasol.

"No stomping tonight, Bri," Richard said. "Just sit back and enjoy the freak show."

"Hippie," Phil razzed.

"Yo' mama a hippie, nigga," Richard said jutting out his lips. We laughed and laughed.

An hour and a half went by, maybe more, and the novelty pretty well wore thin and then out. We did tool with a few chumps stupid enough to get near us, but for the most part playing nice was the rule. Geoff and I headed off to the men's room for a leak. We each took a urinal on either side of a young Middle Eastern gentleman.

"Hey Mike, I think I just pissed on my hand. Could you throw me a towel?"

"Can't help you, Geoff. Maybe Habib here can lean his head over and be a pal."

"My name's not Habib," the fellow sighed. "I'm a Sikh."

"Allah al habbala? Sim salla bim?"

"I don't want any trouble, guys," said Not Habib, zipping up quickly and heading for the door.

"Vell tang you veddy mush!" Geoff called after him. Good times.

As we exited the rest room we spotted the lonely girl at the bar lighting matches and watching them go out in an ashtray. She smiled as her dweebette friend and the skate brat finally made their way back over to her. It didn't last long.

"Hey, uh, Sharon," I heard Nerd Girl say, "how's it going? Listen, I need a big fave."

Poor Lil Thing's eyes were wide with disbelief as her apparent friend told her she needed their dorm room for the evening. Exclusively. "You understand, right? Pay ya back. Promise." And with nary another word spoken, "Marci" and her fine catch of the evening skipped jauntily away into the night. As tears filled the bright blue eyes of that abandoned and forlorn young maiden, as she stood at the bar lost and alone muttering impotent protests to no one at all, Geoff and I literally fell backward against the wall in peals of laughter.

But then … as he is wont to do … Superman swooped in and assed up our fun.

"Excuse me?" Richard said to her leaning in across the bar. The girl peered up at him with a look that instantly brought goose-flesh up on my back. It was a look close to awe, as if she had known of him already from myth or legend or TV and she couldn't believe that he was really there. Couldn't believe that he was talking to her. I clenched up when I saw it. Like I shouldn't have been there to see it. It wasn't for my eyes, and I was an intruder. It was a look that I knew no woman would ever give me (and, to date, none have). I stopped laughing instantly and felt like a cretin for having done so in the first place. Geoff simply shrugged and headed back to the table. Clearly he did not have the same reaction. I stayed, against the wall, in the shadows.

"I'm sorry to bother you," Richard continued, "but my constituents and I were feeling a bit lonely over there in the corner. We were wondering if you'd like to come join us." He pointed to everyone at the table. They all waved. She giggled and nodded.

"Richard Lovecraft," he said.

"Pleased to meet you," she replied. "Sherry Nicolas."

"Truly my pleasure." A line only Richard could pull off.

I walked back to the table a couple of steps behind them. Richard waved me up quickly.

"Sherry, this is my best friend Mikal Fanon."

"Nice to meet you, Mikal," Sherry said. I smiled weakly and nodded. I was, as they say, thrown for a loop. *Best friend? Did Richard Lovecraft just call me his best friend?*

"It's Mikal's birthday today. He's forty-three."

"Well happy birthday, Mikal. You don't look a day over thirty-eight."

Best friend. I heard him say it. *Best friend ...*

Sherry Nicolas was nineteen years old when she came into our lives. She had just started at university with nothing in the world but a fake ID, a few changes of clothes, and a really large poster of Marilyn Monroe. And a couple of smaller posters of James Dean, a young Brando, and a framed postcard of Steve McQueen. She grew up in that part of the burbs that used to be the country not too long ago. This was her first time ever away from home. We were her first new friends. It's hard to know how to feel.

We returned to Richard's apartment with the new girl in tow and you'd have never known we had left. Skrewdriver blasted on the stereo. The drunks were belligerent. Some people were making out. Some appeared to be fighting. Some appeared to do both. Slamming, pilin'-on, diving from the speakers. This baldie Neanderthal I only ever knew as "Meat Cake" was swinging a girl around by her neck. We'd seen them do this countless times before. She would scream and cry but if you tried to put a stop to it she'd kick you in the nuts. Whatever. Some shirtless maniac tossed Fosters oil cans to us all immediately upon arrival. Sherry looked wide-eyed and taken aback by all the goings on ... but something told me she'd seen her share of rip-snortin' hoe downs before. Suzi jumped on my back and doused me with beer. She squealed as I spun in circles swinging her around, her boots whacking some poor sucker in the teeth. Brian and Joe smashed beer cans against their foreheads and dove into the swirling whirlpool of bodies. And so went the remainder of my seventeenth birthday in much the same fashion. After a while Richard and Sherry disappeared. Surprise.

Once the last of the folks had either passed out or gone home Suzi and I retired to our little nest on the screened-in back porch. For my birthday Richard had given me a futon mattress from his parents' house. That night I finally brought Suzi to orgasm for the first time. Or perhaps she just faked it on account of my birthday. Either way …

"I want you to come meet Daddy this weekend," she said lazily as she drifted off to sleep. "I know you'll really like him. He's the most coolest-est."

"Okay, if that's what you want."

"I promise the wicked witch won't be there," she said, yawned, and then fell into instant deep sleep. I pulled the blanket down a bit from her bare back to inspect the series of what looked like razor cuts along her shoulder blade. "Cold," she whined, and pulled the blanket back up. That's just the way it was.

I got up for a glass of water and some aspirin sometime before daybreak. Walking out into the kitchen I heard the unmistakable sound of Wagner's *Die Meistersinger von Nuremberg* spinning on the turntable in Richard's bedroom. That was no surprise. I was also not taken aback by the sound of Sherry Nicolas gasping, panting, and moaning Richard's name. What instead bashed into me from nowhere was my own reaction to it. I instantly crumpled to my knees and covered my ears as tightly as I could. My stomach twisted into knots and a cold sweat broke out on my brow. *But why?* I'd overheard Richard poke plenty of broads on numerous occasions. At the absolute worst it was only ever vaguely annoying. But listening to this girl cry, "I c-c-can't believe … I can't buh-be-believe … you're fucking me! Oh god, you're FUCKING me!!!" … it carved into to my chest like an ice pick. It ripped me to shreds. It was too real. *Too naked.* Too close. *I can't be here now. I'm not supposed to be here now. I didn't mean to be where I'm not allowed …* But why?

Back out on our porch, Suzi whispered to me, "Are they still goin' at it?"

"Yeah," I chuckled, taking my best stab at nonchalance. I must have failed miserably.

"What's wrong, Mikal?"

"Huh? Ain't nothin' wrong, of course. Go back to sleep, Suze."

"Did you have a good birthday?"

"Yeah, I did. Of course I did. Of course."

4.

WHEN I awoke the next morning Suzi was gone. Off to school. There wasn't a woman in the house. I came out to the main room to find a bunch of the boys sitting around inspecting handguns. Richard sat frowning at his framed issue of *Volkischer Beobachter* from 1920, which normally hung on the wall in the hallway. The glass was shattered. I gave him a sympathetic look. He shrugged.

"No big deal. The frame itself is fine. Well worth it for the party we had. Get dressed, Mikey. We're going down to the range for practice."

"I don't have a gun," I said.

"For real, Mike?" Joe exclaimed. "And you were living in Niggerville? Goddamn. You must have a death wish, boy."

"We'll get you a piece," Richard said. "Everybody needs a pistol."

"I don't want a gun," I said flatly. "I ain't going."

"Hmm …," Richard grunted, nodding. "Apparently you misheard me. When I said, 'We're going down to the range for practice,' it must have sounded to your ears like, 'If you think it might be a peachy keen afternoon, would you like to maybe join us?' Reasonable enough mistake, but hear me clearly now. WE. ARE. GOING. TO THE RANGE. FOR PRACTICE."

"Hear me clearly," I replied, "I. AIN'T. GOING." And I turned around and went back to the porch.

As I got dressed, I figured that that was the end of my tenure as a ground soldier in the Racial Holy War. Dishonorable discharge.

After a few minutes Richard came out to the porch and sat on a stack of cushions. He didn't appear angry. He just sat and waited for me to explain myself. When I didn't he finally said, "Okay, let's hear it. What's your deal with the guns?"

"They're just not for me. I don't like 'em."

"A gun is just a tool, Mike. Nothing to be afraid of."

"I ain't afraid. I just don't do guns."

"A tool, you hear me? Like a hammer or a drill."

"I don't do hammers or drills neither."

"Dude, I've seen you use chains and black jacks. I know you carry a switchblade. What's the fucking difference?"

"YOU KNOW GODDAMN WELL WHAT THE GODDAMN DIFFERENCE IS!"

"Mike," Richard said calmly, "tell me what's on your mind."

We sat still in another round of silence. "You know," I finally said, "it's hard to know how to feel when your best friend blows out a man's stomach with a shotgun …"

I told him all about my buddy in Louisville. I told him about Blackchurch and the overabundance of firearms. Going to sleep every night to the *rat-tat-tat*. I told him about watching the boy get shot in the temple and the thigh right in front of me. I told him, in no uncertain terms, I don't do guns. He listened attentively, never interrupted or interjected. When I had said my piece, he replied, "Anybody ever pull one on you?"

"Yeah. Some nig put a rod to the back of my head behind Sunny Mart."

"Did he rob you?"

"No, he just said, 'Is you scared?' I said 'Yep.' He left it there for a couple of minutes, poking into my skull, just to make me sweat. Then he laughed and walked away."

"Huh. Just showing off his big black cock."

"I guess."

"But see, he would have had no power over you if you'd had a big black cock of your own to point back at him."

Touché.

"Rich, I've said what I'm gonna said about this. If you want me to leave I'll leave right now. But I will *never* carry a gun. Even if that means I'll die for being outgunned."

"You're not leaving," he said. "I've heard you out, and I don't agree with your position … but I respect it. You can hang out here today. We'll be back around six and we'll all go get some steaks or something." And that was that.

Staying home alone all morning and afternoon turned out to be a great decision simply for its own sake. It hadn't occurred to me until then, but since joining this crew, virtually all of my waking life had been spent with them. It was an unexpectedly welcome relief to just hang out with myself inside my own head for a couple of hours. I played a bunch of Richard's rare vinyl on the vintage turntable. I ordered a pizza with banana peppers, which I could normally never do since Brian was allergic to them. I played video games. Just because I felt that I probably should, I took a stab at reading *Mein Kampf*, which has got to be the single most skull-meltingly boring book ever written.

I was mightily disappointed when I heard the front door open and somebody inquire, "Anybody home?" It was Sherry Nicolas.

"In here," I said, not taking my eyes off *Sonic the Hedgehog*.

She came in, dropped her book bag in the corner, kicked her shoes off next to it, and peeled off her socks. She sat down next to me Indian-style on the obliterated couch.

"*Sonic*?" she asked.

"The very same. You wanna play?"

"Nah. You here alone?"

"They're shooting."

"Guns?"

"No, they're shoo—yes … guns."

"My brothers and my dad all hunt. I don't care for guns myself."

"Just a tool. Like a hammer or a drill. Nothing to be scared of."

"Guess you're right. I was feeling special cuz Richard gave me a key to y'all's pad, but then I found that the front door was unlocked anyway."

"We never lock it. We're actually hoping some jungle bunnies try to come in and take shit. That would be good times. Don't let that stop you from feeling special, though."

"Richard gets a lot of girls, doesn't he?" she asked, jumping straight to it. Knocked me off balance for a moment.

"Not really," I lied. "You see a bunch of other broads with keys milling around in here?" There was a long pause that I tried to not let distract from the game. But it drove me nuts and I finally said, "So, uh, how is it? College, I mean?"

And out it came a-flooding …

"*Too much.* You know what I mean? It's just too damn much. I'm always lost, always late, always short of money. Like college like life, right? Always have the wrong book, always in the wrong room at the wrong time. Back and forth, back and forth, office to office: Bursar, Registration, back to Admissions, Financial Aid. My name magically disappears from class lists. 'It's NICOLAS! N-I-C- oh never mind.' I don't know anybody and nobody wants to know me. Everyone had already been picked for teams and I didn't even know what we were playing."

"I hear ya."

"And when I finally do get to class it's all ... screeching. Agenda versus agenda. Before I hopped the bus to get here, my brothers joked that I'd need to beware for all the 'commie fag liberals' on campus. Ha ha. But hell, I think I could DEAL with those ... whatever they are. I can't ever get a word in edgewise, and even if I could I wouldn't have anything to say. "You there! Helen Keller. What do you think about the plight of blah blah blah and the rising cost of suchnsuch." Uuuuhhhh ... And the steamroller just flattens me and rolls on. I don't matter. I'm invisible."

"Yeah?'

"Yeah ...," she said, absently fiddling with her ankle bracelet. "Richard sees me, though."

"Hm."

"I like Richard ... a lot."

"So I heard," I said. I could almost feel her face scorch up bright scarlet. It singed my shoulder.

"Oh my god ...," she gasped. "I am so embarrassed now."

"I'm just kiddin' with you," I lied again. "I ain't hear nothing."

"You're lying. I can tell. You're lying to make me feel better. But I know you heard me last night. Ohhhh god." She buried her face in her hands.

"I got up to get a few aspirin at some point and I vaguely heard a bit of rustling around. Y'all coulda been rearranging furniture for all I know."

"Really?" she asked meekly.

"If I'm lyin' I'm dyin'."

"I like your tattoos."

"Do they look familiar?"

"I'mma get a beer, 'kay? You want one?"

"Be careful. There might be broken glass in the hallway."

"I'm in my bare feet a lot. Ah'm jest uh lil ole cuntreh gurl," she said in a horribly affected hick accent. I laughed obligatorily.

When she returned she handed me a beer and said, "I'm hungry. You guys have any eatables? Didn't see anything."

"There's some ground beef in the freezer," I said. "That's about it."

"I'm a vegetarian," she replied. "I can't even be anywhere near beef or I will get horribly sick to my stomach."

"Well, welcome to Shit Creek. I hope you brought your own paddle."

"You got a car?"

"No. You?"

"Nope. God, we're pitiful."

"There's a grocery right out the backyard if you wanna pick up something."

"You reading *Mein Kampf*?"

"Tried to."

"Boring as hell, isn't it?"

"Boy howdy."

"I really like reading about, like, Hollywood Babylon-type stuff. All the dirt and la-di-da about old Hollywood."

"How old?"

"Old old. Like 1950s. And even earlier." She paused contemplatively for a moment, then said, "Richard's kinda got a bit of a 'young

Brando' thing about him. Mixed with maybe Douglas Fairbanks." I didn't know who the second guy was. I still don't, actually.

"Not James Dean?" I asked.

"Dean was queer, you know," she said. That hung in the air like a small cloud for a moment as I tried to figure out where it came from. Inexplicably, she followed it with, "Richard gave me a bunch of vinyl records."

"To keep?" I asked, genuinely astonished.

"Uh huh!" she chirped brightly, figuring out from my tone that this was indeed something of note.

"And you're feeling special about the key? Pffffft. What did he give you?"

"The first Bad Brains record," she answered beaming. "It's actually a pre-print I guess. Or some sort of alternate release. The cover's different and it's got different takes of a couple of songs."

"No way! What did he say when he gave it to you?"

"He said, 'Those niggers were pretty good until they went metal.'"

"I think they're pretty fucking awesome regardless—now, then, and forever."

"Me too," she said. "I think you and I have a lot in common. He gave me bit of classic stuff: Minor Threat, The Dead Boys, Sick Of It All. He insisted I take some other stuff like Final Solution—"

"OI!" I shouted.

"All right, they're good I take it. Okay. He gave me a 7-inch of some group called The Hangmen."

"We actually know those guys. If you're going to be around you'll meet them soon enough. Craaaaazy fuckers. I think they're all inbred. I watched their lead singer eat a dead squirrel one time."

"Ewwwwwww!"

"I swear. We was at a rally on this farm way out in Deliverance country. They played. Some other bands played. I guess this squirrel had tried to jump from the garage to the house and bit into a power line. It had been hanging there from its teeth for like two weeks. So Goat Skinner, that's what everybody calls him, pulls it off the line and chomps right into it. He claimed it was cooked."

"Charming."

"That's just the way it is."

"This music," she asked, "… this is all racist stuff, right?"

"*Racialist.*"

"Okay. Sorry."

"It's the soundtrack for the revolution."

"The revolution … when white people finally take control?"

"Well," I said, annoyed, "… that's a pretty … simplistic way to put it."

"I just don't do hate all that well," she said.

"You know what? I don't really do hate myself. And Richard really don't neither. We're kind of different from other racialists in that way. There's a lot of unfocused aggression in the White Power movement. You'll hear a bunch of people shouting RAHOWA, Racial Holy War, and it's a nice little football chant. But I kind of think—I hope—it ain't necessary. It's like when you hear these rich punk rock kids scream about 'anarchy.' What, and give up that BMW Daddy done bought you? Gets frustrating sometimes, but ultimately it's good to have your troops single-minded of purpose without a lotta, you know, complexities in their thinking. And stuff."

"So where are you guys coming from?"

"We're all about going back to a very simple premise that was good in the past and is still good: complete racial segregation. So-called ethnic diversity is a tragically failed experiment, and it's time for it to end. It is human nature to want to be with your own kind. Chicanos want to be with other Chicanos. Japanese want to be with

Japanese. Forcing everyone together in a pot and saying, 'Okay! Melt!' has only led to violence, misery, confusion, and racial impurity for everyone involved. Being that the US is a predominantly white country, we think everybody else needs to go home. Or we can split up the country. Don't make me no nevermind."

"Wow. That's intense." She flipped the tab on her can and blew into the opening, trying to get a tone. She continued, "It does make sense, though. I always think it's so sad when I see mulatto kids. Like, where do they belong? What's their identity? How could people not think about that before they have those children?"

I nodded and said, "How that ain't considered child abuse straight off I'll never know. Believe me, I lived the experiment. It's a failure. My parents live in a mostly colored neighborhood. I used to live with them there. Blacks, left entirely on their own, shoot each other up like it's a game. I've watched them do it right in front of me. You add Caucasians to the mix, you add gooks to the mix, and now everybody's gotta 'posse up.' It's madness, and it needs to end."

"Look at me," she said. "Fresh into town, and I sought you guys out right away."

"There you go. Everybody wants to be with their own kind. There was a dude in my old neighborhood who became a Black Nationalist, back-to-Africa type. Senbe Shabazz. He called multiculturalism 'pollutin' and dilutin'.' I tell you, I couldn't stand the son-of-a-whore personally, but I agreed with everything he stood for."

"Except," she said, "that he felt that blacks are superior to everyone else. Right?"

"That's cool. Everyone thinks their group is the best one. Fuck, every tribe of American Indian's name for themselves translates in their tongue as 'The True People.' But," I couldn't help but grin, "WE ain't called the Master Race for no reason." Sherry laughed and nodded. "Speaking of Indians," I continued, "I got nothing but respect for them people. They got it right. They keep to themselves in their own communities and maintain their own culture. There's the 'business model,' as Richard says."

"I tell you what, y'all would hate what I see on campus every-day. It's like one big Benetton ad."

"I've seen that shit. Queers, kikes, cripples, rag heads, all hang-ing around together holding hands pretending to buy the world a Coke. That's why Richard dropped out and why I'm never going."

"I was wondering why you're not in school."

"I was expelled. For trying to teach some shaved apes a lesson in reality. There was a lot of hooting and shit-throwing, I'll tell you that much."

"You've got ... quite a vocabulary for slurs."

"It's a talent, not a gift."

"Well, I don't know about 'The Revolution,' but ... I'd like to see a revolution where more than one opinion—read: liberal secular opinion—is allowed at college. It's out of control. My first day of Women's Studies and there's this wacko-left freak in class ... a *man* mind you ... hollering at a bunch of feminists for *not being feminist enough*."

"Ha ha! For all their bullshit about tolerance, they're not even tolerant with each other."

"And there's this black chick everybody's ga-ga over. Oh, she's soooo great. She's just some homegirl with a big mouth, but you'd think she was the fucking Empress of Ethiopia."

"Of course. Gotta reward every little thing they do."

"And just today I had the nerve to mention God in class, and you would have thought I was force-feeding the body of Christ down people's throats."

"You Catholic?"

She paused nervously then said, "You all hate Catholics, don't you."

I laughed.

"We're not The Klan," I said. "I ain't got a problem with Catholics. Pope Pious, one of them, was a big supporter of the Third Reich. At least that's my understanding."

"I didn't know that."

"How could you know? They're not going to teach that in school. That's not politically correct. It might make people ashamed of their religion, or worse yet, might make them stop to think that maybe Hitler wasn't the monster they've been forced to believe he was. Either way it's another symptom of the ... infantilization of our culture. That's why we have to fight."

"Infantilization?"

"You know what I mean. Babyfication ... somethin'."

She giggled, "That's so funny, what you do with your voice."

"What? What do you mean?"

"When it's just you talking, it's all '*mumble mumble fuckin' mumble grumble.*' But then when you go on a tear about THE BIG ISSUES, Professor Mikal steps up to the podium. I just think it's funny. The two yous."

"Hmmm. Yeah ..."

I had completely lost interest in the adventures of everyone's favorite digital vermin, so I shut the TV off. We sat in silence for a moment. After a bit, Sherry asked, "So ... if I join you guys, if you'll let me, do I have to wear those big old steel-toed boots like you're wearing?"

I shrugged. "You never know when you gotta kick somebody."

"I just don't like my feet to be imprisoned. A lot of the girls were barefoot last night."

"Psh. Shows their dedication," I said in mock-disdain. *Surely she can tell I'm joking with her.* If she could, it didn't show.

"Well," she said warily, "I hope I can stay around. I mean, Richard seemed to, you know ... enjoy me." My stomach immediately locked up again. "I'm sorry," she continued, blushing afresh, "I don't know what I'm talking about."

Just then the boys came bursting through the door like a herd of wildebeests.

"Hey you," Sherry cooed to Richard, her voice suddenly regressing to a very high, little girl timbre. "I know you!"

Richard scooped her up off the couch and gobbled on her neck. She squealed and kicked her legs in the air. He deposited her back onto the couch next to me. She kissed his fingers as he slid his hand across her cheek. I could have done without all of that.

"How'd it go?" I asked the assembled mob.

"Killer," said Joe. "We're ready to slaughter people."

"Sweet."

"Yer a fag, Mikey," Geoff announced.

"Really? Is that why I fucked your mother up the ass last night?"

"Yep. Cuz she's a fag hag. Did you draw a hairy chest on her back?"

"I sure did."

"You guys are messed up," said Sherry.

"Duly noted."

"Goddamn," Brian said sniffing. "Were there banana peppers in here? I swear to fucking god just being in this room I'm gonna swell up and die."

"Are you going to explode and splatter all over the place?" Phil asked him. "Cuz if you are, then I gotta leave. These are my good pants."

"If you die can I have your skateboard?" I asked.

"No, cuz you killed me, fucker."

"Why you gotta hold a grudge?"

"Anyway," Richard cut in, "if you niggers are done with Showtime at the Apollo, I'm starving."

"Red meat," Phil said chomping his teeth. "Thick, raw, and menstruating. That's what we need." A chorus of 'Hell yes' chimed all around the room.

"What do you say, Sherry?" Richard asked, brushing a few golden strands away from her eyes. "Hungry for anything in particular?"

"Um …," Sherry replied, "red meat sounds great to me."

5.

THAT weekend Suzi and I went to meet her father. Her eyes lit up like Christmas morning when he came strolling in and she kissed him on the cheek with a loud smacker.

We met at a local greasy spoon because Suzi's mother was home sick with the flu and nobody wanted to be there for that. Suzi had been taking care of her mom to the best of her abilities, bringing her soup and orange juice and whatnot. I guess something or other had enraged the lady, though, because Suzi's lip was split and fattened on one side and her chin was bruised. Something about a flying vomit bucket and I really didn't want to hear any more.

"It was an accident," her father said. "Her mother didn't mean to hurt her."

We ran out of conversation pretty quickly. I don't think Old Man was too impressed with me, not that he had much reason to be, and I'd have to say the feeling was mutual.

"Nice haircut, Mick."

"Mike."

"Mike."

Nothing struck me as particularly wrong about him, but he was no cause for celebration as far as I could see. I couldn't help but think, *Why are you letting this happen? Why are you allowing your daughter to be brutalized?*

"You got a job, Mike?"

"Sort of."

"What do you do?"

"Well … um …"

If you really loved her, you know … you wouldn't … you wouldn't …

After dinner Suzi and I said farewell to Father of the Year and went down to Eldon's Tavern to see a local bluegrass singer named Jasper Highway. The rest of our gang was elsewhere that night, and it was good to be alone. El gave us each a soft drink and said, "No back-talk, you two. Yer lucky I let yuz in."

"Isn't Daddy every bit as great as I said?" Suzi asked me.

Jasper sang, *"I got a heartache, love, deeper than the sea …"*

"Yeah," I said. "Uh huh. Absolutely."

If you really loved her …

That night we tried to have sex in the shower, but it was too slippery and awkward and by the time we got to bed Suzi said she felt dizzy and fell right to sleep. I heard Richard and Sherry stumble in through the front door and head straight into his bedroom.

Suzi rolled over and wrapped her arms around me from behind. I held her hands to my chest and kissed her fingers.

"Mikal …," she whispered, half asleep.

"Yeah?"

"Could you get me a glass of water?"

Goddamn it … The last place in the world I wanted to be right then was out in that kitchen … except for possibly the room adjoining.

"Awww …," I grumbled. "I'm comfortable. Go back to sleep."

"I'm thirsty!"

I mumbled something incoherent in reply and she rolled back over.

"Jeez. What a gentleman YOU are. I'll just go get it myself." And she stomped out into the kitchen. Half a minute later she came back out to the porch and said, "Holy Christ, you should hear—"

"I don't want to hear about it."

Richard had picked up a temp job working on an assembly line and I was looking for something myself so I could start pulling my own weight around the house rent-wise. It was a Monday afternoon and I was sitting in the living room pouring over the Employment page when Sherry came in dragging an old ghost behind her.

"Mikal, I met THE scariest dude ever today. Well, I can't really say I met him cuz I already had seen him cuz he's in my Women's Studies class, right? I told you about that. But anyway, there's this girl in that class named Paige. She's hardly ever there. But when she is there all she does is cause fights. Everybody calls her the Raging Bull-dyke, which is fairly right-on except I think she's actually probably kind of pretty in her own way. Like, imagine young Elvis if he was a woman and had pine-green hair."

"Uh … Okay …"

"Anyway, she's really laying into the rest of the women and I'm staying out of it, of course. She's saying shit like, 'You can't go slurping the enemy's goop and then whine when he doesn't call you the next day,' and all sorts of crap about men that I didn't really understand. And Creepy Guy, he's her friend, he's just sitting there loving it, soaking it all in. But when people start to fight back against Paige he chimes in with all this stuff about 'Sojourner Truth,' and 'Susan B. Whatsherface,' and this other chick goes, 'What right do you have to criticize? Are you a woman? Do you have a vagina?' And he snarls at her, 'You mean besides the one I keep in the mason jar?'"

With that, got to admit, I snorted beer out of my nose.

"Everyone freaks out, right? Bull-dyke Paige is cracking up laughing, and the prof tells the freak to get out. It was CRAZY."

"Fuckin' hell."

"Dude and Paige, they've got this whole circle of friends that are just like that … you remember the Benetton ad? 'Kikes and queers and rag heads' and all. Well, later I run into the guy in the elevator. He held the door for me which was actually really kinda nice of him because I was running late and I had papers spilling out of my arms.

"'So hey,' I said, trying to be friendly, 'you're in my Women's Studies class, right? Seems like a pretty interesting one, yeah?' And he just starts growling, 'Bunch of fucking June Cleavers in that class. Get thin, get sexy, get a rich man. That's what passes for liberation at the end of the millennium.' Or words to that effect. And I'm just a stuttering idiot, talking about, 'Oh … well … umm …'

"'Goddamn *Cosmo* cunts,' he says. 'It's programming, you see what I'm saying? *YM* to *Jane* to *Cosmo* to *Good Housekeeping*. Everybody laps it up. They want the program.' And I'm just staring at my feet wishing the stupid elevator would hurry the hell up so I could get off. He keeps going, 'Cuz, you see, true freedom's just too hard. All the Bettys have now decided that cleaning house, watching Home Shopping, and fucking the mailman ain't such a tough gig. You rushing?' He points at the Sorority postings I had crumpled in my hand. I had no intention of rushing, I just picked them up for the heck of it.

"But he says, 'Yeah, I used to think all those people needed to be lined up and executed, but hey, if date rape and paid-for friendship is your bag, who am I to complain?' The doors FINALLY open and he steps out. Doesn't even turn around, but says, 'Keep your head up. It's sink or swim. Welcome to university life.' Then he disappeared down the hall. I'm all, 'Nice talking to you.' To nobody. Christ."

"What's the guy look like?" I asked her. Even though I already knew.

"Like the devil. Absolutely COVERED in these viney, like, abstract tattoos. Not cool, spare ones that actually mean something, like yours. 'Tribal' I guess you'd call them. And even though it is hotter than the Congo out there today he's layered in clothes like it's Minnesota in January. Leather and flannel. Yeesh. And his hair … is down to his ass, twisted and knotted into the most gnarliest dreadlocks I've ever seen on a white boy or anybody. Like they were dyed with animal blood or something."

"That's what I thought," I said. "He doesn't just look like the devil. He *is* the devil."

"You know him?"

"I've guessed his name." *Jack Curry …*

I didn't say anything more. *I hate the guy. Hate him.* It was that visceral, caveman hate. That hate that sits on you because it can never land on its intended target. Like being in the ocean with a nosebleed and hating sharks. Like hating cancer.

"Well … anyway," Sherry said to fill the empty space, "I'm excited. It's my first farm rally tonight!"

Her excitement was justified. There was a tangible electricity on the farm that night. Sherry was disappointed at first that The Hangmen weren't playing, as they'd been hyped up so much leading up to the day. Alas, their drummer had been jailed for burning down a black Baptist church. In their place was some grunt-core band called Confront whom everybody else seemed to like, but I thought were boring. As far as I could tell, all their songs were called either "Run Nigger Run" or "Die Nigger Die." In fact I think they played "Die Nigger Die" three times in a row, but I'm not sure how one could tell.

Thankfully Richard was there to bring it all home.

He took to the stage *after* the band for a change, the headliner you could say, and I could tell that he had a new spark about him that night. Something had stoked the fire. It wasn't anything glaring or excessive. Just a spark. I could sense that it wasn't going to be the usual "Destroy," "Maim," "Kill them all" skinhead bullshit that night. That night he had a brighter burn.

He began, "A famous colored man once said, 'Move over, or we will move over you.'" Guffaws from the crowd. "Sorry, Stokely." Laughter and jeers … though a number of folks had to explain it to their friends. "Although I appreciate the gumption and gusto, he didn't have the power." Pause. Then, "WE … have the power." Cheers and shouts of "White Power!" rose as if on cue. "We are the power. I think it goes without saying, but in order to be a true revolutionary, you must fight for what you love and love what you're fighting for. I know I do. I love my race, and even more so, I love my country." There was a smattering of claps. "And that's why I fight for them." Clapping and cheering. *Where's he going*? I wondered. I knew that he knew, but would the crowd follow? "I know a lot of Skins are down on America these days. They resent the welfare system. They get all pissy about the lip service paid to 'equality,' 'inclusiveness,' the whole 'open society' catastrophe and all that." Groans and hisses. I chuckled to myself. "Hell, some of us are still sour because America took Hitler out." Laughter and whistling. Richard played with the tension and uncertainty of his audience. Teasing and coaxing when needed, grabbing and throttling when it's not expected. "But I'm here to say that I love America. I'm proud that the U.S. took down Hitler's regime. Don't get me wrong, I have great admiration for Hitler. He's a hero of mine; you know that." Applause. "He did what was right for his people in his time. You must admire that. But he made a lot of mistakes ... and he fell short of the glory." Silence. Only the crickets had a retort, and it went unnoticed. "America can learn from the mistakes of the Third Reich. And we will. And we are. I love America." Cheers. "I'm proud to be American. I'm proud to be a part of America's new golden age, which is just around the corner, people. Just around the corner. The pieces are in place. The gears are already working. The war is already on." Shouts of RAHOWA! began to burst out from pockets of the crowd. Richard dropped the microphone to his side for a moment, grinning and nodding as more and more people hollered RAHOWA! RAHOWA! RAHOWA!!! "We have friends in important places," he continued. "Know that. As we speak, our friends are chiseling away at the communist 'New Deal' leftovers. They're dismantling that toxic doctrine 'multiculturalism' that pollutes our society with a cloud of fake togetherness that is neither necessary nor desired." Cheers and applause. "They are yanking away the free lunches from the lazy and the weak. America will move again. WE are going to get America moving again. I'm proud to be a part of it. I LOVE America." Hearty cheering and shouting. "Old Glory is the new swastika and I am proud to salute her!" An explosion of cheers and applause broke out. "Mark my words, in the next ten years America will succeed where Hitler failed. Fat Willie and his hog dyke wife are a dead breed and we will dump them on the curb with the rest of the waste and America will at last take its rightful place in this world. The Third Reich has passed. The Fourth Reich is in America right now ready to pull out the aces. The Fifth Reich ... is *us*." A deafening roar rose up from the crowd. The stars and the moon above were outshone by the light of Richard's eyes. "We are the power." A deep guttural chant of WHITE POWER filled the air. It rumbled in the ground and shook the trees. I squeezed Suzi's hand. She wrapped her arms tight around my bicep and lay her head on my shoulder. Sherry watched Richard on stage. Enraptured. WHITE POWER. WHITE POWER. Richard saluted "sieg heil" with his hand and mouthed "God Bless America." *WHITE POWER. Sieg heil. God Bless America. WHITE POWER. Sieg heil. God Bless America ...*

From the moment Richard stepped off the stage Sherry was attached to his arm like a barnacle on a ship's hull. As many of the folks began to trickle away, a number of us relocated inside the farmhouse, keeping the fire alive. It was very late, and most of us were drunker than we had really intended to get. Suzi sat on my lap whispering all the things she planned to do to me once we got home, none of which we ever got around to.

At some point Brian walked in the door dragging this grungy dirthead with a black toolbox by his neck. *Hell yes ...* Screwtape, everybody's favorite tat man.

"Hey!" Brian shouted. "Lookit what I almost stepped in!"

Everyone hollered approval.

"I'll be in the kitchen," Screw announced, "if anybody needs a touch-up."

A few of us muscled our way in quickly. Guys proceeded to pull off their shirts, girls peeled off fishnets, sleeves rolled. The room was an ocean of ink-stained flesh. Sherry stumbled drunkenly into the kitchen.

"I want one! I want one!" she slurred.

Screw sneered at her, "Better clear it with your daddy first, little girl."

A few people chuckled.

"Eat me, you faggot!" Sherry snapped at him. Screw jumped back, startled. Those of us who sort of knew her were taken aback as well. It was certainly a side we hadn't seen as yet. We all howled with laughter, and called Screw out as a pussy for his concern. Sherry yanked her shirt up, exposing her breasts to all in attendance and pointed to the swastika on Richard's shoulder. "I want this, right here over my fucking left tit, see!"

Screwtape grimaced and looked at Richard, unsure of what to do.

"Better do what you're told, Screw," Richard chuckled.

"Rich," he pleaded. "Come on. She's drunk as hell. She's gonna bleed like a cherry on prom night."

Richard shrugged and guzzled the remainder of his beer.

"Come on, Tape," I said. "Your reputation's on the line."

"Take a message," he said with a shrug of resignation.

Screw pulled out his needle gun, cranked up the buzz. I stood right behind Sherry, and I heard him whisper in her ear ...

"Listen to me carefully, okay? If anyone asks you what this is, tell 'em it's a sun wheel, you hear me? A sun wheel. That's all. Or ... tell 'em you're Hindu."

I barely stifled a laugh, but Sherry just nodded, hardly able to keep her balance. As Screwtape pressed the buzzing needle against her skin she gave out a little whimper of pain, but held strong, determined to see it through. See it she did not, however, for as soon as the first trickle of blood dripped from her bare nipple, she blacked out and collapsed backward into my arms. I held her up as vertical as I could while Screw finished the piece. Once it was completed, Richard relieved me of her. He scooped her up to carry her out to the car. Laughing, he rolled his eyes, and kissed the top of my bristly head in gratitude. *All in a day's work.*

Once we got home we all crashed hard. Reeba and Phil had pretty well commandeered the abandoned apartment next door and a number of people fell out over there.

As I lay down to go to sleep, Suzi said, "Mikal, let's pretend like we're gonna get married someday, okay?"

"Why pretend?"

"I'd like to meet your folks sometime."

"No you wouldn't. Trust me."

"I bet you're coloring them unfairly. Why do you think they love your brother more than you?"

"Because I lived."

6.

THE next morning I was awakened by clumsy rustling out in the living room. I walked in to see Sherry frantically stuffing papers and books into her school bag. She was decked out: tight Final Solution T-shirt, black boots with "RAHOWA," "white power," and all the necessaries painted on, jeans she must have been stitched into, and a leather tie-off wrapped around her wrist (which I found out later was some bit of a "game" between herself and Richard). I had never really noticed her figure before then. It was indeed worth noticing. She grabbed Richard's jacket, which was too big for her, zipped it up, and rolled down the cuffs of her jeans to cover anything potentially offensive or controversial. She smiled thinly to me. I could tell she was hung over and hating the morning sun like all hell. I was pretty well there myself, but at least I didn't have Beginning Calculus at 9:00 AM.

"Thanks for saving me last night," she said. "I guess I woulda gone splat on the tiles if you hadn't been there to catch me."

"What are friends for," I said. She nodded.

"Reeba's gonna do my hair tonight. I'm thinking maybe a Siouxie Sioux-meets-Annie Lennox sort of look. What do you think? Pretty rad, huh?"

"I don't know who that is," I said. I still don't. Never did keep up with old Hollywood.

"Reeba says she's gonna make me look super hot. I've never looked super hot before."

"Good luck with that."

"Quite a commitment on my part I guess," she said indicating her new look.

I laughed. "The real commitment is, as we speak, scabbing up on your left boob."

"God, it itches so badly," she whined.

"Don't scratch it, you'll fuck it up. When you get home from school put some lotion on it. You'll be all right."

"We'll see," she said, and headed out on her way. "Hey Mikal," she said turning back again. "Did you know that Hitler was a vegetarian?"

"I did indeed, yes. Raised Catholic too."

She smiled and walked out. *Whatever it takes.*

Richard stayed in his bedroom the rest of the morning. He must have had a headache rumbling straight from the bowels of the earth, for he did not turn his music on once. I lay on the couch reading most of the day. Considered continuing my search for a job, *but to hell with it.*

Around noon I heard the phone ring in Richard's room. He walked it out to the living room where I was, hit the Talk button, and chucked it at me. Amazingly enough, I caught it. He lumbered on back to his room without a word spoken.

"Hello?"

"Is this Mikal?" The woman's voice on the other end was hoarse and desperate. She took a deep drag from her cigarette like it was the last she would ever smoke.

"Yeah."

"This is Suzi's mother."

Well well well.

"How ya doing, Ma? Good to finally hear from ya."

"Listen, I ain't gonna bullshit around here. You takin' Suzi away?"

"Sorry?"

"Are you gonna take her away?!"

So much for getting-to-know-you. I let the moment hang. Figured a little sweating it out is good for the soul. She took another suicide drag from her smoke.

"Well," I answered eventually, "I'd like to, yeah."

"GOOD! You gotta do that. Get her far from here. There ain't nothing for her here."

"So I've noticed. Nothing but a lifetime of ass beatings is how it looks from my angle."

"Look," she said, her voice cracking, "I do what I gotta do. I'm just trying to do what's right. I ain't perfect."

"Uh huh, that's one way of putting it."

"Don't you judge me, you little punk!"

"Listen up, you rancid twat, anything I do, any decision I make is gonna be because I thought it was the thing to do. Not cuz the likes of you—"

"Goddamn it! Listen to me!"

"D'you hit her in the face with a bucket of—"

"THAT WAS A ACCIDENT!" She started to cry, which just made me angrier.

"You nasty fucking—"

"I heard that you was a smart boy. You don't sound so smart to me."

"Oh, I think I'm smart enough to know what the score is, mother-dear. Let me guess: Your husband don't pay you no mind these days. Marriage ain't been worth a shit for ... oh, what is it, 'bout sixteen years?"

"You don't get it ...," she sobbed.

"Sure, used to be all rose petals and soft music and holding hands in the moonlight, but since you went and squeezed out a baby it just ain't Paris no more. Am I getting warm here?"

"Oh sweet Jesus ... *sob* ... you just don't uh-unnerstan' ..."

"And I guess you're not only resentful, but downright jealous cuz your daughter and your husband have a close bond and ain't nobody got time for poor little you, am I off base? I'm not, am I?"

She just sobbed and muttered, "Just take her away ... just take her away ... Please ..."

"Okay, Ma, great talking to you. I guess we'll be seeing ya 'round Christmas time."

And I hung up. Richard stuck his head out of his room.

"Who was that?" he asked.

"Mother-in-law."

He nodded and went back in again.

The boys started to arrive about 2:30 PM and they made so much racket that Richard was finally forced out of bed. He cooked us all up a fat vat of scrambled eggs and sausage. Joe had bought a case of Colt .45, which earned him the name "Jamal" for the remainder of the day. We whiled away our youth playing video games and drinking cheap beer.

Around four Sherry called Richard from school. This is what I heard:

"Uh huh. Uh huh. Holy shit! Goddamn. No way! HA HA! That's wild! Nope. Sure wasn't. I have no idea. Uh uh. If somebody from our chapter or any nearby did it, I'd have known. Whoever it was, I'd like to shake his hand. Naw. I'd shake their hands too. I'd show 'em some luuuv. HA HA! Okay. Okay. You coming over? Okay, see you then. You're gonna what? Wow, that sounds like fun. Is that legal in this state? 'Kay, see you then. Bye."

"What the hell was all that?" I asked after he hung up.

"Somebody apparently trashed the Black Student Union on campus. Somebody spray-painted 'white power' and 'tar babies' all over the place. There was almost a riot, the cops came and everything."

"Was anybody arrested for it?"

"Yeah," Richard said, failing to contain himself. "Two niggers."

I don't remember laughing that long and that hard at any one thing before or since. "Them people just can't catch a break, can they!"

But this is what Sherry never told Richard about that day:

Sherry followed Jack Curry out of class like she did most days, staying far behind. *I couldn't help it, he was like a human car crash. It was impossible to not watch.* Usually he'd be in the midst of some ideological death match with someone or other, but this particular day was pretty quiet. At first.

She took her spot on a bench to eat lunch by herself, watching Curry meet up with his friends under a tree off the main lawn. She didn't know them then, but they were Sarabjit Singh, some girl from the Rape Crisis Center named Marissa, and Lin Cho—who was very pregnant at the time—and her fiancé Dave Yoshimoto. (You may know of Dave Yoshimoto's sister Katsumi who used to sing for the Baton Rouge sludge metal band Stigmata Dog. She called herself "Pearl Harbor." Perhaps she still does. They were in a horrible accident on Interstate 71 a couple of years ago and most of the band was killed.)

It was a beautiful September day. People were studying, hanging out, grubbing on caf' slop. Jocks tossed the old pigskin around. Hippies hackey-sacked. All the little stereotypes frolicked in the sun to and fro; it was an idyllic college scene.

That was the first day that Sherry really noticed Niani Shange. She'd seen her around, as it was hard to see Jack Curry and not see her. They were practically joined at the soul. They lived off campus together in a house nestled back from the road. Niani was something of a star around campus, a champion for all sorts of left-leaning issues. Certainly nothing Sherry wanted anything to do with.

It wasn't difficult to see why people were drawn to her, though: a born performer if ever one lived. She had perfected the art of manipulating her voice for any sized crowd. And I don't care who you are or think you are, there was no denying that she was a stunning sight: incredibly dark, her eyes practically glowed against the deep black of her face. *If a barefoot girl in ripped jeans and a T-shirt could look regal,* Sherry said, *Niani Shange did.* Like a true African queen. She was radiant, and otherworldly gorgeous, and Sherry hated her fucking guts. She hated the respect Niani commanded. She hated the attention Niani received. And for good measure she hated her because Richard would hate her. She and her friends were the perfect poster children for the multicultural agenda. *I'm on to your game, girlie-girl. I'm on to you.* Or so Sherry thought. Sherry had no idea at the time of the devastation

Niani would bring. *You could say that I underestimated her. And ... I suppose, you could blame me for everything that happened.*

Watching Jack and Niani together Sherry was struck by how little they actually talked to one another. Their relationship seemed almost telepathic. Or even *mutually parasitic.*

The afternoon's serenity was broken when a young black man came running across the main lawn, screaming, "Niani! Jack! Awwww hell! This is NOT good!"

The Black Student Union was in shambles. "Run Nigger Run!" was painted on the walls, along with a few song lyrics with which we had recently become familiar. *Of course,* Sherry said, *my first thought was* Richard. *Richard was my first thought often in those days, but that was the first time that it wasn't accompanied by unmentionable naughtiness.*

Although no one seems sure of the timeline now, it seemed like mere minutes before police were on the scene. Two black men were led away in handcuffs, screaming about injustice, and Jack Curry narrowly avoided getting arrested (or clubbed) himself before Niani grabbed him and pulled him back from the advancing officers. It did seem a tiny bit odd that no one opened, or even *noticed*, the Black Student Union office until one-thirty in the afternoon. But Sherry could not give it much thought before she was distracted by the two angry mobs—one white and one black—that had squared off on the center green. No violence—yet. Just a lot of vicious words, and tension so thick it was hard to breathe. The crowd outside of the two mobs watched in anticipation. Sherry stood in that crowd. Along the sides of the buildings, anyone who was neither white nor black kept a smart and safe distance.

Jack Curry and Niani ran through the spectators, splitting a path to the center of it all. Someone pushed Niani and she fell to the ground. A black guy and a white guy instantly started throwing punches at one another and it looked as though a full-scale riot was inevitable. Within seconds Curry smashed both guys in the face and they crumpled to the ground, bloody and unconscious. Everyone gasped and stepped away from Jack Curry as if he were a rabid pit-bull. Once again, for a mob, wise thinking.

"Jack! Stop!" Niani screamed, struggling to stand. Sarabjit, Marissa, Dave, and Lin ran to Niani's aid and helped her up. She threw herself immediately into the middle of the closing divide between the black and white crowds.

"Stop!" she yelled at everyone. "You've all got to stop this now!" She continued, ignoring whatever rebuke was coming her way. "I don't know who did that in the center today! And you know what?" Loud grumbling from the mass of people. "I don't care! I don't give a FUCK. It doesn't matter who it was. Whoever they are, y'all sure are making 'em happy! This is exactly what THEY want you to do." A few people shouted, but others quickly shouted them down. She went on, "They played a wack-ass cut, and y'all are dancing to it."

Corny, Sherry thought. But the handful of scattered laughs was enough to shave off a bit of tension. *She knows what she's doing I guess.*

Niani pointed at a group of Asians all huddled together. "Shit," she said. "If I had known this is what it took to get the Japanese and the Cambodians cuddling, I'd have painted 'white power' up in this bitch my freshman year." Lots of people laughed at that and Sherry instantly thought about what was written on her boots, for once grateful for her inherent invisibility. "Please," Niani said. "We gotta be better than this. Please."

In what has to be a gold-star moment in the history of bad timing, just as things were actually starting to calm, city and county police officers came stomping up the hill in full armor toward the grassy field. Niani screamed, "Everybody please! Run! Hurry! Get back to your classes! Get back to your dorms!" Upon seeing the police, people scattered every which way, knocking each other down in the process. Absolute chaos. Niani stepped toward the encroaching policemen, her palms stretched out toward them.

"No need. No need for that. Everything's peaceful here."

And they ... retreated. They listened to her.

There were no beatings, no more arrests.

Hmm. Well, Sherry thought, *no denyin' it. That's impressive.*

But any respect that I may have had for that girl just then vanished the moment I saw her later on behind the Fine Arts building ... sucking face with some alterna-slut.

"You wanna go somewhere?" Niani cooed at the girl, who nodded like a simp, and they wandered off together hand in hand.

Freaks, Sherry thought. *Fucking gross.* She was sickened. And confused, for she had assumed that Niani Shange and Jack Curry were *together* together. *And if they're not ... then what was the deal?* It was none of her business.

But she had to find out.

7.

"MIKAL, change the fuckin' channel, will ya?"

Like a little kid who can't stop picking at a scabbed-up knee, Richard was compelled beyond his will to watch any television program about the "rising scourge of hate crimes in America." He would curse and yell at the TV, holler on and on about the "liberal media" and how "we're being misrepresented."

But the thing is ... we really weren't. I'll be the first to bitch about the mainstream American media, how they're all bought and paid-for, and how they only represent one sanitized point of view. And sure, when they're dealing with the issue of racial "extremism" in America, they can't resist trotting out some toothless flapjack named Buford in a white dress and pointy hat who manages to pull his dick out of his retarded twelve-year-old sister long enough to explain how slavery is justified by the Bible and how whites are the only true humans because we're the only race who can blush. But on the occasion that they deal with Skins, they pretty much nail it. Perhaps they focus too much on the violence and destruction and don't dedicate adequate time to the endless hours spent watching cartoons and pro-wrestling, but all in all it's pretty close.

On this particular night, this particular pixelated Buford was in rare form, and Richard expressed God's gift to the white man full tilt by having a whole mess of boiling blood in his face.

"The white race has proved us selves unstoppable!" Buford exclaimed.

"Goddamn … the fucking Klan," Richard hissed. "Somebody get me an M16 and I will exterminate them all like the vermin that they are."

Meanwhile, the ladies pretty much ignored the whole affair, as they were busy at work on Sherry's makeover. Reeba and Jennie had cut Sherry's hair very short with chin length bangs. It was dyed a pronounced maroon with streaks of her natural blond showing through. She did look very hot and I could tell that she wanted Richard to say so. But apart from a smile and a thumbs-ups he never weighed in on the matter. I considered saying something myself, but thought better of it.

After a commercial break a counterpoint was provided by a very severe Panther wannabe in a black beret, who had apparently not gotten the memo that it was no longer 1974.

"No, we do not encourage violence," said Soul Brotha Number One. "No, we do not preach hate. We simply believe that the easiest, quickest, and most logical path towards peace is segregation. We hope to retain the purity of our race, and I would assume whites would like the same for theirs."

"Finally," Richard said. "A man with some basic common sense."

"Tap dancing porch monkey," Phil sneered. "Go back to Africa, spear chucker!"

Richard chuckled and shook his head. "Settle down, Phil."

"O-bee K-bee, Rich-berd," Phil replied *à la* Mushmouth. Chuckles all around.

"Just out of curiosity," Richard asked, "any of you guys know what became of the Brown Shirts after WWII?" I was about to answer when Richard held up his finger. He looked around at the rest of them. They weren't even paying attention. "Good. That's what I thought." We looked at each other and grinned. I looked over and saw Sherry watching us intently, as if she wanted in on the joke. *Don't you worry your pretty little head, doll face.*

The phone rang. Joe answered it with a "What," because he's pure class, you see.

"Uh huh," he continued, "Yeah. Hold on. Rich it's uh ... the, uh ... Special Olympics." We all snickered like morons. "Um ... they want to know if you'd consider giving them another ... er ... donation."

"Tell them thank you, but I gave all I could last time."

"Awww ... that's sweet," Sherry said, totally oblivious. Anne began to chime in and Richard made a cut motion across his neck.

"Rich," Joe said. "They're ... uh ... crying."

"Hang up, Joey." He did. "Okay," Richard continued, "let's get out of here." That was the last of that.

Barreling down the highway in Phil's behemoth station wagon, we could not have been any more conspicuous had we been shooting a bazooka out the back window. Swerving all over the road, taunting other drivers, openly drinking beer. An older Chinese couple in a Dodge Colt that should have been dragged out back and shot drove steady and cautious as we cut in front of them. We laughed as the old woman pulled out a rosary and began nodding and chanting. Screeching over to the next lane, we jumped behind them, then sped up and hopped in front of them again. Jennie showed them her tits. The old man gave us the finger. Phil pulled back over side by side with them, and Geoff leaned out the window and spat beer at them screaming, "Bonsai!" (which, admittedly, makes no goddamn sense). The beer Geoff spat instantly turned to mist about the highway, but I suppose it was the thought that counted. The couple wisely took the next exit and we headed on downtown.

Hitting all of our familiar haunts, we tried out a few new joints as well, with varying degrees of success. We ran into trouble for underagedness in a few spots and I thought Richard was going to destroy this one bartender for grabbing me by my collar and tossing me out the door. (Lucky for that guy he grabbed me and not Sherry.) Everywhere we went someone in our crew would make a comment about who they thought we should stomp, but except for a few dirty looks from a couple of SHARPs, it was pretty mellow most of the night. Had we been serious about looking for ruckus there were several black and Chicano clubs within walking distance whose patrons I'm sure would've been down for a head rumble, but we just never seemed to make it down that way.

"Pssst. Mikal," Sherry whispered in my ear as we entered this dingy Industrial club called Lucretia's. "If y'all are serious about wanting to lay somebody out, I'd like to nominate that guy." She indicated a young black fellow at the bar surrounded by white people. We watched homeboy and his Caucasian compatriots do a round of shots, and after he had downed his, he licked a line of salt off the hand of some brunette in a white tank top. "That's Trey McKinley. He's in my Economics class and he is a world-class prick. That girl's name is Melanie, and she's always hanging on him like he's Emperor Jones. It's fucking sickening."

"Yep, that's what we call a 'number one.' I wonder if the rest of the boys have seen him yet."

To this day I'm not sure who it was who started the number system, but within our crew we always ranked the various stompable offenses one through ten. Number ten escapes me today, but number one was "black man / white woman." I do remember number seven was "Phish fan."

"Jesus, I don't know if I feel like staying at this joint," Sherry said. "It's packed with fuckers from school."

I was just about to ask, *What did you expect?* when I saw a figure exiting the dance floor, slinking toward the bar. Her deep black skin glistened with perspiration that caught the dim lights of the bar just enough to make her shimmer and sparkle. I recognized her ... but felt I had never seen her before. Ezekial Johnson's little sister. *Niani Shange.* I was so taken with the sight of her for a moment that I hadn't realized that Sherry had completely vanished from the scene. I wasn't one to consider rounded African features or pitch-dark ebony skin in any way attractive. Never. Just not my thing. I choked for a moment when Niani yelled, "Come out and dance with me!" but I quickly realized that she was looking right through me. I didn't exist. And by the time I realized who actually was the intended invitee, I had nowhere to go. *Oh fuck.* Out of the corner of my right eye I saw his multi-colored arm slide across the bar to grab a drink, not a millimeter of white skin to be seen amidst the tribal twists and smears. A bicycle chain was wrapped around his wrist and held in place by a small padlock. I felt his knotted, natty ropes brush against my jacket. Tied into his hair were what sounded like ball bearings, and they clicked against the bar with a *crrritt, crrritt, crrritt.* I froze up, silently cursing my shaved head. Cursing my red braces. Regretting just for the moment all the conspicuous advertising of my politics and my gang, for these were images I knew he'd recognize, and it wasn't beyond or beneath this psychopath to carve that "white power" right off my neck with a broken bottle.

"Come on, Jack," Niani persisted. "You never dance with me. Just this once."

I'm invisible, I thought. *They don't see me. I'm a phantom. I am bar mist.*

"Be there in a second, Lees," he sighed. "Scout's honor."

She disappeared into a crowd of friends and he, after chugging his drink, followed behind shortly thereafter. Walking past he jabbed me with his elbow, which I immediately thought was a message, but he grunted, "Sorry," and went about his way. *I am invisible.*

Lees? Lisa. That's right ... her name used to be Lisa. I thought it odd for a moment that he called her by her old Blackchurch name. Odd, because who else in that bar even knew her given name except the two of them and me? *And I don't exist.*

I vaguely heard Joe say, "Can you believe that baboon cunt actually thinks people are looking at her?"

"Yeah," I chuckled. "Gruesome."

At no point had it been discussed, but we all knew where we'd be heading after Lucrecia's. We all simply knew that we would be visiting that section of town most folks called Candyland. Crawling with "number threes."

It was coming up on 2:30 AM and most clubs were closing down. We rolled into Candyland just in time to watch the flood of queers spill out into the streets, whooping and singing and prancing about. We pulled into a side alley, shut off the engine, and waited. Some play had just closed at the big theater downtown and many of these people were clearly from that production. Often these folks walked the streets in sizable groups and relocated to after-hours parties at apartment complexes just outside the center of town where parking was relatively safe. *Smart.* But there were always a few stragglers. First dates and out-of-towners and one-night-stands eager to get to dessert. That's whom we hunted. That's just the way it was.

Sure enough, separating from the mob were two young dandies holding hands and heading right our way. The one was dressed fairly conservative and, after we exited the wagon and trailed them for a couple of blocks, appeared to me to be a foreigner. English wasn't too strong. Some sort of Eastern European, but I don't know what exactly. The other was American all the way, loud and lit up like Mardi Gras. He wore a huge green feather boa and you could hear his stiletto high heels *click click click*ing down the asphalt from two blocks back. He minced and carried on in this excruciatingly affected high-pitched squeal, periodically calling out to friends across the street as they walked by. Like he was advertising his evening score. Showing off the prize he had won. He cuddled against his new friend and kissed him loudly, calling him either "Jezebel" or "Jessie Bear," I couldn't tell which. All the while we stalked silently behind.

After some time it was only them and us, the clamor of downtown somewhere in the distance. Watching the two of them flaunt and advertise I couldn't help but think about where they might be heading and what they would do once they got there. Would they shower together … work themselves into a lather, as the saying goes. *Play stupid little faggot games.* The thought of it nauseated me, but I had to dwell on it to get my blood to the right temperature. I had to boil. The more I imagined their costumes and sick little role-playing charades the more I wanted rip their throats out all on my own. Psyching myself up for the justice I was prepared to administer. *Will you put his nuts in your mouth, Queen Bee? What about you, Jezebear, do you welcome that cock into your ass?* I felt the vomit rising in my throat as my fists clenched and my pace quickened. Perhaps had these two gents not been so drunk or so smitten they would have felt the weight of doom pressing harder and harder at their backs as we marched ever closer. Perhaps they would have run or called a friend or the police. But they didn't. And by the time they stopped to make out under a streetlamp, it was simply too late.

"Evening, ladies," Richard said casually. The two of them stared at us for just a moment, mouths agape. Terrified, they huddled together, eyes darting every which way for a possible escape. Queenie squeaked out a pitiful "No" just before we rained down Hell and God's wrath upon them.

The girls had a ritual of their own whenever a stomp was underway. Half of them would laugh and the other half would pretend concern, giving us a finger wag and some vague "now now, that's not very nice" attitude. Who played what role was fluid and ever-changing. That night it was Suzi's turn for the latter. Sherry didn't cop to either, however. She was as blank and uninvolved as if she were standing on the curb waiting for the Metro. Like nothing much was going on at all.

Somehow or another the shrieker became mine and mine alone, the rest of the boys working over the bland foreigner who had rolled himself into a ball begging, "Please … to be leaving us … now alone, please." Something about the loud one brought out my rage, and the more he pleaded for mercy, the more he sobbed and howled, the greater my contempt grew. *Slam. Smash.* No matter how hard I beat him, though, he wouldn't surrender the act. *Crunch.* He would not lower his register. *Freak! Fucking freak!* He wouldn't drop the pose. *Sick!* He screamed like a woman, cried like a little girl, and all the thrashing in the world would not turn him back into a man.

"Faggot," I muttered as my boot slammed over and over into his abdomen. "Fuck, FUCK him, faggot."

"Please," he whimpered, his lipstick-smeared face awash with blood. "Please … don't … hurt … my baby."

"FUCK HIM!" I yelled, and buried the steel tip of my left boot deep into his ribcage. His forehead smacked the sidewalk and he fell unconscious, still quietly murmuring incoherent pleading, still in a high girl-squeak. A crowd of people several blocks north began charging down toward us, and we darted off, back to the wagon.

It was an unusually somber ride home. I don't know for sure what accounted for the spontaneous contemplative mood. Perhaps Anne summed it up when the silence became more than she could bear and she blurted out, "Fag bashing is God's work. It's holy duty. Everybody knows that it is the nature of every man to want to stick his cock inside every woman he sees and inseminate her. Queers violate that number one rule of nature. It's sick and it's an abomination."

Something about the word "inseminate" burrowed a hole into my skull and laid eggs there. I don't remember if I had ever wanted to stick my cock inside Anne, but after hearing "inseminate" drip from her lips like sour bile I never wanted to again. She may as well have grown a boil-and-tumor-ridden tentacle from her forehead for how unattractive I found her after that. *Inseminate. Inseminate. No, thank you all the same.*

By the time we had gotten home most everyone was rowdy again, laughing and mocking the two queers with fairly spot-on impersonations of their cries for help and pity. Suzi chuckled a little bit. I guess I did too. Richard did not. Sherry seemed oblivious even then that anything had happened.

As we climbed into bed Suzi said, "I don't feel like having sex tonight. But I'll suck on you if you need me to." "Suck on you" nestled into my brain real snug right next to "inseminate." It was a rather tight and uncomfortable fit. I kissed her quickly and silently and rolled over, bullshitting immediate slumber. Within a minute I heard her fall asleep for real. Girl could fall out on a dime. Must have been all the blows to the head.

I lay there for close to an hour. My muscles twitched and throbbed, locking and unlocking, as the adrenaline drained from my system. I felt the familiar and inevitable emptiness that follows after a hard rush has faded. It's a hollow despair, entirely synthetic, only chemical.

As I walked out to the kitchen I was bombarded with "OH RICHARD! FUCK ME PLEASE! HARDER! HARDER!!!" I ran to the bathroom and heaved into the toilet.

Rolling onto my back on the tiled floor I stared directly into the naked light bulb protruding from the ceiling. Shivering with cold muscle shakes. I felt gummy and white, like a chunk of beef jerky with the juices sucked out. Like a chlorinated open wound.

After what was certainly far too long to be lying on a bathroom floor, I stumbled back out into the kitchen. There I found Richard leaning against the sink downing a can of beer, doused in sweat, completely stark naked.

"Dude, my bad!" I said, retreating back into the bathroom.

"Hey Mikey," he said casually, "you have fun tonight?"

Whatever, I thought. If he wasn't bashful I figured there was no reason for me to be. *Well, I see what all the screaming is about anyway.*

"Yeah, sure," I said, coming out to the kitchen. He offered me a beer. I waved it off and he cracked it open and drank it himself.

"That's cool," he said. "Then maybe you can explain something to me. Beating up faggots. How exactly does that advance the revolution?" I didn't have an answer. He continued, "Are queers creating half-breeds? It seems to me that they are not. So how are they a problem? I mean, I don't really care one way or the other, but this isn't a game. I'm serious about this cause. Are we revolutionaries or thugs?"

"They spread fatal diseases," I offered.

"Good! I fucking applaud that! Look who's exterminated from that disease campaign. Niggers, drug addicts, the flab of the human race. I thought we were in favor of that sort of thing, or was there a meeting I wasn't invited to."

I should have seen this coming. Richard was known for his peculiar perspectives that occasionally flew in the face of the party line. His support for the state of Israel was the most egregious of these points. His devotion to the Republican Party was another sore spot, particularly as anti-government sentiment was on the rise within the movement. "This is no longer the party of Lincoln," he informed a group of bemused elders. "Hell, it's no longer the party of Goldwater or Nixon. You will alienate yourselves from this new rising power at your own peril, gentlemen." I often worried that this sort of thing would ultimately get us blackballed, but no one ever really debated Richard. They did grumble behind his back, old washwomen that they were.

"You said *campaign*," I told him. "Are you buying into the whole government plot theory?"

"This is all I'm saying," he replied, "Something that is destroying the scum of humanity is fine with me, whomever is responsible for unleashing it. Take that for what it's worth. Hell ... I don't give a fuck. If you all get your jollies by beating down a bunch of sissies I'm not going to get in your way. Just don't lose sight of what really matters."

"I don't get it, Rich."

"What don't you get?"

"You love the fucking GOP but you hate the military worse than you hate fags."

"I don't love the GOP, first of all. I just recognize allies when I see them. And I don't hate the military either."

"But we're always fighting with soldiers. You're always calling them 'sheep.'"

"Tough love. I'm getting them strong for the real war."

"Ah ..."

"And all those corporations that you loathe so much?"

"Yeah?"

"We're gonna take them over. We'll do the right thing for a change."

"Is that right?"

"Good night, Mikey. Stay focused. You're my man."

And that was that.

8.

EXTRA credit. That was the only reason Sherry went to Brownard Auditorium that evening. Her Twentieth-Century American History prof was offering extra credit to anyone who attended the special "Civil Rights" hippity-dippity who-hah that evening, and given her less-than-stellar grades in that class, she needed all the bonus points she could scrounge up.

On the bill were a couple of old, local "freedom riders" there to regale the crowd with their harrowing tales of riding desegregated buses through the sixties South. Also on the program, a student was to be honored with a special award for outstanding-community-civil-rights-liberal-activist-whatever. I don't suppose I have to tell you who she was, do I?

Things briefly threatened to get interesting when a platoon of very frightening-looking uniformed black men entered the hall and stood in a solid line along the back wall. Apparently there was a black fraternity on campus that was kicked out some time in the late

1980s for some sort of overly militant activity. They reformed off-campus and remain a fearsome presence to this day, often showing up at open campus events. I believe they are called *Black United!* or *Black Unchained!* but I may have that all wrong. Their chapter head, or Minister of Whitey Killin' or what have you, was none other than childhood chum of Jack Curry, Senbe Shabazz. By then their feud was in full swing. (Had they remained enemies … what would my life be like today? Perhaps it's best not to ponder that sort of thing.)

As soon as Niani and Jack and their rainbow coalition arrived there was immediate tension radiating from the back wall. Curry said something under his breath toward the perfect line of black power, baiting them in some fashion. Niani quickly grabbed him and dragged him away.

What the ancient bus people had to say was probably interesting, but they mumbled, and they were too quiet, and Sherry was bored and didn't really pay any attention. Few others did either, and the collective indifference toward these speakers apparently stuck in Ms. Shange's craw.

Some ridiculously overdressed black preacher served as master of ceremonies.

Now, don't get me wrong, Sherry said. *I had spent pretty much my entire life up until that point faithfully attending church every Sunday. I considered myself a fairly devout Christian lady. But try though I did, I could not understand half of what this fat, sweaty blowhard was yammering on about.*

Really it was just a grand show with a lot of histrionics and casting about, and most of what grunted through his lips was pure gibberish. "… and if we just put our faith in Jesus Christ, our Savior, we shall have no fear. Praise the Lord." The audience clapped and someone shouted *Amen!* and Sherry stared at her watch as the second hand clicked along. He continued, "I would like now to introduce to you all a most outstanding young lady. A woman whose tireless efforts, both on campus and in our community, have kept the work, the memory, and the spirit of the Reverend Doctor Martin

Luther King Jr. alive for us today. Ladies and Gentlemen, it is my honor and my privilege to present the Martin Luther King Christian Student Achievement Award to Miss Niani Shange."

The crowd applauded enthusiastically. Niani calmly stood and walked to the stage. People smiled warmly to her as she was handed her plaque. She took to the podium, smiling politely.

For a brief second, though, Sherry said, *I swear her eyes got all sharp and steely ... and Jack-like ...*

But then she softened again, smiling at the audience.

"Thank you everyone," she said. "Thank you. And let me say what an honor it is for me to just hear my name mentioned in the same sentence as Dr. King's. And I am thrilled beyond words to be sharing the stage with all of these American heroes this evening." Polite applause from the peanut gallery. "I don't see courage like theirs much these days, and that's unfortunate, but we all benefit today from their sacrifice, and for that I thank them all. In keeping with the spirit of the evening, I hope you all would not mind indulging me for just a brief moment ..."

Niani began to recite a poem from some old black writer Sherry had never heard of, *Count Somebody,* she thought, and neither was she terribly interested. Niani proceeded to talk about "Pagan hearts" and "shadowed places" and the like ...

"'Not for myself I make this prayer ...'" And so on, and so on, and so forth. Sherry went about absently doodling in her notebook. *This had better pay off,* Sherry thought.

But, at some point ... Sherry couldn't help but sit up and take notice of the fact that the well-dressed Christians around her were not appreciating the performance all that much.

"'For me, my faith lies fallowing, I bow not 'til I see,'" Niani recited, then indicated with a sweep of her hand the audience before her, "'but *these* are humble and believe, bless their credulity ...'"

A collective squirm began to resonate throughout the hall, and Niani went on. And on. There was no missing the murmur grumbling beneath the surface. She had their attention. No denying. And the vibe was getting ugly.

Sherry was not quite sure what all this talk about "black sheep" and "bastard kin" was about, but it seemed, as best as she could surmise, to be a fairly head-on "fuck you" to the crowd. *Why would she do this?* Sherry thought, torn halfway between sneaking out while the sneaking was still good ... and wanting to see what might be going down. *Why is she trying to piss off the people that are here to honor her?* It just didn't make any sense. It reached a point where it didn't even matter what Niani was saying anymore. *It was how she said it.* Pointed at least. And incongruously venomous. *But still ...*

Niani finally ended with an, "Amen."

Nothing in return. "Amen?" She said again. One lone, nervous cough was heard from somewhere. "AMEN!" she shouted.

Dead silence. Long, agonizing, and thick as a cold fog. Niani looked out and smiled, oddly satisfied.

"In conclusion," she said after a while, "I would just like to say that it will be through perseverance and dedication, NOT blind faith and self-congratulatory complacency, that we will one day reach the promised land. The struggle continues. Thank you."

And with that she left the stage in silence. *Wow. What a bitch!* Sherry thought.

It was hard not to be intrigued, though.

As Niani walked toward the back of the hall there were a few scattered claps. Jack Curry met her in the middle aisle. He hugged her and they turned to leave. People rustled in their seats. A few got up to leave. The reverend rushed to the mic for a bit of spin control. "Thank you Miss Shange for that spirited ... provocative ... blah blah blah ... genius of the Harlem Renaissance ... vigilant and steadfast ..." and so forth.

"*Assalaam-Alaikum*, Sister Niani," said Senbe Shabazz as Niani and Jack walked past.

"*Valaikum-Assalaam*, Brother Senbe," she replied politely.

"What, no 'ma lick'em' for me, Arnold?" Curry said, sour faced, feigning hurt feelings.

"Hello, Mr. Curry," Shabazz said through his teeth.

"Goodbye, Mista Lincoln," said Jack with a dainty wave. (He even managed to make a sarcastic flip o' the wrist into something hideous and creepy.) And with that they left, leaving the Afro-militants behind. Shabazz tightened his lips in anger. The other men remained statues. Sherry exited quickly, not wanting any more to do with this situation. Credits be damned.

"Could you at least try to be civil sometimes?" Niani asked Jack as Sherry headed in the opposite direction.

To which he asked the posse, "Hey, do y'all think if he had read three books he'd have given himself three names?"

I had a feeling right then, Sherry said, *that I would be getting to know that man very well very soon. He possessed what I wanted. What I couldn't live without.*

Meanwhile, Suzi and I had found ourselves in that corner of Relationshipville called "that odd place." Big surprise. Couples always talk about traveling through "that odd place." *We're going through that odd place right now.* And everyone nods knowingly, as if it weren't a completely pointless and ridiculous sojourn. Suzi would say she "wanted more" from our relationship, but would never tell me what that was. "If you don't know, I'm not going to tell you," she'd huff. Her shtick was to stay away for days at a time and not call. When I would do likewise she would break down and cry, "How can you just not call me?!?!" *I'm no good at mind games,* I'd tell her. *You win.* Occasionally she would accuse me of only wanting her around to fuck, which honestly was not true, but it's a hard charge to protest when you're a seventeen-year-old guy. That's just the way it is.

As a result I often had the joint to myself most of the evening when Richard was at the factory, which was a-okay with me. Despite repeated promises never to do so, we'd both started to entertain notions of attending college. Sherry had been on Richard about re-enrolling for some time and it was beginning to take hold. "He's just so smart," she'd say. "I hate seeing him squander that. And you're smart too, Mikal.*" For whatever that's worth.* So notions were at least wined and dined. Mine were fairly abstract, whereas Richard was really getting into the idea of exposing college professors for the Marxists he assumed they all were. When I mentioned that perhaps that was a flimsy reason to shell out such an obscene amount of money he replied, "I can't destroy and rebuild the system from the inside if I'm not inside. I've been to university before. It's not like it's difficult. I gotta get realistic if I'm gonna go big."

"How big are you planning to get?" I asked.

"All the way, my man. All the way. If that pants-shitting retard David Duke can make it, it'll be a cakewalk for me."

"What about all them tattoos you got? You're staring down the barrel of a helluvalotta laser work. How you gonna explain all that scar tissue to your potential constituency?"

"Two words: Agent Orange."

"You're going to lie about being in a war?"

"Oldest politico trick in the book."

"Nice."

I had figured, with Richard slaving away on the assembly line until midnight, Sherry's post-class visits would cease. Or at least decrease. I figured wrong. Between Richard's late shift and Suzi's cold shoulder Sherry and I began spending more and more time together. Just the two of us. Another fairly odd place to be. It's hard to know how to feel.

At first I found her bothersome and obtrusive. Jabbery and self-absorbed and annoyingly insecure. Every day I'd dread the inevitable after-school special. The ritual was always the same. She'd come in, shed her books, her boots, her socks, march into the kitchen for a brew, come back in and plop onto the couch, and start in with, "What a day, I'll tell you what."

After a while, though, I began to expect her at a certain time, and I'd get irritable when she was late. As Richard's right-hand man, after all, I'd be derelict in my duties not to keep tabs on his prized possession, right? I started to worry about where she might be and whom she might be with. Instincts. Ignore them at your own peril.

Her story would usually involve some pompous, asshead prof, a lost loan payment, a combative classmate. But there was often some passing mention of "Curry and Shange and them," which would appear in the form of a single word: curryandshangeandthem, followed by pronounced rolling of the eyes. "I hear that Curry can speak five foreign languages ... but the shit he says doesn't even make sense in English." "Shange is organizing a protest to counter-protest some other counter-protest that's protesting a protest nobody even knows about. Sheesh." As time went on, however, that seven-syllable word curryandshangeandthem morphed into a similar but significantly different one: jackandnianiandthem.

"Richard would want me keeping an eye on those people, don't you think Mikal? They're dangerous."

"Yeah ..."

"I found out where they live at. The two of them anyway. Jamestown St."

"It's pronounced *JAY-muss-ton*."

"You know where that is?"

"I'm familiar."

"Don't worry. I keep a safe distance. They don't even know I exist."

"I believe you." And I did. And I was wrong. Here's the lesson: never underestimate the all-seeing eye of the deranged paranoiac.

I wasn't sure what to do the day she came home teary and red-eyed, her face blotchy with salt burn. I still don't know what I should have done.

"Bad day?" I asked.

"Bad day," she replied.

"Okay … So … what happened?"

"Nothing much. I just get emotional sometimes."

"Hmmmm."

"Richard told me he loved me last night," she said with a sniffle. "I told him that I loved him too."

"Quit changing the subject. What happened today?"

"Jack Curry made me cry today. That's all." A poisonous chill ran through me. *Forever a specter …*

"Uh huh … Okay … Do you just want to not tell me, or are we playing a game here? I'm not into games, Sherry."

"Jack Curry grabbed me today and dragged me into a men's bathroom and slammed me against the wall and ripped my shirt open."

"WHAT?!?!?!?!?!"

"It's not as bad as it sounds."

"ARE YOU FUCKING CRAZY? Not as bad as it sounds?! We're gonna hunt that fucker down and destroy him!"

"NO! Don't do anything! Please, Mikal, please don't tell Richard!"

"Noooooooooooo dice. I HAVE to tell him. You know that."

"PLEASE! Just between us. He didn't hurt me, okay?"

"He dragged you into a fucking bathroom, threw you against a wall and ripped your clothes off, and that's not hurting you?"

"You don't understand."

"He's DEAD. I understand that."

"No—"

"He's not going to see another morning."

"You tell Richard and I'll deny it. I'll tell him you've had a vendetta against the guy for years and now you're lying on me to get revenge. You wanna risk him taking my word over yours? You up for that challenge, Mikal?"

"WHY WOULD YOU DO THAT?!" I was beyond furious. At that point I didn't even care if Jack Curry had raped her. I didn't care if he had rammed his staff right up into her lungs. The fact that she would dare even think of driving a wedge between Richard and I ...

"Why are you taking up for that fucking ... swamp creature?" I demanded. "You fucking him?"

"NO!"

"You wanna fuck him?"

"Fuck you, Mikal! I'm with Richard only. I love Richard. And he loves me."

"You're playing with some serious shit, little girl. You just don't know."

"You're gonna make me cry too. Just like Jack. You both use your tongues like a weapon. You and Jack, you're just the same."

"Don't ... you ... EVER say that to me again, you rank little—"

"Listen to yourself, Mikal. Who do you sound like?"

"You don't know me."

"I do so know you. And I know him too."

"I'll bet you know him all right. I bet you let him nail you in that bathroom. I bet you yanked him off. I bet you licked it off his thigh."

"Keep talking, *Jack*. Same old song. The lyrics haven't changed."

"Get out of my house."

"You wanna throw me out? Huh? You wanna throw me around? Wanna pin me to the wall? You wanna tear my clothes off?"

"Get the fucking hell out of my house."

"This is Richard's house."

"GET. OUT."

"Everybody pushes me away."

She stormed out. I sat there shaking with rage. Why? Why would she put me in that position? What really happened? I wanted her gone forever. I wished she had never come around. I knew I'd have to watch her now. For Richard. And I knew Richard couldn't know that I was watching her. I couldn't risk him knowing whatever she was up to. And I couldn't risk him knowing I was hiding things from him. I couldn't risk him suspecting me. I couldn't risk him pushing me away …

An hour later, she called on the phone.

"I'm sorry."

"*I'm* sorry. Are you okay?"

"I'm okay. Still friends?"

"Still friends."

"Mikal?"

"Yeah?"

"How long do you think you're going to do this?"

"Do what?"

"Where do you see yourself in twenty-five years? Where do you see yourself in ten? Where do you see yourself in the future?"

"I don't."

"Hm. 'Kay. See ya."

And that was that.

9.

JACK did not hurt me that day. Not physically. He hurt my feelings. Maybe I had that coming to me.

Sherry sat in the downstairs hallway alcove of the University Center right outside the bookstore. Watching them.

It was pretty boring, actually. They weren't really doing anything except goofing around by the greeting cards.

Sherry paged through the school newspaper a couple of times without really reading it. The front page contained a picture of Niani and a banner headline announcing "Local Civic and Religious Leaders Outraged by Honored Student— 'Out of Line,' Says Rev. Brinks." Sherry had the hall pretty much to herself, as it was noonish and most folks were in the cafeteria.

Out of line, she thought. *That's a good description of her across the board. Out of line. Out of order.*

Jack Curry and Niani exited the bookstore, bade each other a "see ya at home," and headed in opposite directions. Sherry stood up to go catch a bite when she felt a rough hand grab her collar and whip her around. Before she realized what happened she was trapped against the wall of the little boy's room. She tried to scream but couldn't even so much as squeak. Jack held her shoulders hard against the cold tile wall. She was paralyzed. His face mere inches from hers as he glared right into her. His eyes were like two pitch-black chasms. Nothing behind them.

"So howzaboutya, little ham?" he growled. "What's your story, THINK HARD NOW! Who are you and what the fuck do you want?"

She could barely eke out a sound.

"I ... I ... I—"

"Have been following us? Couldn't help but notice. Somebody send ya? Shit! Didn't think we were that important yet."

He squinted, noticing the top of her tattoo peeking out from under her blouse. He yanked the collar down and a button went flying, rolling across the floor and clinking into the corner. His face darkened further as he stared at the swastika, but he did not look surprised. *He's going to kill me.*

"For, for, for your information," she stuttered desperately, "that's a—"

"Sun wheel? Nice try, piglet. Pull the other one."

Right at that moment the door to the men's room flew open and some neckbone frat boy wandered in. He stopped short, staring at them. The three looked at each other in silence for a fat, stifled moment. Finally the guy just gave a little "my bad" salute, turned on his heel ... and left.

As if suddenly realizing his trespass, Jack backed quickly away and walked to the opposite wall. Disgusted with himself. He turned his back, muttering, "Sorry. Sorry. Didn't mean it to be like that. That's not how I meant it. Not at all. No. No ..."

If I ran, Sherry thought, *would he chase me? Should I say something?*

"Jack ... look. I'm not trying to step on anybody's toes or anything."

"What?" he said turning toward her again. "What the hell are you talking about?"

I don't know.

"I'm not trying to get in the way, Jack. I just want to—"

"Huh? Jack? I've never even met you before! I don't fucking know your name."

I know.

"That girl," she stammered. "That black girl. Your girlfriend. See, I saw her ... and maybe you don't know ... I just really don't really think you know what I ... or, what I mean is—"

"She's not my girlfriend," he said, his voice suddenly hollow. Distant.

"Oh ... I see ..."

Hmmmmm ...

There was a long empty moment, then he turned his glare back on Sherry.

"You little Nazi spunk rag ... Staking out a hit on her? Is that what's going on? Is that what you're doing? Little James Earl fuckin' Ray in a black lace bra? GODDAMN I thought you people were all gone by now!"

"IT'S NOT LIKE THAT!" Sherry screamed. Curry did not so much as blink. "I want to talk to you. Okay? Can we get out of this fucking toilet please?"

So they walked in silence.

I don't know where we were heading, we just strolled along the main lawn as if we had a purpose or destination.

Sherry caught the vibe that Jack Curry was barely tolerating her presence, and the slightest wrong move on her part would bring about dire consequences. So she kept her mouth shut. Across the way they saw Trey McKinley walking with Melanie. They called out to Jack and waved. He gave them the peace sign.

"What up, homey?" Trey yelled.

Painful.

"A'ight T-dog! A'ight Mel!" Jack replied, smiling ... if you could call it that. Up close it was more like a wolf bearing fangs, but Sherry figured that's probably the best he could do.

Said Sherry, *I've always felt that a smile doesn't so much happen in the lips, it happens in the eyes. And looking at Jack just then I couldn't imagine those cold dead stones ever warming to even the tiniest smile.*

As Trey disappeared behind South Hall, Jack quietly sang the "witch's guard" melody from *The Wizard of Oz* ...

"Oreo ... reoooooooo ..."

"Are you calling him an Oreo?" Sherry laughed.

"Not me," he said sarcastically. "That's not nice."

"If he's an Oreo, what are you?"

A thoughtful pause, then ...

"Good question," he said nodding. "Naw, they're cool, though."

"I think he's a prick."

"He's okay."

Another pause.

"So ... Jack, um, I hear that you're fluent in five different languages. Or is it six?"

"Eh, fluent is pushing it."

"It must be wild to be able to communicate with so many different people."

"Heh ... yeah ..."

Guy speaks five languages, Sherry thought, *but can only grunt at me.*

So they walked some more ...

And I began blathering on and on like an idiot. I don't even know how it started. Told him way too much. Where I was from, what my family was like, how hard it was to move away from home and my friends and my safe little cocoon, how Richard and I met. How welcome I felt in his circle of friends. (Shut up shut up! I thought to myself. Dumbass, shut up! But nope, no such luck.) I didn't get into details about the Fifth Reich and pretty much shrugged off the whole 'skinhead' thing as well as I could. I tried to make it sound like stupid little kid's stuff and not really a big deal at all. "It's just punk rock, you know? Pick your pose, get your costume together." I indicated his Napalm Death T-shirt. He didn't respond. I couldn't read him in the slightest. He didn't speak, and gave no indication that what I was saying meant anything to him. So I prattled on and on filling up the silence with whatever. Finally I cracked and started asking him questions head on. How did he and his friends get together? How did they meet? What was his home life like? How long had he known Niani? Had they always been close? What made them tick, whirl, click, and whistle? What's it all about, Alfie? Nothing. He didn't answer me. At all. I finally gave up.

"I just want a little peek inside," I said, small. "That's all. What's your world like. There's something going on in there that's just so totally different and I just wanted to—"

"*Uh huh,*" *he said, stopping me short.* "*Okay. I'm gonna ask this in the nicest way I can think of ... Are you really this fucking dense or is it an act?*" *I was stunned. He said it in such a casual way I had to hit a mental 'rewind' to be sure I heard it right. He continued,* "*So, let's look at the play-by-play. You hooked up with a guy who bashes people's heads in 'cuz you thought he was ooooooo dangerous. A rebel. Leader of the pack. How exciting. But now ... shucks, that's just not enough. Now you need some new honey pot to stick your fingers into. Fill that empty void. Is your life so bankrupt that you constantly need some new bullshit trial? Okay, and what could be more clandestine than for a skinhead's main squeeze to—*"

"*Look, asshole,*" *I spat.* "*You don't have me figured out, okay? I'm not like that. I'm not looking to stick my fingers in any void. You fuck. I love my boyfriend and we've got our thing going and you've got yours.*" *I should have stopped there. Alas,* "*I just thought maybe I could reach across the aisle and say 'hello,' but now I see you for what you are. Scared. You're too scared to even talk to me.*" *I don't know why, but I wanted to push him. I'd heard so much about how unhinged he was, I wanted to see how wide and hard I could make him swing. He tried to stare me down, and I would not flinch. And for a split second ... I wondered if he thought I was pretty at all.* "*Left, right, it's all meaningless to me. Does it mean anything to you?*" *Nothing.* "*It's all about that girl,*" *I continued.* "*You know it, I know it. That girl who's not your girl. The one that's so close ... oh, but just out of reach. It's ALL about her. But ... she's not with you. So why can't you let me in a little? You're never going to be happy like that anyway.*"

Oh my god, why did I say that? Like water on a grease fire—

"*YOU DON'T KNOW A GODDAMN THING ABOUT FUCKALL, YOU INBRED COUNTRY FRIED TWAT!!!*"

"I've seen your type before. All your life you've walked in a haze with no thoughts of your own. Somebody else's fucking opinions, some pre-fab beliefs. A little sucking and squeezing in the back of a letterman's pick-up or Pappy's outhouse and you think you know what's what. Now you're out in the 'real world' to find yourself and get your learn on but you're still too bottled-up Catholic, afraid God and your dead relatives are watching you masturbate. Can you hang with all the freakos and faggots and darkies running about? Wanna take a trip to the nigger side of town so long as you can go home after, right? What? Why you still here? What do you want from me? Go on, then! Run on back to your fucking boyfriend!"

"You're such a fucking jerk! People say, 'Oh, that's Jack. He looks like a monster, but he cares about folks.' But you don't care about anybody! You don't help anybody! You and your poseur bleeding heart friends just put on a big show to impress fuckin' everybody. But it's all BULLSHIT! You are just as cruel as anyone else, you hypocrite! Stop it. Shut up."

I started to cry. "I said stop it, you fucking bastard, I just wanted to talk. Fuck you! Can't we just talk?"

I was really bawling, and that just made him meaner.

"Oh is that what you are?! Is that where you live at?! SHUT UP! I'm leaving now, all right?! I'll leave you alone! I don't want anything from you! I don't want anything!!!"

He snarled boyfriend *and began goose-stepping and throwing the salute. "Sieg Heil! Sieg Heil!" I covered my ears and ran away as fast as I could, sobbing, terrified and humiliated. "Run on home, Eva Braun!" he yelled. "Go on, Ellie Mae Clampett, you hillbilly slut, go let your brothers gang fuck you some more! Run on back to the sticks, YOU FUCKING HICK!!!"*

Some would probably say that that should have been enough to keep me away for good.

But it wasn't.

10.

Suzi called me around 9:30 PM. The waiting game was, apparently, over.

"You home alone?" she asked.

"Yep."

"Miss you."

"I'm always here. You can come over any time."

"How's about now?"

It's a peculiar thing, you know, how confident I was that everything between us would work out in the end. I was sure we'd weather any storm. Make it through the trials and tribulations. Uncertainly and strife, Mars and Venus, bend in the road's not the end of the road, all that dog shit. There was never a doubt in my mind. *Wait it out, it'll all be fine.* When I opened the door for her that night and she practically dove into my arms I thought to myself, *Nicely played, old chap. Jolly good show indeed.*

Without a word spoken we rushed to my room on the back porch, freed each other of any and all burdensome clothing, and fell in a naked heap onto my futon, gobbling each other alive.

"Wait!" she gasped. "Do y-you ... really want to ... really t-take me there?"

"Yes! Of course! Anything you want!"

"Go g- ... get ice."

I ran out to the kitchen and yanked an ice tray out of the freezer that had frozen, frost covered, onto the door. Contained therein was exactly one cube. When I got back to the porch she had already started without me, working her fingertips between her thighs, curling her wrist in circles.

"Round off the edges for me," she whispered biting her lip, here eyes shut tight. I put the cube in my mouth, twisting it back and forth in my lips, melting it into a workable dome shape. From there I simply did as I was told, following her every instruction to the letter. "Rub it here ... Oh yes, that's it, right there ... Slide it back in ... deeper ... Just like that, in a circle ... oh god yes, right like that ..." She shuddered and squirmed, her arms locked stiff as she grabbed hold of the sheets with both hands. Her moaning got louder as her breaths shortened, her head jerking back and forth across the cushion. "Oh god, Mikal, I don't know ... if I c-cuh-can taaaaaaake ... much more!" All at once she arched her back, bucking hard against my hand. She screamed, thrashing up and down on the mattress as I felt the diminishing ice cube disappear into oblivion. She rolled away from me, curling up into a ball at the top right corner of the futon, shivering and cooing. "Oh fuck ... Oh Jesus ... that was amaaaaaazing ... Ooooooooo my god, it's shooting all through my body. Little micro-gasms all over. I can feel it in my toes!" I sat back beaming, feeling fifteen feet tall and cast-iron. I don't know how much I could honestly have taken credit for, but I was proud to be a part of it at any rate. "Oh fuck yeah ..." she continued, panting, wiping a tear from her cheek. "That's it right there. That's just how HE does it. Yeah. That's what he does to me. And she's so jealous. She's jealous of me."

I sat granite still, dumb-struck, my mouth gaping open like a mounted trout. She didn't even notice.

"Oh yeah," she said. "She is so jealous of what we share."

And that's how she opted to tell me.

But let's be honest, I kind of already knew, didn't I?

11.

NOT many people know about my brother. Kaleb was his name. Two years my junior. I barely remember him. Died when I was eight. I've since met a number of people who have survived leukemia, but when Kaleb was diagnosed I don't remember death being anything but a forgone conclusion. He fought like a champ, you know. But he was just so goddamn little. My people are slight folk as a rule on both Mom's and Dad's side, and he was tiny even by our standards. I don't even remember going to his funeral. Perhaps I didn't go.

We were still living in Louisville, I was ten or eleven, the first time I ever stood up to my father. I don't recall what set him off, but he was whaling on Mom with a curtain rod. She shrieked and blubbered, curled up on the kitchen floor, and I ran in and jumped between them. Dad didn't so much as pause, he simply kept whacking—on me instead—as I was in the way.

"Get the fuck out, Mikal, or I'll beat yer ass bloody!"

I didn't flinch, though it stung like a thousand hornets. I called him a "weak asshole" and told him if he touched my mother again I'd slit his throat while he slept. "Don't sleep, you weak asshole," I said, short on words just then. He called me "tough guy" and pulled out his .357. Of course it was loaded. It always was and so was he. My mother crawled up on her knees and threw her arms around me, sobbing, begging him to put it away.

"Ya heard 'im threaten me, Tanya!" he yelled, waving the gun back and forth between my mother and I. He stumbled a bit in a deep vodka drunk and cocked the piece. My arms and neck throbbed. The bass drum in my ear needed tuning.

All at once he fell to the floor in a weeping heap. He dropped the gun under the table and I had a mind to grab it and shoot his face clean off.

"I love y'all so much," he cried. "I'm so sorry!" He began cradling his arm, rocking back and forth, snot, tears, and drool spilling down his face. "My baby boy," he sobbed into the negative space in the crook of his arm where a baby would be. "My baby K ... where's my baby K at ... where's he at ..."

"You let him die," I said. "He could have lived, but you let him die."

"Where's he at, my tiny little baby boy ..."

I spat on him and called him out for a "queer." Mom grabbed me and we ran out of the house. Nowhere else to go, we stayed in a gnarly-ass roach motel called The Pit Stop Lodge.

She called him that night. Of course. He pleaded with her to come home. He promised he'd never hurt her or me again, and he swore he'd never pull the gun on us ever again, and he vowed on his mother's eternal grave to get rid of the gun once and for all. But he did, and he did, and he didn't. That's just the way it is.

"Suzi, this has to stop right now!"

I paced about in a frothing rage, flinging my arms aimlessly about as she, cool and calm, got dressed and prepared to leave.

"You just don't understand, Mikal. You don't understand the bond that we have, him and me. The love that's between us. I'm sorry. I never wanted to hurt you."

"Hurt ME?! I ain't the one who's fucking HURT, Suze! We got to go to the cops! We can't let that diseased bastard get away with this!"

"Don't you talk about Daddy like that!"

"How can you call that fucking cretin 'Daddy'?! This is the most morally di—"

"Ooooooooooh morals." She threw up her hands in a grand display. "That means a FAT lot coming from you, Mikal. Mister Aryan Nation. How many times have I watched you attack people—who never done a thing to you—and beat them half to death? Huh? How many times? How many people have you hurt? Not for your so-called 'revolution,' but just because it got your rocks off. And you want to lecture me about morals? You've got balls, my love. Big, heavy, metal balls swinging right between your knees. Morals. Ho ho ho. Too funny for words."

"You want me to quit, Suzi? Do you? Cuz I will. If it bothers you, then I promise on my life that I won't never harm another person so long as I live, no matter what. Okay? I'll give it ALL up if that's what you want. All of this. Okay?! I would do that *for you*." And I meant it.

"No, I don't think you will, Mikal. And for the record, I don't care what you do and I don't care who you stomp. Some people are sub-human and they get what they deserve. But that's beside the point. I don't think you ever would quit, no matter what you say. It's not because I don't think you're sincere. It's because I know in my heart that I'm not your first love." She indicated Richard's bedroom door. My face burned so hot you could have lit kindling off my forehead. I wanted to grab her and slap her hard for crossing that line. I wanted to scream at her and shake some sense into her. But I simply stood rigid, and with all my strength forced a meager smile.

"Yeah, Suze? Well … I know I ain't your first love neither."

"You're damn right you're not." And she walked out. And that was that.

I never saw her again.

I didn't tell anyone why Suzi and I had broken up. "It just happens, you know. People grow apart." I figured they would find out on their own someday anyway. I was right. But that next night it was all about Cheer Mikey Up, so we hit the town running, everyone promising to buy me a drink. A promise they all made good on, though I now certainly wish that they hadn't.

Yeah, we painted the town red, all right. And we had help. At about 1:30 AM, after hitting every bar that would let us in, we headed across the viaduct to the West Side. See what was shaking at that guy Meat's place. We never made it that far.

I still don't know where exactly we were, but I was the first to spot them.

"Hey, Sssshurry," I slurred, pointing out the window as we stopped for a red light, "ain't that that nigger you wanted us we should stomp up the uth'r night at Lucree … sha's … ?"

"Yup," she said. "That's old Oreo Trey and his white chocolate arm candy Melanie."

With that, Joe threw the van in reverse, slammed it in drive, and peeled up to the sidewalk.

"I think these number ones need a lesson," Joe announced. "Do I hear a 'nay'?"

With that everyone poured out of the van. Upon seeing us, Trey and Melanie froze in terror. I don't think anyone spoke.

There was no pause or hesitation. We all just immediately lunged for the guy. We beat him to the ground and went in for a circle-kick. Melanie ran off screaming and Richard yelled at the girls, "FUCKING GET HER!"

Sherry said:

Little girl was quick. Must have been an athlete or something. She kicked off her high heels and was definitely faster barefoot than we were in those big, clompy boots. At some point she was so far ahead of us she was completely out of sight. By the time we caught up to her she had wedged herself L-shape into a phone booth, already talking frantically to someone. It suddenly occurred to me that this chick could identify me. Plus I'd have to see them at school Monday, or eventually anyway. So I stayed back as Anne, Jennie, and Reeba all went flying at the booth.

"Get out of there, bitch!" one of them screamed at her. The three kicked furiously at the Plexiglas booth, successfully breaking in one side. Melanie cried and wailed, pressing her bare feet against the glass to keep them out.

"Hurry, please!" I heard her sob into the receiver. The scene was starting to attract attention from the locals, so we darted off.

"I understand the bind you're in, fella," Richard said to Trey McKinley, who was barely conscious. Trey attempted to speak, but only succeeded in creating a low gurgle, and tiny bubbles of blood. His face was beaten so out of shape he barely looked like the same man. The smell of blood collided with the copious amount of alcohol sloshing about in my stomach and I began to feel dizzy and sick. "I mean," Richard continued, laying on his fake *I'm reasonable* routine, "black women are some surly, ugly, nasty bitches. I know that. I see 'em flashing their shit on the street corners downtown. 'Hoes' you call 'em? No doubt. But that simply does not give you the right to pump your filthy seed inside *our* women. Are you straight hip to my lingo, brutha?"

"Ha ha, yeah," Brian snorted. "Are we down, homey?"

Duty done, we were about to leave him there sleeping on the curb and go find the girls, when suddenly this huge brown Cadillac screeched to a halt right next to us. Out stepped Jack Curry, this young Japanese headbanger I later found out was named Yoshimoto, and six of the biggest, darkest, hardest homeboys who ever lived. These guys had a good ten years on us, probably hard-time, and countless pounds of muscle. *Oh fuck fuck fuck ... Blackchurch ... represent ...*

"Just hang tight, lil cuz," one of them said to Trey, who likely did not hear him. They all began to circle us. My head was spinning and I stumbled, like I had just stepped onto a moving carousel (a feeling to which I have grown quite accustomed).

"All right then, T," said Yoshimoto. Some wet mumble burbled from the sidewalk.

"Don't worry, Trey," said Curry. "We'll have you up on two and voting Republican again in no time."

We were completely walled in. No escape, but it did occur to me, even in my drunken state, that in that formation they likely didn't have guns. I'll take my pluses where I can get them. I heard a click that I knew was Richard's switchblade.

"Okay," Richard yawned, "let's get this over with."

To this day I don't know what he was thinking. There was no way we could take these guys and no way out. Did he miscalculate? Had his head gotten too big? They came down on us like collapsing walls. I barely got one swing in when I felt a wrecking ball slam into my stomach from two counties over. I hit the pavement knees first, spilling a river of blood and booze vomit out into the street. I felt a boot heel jam into my kidneys and another crack the back of my skull as I flew cheek-first into a rusty wheel well. A slam to the chest and two pops to the face and that was it for me. There was a lot of "Whatchoo thought, fool!" and

"Betta reckonize, punk!" kind of chatter. *Feels like home, by gum.* I crawled up to the sidewalk to see someone scoop up Trey and carry him to the Caddie, which proceeded to squeal off into the night. My boys held their own, more or less, but it was the most brutal beat-down any of us had ever caught. I appeared to have been deemed either out of commission or no longer present as I lay there watching through blurry, swelling eyes. Closest to me Curry and Phil were doing a number on each other, Phil managing a solid whack to Curry's shoulder with a thick metal chain. In a flash Curry got the upper hand and slammed Phil's face into the bumper of the parked car. From there he brought his boots down on Phil's wrists, one then the other, the second *smash* even more devastating than the first. Phil shrieked in agony. He continued to howl as Curry dragged him into an adjacent alleyway. From there all I heard was the occasional dull grunt and the moist pounding of beef being tenderized.

Sirens began to wail in the distance. Rapidly approaching. All present tore off into the night every which way. Except for me, of course, and whatever unspeakable horror was taking place in the alley. I attempted to stand, and fell immediately again onto the sidewalk. I tried to speak and hacked up more blood instead.

Sherry said:

The girls and I panicked when we heard the sirens. We freaked when we saw the rollers speed past, heading in the direction of where we had left you boys. We went to hide out at a nearby gas station and screamed at each for a half an hour about what to do. Finally Reeba called her brother Kevin and he came to pick us up. We were too afraid to go back to Richard's place so we ended up staying at Kevin's house on the West Side until about five or six AM. I called and left a message for Richard telling him where we were and to please call or come over as soon as he could.

The rest of the girls fell asleep after a while, but I couldn't, so I sat in the kitchen all by myself. At some point Kevin came in. He

*was nice at first, asking me if I was okay and if I needed anything.
He handed me a beer from the fridge and asked if I was hungry.
Then he asked me if I felt grateful ... and in a flash I wanted to run.
I didn't say a word.*

*"Don't look so freaked, pretty girl," he said, lighting a ciga-
rette. "Yer safe now."*

"I'm just a little ... shook up."

"That'll teach ya not to play where you oughtn't."

*He came right out with it that he would really like to butt-fuck
me and I should let him because if it hadn't been for him, "the
niggers would be sucking the meat off your bones right now." He
pulled his penis out of his sweat shorts and presented it to me like
an offering. It was half-hard and hung crooked. I gave it a few
awkward pulls and felt it stiffen in my fingers. I started to cry. He
snorted in disgust, stuffed it back into his pants and shuffled off
back to bed. I made a mental note to tell Richard about it later and
have him settle that piece of shit but good. I never cashed in on it.
Call it a lost opportunity.*

*Desperate for some shut-eye, I went out to the living room and
scooted Anne over so I could grab a bit of couch space. She rested
her head on my shoulder and cuddled against me, never waking. I
closed my eyes and pretended she was someone else.*

*When I heard later how things had gone down and what Jack
had done to Phil, I wasn't surprised. And it was hard to know how
to feel.*

I hadn't felt it at first, but the jagged corner of the wheel well
had lacerated my cheek, and it throbbed and pounded as I crawled
slowly on my elbows toward the alley. I saw Jack Curry prop Phil
into a sitting position and kneel before him face-to-face. Phil tried
desperately to punch him, but his crushed wrists made it a futile
effort.

"I am so happy for you, man," I heard Curry say, his voice hideously giddy. "You must be so excited!" The sirens grew ever closer. I dragged myself up and fell against the brick wall. "You're gonna love this, dude," Curry said like a sugared-up ten-year-old. "Scout's honor."

I saw his hand slide into Phil's front pants pocket. Rooted about for a moment, then pulled out Phil's brass knuckles. I tried to yell, but I still had no wind in my lungs, and retched up a thin string of blood instead. I lunged forward and hit the pavement once again. *Pathetic. Pathetic!* Curry did not notice, or didn't bother to care, but Phil saw me. Our eyes met, and I'd never seen him so terrified. I'd never seen *anyone* so terrified. Even those two queers we stomped in Candyland weren't as afraid of us as Phil was of Jack Curry just then. And with good cause. Those queers likely recovered in a couple of weeks. No such luck for Phil.

"No!" Phil begged "Please! Please don't!"

Curry just laughed.

"Love it! You'll love it. Trust me. Don't worry. I'm a man of peace."

SMAAAAAASH!!! The sound of a brass-knuckled hook punch square into Phil's mouth. The echo of his jaw shattering bounced from building to building, reflecting all throughout the streets. Gushes of blood and fragments of broken molars spilled from Phil's open mouth as he gurgled in incoherent misery.

"Awwww ... fuuuuuuuuuggggggg ..."

Curry proceeded to slam him twice more in his already pulverized jaw. Just then two squad cars barreled in, blocking the street both ways. Curry picked up Phil and tossed him out into the road, then darted the opposite way down the alley. I closed my eyes and they fused shut.

"Jesus, boy," I heard a voice say. I didn't know if it was directed toward me or not. "Can you talk?" Phil's ability to speak, or lack thereof, should have been obvious, so I proceeded to tell the disembodied cop voice,

"We was jumped. Big gang of blacks. A drug gang I bet."

"You have any drugs on you now, son?"

"Oh NO, sir. Never."

It was true. No weapons either at the moment. I'll take my pluses where I can get them.

Phil was rushed to Mercy Hospital (and so had been Trey McKinley). I was taken to the police station and given an obscene amount of ancient, tar-thick coffee. After I became more lucid I gave the police my report. Seems my friend and I had been driving home from a party when we were car-jacked by a gang of thugs. The leader had a mouthful of gold teeth and said something about payback for Rodney King. Then they beat us up and stole my 92 CRX hatchback, which my friend had been driving for me. And that's exactly how it was, officers, I swear to The Good Lord Above.

"Well, what did y'all expect driving through that neighborhood?" A cop scolded. "You boys should have more sense when it comes to those people." They bought it. Cops always buy that story. Try it, you'll see.

"Believe me, sir," I said, laying it on, "we tried to get through there as quick as all git-out, but the car ahead of us stopped to talk to another driver coming the other way. They was blocking traffic both ways! We was sitting ducks."

"That sounds about right," the officer said nodding. Hook. Line. Sinker. Almost too easy.

They decided that, although I'd probably be pissing blood for a couple of days, my injuries were relatively minor, provided my tetanus shots were up to date (not likely). I did get a stern lecture about being an underage drunk. "Son, you're playing a loser game here." Thinking they were really giving it to me tough they threatened to call my folks, then proceeded to do just that. I pretended to be all worried and scared straight. It was hard not to laugh when the officer who called my parents came back looking vexed and perplexed.

"I ... don't ... think ... your father is in any ... condition to drive."

I offered to call "my brother" to come pick me up.

Richard arrived at the station wearing a baseball cap and varsity football jacket from some school I'd never heard of. I suppose that was his stab at looking like a "regular guy." He yelled at me in front of everybody about being intoxicated, then said we had to "pray extra hard at church tomorrow." It was simultaneously overdone *and* half-baked, but the boys in blue ate it up.

All joking around had blown away on the early morning breeze by the time we got out to the van, however. The rest of the guys sat there huddled down, beaten to shit, bashed, and bandaged up.

"Well ... that went good, huh?"

"We didn't want to leave y'all, Mikey," Brian said.

"It's all right. You did what you had to."

"Fucking niggers," said Geoff.

"They did what they had to," Richard replied.

We didn't speak again until we pulled up outside Reeba's brother's house to collect the girls.

"From now on," Richard said in full boss voice, "No one leaves the house without a pistol." He looked right at me as if I had done something wrong. "No one."

As shotgun it was my job to run up to the house and do the collecting. Reeba's brother Kevin answered the door. Seemed like a nice enough guy.

As we slid the van door open to let the girls in, Reeba instantly noticed Phil's absence and fell into screaming hysterics. I wanted to slap her.

Shut up, cunt. Nobody asked for your input.

12.

It was a long night. Sherry was exhausted. She felt grimy and sick. It was close to 8:30 AM when they entered Mercy Hospital. They were told Phil would get into surgery as soon as possible, but there was no point in waiting around.

Richard dropped Sherry off at her dorm and they made plans to go see Phil later.

Had she not been so exhausted Sherry would have laughed out loud when her roommate Sarah laid eyes on her. It hadn't occurred to Sherry until just then, but this was the first time they had been in contact since her "makeover."

"Sharon?" Sarah asked blinking.

"It's hell out there kid," Sherry replied, re-hanging her giant poster of Norma Jean that had obviously been ripped down. "I'm going to sleep for long, long time. You wake me up and I'll suck your eyeballs out of your goddamn skull."

Richard, Reeba, and Brian came to pick Sherry up around 7:45 PM. It was after visiting hours, but Richard had worked something out so that they could see Phil. It was hard not to notice that Reeba had already begun the process of "unloading Phil," and Brian was perfectly willing to fill that vacant hole.

"Don't worry, Phil," Richard said. "We'll find the cocksucker who did this. He'll be maggot breakfast by end of the week."

Phil lay in bed with both his arms elevated and his swollen jaw bandaged and wired shut. I'd been at the hospital all day. Promised I'd stay by him. I don't know why exactly. I felt that I owed it to him.

"Shorget adout it, Rish. Goezh wit ta territory."

He looked deformed. Misshapen. His left eye was swollen closed. But the worst bit of it, and he knew it, we all knew it, was that he was *different* from us now. He didn't look like us anymore. He couldn't do what we could do. He was no longer a soldier. He was a cripple. Even in the world of low-rent fascism, there's nothing lower than the cripple.

He looked up at Reeba with his one working eye. She ran her fingers lightly over his ravaged, broken face. He knew she wasn't his any more. Brian would fuck her and that would be that. He'd never have her again. And he'd have to choose between sitting around eating through a straw, with his hands so bound and bandaged he can't even jerk off, while the woman he loves is gobbling his friend's cock in the next room ... or he could leave for good and be completely on his own. Tough call.

After a while, whatever Richard, Brian, and Reeba had to say to Phil became nothing but low static to me. Sherry and I stared silently at one another. Pretended we weren't. It was ridiculous, but we shared a secret. *A stupid, pointless secret we shouldn't be keeping. Tell them, or I will. Tell them, or I will.* But I didn't.

When it was time for everyone to leave I walked down to the lobby with them. Richard said he would come pick me up in the morning. I said okay, although I planned to be alone the next day and would just as soon take the Metro. Whatever.

Heading back to Phil's room I stopped in the men's room, sweating and anxious. Anyone who can watch a stream of blood spray out from the end of his dick and not want to take his own life right then and there is a stronger man than I. As I steadied my left hand against the wall and prepared for the searing gasoline burn of another red piss I wondered how many blows to the kidney I had delivered in the past couple of months. Twelve? Fifteen? More? I tried not to think about it. *Fuck it! That's just the way it is! You take it as it comes.* The second an Aryan Warrior starts sweating about karma is the moment he may as well cash it all in for tie-dye and some groovy crystals.

As I walked down the hall toward Phil's room I heard him trying to yell at someone. I ran in just in time to hear, "What shou want? Tanks?! I owe 'ou shit, houshe nanny!" And catch Niani Shange walking out. *What the hell?*

"Excuse me," she said as she squeezed past me out into the hallway. I didn't breathe. I shut my eyes. Even for such a brief moment, it was surreal being that close to her. *Be gone.*

"Dring ne ny dinner too, cunt!!!" Phil hollered.

I walked into the room to see a milkshake sitting on his tray table.

"Strawberry?" I asked. He turned his head away from me.

And then she spoke …

"Mikal? Mikal Fanon, is that you?"

I spun around to see her standing in the doorway. My mouth went completely dry and I felt like I would choke if I tried to swallow. She looked right at me. Right into my eyes. "Mikal Fanon. It is you, isn't it. I remember you from the old neighborhood. How are you? It's been a long time. Couple years anyway." I was stone cold silent, staring at her like a feeb. "Do you remember me? I lived in the house three down from you. On the left." Nothing. "What have you been up to?" I opened my mouth but there was no sound. *Talk! Speak! Grunt! Gesticulate! Something!!!* "Do you remember my brother 'Zekial?" *FUCKING RETARD!* "How are your folks? How is your dad's hand? Is he better?"

Nothing.

I ... got ... nothing. I got nothing for you ...

Finally she just nodded. "Okay," she said.

And she walked away.

I went and sat down in the chair next to Phil's bed. Not a word. Still. He made no indication that he wanted a drink of the shake. It just sat there. With my throat hot and dry like the goddamn Mojave I had half a mind to just grab it and slurp it all down. But I didn't. So we sat there in silence as the shake melted. Then it got warm and spoiled.

I turned on the TV and it all sucked. I turned it off again. I was just about to curl up in the chair and try to get some sleep when the last visitor of the night crawled out of the hottest pit in Hell and popped by for a "sweet dreams."

Upon seeing Jack Curry, Phil panicked and went to reach for the nurse call button, which was attached to a cord by his right hand. Jack grabbed it and stopped him flat.

"Hey hey hey. No need for that now, buddy."

"Whak ta fuck do zhou wonk?"

"Just stopping by to see how you're doing. That's all."

I wished I had a knife. For just a moment ... I wished I had a gun.

"Dey hat ta show ny fuckin zhaw shuk!"

"Sewed your jaw shut, huh. That's a pisser."

I stood up and was about to lunge at Curry when he said, cold as a reptile, "Sit back down or I'll slash your throat all the way open. Go ahead and test me." He didn't even look my way. I doubt he even saw me out of the corner of his eye. He just sensed me. I didn't sit, but I stood paralyzed. Paralyzed and mute. *And stupid. And worthless.*

"GET TA FUCK ARAY FRON NE!!!"

Curry put his hand over Phil's mouth. Phil thrashed and shrieked in agony from the pressure.

"If you settle down, I'll take my hand away."

Phil tried to calm himself as tears began to stream down his face. I couldn't move. *I'm a lifeless fucking husk.* I wished I was dead.

"You know ... Philip is it? You know, Philip, I understand the bind you're in. I mean, shit! You're white! You should be running the damn show, correct? Your ancestors kicked ass. Massacred, enslaved, and infected everybody. So why aren't you calling any shots. Poor? Ignorant? No education? Couldn't keep a decent job even if you could get one, right? God. It's just so unfair. And the minorities get everything handed to them on a silver fucking platter, don't they. I feel for you, my strong white brother. I really do."

"Shou're a got tan rayshe traitor," Phil hissed.

Curry laughed.

"Race traitor? Did you say 'race traitor,' Philip? Do people even still say that? Guess you do." He slapped Phil in the jaw. Phil winced and shook off the pain, trying to stifle the scream welling up. I looked about the room for something to smash over Curry's head. "I'm sorry. Shouldn't have done that. I'll make it better." He bent over and licked a teardrop that was streaming down Phil's cheek. Just at that moment, a nurse walked in … froze in her tracks … giggled … gave a little "my bad" salute … and walked away. And Jack Curry laughed and laughed. And Phil shook with rage. And I wished I was dead.

"I'll be seeing you guys," he chuckled. "Stay strong. The white race needs men like you." And he was gone.

You're fucking worthless, I thought to myself. *Goddamn fucking worthless.*

"What tah fuck, Nikal," Phil said softly, sniffling.

"I'll kill him for you, Phil. I promise. I will kill him."

It was late. Midnight maybe. Maybe one. Hospitals at midnight are like sterile catacombs, but without the comfort of knowing the worst is over. I went for another fire piss. Not as horrible that time. *Let the healing begin.*

I didn't want to go looking for Trey McKinley's room. But I knew I would. Auto-pilot took me there.

I stood in the doorway watching him sleep. His neck was braced and his face was bruised, both eyes puffy and knotted. But he didn't look too bad. It certainly wasn't his best day, but he didn't look all that bad. And he appeared to sleep in relative comfort. Cards and flowers all about the room. Already. An empty milkshake cup in the trash.

"I ain't sorry," I growled under my breath. "You got what you deserved. You hear me, nigger? I said, I ain't sorry."

"I hear you," he said without opening his eyes. And I wished I was dead.

13.

THE phone rang at about 11:30 AM. To say the very least, I was not entirely awake.

"Helluh? I'm lookin' fer Mikal Fanon."

"You found him."

"Dude!"

"Holy shit! How you been, man? You still living in Louisville?"

"Yep 'er. Can't complain too much. I've had a bitch of a time tracking you down, hoss."

"Yeah, I'm off the radar these days."

"Chup to?"

"Nothin' really."

"School or anything?"

"I'm a Fifth Reich Skin."

"A who?"

"Yeah."

"Is … that what, like a gang?"

"Yeah … sorta …"

"Like the Crips?"

"Yeah … well, no … kind of …"

I don't know how long we talked. Maybe and hour. I kept falling asleep. He was working in his dad's auto shop. He got married, had a son, all that dull shit.

"Hey Mikey, you remember that guy I had to … you know, the guy I had to shoot?"

"Uh huh."

"I got a hold of his autopsy photos. You wanna see 'um?"

We made plans to get together. I never followed through. I try to make it a point to leave the past in the past. When possible. Talking to him, I walked past the bathroom and looked in the mirror at myself. *This isn't even the guy he knows,* I thought. *So long, bud. Best of luck to you.*

The angry gash in my left cheek kept me from shaving, which yielded a thoroughly unimpressive teenage beard. It was enough for Richard to start calling me "Jerry Garcia," however. I actually earned a string of nicknames at that time. Although I was no longer shaving my face, I was still shaving my head, which was not a good look at all, so I had taken to wearing a knit skull-cap. And so I became "Johnny Grunge," "Mikal-In-Chains," and one of Sherry's invention, "Mudhoney," which everyone thought was hilarious but only Richard understood. Because of said misunderstanding I also ended up as "Mud Pony," "Mud Bunny," and often just "Mud." I was a good sport about it, though, and danced about singing the song "My Name is Mudd," which also no one got. Good times.

The first week after the downfall of Phil was fairly rough for me as Brian and Reeba had taken to spending all afternoon in the abandoned apartment next door rutting and caterwauling like feral felines.

"Goddamn," Reeba said to me passing through to get to the fridge. "I never knew it could be that good."

"Your thighs are bruised up."

"Why you lookin' at my thighs, Mikal-in-Chains?"

As I would sit there turning up the TV or the stereo as loudly as I could the thought crossed my mind that perhaps having to listen to other people fuck is my lot in life, my destiny, and maybe it's punishment for some wrongdoing from a past existence. I also wondered if that thought had ever occurred to Suzi's mother.

The heavens did smile upon me after that first week, however. Reeba's brother Kevin and his wife and two daughters had decided to take an extended trip down to Huntsville, Alabama to stay with some great-grandaunt who was dying of throat cancer. So Reeba and Brian moved in over at their house to keep an eye on things.

I got to enjoy being home alone more and more, and I found that the time spent completely by myself was by far my happiest. Richard and I, by that time, had become something of a crotchety old couple, not really speaking around the house except to bitch about there being no food or the place being a mess. I'll admit that I've never been much of a housekeeper, but I usually kept the kitchen pretty well stocked. We lived right behind an IGA and I'm a fairly skilled thief. It's a talent, not a gift. It pissed me off when he griped about the food situation because I did my best to make sure we always had his favorite things, even at the expense of my own preferences. And it was my ass risking arrest every time I went "shopping." But it was never good enough for him.

I was rummaging through Richard's room one day looking for the phone when I discovered his chest o' weapons. He kept everything in fairly neat order: knives in sheaths, firearms in shoe boxes. I pulled out his nine and inspected it top to bottom. You always hear how heavy those things are, but you really don't think about it until it's in your hand. Richard's was perfectly polished, of course, oiled, and well maintained. And loaded. I flipped the safety off, slid the long barrel into my mouth, and pressed the muzzle to the back of my throat. It clicked against my incisors, which almost made me bite down reflexively. I cocked the hammer back and shut my eyes tightly, trying not to gag, rubbing my index finger against the trigger. Just then I heard the front door slam.

"Mikal?"

"I'm in here, Sherry."

"Can I come in?"

"No. I'm sleeping." I put the gun back in the box and closed the chest.

"Are you naked?"

"What?"

"I'm tired too. Can I go sleep in your bed?"

"Knock yourself out."

I came out to the living room and found her usual heap of stuff by the door. Why I decided that day to look through her book bag I don't know. But I did. That's just the way it was. Usual stuff: textbooks, floppy discs, crumpled up papers. There was also a small plastic bag of weed. *Huh* ... I unrolled it to take a sniff, then closed it back up again. I didn't want to get a contact buzz. I also found a flyer for a party that Friday night. An "all-campus block rocker." "Come one come all." On Jamestown St.

I went out to my room and found her sleeping on my futon in nothing but panties and a white T-shirt. Her dark black swastika tattoo screamed through the thin cotton.

"Uh," I said. "I'm up now, so you can go to Richard's room if you want. Probably more comfortable."

"Okaaaay," she mewed, not opening her eyes. She rolled over and wrapped her thighs around a pillow. "Your bed is gross." But she made no move to get up. "Will you cover my feet up, Mikal? They're freezing."

I covered her with a quilt and turned to leave.

"Oh, hey," I said. "I don't know if you know, but there's a big party at Meat's on Friday. Kind of a 'Get Better, Phil' thing."

"Sounds fun, but I gotta study all weekend. Big test Monday. Soooooo tired."

"All right."

We'll see.

We'll see ...

Friday morning Richard woke me up before leaving for work.

"Mikal, I picked up all the literature about starting classes in Spring. It's on the coffee table if you wanna look it over."

"I still gotta take the GED."

"I'll help you. You'll ace it no problem."

"Man, you up for it really? Putting up with all those liberal PC assholes every day?"

"Dude, I love PC. Political correctness is one of the greatest things to ever happen to the Movement. Whenever society as a whole decides to give words more weight than they warrant? Advantage: us. Whenever people think language is our master and we're its servant and not the other way around? Advantage:

us. Hell yeah I'm excited to face those douchebags every day. They've handed me all the weapons I need. Thank god for PC."

"Huh. Yeah. Plus it gives the ... what would you call it ... the 'respectable right' the chance to play the First Amendment martyr card."

"Exactly. See, you're catching on. You going to Meat's tonight?"

"Maybe."

"Maybe? What do you mean maybe?"

"Maybe. I'm not in a party mood. I want to talk to him. But I want to talk business."

"What kind of business?"

"Bombs. Pipe bombs. Cocktails. Chemical shit."

"Well, Meat is the man as far as that goes. He'll be excited to chew the fat about that stuff. I'll see you there tonight. Get a ride with Joey. Oh, and by the way, we're *completely* out of grub."

"I know."

So I spent the rest of Friday morning looking over college literature and thinking about bombs. It's hard to know how to feel. I didn't really feel too much.

Three o'clock rolled around. No Sherry. Five. No Sherry. Eight-thirty. No sign of her. And I thought some more about bombs.

14.

FRIDAY evening I took the last bus into town, got off at Fourth and Jamestown, and followed the noise from there. A "block rocker" it was indeed. Even the front yard outside the house was packed with people. As I buttoned up my flannel and adjusted my knit skullcap it occurred to me that I looked more like a longshoreman than an Aryan Warrior just then, which was certainly the right way to go. Like any self-respecting Skin of the time I loathed Seattle "grunge" rock and whatever it may have stood for, so sans red braces and geared in everyday hiking boots, I felt undercover and in disguise. *Even more anonymous than normal.* Perfect.

Thinking about it now, I had to have been an imbecile walking into that house party alone and without an Uzi at least. Talk about enemy land. This was a bacchanal hosted by The Devil himself, and it was everything I had trained myself to hate. The air was thick with weed and cloves and my fear of the contact buzz had to be addressed and discarded once and for all the moment I walked in the door.

The placed was loaded with multi-cultists, and they danced to rap and funk and world beat and even the heavy stuff was infected with tribal drums and third world ooga-booga. College chatter every which way about books I had never read and issues that don't come up in my house, with my clan, around my campfire. These people were for all intents and purposes my peers, and yet they might as well have been from the Fifth Dimension. The twilight zone *or* the band. Either way. I overheard a couple of people talking about counter-protesting a demonstration by the local chapter of the Ku Klux Klan at the end of the month. Seems the Klan, in a desperate move to remind everyone they still existed, had won a permit to march on the square. *Poor, sorry, cousin-fuckin' bastards.* I did feel naked and spotlighted and *persona non grata* for a just brief moment until I realized just how inconspicuous, incognito, and inconsequential I truly was. And as for The Devil himself, I had sworn to end his life. But I didn't even bother to case his house for a bombing, as initially planned. I was there instead about a girl and a secret and that's just the way it was and it seemed to make sense at the time. A girl who wasn't mine. A secret with its own designs. In the house of The Devil and a one-sided holy war. Like I said, it seemed to make sense at the time.

There was a front yard and a backyard, two floors plus a basement, and a couple hundred bodies to wade through. That house was as good a place as any to lose myself, and that's just what I did that night. Stands to reason, as I had already lost all sense of perspective and I must have lost my mind. I had certainly lost Sherry, as if she had ever been mine to find or keep in the first place. I didn't even know if she was there.

I wove through the crowd out to the backyard to find a large bonfire and a mammoth grill cooking up barbecue. A well-worn boom box blasted out some old-style hip hop I recognized from my Blackchurch days. I grabbed a plastic cup, made my way to the keg and pumped out some domestic swill.

"What can I get you my man?" this red-headed Jew-fro'd hippie minding the grill asked me, then proceeded to sing along with the radio, "Excuse me Doug E ... Excuse me Doug E ... Excuse me Doug E. Fresh you're on! Uh-uh, On ... on ... on ..."

I wanted to say "nothing," but I hadn't eaten all day and the fixings on the grill smelled like it had been cooked up by the Almighty.

"Well," I replied, "is this meat or, uh, like, tofu meat substitute?"

"It's fucking *meat*, dude," the hippie laughed, feigning offense and flipping a rack of ribs. "*Tofu*. Pshhh. Hey Greg, did you hear this fuckin' guy?"

"Greg," a Korean in a jester's cap and Stigmata Dog T-shirt, giggled like a moron and gave the thumbs-up. I chuckled and shrugged.

"All right. Just had to make sure. Pull me some of that pork."

"Right on right on. Get you a bun. This shit is the bomb-ditty-bomb-bomb."

??? Okay ...

"Hey, y'all know a girl named Sherry Nicolas? I'm supposed to meet her here."

"Naw, doesn't ring a bell. Look around the house. There's a lot of smokin' *boo-tay* here tonight, so even if you don't find her ..." They then broke into a fit of giggles. I opened the bun on my plate and saw that it was saturated with a thick, pungent goo. The hippie slopped a steaming heap of tangy pork onto my bun. "Haw yeah ...," he said, licking his lips.

"What's this stuff on the bun?"

"Green butter, baby. Buh-ZAM! It'll make you the happiest motherfucker in the world, dude. Guaranteed."

Aw fuck ... Awwwww FUCK ...

I thought about throwing it out right then and there, or maybe pretending to take a bite then tossing it away when I got back inside. But my stomach twisted and growled and demanded I eat at least a bit of it. I brought it to my lips, intent on taking just a nibble, but instead I chomped into it, munching it all down in two full bites. It was, bar none, the most delicious sandwich I had ever tasted, and if it had been seasoned with Strychnine I would have done the same.

"Goddamn, bottomless pit!" the hippie hollered. "You want another?"

"No, I'm good. Shalom."

"'Kay. Whatever."

I guzzled my beer, grabbed another, and headed back into the house.

"Wow. That's fascinating, Chad," I heard Niani Shange say. I peered into what was probably meant to be the dining room to see her hitting a joint and passing it to this pasty, preppy neckbone in a polo shirt and sandals-with-socks. Niani wore a tight black pullover shirt and an ankle-length peasant skirt. Her hair hung in kinky ringlets, ornamented with colored wooden beads. I wondered what her hair felt like.

"Essentially," she continued, "whatchoo, whatchoo, what you are saying is ... we can't give welfare to the poor because then they'll lose their drive to work. But ... we MUST give welfare to corporations or else THEY'LL lose their drive to work. That's just. Wow. Brilliant. It really is."

"You're twisting my words, Niani!" The neckbone protested and coughed out a cloud of white smoke, and I felt like I would really like to get in on that conversation myself, but I quickly skittered away down the hall. I couldn't trust her to not recognize me. Unlike Jack Curry, whom I ran into head on.

"My bad," he grunted, obviously already on his way to Blitzville. He swigged hard off a bottle of Jim Beam, and handed it, more or less, in my direction. I didn't take it, step back, or even startle, because I knew he didn't know who I was. His eyes weren't even open.

"S'cool," I said tossing on a character I just yanked out of the air. "Killer party, dog." He didn't hear a word that came out of my mouth. He also wasn't aware of the knife I had pulled out of my pocket and held up to his back. I waved the blade right around his belt line. It brushed lightly against his dread-locks. With the sharp silver tip I made circles in the air, right outside his kidneys. *One stroke and you're dead, fucker. One stroke. One stroke.* I flipped it shut as that guy Yoshimoto turned the corner holding a glass of milk. As it was, I couldn't have gotten away with stabbing Curry anyway. I would not have even made it to the front door alive.

"What's with the milk, son?" Curry slurred.

"We're pregnant," Yoshimoto replied defeated and resigned. I was surprised for the moment that he didn't talk like an extra from *Godzilla*. There's just no telling.

Curry proceeded to dump a quarter bottle of whiskey into Yoshimoto's milk. Yoshimoto stared at the glass stunned and speechless.

"*Kaketsuke ippai*," Curry said and stumbled on his way.

Kaketsuke ippai. Drink up to catch up.

Yoshimoto looked up at me for a brief moment and squinted.

"Cheers!" I said, hoisting my cup of beer. He nodded and walked off.

A wave washed over the front part of my brain and trickled down through my body. I didn't know if it was the butter getting on top of me, or the quality of the air itself, but I felt suddenly coated in a thin slather of Novocain and encumbered by the overall gelatin-like state of the atmosphere. The motion around me clipped to slo-mo and I realized I was walking down the hallway in time with the music, slogging through space, knee deep in cheese casserole. I sank into an available easy chair and shut my eyes, my head bobbing to the pulse of something reggae-esque but strangely alien.

"Hey, are you all right?"

I opened my eyes to see a nice little punk pixie sitting on the armrest of my chair. She was skinny and slight, just the way I liked them then, with short, spiky green hair. A thin gold ring pierced her septum.

"Gimme a sip of your beer and I'll be perfect," I said. She handed me her bottle of Killians. I took a bigger swig than what was likely polite, but for some reason I felt entitled. Just the way it is.

"So are you a friend of Jack's? " she asked.

"Aw, hell yeah. That crazy bastard and I go way back."

"What's your name?"

"Um, Don Willis."

"Oh yeah! I've heard of you! You're a twin, right?"

"Yeah. Zary is my brother."

"Is he here?"

"Naw. He's in jail."

"For some reason, to hear Jack talk, I assumed you were black."

"Who's to say I ain't?"

"Well," she shrugged, "not me I guess."

She was the first girl I had talked to since Suzi, and I couldn't really gauge how I was doing. But that question pretty well answered itself when a boho-looking Indian girl slunk by and put her arm around my new friend's shoulder.

"Hetel," Greenie said, *"mere dost se miliye* Don Willis *aur mere dost—"*

"You know," the Indian girl giggled, "I CAN speak English, silly-billy."

"Argh! She never lets me practice my Hindi!"

"Good to meet you, Hetel," I said, trying to mask my disappointment.

"You're Don Willis?" Hetel asked. "Of the Willis twins? I thought you—"

"Was black? Yeah, I get that a lot. Hey," I turned to the green-haired girl. "Your name ain't Paige by any chance, is it?"

"Yep. Why?"

"I think you're in Women's Studies with a friend of mine. Sherry Nicolas?"

"Uh … okay …"

"Punk rock chick. She's got, like, short maroon hair with blond streaks."

"Oh yeah. *Helen Keller*. She's around here somewhere."

"Cool."

I couldn't lift my head, but I saw a very pregnant belly waddle through my peripheral vision. "Anybody seen my brother Greg?" it asked. "I'm looking for Greg Cho. Anybody?"

"Outside," I said, as I felt myself begin to hover maybe a half-inch above the chair. "By the bonfire."

"Thanks." And the belly waddled away.

"Come dance with me, baby," Hetel cooed to Paige. And I spun my useless third wheel.

"Good to meet y'all," I said.

"Ditto," they chirped in unison, then proceeded to get some manner of freak on.

Nicely done, Jerk-off. First chick you try to talk up and she's a goddamn dyke. And with a tongue for the darker magenta no less.

I watched the two of them dance close together until a brighter vision caught my eye. Niani. Twisting and twirling. Surrounded by a little crowd of folks just thrilled to bask in her glow.

You're a sitting target. Keep moving. I wandered out to the kitchen to once again see Jack Curry's back. He was an easier kill this time, all alone and right by the door. He held the phone's receiver nearly half a foot from his ear and hollered, "Man, it's BUMPIN', D! And all the honeys be sayin', 'Where Daddy Molotov at?' Man, I ain't lyin'! So git yo' ass on over here. A'ight. A'ight cool. See ya in a minute. Peace."

D ... D ... D ... D? D ...

He stumbled off through the screen door to the outside and I once again missed the opportunity to carve him up like a Christmas goose. My heart was no longer in it anyway. Surprise.

A disembodied hand waved a joint in my face. I pinched it between my fingers and took a deep drag, coughing and sputtering. The hand laughed and took the joint back with a, "Right on, dude!" And I heard it shuffle away singing along with the music.

"Thank you, Thing," I said, my lungs burning and itchy.

I turned around and leaned against the kitchen doorway. Two frat boys stood next to me holding up the wall. They looked so much alike they could have been the same guy in split screen (and yes, the irony of a Skinhead saying that is not lost on me).

"Hey," one said to the other, "you see that hot looking black chick? The one freak-dancing with everybody? I'mma try to FUCK that pussy tonight! I heard she's a sluuuuuuuut. Straight up cum dumpster, for real though. Some cat in Astronomy told me that last quarter she let him bang her doggie-style while … git this … she ate out his girlfriend, dude! DUDE! He was calling her all 'Aunt Jemima' and grabbing her hair and slapping her ass and shit, and she was loving it! Begged for it! GOD, let me hit that!"

I felt my heart suddenly kick into overdrive and my teeth clenched hard like a vice. My hands balled into fists so tight I thought for sure that my nails would cut my palms open. *He ain't got no business talking about her like that.* He didn't deserve to breathe her air, let alone jab his worthless cock inside her. *I'll kill you, you white ball-cap wearing bucket of swine vomit. I'll kill you before you EVER touch her.*

"Yeah, I'd split her like a wishbone," the other replied. "But watch out, 'cause, man, y'know that psycho grit that lives here with her? Fucking *murdered* a guy. That's what I heard. Cut his throat or blew up his car or some shit."

I'll hack you apart. You will know pain, you fucks. I'll yank your goddamn guts out.

"Hey …," the second one whispered to the first, "did you hear what that guy just said?" They turned to look right at me.

HOLY SHIT!

The chatter in my head was apparently leaking out. They both glared at me, ready to pounce, and I figured I'd have to make a move. I pulled down the collar of my shirt and showed them the "white power" tattoo.

"Heads up, kids," I growled. "I'm about to make a phone call and it's about to get evil around here. I'm warning you cuz you're white brethren and I'd hate to see y'all caught in the crossfire. You might wanna amscray." So they did. And quick. Good thing too because I'm pretty sure my bones had turned to licorice rope by then, and I was truly in no state to fight. So I stood alone, wondering what the fuck that was all about anyway.

From the opposite hallway I watched Niani pass through the kitchen and out to the back deck. I followed her as far as the screen door and watched as she sat down on the top step behind Jack Curry. She wrapped her arms around him from behind and rested her head on his shoulder. I wanted to die. I felt a bolt of rage shoot through me before I realized that I had no right to it. Not mine to have. That's just the way it was. The yard was empty by then and the three of us watched in silence as the bonfire died away. Finally Niani said to him, "He's coming over."

"Great."

"Y'all could finally patch things up."

"Yeah right."

"He misses you, you know. Why else would he come?"

"Arnold? He just wants to pick up some easy sorority girl and punish-fuck her for the sins of the white man."

"That's ugly, Jack."

"It's an ugly world, Lees." I had to agree.

"That's quite a *teenage* attitude," she said to both of us. Even though I didn't exist.

"I just called Philips back. He's coming by."

"Oh. Wonderful. It'll be like a Blackchurch family reunion up in here."

"Yeah. Gats out, posse up."

"But see, I KNOW nobody's tryin' to act a fool up in MY house."

"It'll be a'ight."

I stood there playing out this whole ridiculous scenario in my head wherein it was me on that step with her and not him. I'd tell her that I'd protect her and I'd never let anyone hurt her. I'd keep all the evil spirits away. *I am a gargoyle. I can be **your** gargoyle.* I imagined my crew skulking around, bad talking her and threatening her and I'd fight each of them one by one. *I'll keep you safe.* In my mind I hadn't yet gotten to fighting Richard when I heard that *voice*:

"You're jealous, aren't you."

I turned my head and Sherry stood with her face inches from mine holding up an accusatory index finger.

"Is that loaded?" I asked.

"You just had to follow me," she continued. "You can't ever leave me alone. It's cuz you're jealous."

"Why are you here?"

"Because I fell in love and I can't help that. How about you?"

"Nope."

We looked out through the screen door at the two of them sitting there. If they felt our eyes they made no show of it. The party seemed miles in the background and I stood there feeling like a stalker. *At least I ain't the only one.*

"Fuck," Sherry muttered as she watched them, her eyes welling with tears. "Fuck fuck fuck." She punched the wall with her left fist and yelped in pain, but reared back to punch again. I grabbed her wrist mid-air. "Let go of me, Mudhoney."

"Stop it. So what, you don't want to be with Richard no more?"

"I don't know. I don't know what I want. Well, I know what I want … but I don't know what to do."

"You talked to him?"

"No."

"Cuz you don't just *break up* with Richard Lovecraft, you know. I hope you understand that."

"I know."

"Especially … well, it don't make no difference. You just don't break up with him."

"I'm not anybody's property."

"See, that's where you're wrong."

"You want a beer, Mikal? I'm going to go get us some beers."

And off she went. My entire body buzzed, and I felt my fingertips pricked with tiny plastic pins. I felt *watched*, and decided it was time for me to leave. Oriental Greg with the joker's hat came stumbling into the room saying,

"Anybody know a Mike Shannon? Mike Shannon." He turned to me and asked, "Dude, you know a cat named Mike Shannon?"

"Never heard of him. Why?"

"He's got a phone call."

Whatthefuck …

I headed for the front door just in time to see D'antre Philips walking in. One hundred and eighty degrees and off I went in the other direction.

Back to the kitchen, out the screen-door, to the deck and ready to break into a sprint and there she was sitting alone on the top step.

"Hi Mikal Fanon," Niani said. "It's wild that you came here." I hurried past her down the steps, out into the yard and the near-pitch dark. *Run! RUN!* "Hold up for just a minute," she said. And, dutifully, I froze in my tracks.

"You … can't see me," I said. "I'm invisible."

"Well, I thought ya knew I'm wearing my magic glasses today."

"Curses. Foiled again."

My head was strapped tight in on a tilt-o-whirl. I wanted to run away. Into the night. Into the nothing. I wanted to kiss her. I wanted to hit her for making me want to kiss her.

"I saw your folks not long ago," she said. "I usually see them in Blackchurch when I'm down visiting mine's. They're always really kind to me when I see them."

"Don't be fooled," I said. "It's just fake-friendly, mid-western 'howdy neighbor' bullshit. I promise you, they think you're an animal."

A streak of hurt flashed across her eyes and I wanted to pull out my knife and slash my own wrists open right then and there for making that happen.

"Well," she smiled, "They do a good job covering it up."

"Lee … Niani, I'm sorry I … I didn't wanna have nothing to do with hurting your friend, but … it's like …"

"He's fine. He's here in fact. You want to meet him?"

"No, I sure don't. And he ain't fine. I know it. That's the thing. He ain't never gonna be fine. It ain't just about damaging the body. You know that. If it was then there'd be a lot more racially moti-vated murders than there are. It's about *terror*. It's about scarring the *insides* all up. Setting up and maintaining the dividing lines. Perpetuating the fear and the hate. Keep it alive. Keep it burning on all fronts. The racialist's biggest fear is …"

"Obsolescence."

"If that means what I think it means, then yeah."

Why was I telling her this? *She's the enemy.* She was ev-erything I had to hate. Everything … in one dark and beautiful package.

"You don't need those guys, Mikal."

"It's just a thing, you know. Whatever."

"You don't need them."

"You gotta ... believe in *something*."

"Why?"

"Because ..."

"Oh, you little boys and your plastic armies."

"It ain't ... about that at all."

"You don't need those guys, Mikal."

I thought about Phil. I thought about myself in his place.

"I ..." I saw myself smashed up, destroyed, and alone. "Yes ... I ... do."

"You high right now?" she asked.

"Yeah."

"Me too. Getting high makes me happy. So why are you so sad?"

I held up my hands to my face and was shocked to feel that it was damp. *What the fuck?* I examined the moisture on my fingertips as if I had no idea from whence it came.

"You don't need those guys, Mikal," she repeated. *She's manipulating you.*

"You ought to go stay with, with, with your parents," I stuttered. "You ain't safe here. She's gonna bring bad things to this house."

"She who?"

"Crossfire ... you know ..."

"What are you talking about?"

She stood up and walked slowly toward me. My chest locked shut.

"They're gonna hurt you," I whispered.

"You won't let them hurt me, will you?"

Acid tears burned rivulets down my cheeks. She slid the cap off my head like revealing a secret. I could only breathe in syncopated jags, and I was so goddamned furious at her right then. I'd spent a long time building up a good solid wall, and she burned through it like tissue paper.

"You like this music, Mikal?" I hadn't even heard it until she pointed it out.

"Yeah. It's Burning Spear, ain't it?"

"They and them does hate I ..."

"Yeah."

And Spear sang, *"They and them does fight against I / You should see them rejoice / And tell I to run to run to run / I will never run away ..."*

And I knew that it was just the drugs that had me shaking like a lost, cold pup ... and she used that against me. She cradled my face in her hands and stared right into my cloudy, scarlet, salt-singed eyes.

"I ... I ..."

"I see you," she said.

"... Weeping and wailing / gnashing of teeth / you got yourself to blame ..."

"Don't touch me, you fucking NIGGER!" I grabbed her shoulders and pushed her as hard as I could. She tumbled backward, landing in the grass. "Fucking slut." I growled. "Don't trick me, you fucking dyke nigger SLUT!"

"Which is it, Mikal? Am I a dyke or a slut? You gotta pick one."

"Oh, whatever it takes. Whatever makes that money. Niggers are the fucking termites of society. Cockroaches! Feeding on filth and spreading disease. Take, take, take, breeding like sewer rats—"

"Do you even know what you're talking about? Do you understand the words you're saying?"

"Spitting out litter after litter of little niglet pickaninnies to gobble up all the fucking welfare. All the tax money! LEECHES!"

I came completely unglued. My vision was a blur. I paced around, venom dripping from my lips as tears poured out of my eyes.

"Why is it so hard for you to say that, Mikal? Why does it hurt you so bad to say it?" And she didn't break in the slightest. "Seems like you've got a job to do then. Come on. Kick me. Right here. As hard as you can."

I couldn't have stomped her even if I wanted to.

"The Jews and the socialists use the niggers as cheap labor and grunt soldiers on the front line to undermine White Christian America—"

"Here's your chance to be a hero for your race, Mikal. Stop me before I have a chance to breed like a sewer rat."

"To exhaust resources and dilute the purity of the white race through perversion miscegenation mongrelization—"

"Come on! Kick me! Kick me as hard as you can!!!"

I couldn't touch her …

You're hurting her! YOU'RE HURTING HER!!!

"Every new generation of a completely dependent criminal class further advances the elite Zionist agenda—" *You're hurting her! Kill yourself, you maggot!!!*

I truly did not follow my own logic at that point. The words coming from my mouth were not mine. I was a pre-recorded broadcast.

"Kick me, goddamn it!"

Pull out the knife and jab it into your throat! You don't deserve to live! KILL YOURSELF!

"To usurp power from the rightful stewards of the homeland!"

"Stop me before any pickaninnies of mine can wreck your precious White America!"

I couldn't even hear myself anymore. It was all just jabbering, babbling static vibrating from my lips and buzzing in my ears. *WHITE NOISE.* Chattering, blathering meaningless words and concepts like vomiting bile, I paced and shuddered, crying and shaking like a five-foot-ten newborn. I must have stopped at some point, because after a while all I could hear were my own sobbing breaths. (And maybe a bit of Funkadelic way off in the distance.) I was broken.

"Well," she said finally, standing and brushing herself off, "I'm really glad we had a chance to have this little chat." She turned around and headed back into the house. She turned back one last time to say, "If you ever need me, Mikal Fanon, you know where to find me." And she was gone. And she won. I stumbled off through the yard to the back road. *She's still got your hat,* I thought. *Gotta get that hat back.*

I staggered down the gravel alley behind the house toward Fourth Street. I felt like I had been walking for an hour at least, but it couldn't have been but a minute. I could still see the house when I turned around. I heard a voice say, "Yeah that's one uh them that fucked Trey all up."

Out of the darkness, lurching, came two young black gentleman of moderate build, and one gigantic Magilla-looking sumbitch. The first two I recognized from the hood, the third I must have met one fateful drunken evening on the West Side. I gave an exaggerated wave.

"Hey! I guess y'all are wearing your special glasses too, huh?"

"Psssh. Damn, Shabazz, this boy trippin'."

"What up, Arnold?" I slurred. "What up, Don? Hey Don, I just softed two hoes up for you, man. No charge."

"I don't know you, punk."

"Yeah … that's just the way it is."

"So," Gigantor grunted, "why you gotta go messin' up my cousin Trey, huh? Lil cracka-ass cracka."

"Misunderstanding, my man. We was thinkin' he's Jewish."

I barely remember the tornado of fists. I really only felt the first blow, which opened up my cheek wound like the South Fork Dam, and turned the collar of my flannel into Johnstown, PA. After that it was just a series of dull thuds landing somewhere near me. It was painful, but only in the abstract. I was well anesthetized. *Thank god for that Yid hippie and his drug butter. God bless that pork-dosing heeb.*

Once they got bored with pounding on my lifeless shell, they headed off to the party and likely had a swell time. I spent the rest of the morning stumbling home, bloody and dazed. By the time I got to my front porch, the sun was just starting to rise, and I thought, *She's still got my hat. She's still got my hat …*

15.

WALKING in, I wasn't sure if I had the skill or balance just then to negotiate the obstacle course of bodies. And exactly as I had to just now to reach my den to write this, I had to creep carefully and silently over and around sleeping friends and random ne'er-do-wells (I suppose some things never change).

I was just about to my room when I heard Richard's voice.

"We missed you at Meat's last night."

"Yeah," I said turning slowly so as not to wrench my already damaged neck. "Shit came up."

"What happened?"

"You remember them niggers that jumped us? Well, see, I went to go settle up."

"By yourself?"

"Made sense at the time."

"Did you bring a gun?"

"Meant to. But I forgot it."

"Yeah, I know. You left it cocked in my drawer."

Fuck.

"Well … live and learn."

"Get some sleep, Mikal. We've got a lot to discuss tomorrow. Or rather today."

"Rich, I gotta tell you something about Sherry."

"Yeah? What about her?"

Just then Sherry popped her head out of the bedroom right under Richard's arm.

"Jesus, Mikal!" she gasped. "What happened?"

Speedy little bunny ain't ya ...

"You should see the other guy."

"What about her?" Richard asked again.

"Well … she wanted me to tell you that she ain't coming to Meat's party because she's got a big test Monday, but apparently you already knew that, so message delivered and I'm going to bed."

Richard chuckled, rolled his eyes, and disappeared back into the bedroom. I looked down at the floor and watched the wood panels ripple like water. I could really only see out of my left eye, and even that was hazy. My right ear rang so loudly, it would likely have been audible to someone standing nearby. Sherry emerged from Richard's bedroom holding a bottle of rubbing alcohol.

"You. Me. Kitchen. Now."

I followed as well as my busted equilibrium would allow.

She dabbed a cotton ball filled with searing hot lava against the cuts on my face. I didn't flinch.

"You look like shit, Mikal."

"Fuck you."

"Aw, whatsamatter? No joy in Mudville? Hold that ice on. It'll keep the swelling down."

"Some hot party, eh Sher?"

"Is that a threat?"

"Did it sound like a threat?"

She opened the freezer and removed a piece of steak. I watched her try not to gag as she pulled open the plastic wrap.

"I don't know if this even works or if it's an old wives' tale, but that eye is nasty, so here we go." She held the frozen steak to my eye, swallowing hard to keep the puke at bay.

"Is the steak supposed to be frozen?"

"How should I know?"

"I can hold it."

"You mind the ice pack."

"Ow!"

"Sorry." Pause. "Mikal, I said some things last night that I didn't mean to say."

"Did you *do* anything you didn't mean to do?"

"No. Did you?"

"Hell yes. Well … There was shit I meant to do that I neglected to. I meant to case the house. Didn't. Meant to bring a gun. Whoops. Meant to gut Jack Curry like a wild boar. Maybe next time." She drew a hard shudder-breath on that last bit, and shut her eyes tight. "So you done fell in love with that nigger, huh?"

"What?!"

"I mean that figuratively, of course. It ain't even a race thing to me no more. Nigger is a state of mind."

"Well, you should know. Good night, Mikal. Bob's your uncle."

And she padded off to bed.

"Yeah, I guess he is."

16.

"Wait a second. I just want to talk, Jack. Please. Can we talk?"

"Sherry … relax, all right? I'm not going to fuckin' hurt you."

"Don't scream at me either."

"Okay."

"And don't send me away."

"You got a lot of nerve coming around here, girl. I can see that goddamn scar on your tit from here. Sickening. Shameful."

"I'm not ashamed."

"You should be. Lot of nerve coming around here."

"Jack, I can't help who I fall in love with. I'm sorry."

"You're just … confused."

"I'm in love. Madly. Blindly. It's the only thing I'm sure of, and it's fatal."

"That's fucking crazy! You're with whatsisname. Dickie-boy."

"Can't I be in love with two people?"

"No. Well … I don't know. Can you? I can't. But we're different."

"No, that's the thing. We're not different. I know you feel exactly the same way I do. Exactly."

"I'm not in love with … anybody."

"Yes, you are! I know you are! And I'm sorry. I'm so sorry. I don't want to see you hurt! But you can't help the way you feel any more than I can."

"You're really fuckin' bold, you know it?"

"I feel like I don't even know who I am anymore. Do you know who you are, Jack?"

"Yeah, sure."

"Maybe I've never known. But I know how I feel right now. I've never felt so sure of anything in my life."

"Too crazy …"

"It ripped me apart seeing you with her tonight. It tore me up into little tiny pieces. She had her arms around you so tight and I told myself, It's nothing. They're just like … brother and sister. Right? Just old friends. Right? But I felt like I was dying inside. I can't help that I was jealous. I can't pretend I don't feel the way I do."

"How do I know you're not going to flake like you did on that guy? I'm gonna see my whole world torn to shreds and you're just going to just … float on to whatever's next. Huh? Or maybe it's a set—"

"It's not a set-up! I've never felt in my life the way I feel now. It's real. Don't you understand that? I don't want to *destroy your world.* I don't want anyone to get hurt. Believe me, I don't. I'm sorry."

"It's the DMC isn't it. Quite the aphrodisiac. Power. Strength. Charisma. Devastating mind control. Gives you a panty-tickle doesn't it."

"You're a nasty, mean, rotten bastard. You know it? Are you proud of it?"

"No."

"Who hurt you Jack Curry? Somebody cut you up bad."

"Wrong. Nobody touches me."

"I believe that."

"You're not the first, you know. Not even close. LOTS of girls have come before you. I've lost count."

"I realize that."

"Boys too. There have been boys. Does that bother you?"

"It doesn't make me happy. But oh well. The past has passed."

"Just so you understand."

"I'm out in limbo here. It's cold. Help me. Let me in."

"I couldn't stop you if I tried."

17.

I woke up to find all the guys packed tight in the front room. Every Skin in the area with whom we had even the slightest connection was there. And of course, it was a "no girls allowed" affair.

The vertigo was actually worse than it had been before I went to sleep, and the floor kept moving and dodging under me as I tried to walk. Someone handed me a beer and I handed it right back. Thankfully, at least I had regained full use of both eyes, such as they were. I found that if I didn't move them or my head at all I was fine, so after slapping a West Side newbie out of my favorite seat, I took to sitting perfectly still and trying to keep my eyes open. That's not to say that I was paying attention, however, for memories of the evening prior and the screeching and whining in my right ear dominated my focus.

Phil looked at my bruised-up, beaten-to-hell face with a knowing smile. As well as he could smile with all the wires and clamps.

"Relcome choo my 'orld, shun," he said. He gave a plaster-casted thumbs-up and resumed drinking his Fosters through a bendy straw.

"I'm glad you're all here," Richard said. "There's been some issues bugging me lately and I thought it best that we all convene so they could be brought out and kicked about. As many of you know, the local chapter of the Ku Klux Klan, who at last count are eight strong—" An overall snicker of derision filled the room, and Richard chuckled along in agreement. "Yeah, I know, I know. Anyway, the Klan will be marching on the square next Saturday afternoon. And it's no stretch to say that this will be a great joke to a lot of the locals, and fair play to them I say. But what we some-times forget is most people don't make the distinctions that *we* might about the Movement. So when they're laughing at the Klan, they're laughing at *us*. They're laughing at White Power. And that can't stand. I feel like we've been treading water for a long while, guys, sticking with our own and really not rising above basically thug-like behavior when we do act at all. A notable exception was Mule of the Hangmen bringing down that Baptist Church. So, re-spect to Mule. We will miss his great music." Richard tap-danced right on past the fact that, respect or no, Mule will not be breathing the sweet air of freedom until he's forty-five years old. And that's providing that he actually survives Lucasville Prison. Richard continued, "I think it's time we made some tactical strikes. Hits that send a clear message that we are not playing around, and we will not be ignored. It doesn't have to happen today, this week, or even this month. But when we hit, we will hit with full power. If anyone has any good targets in mind for a strike, or even a test strike, please let us know." I could have spoken I suppose, but I kept silent.

Meat Cake's younger brother, this jittery little rat-faced boy named Stevie, got up to talk about building homemade bombs. I pretty much fazed out at that point. His wiener-dog-like yip was no match for the pounding and screeching inside my head. He started off yakking about using soda bottles as hand grenades as well as ground bombs, and he pulled up his pants legs to show the scars on his calves illustrating what can go wrong when dealing with volatile chemicals. By the time he got to the mechanics of dousing someone with gasoline and setting them on fire, I had to excuse myself and go back to bed. I thought Richard would protest, but he just nodded, and off I went.

"I call that giving someone *the shower*," I heard Stevie say as I left. "Careful you don't get cleaned yourself."

I woke up some hours later to find the house empty. I was able to keep the head spinning down to a workable level by walking with my neck locked into one position. I headed out back, through the rip in the fence to the grocery store. Not on my A-game just then I actually *purchased* some items for a change, and came back to the house with macaroni and cheese and a two-liter of red cream soda in tow.

That night, as Phil sat in the front room watching some porno video called *Anal Virgins in BangCock,* I shaved my head with a cheap pair of clippers I had stolen the month before. *If you're gonna steal, why grab the cheap ones?* Only god knows.

"Ooooo! I come now rong time rong time!" said a ridiculously over-the-top "Asian" voice.

"Sounds pretty sexy in there, Phil," I said. "It's a damn shame about your hands."

"Eat a hot dick," was his reply, and I stopped to marvel at how clear it sounded. "Eat a hot dick" may very well be the most perfect sentence to say for a person with his jaw wired shut. There's just no telling.

I didn't know it then, but that would be the last time I ever shaved my head.

Wednesday afternoon I called my mom at work to see if she'd like to get together around six o'clock for coffee and a bite to eat. I hadn't seen her in a very long while and thought it might be good to catch up a bit. She said yes and we agreed to meet at a diner nearby. I got there at 5:40 and waited for two-and-a-half hours. She never showed up.

Walking home I thought about Niani. I didn't want to and I tried not to, but apparently it wasn't up to me. I couldn't shake her. *Maybe she set you up to get jumped.* But that just didn't seem true. "I see you," she said. She broke me. She called my bluff. *She called you out for the rodent that you are.* I wanted to find a way to redeem myself. Pay the fine, do the penance, *make peace.* Only with her. The rest of the world could burn away and die. But I wanted her to see me again. *Better than I am. Better than I deserve.* And I knew I had blown that chance forever.

As soon as I walked in the door I could feel that something was off. Sherry's usual pile of odds and ends sat in the corner as I had come to expect, but she was nowhere in sight, and the place had an exotic aroma about it ... both completely new to me, and yet strangely familiar. I noticed it first at the party on Jamestown Street. *Marijuana, yeah, but something else too.* A flowery soap smell that gave the air a peculiar thickness. I could hear the sounds of the Bad Brains coming from Richard's room. I knocked.

"I love I Jah, yeah yeah / I got to keep that PMA ..."

"Sherry?" I tried to turn the knob, but the door was locked.

"Yeaaaah?" she drawled.

"Unlock the door."

"Come back later."

"Open up."

"I'm masturbating," she said casually. "Leave me alone."

"Come on. Open the door."

"Go away."

I commenced to knocking on the door in triplets, over and over and over, in the most irritating fashion possible. "All right all right," she sighed. I heard her get up and pad a-rhythmically across the room. The door unlatched, and I heard her pad back again. "Come on in. It's open."

"Wait a minute," I said. "Are you decent?"

"Am I *decent*? Are you queer? Come in for fucksake."

So I walked into Richard's bedroom and into a fog of white smoke. Sherry sat on Richard's bed with her eyes half-closed. She was wrapped up in Richard's Nazi flag, and all of her clothing lay on the floor in front of her.

"What's going on here?" I demanded.

"What do you mean?" she asked dreamily, her voice floaty and sing-song.

"Holy fuck. I can't believe you're smoking drugs in Richard's house. He's gonna know. He's gonna murder us both."

"Richard Smichard. Bo-bitchard."

"Hmm … yeah … well, I guess I can't argue with that logic."

"Damn straight," she said. "Or not." She lifted a glass pipe to her lips and took a deep drag. She offered it to me. I declined. She shrugged and hit it again, sparking it with a lighter.

"What is that anyways? It ain't just pot."

"Shiny black rock," she replied. "It's glooooorious. Makes me tingly."

"Black rock? What the fuck is that?"

"Ooooooh peeeeeee yuuuuuuummmmm …"

"Oh god …"

"Have you ever heard of astral-telepathy?"

"Oh … fucking *god*!"

"Me neither."

"So what, are you a junkie now? Who gave it to you? No. Wait. Don't tell me."

"Jackie gave it to me. He's a candy man."

"Yeah … real sweet. That's the guy who pretty much crippled your friend, remember?"

"He gave it to me to give to Phil. Said it would make him feel better. But I knew Phil wouldn't use it, so fugg'm."

"I'mma kill that guy," I said through my teeth.

"So you've threatened. Jack's pretty scaaaaary, huh?"

"Yeah … So, uh, are you naked?"

"I've got the flag on," she said, her eyes all a-roll. "Prude."

"Richard's gonna kill us. Why?"

"Why?"

"WHY?!"

"I *told* you, goofball. I was touching myself. Taking matters into my own hands. What, don't True Aryan Warriors ever tug on their little thingies?"

The record ended and the arm lifted up and returned to its resting-place. The disc continued to spin and crackle on the wheel.

"Why don't you get dressed, Sherry? I'll make us some coffee and we'll talk some more out in the front room."

She stretched her bare legs out in front of her and stared at them, deep in thought.

"I have something not a lot of people have. A really early glamour shot of Norma Jean. Before she became "Marilyn." She was born with extra toes, did you know that? As soon as she was able, she had them surgically removed, and most of those early pictures with the offending digits were rounded up and destroyed. But I have one."

"Well I'll be damned."

"Yes you will. I just think it's interesting. Here she was, icon of her generation, pretty much the gold standard for beauty, but she'd had herself carved up and mutilated in order to be like everybody else."

"Yeah … that's just the way it is."

"Do you ever feel like you've cut off parts of yourself, Mikal? I do."

"I'm pretty well intact. Besides my hair."

"Good for you."

"Good for me."

"Do you want to kiss me, Mikal?"

"No."

"Do you want to kiss Richard?" I didn't even bother to dignify that with a response. "I know you hate me."

"Sherry, I don't hate you."

"Yes you do. You hate me because when you look at me you don't like the way you look in my reflection. You hate me for the same reason Jack hates me. Because you're afraid I've come to steal your light away."

"I think you're needin' to sober up."

"There's a select few people. Just a few, who give off a great, shining light. The rest of us can only bask, or burn, blistering, blinded, trying to dance in it."

"You are higher than weeping Jesus."

"You wanna dance, Mikal?"

"Christ Almighty …"

"I'm sorry to say it out loud, cuz I know he doesn't want to hear it said, but I know Mikal is obsessed with Richard. More than just fond, more than impressed, he's captivated by him. He's *taken*. Richard is powerful. Charismatic. Handsome. And *evil*. *Sooooo* evil. And Mikal wants a piece of the dark light. No different from Jack Curry ... whom Mikal *claims* to despise. Been afraid of him for years. Fear, love, worship—to Mikal there's very little difference. He's awfully Catholic in that regard."

"Or maybe you need fucking therapy. I'm standing right here. You ain't got to talk about me third person. And you don't know shit."

"Just tell me ... honestly ... If some night ... by chance ... he invited you into his bed, would you refuse?"

"You know what? Maybe I do hate you after all."

"Do you know who you are, Mikal?"

"Yeah, sure. Of course I do."

"I don't know who I am." She lowered her head and began to cry. "I don't know who I am. *I don't know who I am*."

I stood there and let her cry. I wasn't really sure of what else to do. Looking back now, I still don't know. I eventually turned around and walked out. Took a bus to Reeba's brother house. They had a spare room for me.

Sherry and I spoke once more on Saturday, and that was that.

18.

SATURDAY. Klan rally on the square. Torrential downpour all day. Good times.

The day started off with this message on the answering machine:

"Hi Mikal. It's Tanya. Sorry I missed you at the diner the other night. Totally slipped my mind. I ain't thinking too good these days. I would like to see you, though, so give me a call."

Tanya. It's Tanya. She couldn't even bring herself to say, "It's Mom."

I never called her back. I couldn't. That was the night that I fell of the edge of the Earth.

Around 3:00 PM Brian drove me back home so I could change clothes. The house was empty, as Richard and Sherry had headed over to Meat's to rendezvous with the extended crew. Geared up and ready to roll, I picked up the phone to call my mom about a rain check. A fierce headache overtook me, a fog rolled in over my eyes, and I fell to the floor. I couldn't remember the phone number. I couldn't remember my own phone number. I grasped for any handle to pull myself upright, and ended up yanking the phone out of the wall and splitting the cord. The answering machine fell off the end table and shattered.

"Hey Mikey!" Brian yelled from the front porch. "Let's roll!"

I lay there, watching the room spin above me. Within a minute or so my head cleared and I regained my balance. *Just take it as it comes.*

We met up with everyone down at the square, which was already packed to the splits with protesters, counter-demonstrators, and general rubbernecks. To this day I don't know what purpose we thought was served by our attendance. It did solidify a number of people's respective destinies, mine included, so I suppose the fates know what they're doing.

I heard Niani's voice through a megaphone: "Well, I am quite embarrassed that we've all shown up this afternoon to give so much free publicity to this pitiful excuse for a Klan march."

The crowd laughed. Cries of "you're welcome" were aimed at the Klanfolk across the street. There were exactly five of them, all dressed in their white sheets and hoods. Two men in their mid-fifties, a woman in maybe her early forties, a man who looked to be in his late nineties who was so locked in the clutches of senility that he smiled and waved to the crowd, and a young boy of about twelve. The boy was wide-eyed—enraptured with the entire scene. He appeared to feed off the negative energy. Silently mouthing, "nigger, nigger, nigger, nigger, nigger …" I found it rather chilling. I found it rather familiar.

Niani continued to speechify about how "love always over-rules" or some such drivel that I doubt she really believed, and it was met with warm and enthusiastic applause. She turned her megaphone over to an older black man who looked like a former prize-fighter. He commenced to leading the crowd in a rousing, though somewhat confusing, rendition of "I've Got a Robe, You've Got A Robe (Goin' to Shout All Over God's Heav'n)," or so I've been told. It just sounded like nonsense to me.

A couple of the lads had taken to shouting "Sieg heil!" and goose-stepping, trying to make a scene, but the crowd was so large and preoccupied with singing that no one paid any attention.

"Knock it off, fellas," some cop yawned. "That's irritating."

We milled about for an hour or so, cold, wet, miserable, hopelessly outnumbered, bored and frustrated. A couple of pre-teens on scooters rode by and laughed at us. I couldn't tell if Richard was lost in thought … or just lost. He didn't even seem to realize when Sherry slipped away into the crowd. But I did. And, I couldn't help but notice, so did Phil. Since the beat down Phil's status had all but withered to nothing, and many of us wondered when the day would come that Richard would drive him out into the woods and leave him there like a useless old dog. But Phil had an air of ambition about him that day. He wasn't going to go quietly or without bloodshed.

"This sucks," Richard said finally. He turned to me and said, "Go collect Sherry. It's time to go."

"And you're thinkin' my name's Tobey? Cuz it ain't Tobey."

"What did you say?"

"You musta mistook me for a slave. But my name ain't Tobey."

"All right," he sighed. "Fine."

"It's Kunta Kinte."

"Whatever," he replied, glaring at me.

"I'll get 'er," Phil said, and trudged off into the sea of bodies.

"Guess he's not worthless after all," Richard said to no one in particular.

It occurred to me just then that shaming Richard in front of his soldiers wasn't my smartest decision ever, so I went off to assist Phil in his mission.

Thunder crashed and the rain began to slam harder than ever. It sent many people on their way. The Klan quintet departed as well, prehensile tails between their legs.

As a large section of the crowd broke, I saw *them*. All together there huddled under an awning. And it all fell into place in my mind. I saw them: Jack Curry, Niani Shange, Yoshimoto, Lin Cho, Paige, the whole host of them. The whole lot. And Sherry, right in the middle. She looked comfortable with them. At ease. At *home*. I saw her tug on the Demon's dreadlocks, and he laughed. Niani whispered in Sherry's ear, pointing at Curry, and Sherry covered her face, *blushing*. I'd seen that maneuver before. Even from afar, I could read *that look* in Sherry's eyes. That look she used to have for Richard. That look of awe and instant devotion. *That look I shouldn't see.* I watched Sherry toss up the nazi salute in an exaggerated fashion, and they all laughed. I should have felt betrayed, perhaps. Threatened even. *Sherry could lead them to us. They could case our house like I should've cased theirs.* But I didn't. *She's out of your reach.* I didn't feel anything. *She's a stupid little girl with a stupid little crush.* And I accepted defeat.

A small gust of fear blew briefly through me when I saw Senbe Shabazz and his Raging Black Fist! or whoever they are. But I was far enough away to not be present in their world. Shabazz chucked Curry on the shoulder as he walked by. Curry chucked him back. It was casual. Friendly even, but non-committal. The black army marched away. I felt as though I were watching it all on television. I may as well have been.

"SHERRY!" we all heard Phil bellow. "SHERRY NICOLASH!" He was far enough away that he couldn't be seen yet, but the third "SHERRY!!!" was closer. And the fourth closer still. She quickly gave them all hugs, lingering on Niani long enough for Niani to whisper again in her ear. Sherry nodded, and then she darted off. Away she ran, and I circled around the perimeter of the square to try and head her off.

"I was looking for you!" I shouted as I ran up to her.

"Surprise," she replied.

"Let's just—"

"Bark like a good little puppy, Mikal. Bark for your master. Fetch, boy! Fetch!"

And from out of the ether Phil appeared.

"It'sh time to go. Rishard wantsh to shee you, Sherry. Get going."

"Ooooo," she said waving her arms in mock hysteria. "Best not keep *His Highness* waiting." And off she went. I began to follow her when Phil stopped me.

"It'sh over, Mikal," he hissed under his breath. "I'm blowing the whishle."

"Huh?"

"I know you've been following 'er. I know you've been watching 'er. Cuzh I've been watching *you*."

What the fuck ...

"You'd better start making some sense, Phil. Clock's ticking and I'm tired of getting wet."

"I've been watching. I know pretty mush everything you know. And I think it'sh time for shome people to die. Don't you think death ish calling, Mikal?"

"Phil, what are you—"

"Why didn't you tell Rishard?!" he demanded, shaking. "About her? About *HIM*?! That cockshucker who did thish to me!" he indicated his face. "Why have you been keeping shecretsh?"

"I … I …"

"Who are you protecting?" He grasped his mouth with his fingertips, wincing in pain. Apparently trying to holler with a broken jaw is none too pleasant.

"I …"

"Doeshn't matter. *I'm* telling 'im. Tonight. I'm telling 'im everything I know. And I don't think Rishard's going to be too pleashed with you."

Maybe I should have been worried, but instead I was merely irritated. *Go die, Short Bus.* And being smacked by stinging rain and damp wind helped not a bit.

"Fuck it. I don't care. Earn your little brownie points if you want to, you pathetic gimp. So yeah, I know who crippled you. I hope he gets what's coming to him. Meant to bring it up before, slipped my mind. Whoops. Oh, and Sherry's got wandering eyes behind Richard's back? Fuck her. I hope she gets hers too. I don't care about her, I don't care about that rope-headed tat freak or his nigger cohorts, and I don't care about *you*."

"But," he growled, "there ish shomebody you DO care about." From out of his jacket pocket he pulled the party flyer. *Jamestown Street. Come one, come all!* My heart stopped cold.

"You … leave her out of this, Phil."

"Why the conshern?"

"Fuck you. She don't matter none."

"Nigger dyke with a big mouth. Sheems like a good hit to me."

"No. Leave her be."

"Two birds, one shtone."

"Look, Curry's who you want. We'll catch him on the street somewhere. Do him proper. I know where his family lives at. We'll case his mama's place, okay?"

"Too complicated. Too long to wait. I want to hit 'im now."

"Stay away from that house, Phil. I'm telling you. You stay the holy fuck away from her."

"Whatsha matter, Mikey? Little monkey twat caught your eye? Don't you like the way black shkin burnsh?"

I dove at him head on and tackled him to the concrete. He screeched like an animal as I forced both of my hands down against his mouth. His blood oozed out between my fingers and washed thin in the rain, dissipating into the cracks in the sidewalk.

"I'LL KILL YOU, PHIL! I'LL KILL YOU BEFORE YOU HURT HER!!!"

He smashed the plaster cast on his left wrist full on into my temple, and the fragile little stones in my ear that balance my equilibrium dislodged once again. The universe tumbled and crashed about me as I pummeled his face and stomach with my fists. Somebody lifted me up at my abdomen. I saw Geoff and Brian help Phil to stand and with all my strength I kicked out and slammed the heel of my left boot square into Phil's jaw. It impacted with a sickening *CRUNCH* as his metal wires popped. He screamed with a spray of crimson that splashed across Brian's face. Phil spun one-eighty on the rain-slick sidewalk. Brian froze in horror as Phil's blood ran down his cheeks and forehead. We all watched Phil loping away down the street, groaning and wailing all the way. Joe started to chase after him but Richard stopped him short.

"Let him go, Joey. He's finished. There's nothing left for him anyway."

I never saw Phil again.

(If you're reading this, Phil, I hope you realize that I may have saved your life that day.)

I expected immediate static, but it never came. No one said a word to me. *Stomping a cripple. It don't get much more Skin than that.* As we walked back to the cars, a cop approached Richard and said, "You'd outta keep better control over your children, Richie."

"Yes, Mr. Hansen," Richard replied, and the cop strolled away. Richard patted me on the back and said, "See ya later." I nodded and got into Brian's car with Reeba, Geoff, and Jennie. I watched Richard and Sherry kiss in the pouring rain before they got into Meat's LTD.

Brian was too freaked out to drive, so Geoff drove us back to Reeba's brother's house. "Goddamn, goddamn, goddamn," Brian muttered the whole way home, furiously wiping at his face trying to rub all of Phil's blood away. He did not succeed. "Goddamn. Goddamn, goddamn."

19.

THE storm raged on the rest
of the night. I drank a couple of beers, which did nothing to ease my
vertigo, and went to sleep in Reeba's niece's room. I lay there with
my eyes closed for an hour, maybe more, trying to ignore the spinning
room. Trying not to think about Niani. About her smile. Her voice.
That sad, hurt look in her eyes. I wanted to tell her that I was sorry
for what I said to her. That it was all bullshit. *Just one more chance.*
Please. I just wanted to be close to her one time, like Jack Curry on
the back porch steps. Like Sherry at the square. *Just once. Let me just*
hold you one time. I wanted to tell her that I'd begun my campaign to
protect her from the evil spirits. *One down, however many to go.* But
I never would. I thought about going to the house. I had missed the
last bus, *but I could walk. I could walk to Jamestown ...*

I had missed the last bus, so I walked to Jamestown, Sherry
said.

Sherry and Richard had been dropped off at the house. She begged him to take her back to her dorm.

"Car is at Meat's, babe," he said. "We'll get it in the morning."

Richard then proceeded to get drunk and pass out on the couch listening to Wagner. She was stranded. Last resort of last resorts, she thought to call her roommate Sarah, but the phone was destroyed, yanked from the wall.

So around about eleven o'clock, Sherry wrapped herself in Richard's jacket and headed out into the storm.

Lightning had knocked out most of the streetlights. No stars, no moon, just the cold black of the night and the hard, brutal rain. But she walked. All the way to Jamestown.

Within a mile, her boots were full and heavy, gushing over with freezing water. She tried to resist the urge to yank them off, but gave in before long.

Sherry said:

I sat down on the curb, pulled off those worthless clompers with their stupid swastikas painted on, and dumped them and my socks into a trash can. My bare feet froze numb, I couldn't feel my toes, I could barely feel the sidewalk.

It was worth it.

That was the first night that we ever made love.

Meanwhile, I tried to get some sort of rest at Reeba's brother's place. To no avail.

"Mikal, wake up."

Reeba nudged me awake, whispering, her voice warbling with panic. "Come on, Mikal. Please."

"What? What's the deal?"

"Shhhh! Whisper. Richard's here. Something's *wrong*. I don't know what's going on, but it's bad. Oh god, it's bad."

I looked her over. She was wearing a large, men-size, button-down shirt, and nothing else. Her lip trembled, her eyes floated in deep pools of fear.

"Where's Brian?"

"He's sleeping. Geoff and Jennie went home. I was just sitting there watching TV when Richard came banging on the window. Whatever he's plotting, I don't want Brian involved."

My stomach knotted.

"What he's plotting?"

"He's crazy, Mikal. He's not acting himself. He barged into the house, demanded I wake you and Brian up, and then smashed an ashtray with his fist. Then he called Meat, left this horrible message about burning people to death, and now he's sitting out there in a rage waiting for Meat to call him back. He's just sitting there shaking, muttering to himself over and over. You've got to stop him! I don't want Brian mixed up in this. Whatever it is. You've got to do a better job than I did." She put her face in her hands and began to cry. She pulled the shirt down to cover her nakedness. "He didn't want what I offered. He just pulled my hair real hard and called me a 'gutterslut.' I'd do anything to protect Brian! Anything. I don't want to lose him."

"What's he muttering?"

"It's awful."

"What's he saying?"

"'Kill the bitch. Burn her. Kill that fucking cunt bitch.' Something. Does he mean Sherry? Why? Why is he going to kill Sherry?"

"He's not talking about Sherry."

20.

SHUDDERING, wobbling and numb below the ankles, drenched, and chilled to the bone, Sherry finally made it to the house on Jamestown Street. Before she could so much as ring the bell, the door flew open.

"Hurry quick inside!" Niani said. "Before you get pneumonia." She didn't have to tell Sherry twice. "You didn't walk here, did you?" Niani asked. Sherry simply shivered in reply. "Well, why didn't you call?"

"Ffff … ffff … phone's b-b-broken," Sherry stuttered, her teeth chattering. "No car."

"Damn, girl …"

"But it's … it's all g-g-good!"

"Oh … kay …"

Jack was away at work. The late shift. Sherry knew that. That's why she came. That's why she walked. Through a hard, metallic rainstorm. Like needles shot out of a cannon.

"N-nice p-p-p-place you got."

"I'm glad you're here, but, you didn't really need to …"

I would have swum through magma to be with you, Sherry thought. *I would have crawled on broken legs.*

"Come on upstairs. Let me find you a towel or a blanket."

I love you. I love you.

Niani wore gray sweat pants and a Malcolm X T-shirt, wooden bracelets, and silver rings. Somewhere in the house Nina Simone sang on a vinyl record …

"Black is the color of my true love's hair …"

I wanted to kiss her so badly, but I didn't know how to go about it.

"Girl," Niani said, "we need to get you out of those clothes."

Sherry gasped. "Wh … what?"

"They're soaked. Go take you a super-duper hot shower. I'll put that stuff in the dryer and make us some cinnamon tea, all right? Sound good to you?"

Good to me …

Sherry cranked the shower dial as far to the left as she could stand.

I felt the chill drain out of my bones, from the top of my head all the way down my body and out the tips of my toes. I'm in love with you, *I thought.* How do I tell you that I love you? *I didn't want to frighten her. I didn't want her to think I was crazy. But I was!* You make me crazy. *From the moment I laid eyes on her I loved her. I couldn't help it.* I'm out of my mind. *It was out of my hands. I fought it. I lied to myself about it. Tried to convince myself that I couldn't, she wouldn't, it's impossible, over and over and over and over.*

Through the glass shower door Sherry saw Niani's silhouette enter the bathroom and place a stack of fresh towels and some manner of dry things for her to wear. She stood perfectly still for a moment, soapy and poised, knowing Niani was watching her. *I hope you like what you see.* Apparently she did. But like a lady, Niani quickly turned on her heel and left.

And Sherry forgot, for a while, all about Richard.

Which was a dreadful mistake.

21.

I walked out to the living room to find Richard pacing about.

"Beautiful night, eh Rich?"

"Go wake Brian up."

"Reeba says no."

"Reeba can suck my dick."

"Wasn't that on the table already?"

"Shut the fuck up and go get him. I'm not playing around." The phone rang and he snatched it right up before it completed the first chime. "Meat? Yeah, you heard me right. Bring it all. Whatever you got. Call everybody. Everyone needs a piece too. This is no joke. I'll see you in forty." And he hung up.

"I ain't carrying no gun, Richard. You know that."

"Mikal … You're a very small man. I suggest you don't stand in my way."

"Tell me what's going on."

"WHY DON'T YOU TELL ME!!!"

"What?"

"You're the guy who knows everything, right?!"

"I don't know nothing."

Brian came stumbling out of the bedroom half-asleep, Reeba trailing behind him.

"What's goin' on out here?" he yawned, squinting.

"Nothing, baby," Reeba said. "Mikey and Rich are just leaving. Come back to bed."

"Get dressed, Brian," Richard said. "We've got business."

Without a blink or a question, Brian hurried back to the bedroom.

"Please, Richard," Reeba begged. "Please let Brian sit this one out."

"Mikal, would you shove something in this cow's maw so I don't have to listen to her?"

"I hate you," she cried. "I *hate* you."

"I don't even know what the deal is," I said.

He removed the tattered remains of the flyer from his pocket. It was so faded and rain damaged that it was hardly legible. "You know this house, Mike?"

"No."

"How could you lie to me like that?"

"I ... I mean, I've been there. But—"

"Well, you're going there again. And we're having a barbecue." He pulled out a small handgun and presented it to me. *No.* I didn't budge. "You really don't want to defy me right now." Nothing. *I can't.* "Don't go breaking my heart." *God ... no ...* "I'm not telling you again, Mikal." I took it and shoved it into my pocket. Brian returned fully dressed, and Reeba grabbed his arm.

"Brian," she sobbed. "You don't have to go. This isn't going to—"

"Brian," Richard interjected, "I think it's time you dumped that used cum sack out on the curb with the rest of the garbage. Those holes were worn out busted and spent back when *I* had her."

Reeba's face scorched up bright scarlet and tears streamed down her face. "You bastard," she spat. "You fucking bastard."

"Drop the wench, Brian," Richard continued. "You don't need it. There are better whores out there with way less cock damage."

Brian looked at Reeba.

"Brian, no …," she cried.

"Look at her. Look at her stomach. She's swallowed so many loads she's getting spunk fat. Lose her."

"Okay, Richard," Brian said, "I will. Bye, Reeba."

And with that we left. I heard Reeba collapse to the floor, sobbing, as we walked out the door. I never saw her again.

22.

WIPING a bit of condensation from the mirror, Sherry inspected her tattoo. It was rough and hideous. Artless and spotty. *Embarrassing*. She chuckled to herself when she saw the clothes that Niani had left for her: a pair of men's boxer shorts that must have been Jack Curry's, and a tight black T- shirt. It read:

The Blacker The College The Sweeter The Knowledge

Sherry joined Niani on the couch in the upstairs living room, where she was greeted with a mug of piping hot tea … *which I proceeded to spill on myself like a clumsy dork.* Niani giggled. Sherry's heart slammed around inside her chest. She felt dizzy. Niani got up to drop a new platter on the turntable. This time it was Ella Fitzgerald's turn, and she sang:

"I tremble at your touch …"

"So ... um ..."

"Yeah ..."

"I want you oh so much / I know I shouldn't / but that's the way it is ..."

"It's quite a ... a thing, you know?"

"For real."

"Quite an evening."

"Pretty wild day overall."

"So ..."

"Yeah."

"Yeah ..."

Sherry thought about making a break for it. *I thought about running away. For the second time in one night. Barefoot. In freezing rain. And pitch dark. Half-naked, in men's underpants, and with no where to go. I considered it.*

"It's really ... cold ... outside."

"Uh huh."

Sherry didn't know what to expect to happen. She blew on her tea and swayed to the music. Niani took a sip of her tea. Sherry did likewise and burned her mouth.

"You okay?" Niani asked.

"Yeah ..." *I felt like an idiot.*

Niani sang along with Ella. Sherry swayed back and forth to the soft, shuffling rhythm. *I wanted to ...talk to her. I* needed *to talk to her. But about what?* So instead she intently sipped at her tea as if that's all she wanted to do.

Sherry had watched Niani at school, on stage, out and about, so confident and sure in front of hundreds of strangers. She always seemed so radiant and in control and one step ahead of the rest of the world. But on that couch, she seemed so small. *Tiny ... just like me ...*

"Thank you for inviting me over."

"Thank you for, you know, coming."

"I'll love you forever / though it may never be / but that's the way it is with people like you and me ..."

"Wow." Sherry said. "That's a sad song."

"You want me to change the record?" Niani asked. "I could put something different on."

"No, it's pretty. I like it."

"You sure? I got lotsa stuff."

"Uh uh. It's good."

But then, alas, the very next tune started in with lady Ella, in no uncertain terms, begging her lover to *"Make love to me my darling ..."*

Oooooooooh my ...

"Uh, so," Sherry interjected over the lyrics, "what's up with this guy?"

She indicated a large framed black-and-white photo hanging on the wall of an odd looking black man with wild, silver hair. Bayard Rustin as it turns out. Gay. Black. Communist. Friend of MLK's. *Who knew?*

"He's a hero of ours," Niani said. "Jack's and mines. We decided we needed one good icon for the wall in here."

"Must I extend an invitation / to make love to me my darling ..."

"Of course," Niani continued, blushing if she could blush, "Jack campaigned for Harriet Tubman because she, quote, 'lead her people to freedom with a gun to their heads,' unquote. He bought this huge painting of her at a flea market. But she seems a little, I dunno, obvious, yeah?"

"I've got hero posters on my walls too," Sherry said.

"Who do you have?"

"Just old dead people."

"Of course."

"That's an impressive record collection you've got here," Sherry said, still attempting to reflect attention away from Ella laying it all out. And indeed it was. Twice the size of Richard's, if not more.

"Ah ... vinyl," Niani sighed. "Why listen to anything else?"

They sat speechless, again, sipping at their cinnamon tea, letting Ella do the talking. After a good while, Niani stood up and walked over to her record wall. Flipping through the discs she began to dance to the music ...

"Before the mood that I'm in changes—"

"Sherry?"

"Make love to me—"

"Yes?"

"Make love to me—"

"You want to dance?"

"My darling ..."

"Uh ... no. I—"

"Yes you do."

"No I really—"

"Yeees you dooooo."

"I'm so—"

"I ..."

"in love—"

"Dance with me."

"with youuuu."

"I got two left feet."

"But they're such pretty left feet."

I'm so in love with you.
"Okay."

So they danced. Slowly. Each song inching closer and closer together ...

And by the time the album was through, I was not only mad for her, I wanted to sleep with Ella Fitzgerald as well. She smelled like heaven. She tasted even better. And when she lead me by the hand down the hallway to her bedroom, I had to follow. I would follow you anywhere. *Holding her body against mine, smoldering hot and delicate and smooth as wet silk, I felt the woman I had been, whomever she was, melt away into nothing.* Goodbye, and good riddance to me.

Oh god did she ever make love to me that night ...Never felt anything like it. Only the finest opium can come close ...and even that's a bunch of jive.

I'd been searching for a shining light to dance in, to bask in, and she was the brightest I've ever seen. A golden fire that would shimmer, sparkle, shine, or ignite, shaming the rays of the sun itself. I couldn't help but be drawn in ...even if it meant burning alive.

Niani ... my love ... I'll forever be dancing in the light of you.

23.

BULLET rain pelted the sides of Meat's LTD. It's seemed to fly at us from all sides, rocking the wagon like a tugboat lost at sea. Some neighborhoods were even without streetlamps. We were a caravan of three station wagons and four large vans. An army, setting off to wage holy war on a tiny, oblivious, unprepared enemy. Death rode on the wind like smoke and napalm.

"Mikal," Richard asked examining the address on the flyer, "is this a four or a nine?"

"It's a nine."

"Four it is."

"Whatever."

Meat drove. Geoff rode shotgun. And as we hit the first red light rolling into downtown, he threw open the passenger-side door and ran off into the night. No one blinked. Meat leaned over, shut the door, and away we went.

"So long Geoff," Richard said to himself. "For your sake I hope we never meet again."

24.

SOMEWHERE far, far away Sherry thought she heard Etta James singing "Tell Mama." *But that may be just my imagination.* Mostly she just heard her own heartbeat, and her deep, contented breaths. *And hers ...*

"So ..." she said finally, "your real name is Lisa Johnson?"

Niani chuckled. "There are only two people in the whole world who call me 'Lisa.' My grandmama and Jack. I wasn't born with my *real* name."

They lay in bed cuddled close together, sharing a large Santahead mug of White Zin.

"Sorry for the mug. It's all I could find that's clean."

"Cool with me."

"It's so inelegant."

"Hey, this is classy where I come from."

"Yeah … me too, actually."

Niani took a sip and handed it to Sherry. She gulped it too fast and coughed. Niani giggled and smoothed Sherry's sweat-soaked hair. "You can too, if you want to. You can call me Lisa."

"No, that's okay." Sherry smiled and kissed her. "I love *Niani*. So beautiful." She attempted another drink, but her fingers were slippery with perspiration, and she ended up spilling it on herself. "Aw, Christ!" Wiping her bare chest with her hand, she had to look once again at that hideous black scar that mocked her from her left breast. "Figured no point in trying to hide this from you," Sherry said softly. "But I swear, I'm going to get it lasered off as soon as humanly possible. I promise."

"No. Don't, Sherry. Don't ever get it removed. Scars are important. They remind us were we've been. You know? Don't tamper with the map."

Niani leaned her head down, gliding her lips across Sherry's skin, tracing the broken cross with her tongue. *Ohhhhh … sweet Jesus …*

"Mmmmm," Niani cooed. "Zinfandel."

They heard the back door slam, and decided it was probably time to get out of bed. Niani put on her sweat pants and a robe. Sherry got back into the T-shirt and boxers, and they headed downstairs to investigate.

Down in the kitchen they found Dave Yoshimoto and Jack, dripping wet, rummaging through the cupboards like mangy street mutts.

"Fuckin' starvin," Jack said.

"Aren't you supposed to be at work?" Niani asked.

"Fuck 'em."

"Fair enough. Hey Dave. You want a beer? You remember Sherry?"

"Yes, I would like a beer and yes I remember Sherry. Hey Sherry. Good to see you again."

"Ditto. When's your baby due?"

"Any day now," Dave answered.

"Are those my boxers?" Jack asked.

"You know I've been dying to get into your shorts, Jackie," Sherry said. Everyone laughed.

"Keep 'em," he said. "Don't say I never gave you nothing."

"I would never say that."

Dave and Niani retired to the front room with their respective beverages. Sherry was about to follow when Jack Curry put his hand on her shoulder.

"Happy?" he whispered in her ear.

"Very."

"Scared?"

"Very."

"Cool. You should be. On both counts. Just listen up. That's my girl in there. Love of my life. My Siamese twin, okay? I've got a good feeling about you, so I'm happy for you. But you ever do something to hurt her, you bring any kinda pain down on her, and we fightin'. Ai'ight?"

"Ai'ight," she answered, *but it sounded stupid coming out of me*. She turned around and hugged him tight, his long, soaking wet hair enveloping her like a drenched curtain. "Thank you, Jack."

"Um … okay …"

And just at that moment a Molotov cocktail smashed through the front window, shattering against the living room wall and setting the sofa ablaze.

25.

OUTSIDE, rocks and bricks flew overhead toward the house as lightning flashed across the sky. The storm raged and the Fifth Reich marched into battle. Using the party flyer, Richard lit another cocktail and heaved it through a downstairs window.

"Someone station the back of the house," Richard said.

But there was little cohesion to the operation. More cocktails followed. No one drew a gun as yet, and the taunting and screaming of epithets was kept, surprisingly, to a minimum. At first. They were trying to draw the inhabitants out. I thought about Niani. I thought about Sherry. And I hoped that they had already left. *Run.* I could only stand by and watch. *Worthless.* Stevie pulled a tank of gasoline from the back of an old blue van. Richard nodded to him.

"First person you see come out gets the shower."

This was certainly a fork in the road. *The fates have laid the paths, and we flip a coin and move.* A moment of still fell across the yard, and I'd like to think everyone contemplated for that moment the commitment they were making just then. *There's no turning back from this.* Is this truly what everyone wanted? *Is this the revolution?* I'd like to think everyone gave it a second's thought, but perhaps it was only me. How many armies have marched off to kill and die on such flimsy pretense as this? How many wars have been waged over backed up jism, blue balls, and a bruised ego? *All of them. All of them.*

"You know," I offered finally, "there is a back door ... and a gravel road at the bottom of the hill."

At that moment, Jack Curry came flying out the front door, shirtless and wild, .357 aimed right at us, as a troop of armed black men emerged from behind the house. Guns at the ready. Sengbe Shabazz in front. Skins all drew frantic pistols. Some ducked behind cars. Most, like Richard and I, were caught exposed in the open air. Instinctively I pulled the snubnose from my pocket and set it dead aim on Curry. Richard did the same. And as the thunder crashed right on top of us and the house fire roared against the night, we all faced off like opposing chess pieces.

"Do I know you, Hippie?" Richard asked Jack Curry. Jack laughed.

"You're staring down the barrel of a fully loaded .357 Colt Magnum Carry. Do I really look like a fucking hippie to you, Cro Mag?"

"No sweat, lads," Richard said to us. "Like shooting monkeys in a barrel."

"Uh, excuse me, Mr. Shabazz?" Curry asked, as cocksure and snide as the Morning Star.

"Yes, Mr. Curry?" Senbe replied.

"Your men here, they're all trained marksman, yes?"

"Why yes, Mr. Curry, certified sharp shooters every one."

"Oh fuck, Rich!" someone jabbered in a panic. "Oh fuck!"

"Tsk tsk. Not looking too rosy for you, Mr. Lovecraft," said Curry. "Not too rosy." His cool veneer cracked open right then, and he yelled, "You hear me, Dickie?! You're gonna die for pussy tonight! Girl got heroin in her snatch? Was it worth dying for? All you baldy-roughneck-knuckleheads are gonna die bleeding and shitting yourselves cuz your dude here lost his pussy!" And he laughed this hideous, staccato laugh.

Die, you fuck.

"Say there, house boy," Richard said to Shabazz, "yo' massa sure likes to surround himself with lotsa black cock, doesn't he? Does he make you suck him? Guess he wasn't getting much off that dyke mammie he had housed up here, huh? What's it mean to you? He feed your crack habit? This'll all be over if you tell me where—"

"SHE'S GONE!!!" Jack bellowed. "YOU LOST HER!!!"

And I wonder today, if he was talking to Richard, or himself. He could have been talking to me. *She's gone. You lost her.*

Without realizing what I was doing, I moved my aim—up to then trained directly on Curry's face—to the back of Richard's head. Snapping to, I quickly moved my focus back to Curry. But the muzzle drifted again to Richard's skull. *You can stop him. You can't let him hurt her.* Back to Curry. *Point it at yourself.* The pouring rain made my trigger finger slippery.

Suddenly, the yard was awash with floodlight, sirens blaring, and rollers spinning. Cruisers and meat wagons screeched onto the scene as police jumped from their vehicles, weapons drawn. Fire engines came wailing up the back street behind the house just in time for the building to collapse in flame. The officers hollered for everyone to drop their weapons and hit the ground. My head slipped from its axis as the scene became a wash of noise. It became television. A vaudeville show. A staged moment strictly for my observation. *I am not party to it. I'm invisible.*

The stalemate remains. The cops scream their final warnings.

"All of you! Drop your fucking guns now!"

No one moves.

"We will be forced to open fire!"

Nothing.

The rain falls to a steady pour. The thunder subsides.

"This is your last chance!"

Last chance.

Last ... last chance ...

Last chance ...

Then it starts. A gun falls to the mud. And then another. And another. Gradually, one by one, everyone drops his gun and lies flat on the ground. I do. Meat does. Joe does. Stevie does. Shabazz does. All his men do.

I forget why we are there in the first place. None of these people are familiar to me. Something about a girl. I don't know which one. I know I loved a girl once. I think I did. Don't know her name. Maybe I used to know. Maybe I just saw her picture one time and made the whole thing up.

We all lay on the ground and put our hands out flat. Only Jack and Richard remained standing; their weapons still pointed at one another ...

"You two, drop the fucking guns!"

"Drop 'em now!"

"Drop 'em and get down!"

"I know your parents, Richie! Don't do this!"

"This is your last fucking chance! Drop 'em or we open fire!"

They won't give in. Neither one of them will submit. They will never surrender.

"Okay!" Jack hollered suddenly. "Okay … it's all over now!"

He slowly began to lower his gun to set it on the ground. *Could he really accept defeat? Could he?*

But before that pistol left his fingers I would swear on Tanya's eternal soul, whatever it's worth, that Curry flashed Richard one last murderous look and that barrel was aimed right for him. Richard pulled his trigger, and the bullet smashed through Curry's thigh, shattering his femur.

The police line lit up on Richard …

Lucifer …

And I watched my best friend fall to the ground in a spray of gunfire …

The harbinger of light.

Each shot a cloud of powder, a spurt of crimson, a sprinkling of pulverized bone.

Curry did not drop his gun and instead lay on the ground, twitching, gurgling, waving his weapon in the air. A cop's bullet tore through his wrist, dropping the gun to the grass. Another officer ran up and bashed him in the head with a baton to subdue him. White as death. Gasping and gurgling in heavy shock. But he would *survive.*

Sherry said:

Everything after the first firebomb is such a blur in my memory. Jack called Senbe. The living room burned. Niani and Jack screamed at each other. Smoke and fire. Jack refused to leave the house. Dave grabbed Niani and picked her up, dragged her through the back door kicking and screaming. I sobbed. Followed close behind. And we ran ran ran. To Dave's car and gone. We heard the gunshots far in the distance. Niani screamed JACK! She cried WE GOTTA GO BACK FOR HIM! Sat in the back seat. I cradled her in my arms crying, Please don't leave me. Please don't leave me. Dave drove us to his apartment. Safe harbor. I knew Richard was dead. And I didn't know how to feel.

Richard and Jack Curry were loaded into an ambulance as the rest of us were handcuffed and tossed into the backs of waiting cruisers and meat wagons. I felt the metal cuffs clamp onto my wrists behind my back, and I was lifted into the air by unseen hands. I shut my eyes to stave off the spinning as I was dropped into the back of a cruiser alone, freezing and drenched, caked in mud and gravel. I heard Jack screaming, "I'm sorry, Arnold! I'm so sorry!"

Shabazz's voice replied, "Jack! Stay up, brotha! Keep strong!"

A cop said to him, "Shut the fuck up, boy," and there was no more Senbe to be heard.

"I'm sorry, Arnold! I'm sorry!!!" and the ambulance door slammed shut and we all disappeared into the night.

I lay curled up in the back of the cruiser, feeling every bump in the road. My mud and rain-soaked face glued to the vinyl seat. *Ah ... vinyl ...*

I knew Richard was dead. And I knew Jack Curry would live. And all I could think was that Richard was the strongest man I'd ever known. He was the bright light. The shining star. *That Richard's just got a way about him. Richard's just got a way.* The brightest. The quickest. The living Power. And even he couldn't bring The Devil down.

Sherry said:

I grieved for a long time, Mikal. Believe that I did. I was hurt and I was guilt-ridden and I was furious. I was angry at him. And I hated him. And I missed him. And I was angry at myself for thinking that the world was better off without him. I still am. And I still do.

Mikal, I'm so sorry. Please don't hate me. I know you loved him. I know how much you loved him. And I understand. We love the wrong people sometimes. That's just the way it is.

26.

WE all did time. All of us.
Surprise. Some did harder time than others. I don't have to tell you
which people those were, do I?

"Them people just can't catch a break, can they!"

There was some debate about whether or not I should be tried
as an adult. I was not yet eighteen, but my involvement in the incident, the extent of my trespass … and so forth. I ended up being
tried as a juvenile which, more than likely, saved my life. It's not
that juvie was a day at the Magic Kingdom, but some of my old
crew who went to big boys prison are dead right now and they left
bad looking corpses and that's just the way it is.

After that night, I never saw any of them again. I didn't visit
anyone. I didn't keep in touch with anyone. I don't to this day.
Thinking about it now, I can't even remember how each of them

looked individually. In my memory they're all just slight varia-
tions on a theme. I doubt I'd recognize any of them on the street
today. I don't even recognize me.

I'd heard through a tangle in the grapevine that Phil Reider
and Joe Briggan both attempted to enlist in the Army. Phil did not
pass the physical and today works as a mechanic in Cleveland.
He's married and has a daughter with cerebral palsy. Joe successfully joined up and just recently returned home from combat in
Iraq in multiple pieces. He's alive, more or less, and does have
most of one arm left.

All told, I was a Skin for barely a year. And yet, it's the
thing that I carry. It defines me more than anything else. Sixteen.
Seventeen. Most folks wear a thousand hats during that time, trying to find out what fits them best. No consideration, no contem-
plation, just dive in and try it out. Most are discarded and folks
move on. I happened to have worn a costume with consequences.
So I continue to carry it with me. That's just the way it is.

I couldn't point to a specific spot on my personal timeline
where I stopped being a True Aryan Warrior. I just became, gradually over time, less true. It was difficult in juv, because there were
baby Skins there already, and I was a legend.

"There he is. That's Richard Lovecraft's right-hand man. He
was with him *that night*. RAHOWA!"

I kept my distance from them as much as possible. One particularly zealous fan ended up with a broken nose. My officially
stated reason for punching him was, "He begged me to let him
suck me off." Which was, in fact, the truth.

I spent my first month and a half perpetually in the dog-
house for fighting. The worst was with a trio of Chicano brothers.

Apparently they didn't much appreciate being called "beaners." Live and learn.

But that eased up after a while, and the little Brown-Shirts-in-training learned to leave me be. There was really only one Skin who caught and maintained my interest. Henry Fulson: fifteen years old, locked up for ethnic intimidation and vandalizing a black-owned restaurant.

"Hey Mikal, we can resurrect the Fifth Reich. You and me. The time is now."

"I don't think so, Henry."

To this day I never fully deduced the origin of that kid's enthusiasm for the White Power movement and his dedication to fascism in general. But he was definitely devoted. It was a commitment to which even I could not relate.

"Hey Mikal. Have you read *The Turner Diaries*?"

"Of course."

"Awesome, ain't it."

"I think the prose is kinda clunky, actually."

I had at that time developed a growing interest in writing. I read everything I could get my hands on, kept a notebook with me all hours of the day to write down memories, impressions, little bits of thoughts and recollections—some of which ended up in this very book. Henry was really excited by this, as he hoped I was penning a manifesto of some sort.

"Hey Mikal. Do you think, if Richard Lovecraft was alive—"

"*Were* alive."

"Were alive today he would have let me run with you guys? I can stomp like no one else. Yids, niggers, gooks—as soon as I'm free again the rampage begins."

"No, Henry, I don't think Richard would have welcomed you."

"Hey Mikal. How come?"

"Because … dude … you're fucking *black.*"

Wherever one might fall in the spectrum of racial politics, it should be universally agreed upon that self-hatred of that magnitude can only bring about an ill conclusion. I have to hold to that. One morning at breakfast I tried explaining that to Mr. Fulson. This is how he replied:

"Hey Mikal. Look at this."

He pulled down the collar of his shirt and pointed to a discolored patch of pink skin about the size of a silver dollar right below his neckline.

"That's vitiligo, Henry. It's a skin disorder."

"No. You're wrong. That's the *white trying to come out.*"

"Okay man …"

"Hey Mikal."

"Yeah?"

"Sieg heil!"

"Yeah."

Even in death Richard cast a shadow. And I wanted out of it. I'd loved him like a brother, no doubt, for whatever it was worth. I wanted no part of his ghost. I studied hard in juv, got my grades in good shape and earned my GED while still in lockdown. Although I never consciously sought to leave behind the person that I had been, it subconsciously became my abiding purpose all the same. *Good bye and good riddance to me.*

I saw the last shroud of that life fall away one night in lockdown, a week before my eighteenth birthday. I sat in rec watching TV when the local news came on. I was just about to leave when I saw a familiar face appear on the screen, standing before a judge begging for leniency: *Father of the Year*, my Suzi's favorite daddy. Seems his beloved daughter had decided one day that all that love and affection was more than she could bear, so she took his gun out of the sock drawer, locked herself in the bathroom, and emptied out the contents of her skull all over the tiles. When asked by the judge why he felt he should receive mercy from the court he replied, "Because I've already been handed the worst punishment of all. The loss of my daughter. *More* than a daughter, really."

Three bailiffs had to tackle Suzi's mother and drag her from the courtroom screaming. Then they cut back to the *tsk*ing anchorfolk and a commercial break and I don't suppose anyone else really cared. And that was that.

Sometimes, late at night, when I'm the only person in the apartment awake and my vertigo is so severe that all I can do is lie on the floor and cover my head, I'll hear that woman screaming deep in my mind. *Shhhhhhh, Ma. Not so loud.*

Go to sleep, Suze. Sleep tight, hon.

"Mikal, let's pretend like we're going to get married someday, okay?"

Sure thing, sweetheart. Anything you want.

I couldn't have saved her.

But, you know, I coulda tried.

27.

"**MIKAL.** Psssst, Mikal. Ya know sump'n?"

"Hey Kaleb. What's goin' on, buddy?"

"Look at my knee. It's all skinned up."

"That's pretty bad-ass, dude."

"Go long. I'll frow you the ball to you."

"Gimme a hug first."

I go to squeeze him but he's just made of water and now he's gone and my shirt's all wet and I wake up crying with blood dripping from my nose and I hope to god I wasn't talking in my sleep.

"You okay, babe?" Darcy asks. She rolls over and hugs me from behind, tosses my hair out of the way and kisses my neck.

"Yeah. It's just … sinuses … allergies …" I wipe the line of blood onto my hand and lick it off so she's none the wiser.

Life after juvie was not much but a series of shit jobs for quite a while, each louder and hotter than the one before: kitchens, factories, roofing, asphalt. Three-odd years passed without my recognition. I was on auto-pilot. Numb. Maintaining an open-door policy on friendships kept me in places to stay as I shuffled from job to job, apartment to apartment, often living with groups of guys fresh from the joint who had done much harsher time than I. But they accepted me as a fellow ex-con and that's just the way it was. Often I was the only white. What can you do? *How did I come full circle?*

With few additional expenses I put aside a couple of bones every month for ink work. I had a lot to cover up, and opted for mostly black and red tribal vines and shading to mask the crude bluish stains I'd come to loathe. You can still make out the swastika over my heart today if I point it out, but they're as gone as I could hope for.

Don't assume I had turned any leaves or corners. Nope. I was the same person I'd ever been, *whomever that was*. Quick to anger, quick to fight, I kept my tongue sharp and loose in case someone needed a cutting (and plenty did). Even to this day I don't *feel* appreciably different. And of course I've left a string of frustrated, unsatisfied women in my wake.

"You're a fucking zombie, Mikal!" said *Whatshername.*

"I'm sorry, did you say something?"

Forever alone in a crowd. I'd simply learned at last to accept and embrace that that's how I am and that's the way it is. I'm good on my own. Today, as I was in '96, I'm surrounded by friends. Always. Lucky that way. But I'm just fine on my own all the same. I'm not a soldier, I've never been a soldier, and no costume will ever make me one.

"Do you need to take something, Mike?" Darcy asks me. "Are you feeling dizzy?"

"No, I'm okay, hon. Go back to sleep."

I was diagnosed with chronic positional vertigo. Thanks to repeated head and neck trauma, and some fairly nasty inner-ear damage, I'll likely have to deal with bouts of it for the rest of my life. It comes and goes, and it's not as bad these days as it once was. The headaches and nosebleeds have largely subsided as well. All I can say is, thank god for sweet Mary Jane. She keeps me sane. I don't smoke a lot, just a joint here, a bong hit there. But it helps me keep my balance and perspective.

After some time had passed, I found myself becoming more and more cognizant of the damage I had been party to. The pointless violence, the *terrorism*. It would dawn on me in waves and spurts and I'd see in my mind the screaming, pleading face of someone I was about to smash.

"Please no. Please. Please don't, dear god!"

I'd wonder where they all were today, how they'd recovered, if they'd recovered at all. So much suffering I had caused so many people … it began to claw away at me. Devoured me from the inside out. I'd try for anger as an easy grab, putting the blame on them for whatever wrong I'd pretended that they had done. But that was fruitless.

"Say yer sorry, Mikal. Tell 'em yer sorry and you won't do it no more."

"How, Kaleb? Who do I tell?"

"Do yer punishment, Mikal."

"For how long?"

Drinking myself unconscious seemed like the right way to go. But all that did was render me unable to distinguish when the vertigo was on top of me and when it wasn't. And it turned me into my father. *Life ain't nothing but listening to other people fuck and watching other people die ...*

There was no penance I could do ... there's none now ... there never will be.

"I'm sorry ... somebody hear that I'm sorry ..."

Sometime late into 1998 I began gradually making my way toward Columbus where, without fully realizing why, I would find myself at community activist meetings organized by students from OSU. My lifelong interest in environmental concerns lead me to ECO and Corporate Watch and other grassroots organizations whose mission it was to monitor what Big Business was shitting out all over us. Neighborhood clean-up projects in low-income areas also became an abiding concern.

It was at one of these meetings that I met Darcy. She was so unlike any of the girls from my past. Soft and light and kind of rounded. Quick-witted, compassionate, intelligent. Delicate, but not the least bit fragile. I remember seeing her first as she held the conch about staging a demonstration on campus. About ... something or other. I've forgotten her words today, but I remember she was a pretty terrible public speaker and no one really listened to her. She's not a commanding presence, and I love her for that. Seeing her try to hold the attention of a room full of people and having them all but ignore her, I knew she'd be my wife someday. Her shoulders are unburdened. Her eyes are uncluttered and I don't think she's ever really known any deep or lasting pain. I love her for that. There is nothing pointy or jagged about her. She's soft and rounded. I hope, if and when she ever reads this book, it doesn't upset her too much. I'd rather she didn't read it at all.

Darcy's family are old-money Taxachusetts liberals. They're very *nice* people and I mean that in all its benign blandness. Sometimes I wonder if they live on the same planet as the rest of us. It's rarefied air they breathe, and it'd be useless for me to ever argue with them or try to tell them where I've been. They'd be sickened. Rightfully so, I suppose. But they've accepted this tatted-up white-trash hooligan into their clan with open arms, so I'm certainly grateful. In fact it was Darcy's father who helped me apply for the Appalachian scholarship that enabled me to attended Ohio State. Full ride. I'd likely have never gone otherwise. Darcy and I both graduate this year, she with a degree in Poli-Sci, me in Creative Writing. For whatever that's worth. It's more than I could have ever hoped for and a good piece better than I deserve.

"I wish you'd quit saying that," Darcy says. "You're a good person and you work hard."

I'm glad you don't know me, sweetheart. I hope you never do.

I'm holdin' like Caulfield, you see. I'm here to catch her. I need to protect her from gargoyles like me.

I try to go back to sleep, but my baby brother has morphed into D'antre Philips who has morphed into my father who has morphed into Suzi's father who has morphed into Vice President Dick Cheney who is shooting fire and napalm out of his cock porno style, and I might as well wake up. That decision is clinched when a one-hundred-fifty-pound sack of hair and muscle lands on me from nowhere and I'm slapped repeatedly in the face with a large slab of hot balogna.

"Igor! Gah! Off the bed!"

The mammoth Shepherd growls in protest and continues to lick me about the chin.

"He just wants to love ya," my wife murmurs half-asleep. "Doncha, Doodlebug?" She coos, "Yessss him doessss."

"Jesus! What the fuck did he roll in?"

"You don't want to know." And back to dreamland she goes.

So I get up to go to my den, maneuvering through the gaunt-let of sleeping bodies once again. Igor pushes my friend Daron off the futon and hunkers down next to Daron's boyfriend Chang. Chang scratches Igor's chest and the mutant beast happily kicks his leg in the air.

"Hey don't mind me," Daron says, rubbing his boney, carpet-burned elbows. "I'm fine here on the floor, ya dig?"

And all is right with the world. I'm very fortunate to have the circle of friends I have these days. As crowded as my apartment is right now, I'm glad that they're all here. A religious person might say that I'm *blessed.* I'd simply say that the fates have been chari-table, if not fair.

Interesting group assembled here. For as young and diverse as we all are, there are a lot of skeleton-packed closets amongst us. I think my wife may be the only person in this apartment tonight with no grim secrets or heavy baggage. I love her for that.

Daron follows me to the den. He packs a bowl with some particularly sticky green and I hit Random on my CD player. It's a *tragic* mix tonight. All music by bands who've had members die violent deaths. Pantera. Joy Division. Acid Bath. Stigmata Dog. Run DMC. *Good times.*

"How's the book comin, yo?" Daron asks choking out a cloud of smoke. "Am I in it?"

"You are now," I say as he hands me the glass pipe.

"Always meant to write a book."

"So do it. Write about your times on the road. Although ... I guess that's kinda been done, huh."

"Yeah. All I got is poetry ... and I hate books of poetry, ya dig?"

"I guess."

"So hey, we gotta celebrate this weekend, right? You and your better half are gradumagatin', Shay got a job, and it's coming up on Chang's and my anniversary. Four years, yo, can you dig that?"

Daron and Chang have been underground since the beginning of the millennium. Their fingerprints are on a couple of fairly high-profile piles of rubble, and they've rubbed shoulders with a rather frightening array of militants, destroyers, and unstable misfits. *But, of course, that's all in the past, right? Sure it is.* Although still devoted and die-hard left wing radicals, they've since denounced violence wholesale and are heartily committed to complete pacifism. Admire that though I may (and I don't really know how I feel about it), I can't truthfully say the same for me. And despite the millions of dollars in property damage they've been party to, there's never been an injury or death as a result. I, of course, once again, cannot say the same.

"All that shit's over and done with, yo," Daron says. "Chang and me, we're just a bitchy old couple nowadays, right?"

"And if the shit goes down you can say it was all Chang's fault anyway. Heh heh."

"No doubt, man. I'm innocent, ya dig? Course I gotta be grateful to my baby. If I'da never met him I'd be just another midwestern faggot married to a fat girl." We laugh.

"All right, get the fuck out. I got work to do."

"Your devil dog pushed me outta bed."

"As skinny as you and Chang are, there's plenty of room on that futon. Or you can sleep on the couch with Shayla."

"Dig, you know I love Shay. But I'm not trying to lay that close to a *female*, right?" He gives an affected shudder and I chuck a rubber dog toy at him. He runs off with a squeal.

Shayla is another dear friend from the wrong side of the law. A runaway since she was eleven, my girl whored until she was fifteen. That makes me sad. But she's one of the toughest people

I've ever known. After my wife, Shayla is my favorite person in the whole world. Darcy would likely say, "After Shayla, Mikal is my favorite person in the whole world." That's just the way it is.

There's a select few people who give off a great, shining light. The rest of us can only bask, or burn, blistering, blinded, trying to dance in it.

I think Shay is one of those people. It's hard not to be drawn to her. And it's hard to know how to feel. I promised myself to purge those folks from my life. But at the end of the day, we're all just giant moths compelled by the light. That's just the way it is.

And in fact, speak o' *de debbil*, here she is right now, reading over my shoulder as I'm trying to write.

"I ain't readin' over yo' damn shoulda. I'm just lookin'. Hey, and don't be typin' ever'thang I be sayin'. I don't talk like 'at anyhow. Uh! You ain't right!"

She sits down in the purple beanbag chair and sticks out her tongue at me. I cackle all Snidely Whiplash.

"You ain't right, Mikal." she says again.

"I ain't left either."

"How come you write my name as *Shayla*?"

"It's pretty, don't you think?"

"Yeah, I like it a real lot. But you can use my real name if you want to. You almost finished?"

"I think so."

"I want to read it."

"I'll give you a copy. Promise."

The music plays a bit too loud for this time of night / morning. Shayla rocks out to Pantera's "By Demons be Driven," banging her head and throwing the horns.

"Beckon the call ... beckon the call ..."

"Work it, girl," I say.

"Love that stuff!"

"You nervous about starting work?"

"Yeah. It's funny. All the shit I done for money befo', and I'm scared of working at a bookstore."

"Yeah ..." It makes me sad when she brings that up. But the past has passed. I hope.

"It's cool, though."

"Just take it as it comes."

"I done *that* already," she laughs.

"Not what I meant."

"Ai'ight, Mikey-Mike," she yawns. "I'm goin' back to sleep. G'night."

But I know she's not going to sleep just yet. It's the same routine every time. She says "G'night," then she goes to the kitchenette and puts on a pot of coffee for me. Sure enough, I hear the bean grinder right now.

I think about the Mikal who appears in this book. Mikal The Bald. Mikal the Holy Warrior, skinny and scum tatted, sleeping in combat boots, *cuz you just never know when you gotta kick somebody.* I still have his boots around here somewhere. I try not to imagine what he would do to the people in this apartment if he were to walk in here right now. *Nothing, if he was by himself. But with his army ... with his army ...*

Shayla places a steaming mug of pure Colombian heaven on my desk and flips the disc changer to Stigmata Dog.

"That oriental girl is so wild lookin'," she says, looking at the CD's inlay card. "The vocalist. Pearl Harbor."

"She's Japanese. It's funny. At first I assumed she was a man. Or a young boy anyway."

"What ever happened to this group?"

"Bus accident. About three or four years ago. She and a guitar player survived, barely, rest of the band went splat on the highway. Not far from here really. Just north."

"That's how rock stars go out, ain't it."

"Just the way it is." I lift the mug to my lips and take a cautious sip. Perfect.

"I know you like yo' coffee like you like yo' women," she says. "Hot and creamy with two lumps of sugar."

"I do like my coffee like I like my women. Cold, black, and bitter."

"You so *wrawng*," she groans, twisting my greasy, unwashed hair into a braid. "It ain't a braid," she says. "It's a *fishbone*. Four ropes instead of three."

"I see."

She hugs me goodnight from behind and turns to exit.

"I'mma give poor Daron the couch so he ain't gotta sleep on the flo'."

"Score!" We hear Daron shout and he dives onto the couch.

"Cool if I go sleep with Darcy?"

"You're gonna sleep with *my wife*?"

If a black girl could blush, she does.

"You *triflin'*! I mean, y'know, sleep in your bed. You ain't goin' back to sleep, I know that. You won't sleep for another three days 'n shit. Ain't nothin' funny goin' on."

"I think it's funny."

"Ugh. Good night, Mister Triflin'-ass. Oh hey, I forgot to tell you, some girl named Sherry called for you. Said she'd call back."

And she does.

"Mikal?"

Well I'll be damned …

"Hey Sherry. Long time."

"Wow. Yeah. God, you sound different."

"Nine years."

"So you got my letter."

"I did, yes."

"What time is it in Ohio?"

"Sun's coming up."

"Is it too late to talk?"

I tell her of course not.

But … maybe it is. It is too late. Too late in our lives. Too late in the game. *Nine years.* We try to play catch up. But she doesn't really want to talk about her life today and I don't want to talk about mine. We banter in vague *nothingmuch* for a while, then simply sit in silence, piling up long distance minutes.

"So … um … thanks for writing back," I say. "That was a big help. And I really enjoyed, you know, getting your side of things. It was … illuminating."

"Did you makes any changes?"

"Well, I kinda … tightened some screws. Or some … bolts."

"Okay … but were you honest?"

"Tried to be. But I don't know. You know? I mean, is that even possible?"

"I don't know. Maybe not."

"Maybe my memory lies."

"Maybe mine does too. Are you using my real name?"

"Do you want me to?"

"Up to you. You're the writer, you make the decisions. We're all in your hands now, Mikal. You write the history, you control our fates. You're the boss. That's what you always wanted, isn't it?"

No ...

"I don't open the can of worms, Sher, I just kick it over."

"Fair enough."

"Tell me something."

"Hey look, it's been great to talk to you, but I gotta go."

"Hold up a minute."

"Mikal, I've told you all I can."

"Just tell me ... Did you stay together?"

"What?"

"You and Niani. Was it ... true love and all that horseshit?"

"I'm ... very happy today. Portland's—"

"Are you still *together*?"

"You haven't let go, Mikal, have you."

"Yes I have. What's done is done. But ... I just can't help but think that ... that if you two stayed together, then at least it wasn't all ... pointless."

"Mikal ..."

"Just tell me, all right?"

"This is more of your *destiny* bullshit. Fate and whatnot. I don't believe in it. Life is chaos, Mikal. It doesn't mean anything."

"That's not very Catholic of you."

"Fuck no it's not. And thank god, or whatever, that I left that rubbish behind. It's all random. Period."

"No, it's not. We have free will to choose our paths, but the paths themselves are set."

"One big *Choose Your Own Adventure* story, huh?"

"That's a pretty ... simplistic way to put it, but yeah."

"You still love him, don't you."

"What?"

"You're trying to make his death mean something. You want it to matter. Well it does. Okay? It does. But only for its own sake."

"No. Listen—"

"You still don't know who you are, do you, Mikal."

"That's not fucking it! Sherry ... listen to me. At least if you two were really *meant* for each other, then—"

"Then what? Nothing I tell you is going to satisfy you. I-I can't ... I can't let you open up any more hurts in me, Mikal." She starts to cry. "I'm all cut up again. Nine years! Nine years. I don't blame you, and I'm glad I was able to help you, but I can't do this any more. I thought I had healed over, but I'm bleeding again. And you are too. You've got to stop bleeding, Mikal. Let's not do this to ourselves."

"Just tell me. Tell me and it's over with. It'll be done. Forever."

"It's over with now. I wish you nothing but the best—*sniff*—I really do. And I, I'll be watching the book shelves for your name. I sure will. Take care of yourself. Okay? Write your ending, Mikal. It's yours to write."

And with that she hangs up. I check the caller ID. Unlisted. *Just as well.*

I pace a bit. Turn the music off. Light a joint. *Wish I had some black rock.* Igor moseys in and head-butts me in the thigh. I rub him behind his ears. I catch my own reflection in the full mirror hanging on the wall and undo the fishbone. I'm shirtless. My viney, abstract *faux*-tribal tattoos weave all about my arms and torso. I'm not as skinny as the boy in the book. Not any more. My hair hangs in greasy strands down my back. I can't even read the look in my

own eyes. Colder than they feel in my head. Rather dull. Lifeless.
I may not know who I am … but I know who I look like.

Write your ending, Mikal. It's yours to write.

FIN

DAS ENDE

THAT'S JUST THE WAY IT IS

THE END

AFTERWORD

LORD, *spare me from any*
more Blackchurch funerals.

It's been a while since I've written anything here. Life has sol-
diered on, as it is wont to do. My friends have all hit the road once
more and I'm alone again. Naturally. I miss them all of course,
and I look forward to seeing them again at some point … but *these*
are good times. On-my-own times. Even my wife is off visiting
old high school chums in Boston. And, due to some sort of elec-
tromagnetic gravity pull science has yet to fully explain, I'm back
in Blackchurch.

The place is thick with ghosts and phantoms this weekend.
I've brought Igor down to see my folks, as he's probably the closest they'll ever come to having a grandchild.

It's Monday afternoon as I write and I'm packing up to head
back to Columbus. Yesterday was funeral day as it often is in

Blackchurch. The host and guest of honor for Sunday's affair was a chap named Rakeem Hollis who had recently run afoul of local law enforcement. Apparently said police felt that sixty nightstick blows to the skull were necessary to convince Mr. Hollis that he had the right to remain silent. I didn't really know Rakeem, but I attended the funeral for my mom's sake, who attended for the sake of Rakeem's mother Yolanda. The Hollis's live across the street and over one. Dad came as well, but bitched about all the "Blackchurch voodoo and ooga booga." He's referring, of course, to the screaming, fainting, and general bedlam of African-American funerals. I have to admit, it's a little hard for me to take as well. But that's just the way it is. You really can't beat the music, though. It does give the spirit a good washing, for whatever that's worth.

I felt as suitably out of place in church as I do in *'Church.* As well I should. Scanning about the room I looked for familiar faces. Trey McKinley was there with a very pregnant blonde. Ezekial Johnson and his parents sat in the third pew on the right side, and I held to some strange hope that maybe Niani would join them. It was in vain. *Just as well.*

Sitting there as people cried all around me and some fat, sweaty preacher said something or other about God welcoming his child home and choirs of angels and whatnot, I felt that it wasn't just Rakeem's funeral I was attending just then. It was all the funerals I should have attended and didn't.

Sleep tight. Sleep tight.

The choir sang:

"And he will raise you up on eagle's wings / bear you on the breath of dawn / make you to shine like the sun ..."

It occurred to me that I could have dressed a little nicer. Then it occurred to me that, no, I could not have. This beaten old blue suit is the best that I own. Just the way it is. And fat preacherman said something about one day all of God's children will sit together at the banquet table under the banner of God's love. Or words to that effect.

"Bullshit on a stick," muttered my dad.

"Amen," I said. *Amen.*

After the service everyone milled about out on the sidewalk for a very long time. I could tell my dad was getting antsy, eager to get away from this throng of Negroes and home to his gin bottle. Tanya delivered all the necessary hugs and condolences and they headed home. No telling why, but I decided to stick around and told them I'd join them later.

Eventually those of us who remained all marched down Churchwalk to the cemetery. Some folks sang:

"Sometimes I feel / like a motherless child / a long way from home ..."

There at the grave site folks mumbled more prayers. More singing, more consoling, but I can't be sure that I was really there. I felt like an observer, at least one step removed. *This is a sad show. Somebody change the channel.* Rakeem's grandmother fell backwards wailing and a little girl threw dandelions into the grave.

"Tiesha, you stop that," her mother said. "You leave Rakeem alone. He sleepin'."

Sleep tight Rakeem ...

I finally got up the gumption to approach Trey McKinley and his pregnant lady friend. *He's still a little scarred up about the face.*

"Trey McKinley," I said, my voice shaking more than I antici-pated. "It's been a while. How you doin'?"

Trey turned his head with a questioning look. "Uh, hi." He shook my hand. "Have we met?"

"Long, long time ago. I'm Will and Tanya Fanon's son. Mike. I live in Columbus. But, um, hey, I just wanted to say ... that ... *I'm sorry.*"

"Thank you. I appreciate that. Rakeem was my dude. He'll be missed."

"Yeah. Yeah. I just wanted to tell you ... how sorry I am."

"Cool. Take it easy, Mike. Church."

"Church."

Time to go. Mission accomplished. One step at a time. Time to go ... But not before *that voice* sneaked up behind me.

"How 'boutcha, whiteboy." *How 'bout me.* "I been wantin' to talk at you for a minute, Mikal." Against my stronger instincts I turned around slow and casual. *I will be damned.* "You recognize me, bruh?"

Goddamn ...

"Sure. Yeah. How could I forget?" He hadn't aged a day. We shook hands. "How, um, how ya been, D'antre?"

"Been better. I'm tired of buryin' my niggas, ya heard?"

"Sure."

"This be my third funeral in two months, son. I ain't havin' no more of it."

"That's hard."

"You know how it is, buryin' your friends."

"Yeah ..."

"I done read your manuscript."

Fuck ...

"Zat right?"

"Whatcha say you 'n' me grab us some drinks down at the Soul Lounge. I'm buyin'."

"Wouldn't say no."

If you look up "ghetto dive" in any respectable dictionary you will find a picture of the Soul Lounge. It's a tavern stuck in time, replete with dark, life-beaten, yellowed-eyed characters who are also stuck in time. They don't take credit cards, the jukebox is stocked with 78s, and if you'd like to sit in the non-smoking section you'll be pointed in the direction of the broom closet. Good times.

Turns out D'antre had acquired a copy of the manuscript through Shayla. He'd been up in Columbus doing a drop-in book signing for *Princess Africa Jones* at the shop where Shayla was working. They became fast friends and she even stayed in Blackchurch for a while. I had lost touch with her by that time, and the last D'antre heard she had headed off for Baton Rouge, Louisiana. I'm kind of sad about that, and I hope I get a chance to see her again someday.

"Guess shit got a little fiery between y'all, eh? You an' and Shay an' your old lady."

"I don't want to talk about it," I told him. He nodded and ordered us two Wild Turkeys on the rocks.

"Tell me somethin'. The first time we 'met,' or whatever you'd call it, did I really say to you 'Welcome to Niggatown'?"

"If I'm lyin' I'm dyin'," I said.

"That's funny."

"Why's it funny?"

"I just think it's funny. I don't remember that at all. I do remember poor lil Artiz gettin' shot up."

"*Artiz.* Huh. I always wondered, whatever happened to him?"

"He survived, but he got a bad blood infection, son. Nasty shit. The head shot did him no favors neither, ya heard. He done been in a wheelchair ever since. And he don't talk too great. Here: a toast." We raised our tumblers. "To absent friends."

"To absent friends. Cheers."

"Mud in your eye."

"D'antre, man, before we go any further with all this, I just want you to know that … I'm not the person I used to be. All right? So whatever you might be thinking after read—"

"Hey," he shrugged. "Who is, ya heard?"

"Right. Right."

"I was feelin' your story, dawg. Believe dat. And it got me thinkin' … bout lookin' at my own self, ya heard. It's hard puttin' your friends in the ground, ya feel me. Hard. It's hard when they die … but in a way I think it's harder when they kill, right? I've had both, knahmsayin, just like you. It's harder when they kill and they live cuz in a way it's like they are dead to you now, or half-dead, but you still gotta hang with they ghost and perp like ain't nothin' wrong."

"I know what you mean. It's hard to know how to feel."

"It's hard to know how to feel. Dead up. Before Rakeem, the last cat I had to bury, we was real close, ya heard. I had mad love for him like a brother, knamean, but he done some *ill shit*. Just wrong shit, son. All fucked up in his head, a soldier ya heard, a vet, all fucked up with the gov'ment's poison … And when they finally brung him down, cuz they had to … I was … relieved. And I got hatred for myself for that. At least he died free, whatever that's worth."

"Yeah …"

I bought us another round. We sat in silence for a long time. When he spoke again, it was a completely different voice. Clear, precise, almost mannered.

"You know, Mikal, it's a peculiar thing," he said. "I'm staring down the barrel of forty-years-old. It seems like I should have found my *space* by now. But I feel like an alien. That's how it is. These past couple of years I've been renting an apartment in an old converted church. THE church, the big one, the original *Blackchurch*, on the corner of Blackstone and Desmond."

"Churchwalk."

"Churchwalk, yes. Heart of the neighborhood. The namesake, for chrissake."

"Dude, I saw that! I saw it when we were walking down to the cemetery. You live there? There's police tape all around it."

"They converted it some years ago to a community hall, bingo and theatre and whatnot, and there's a little apartment for rent on the second floor, and that's what I've called home for the past couple of years. Hoo boy. Thirty-six years old, a published author, and I'm living like the hunchback of Notre Dame." We laughed. He shrugged, matter-of-fact. "And now, thanks to my boy, R.I.P., and his demons, there's police tape around it and blood on the inside."

"Damn, that's one of those moments when you gotta step back and take inventory, right?"

"Yeah, so let's see: most of my friends since childhood are either felons or fertilizer. My wife and my baby girl moved away to Madison, Wisconsin ..."

"I didn't know they even *let* black people live there."

"News to me too. I live in a bloodstained church with a devil-possessed blast furnace. And now ... I'm sitting in a nigga-only ghetto bar with a cracker-ass neo-nazi."

"Yep. Somebody took a wrong turn somewhere."

"And I think it's me."

I wasn't sure what to say. I'd always thought of D'antre Philips as the toughest, cockiest motherfucker in the world. *But here we are. He's got his small moments too.*

How did *we end up here? What kind of twist in the road did I miss? Maybe the paths aren't set after all. Maybe there are no paths. Maybe it is* all random. *Chaos ... absolute freedom. I could learn to enjoy freedom on my side.*

"Well ...," I answered finally, breathing deep and coughing a bit on the stagnant Soul Lounge air. "There's really only one thing I can say about all that, my man."

"Yeah? What's that?"

"It's gonna make one HELLBOMBER of a book when you write it, son!"

We laughed heartily and clinked our glasses together.

"You goin' in my book, muthafucka," he cackled, his voice returning to "normal."

"Fair play to you," I replied. "You're in *mine.*"

Just then the tavern door swung open and I noticed that evening had completely set in. Slumping in the door, stooped and limping on a cane, was a rough-looking peckerwood with stringy, shoulder-length hair. A graying, too-tight Judas Priest concert tee struggled to contain his rather sizable potbelly. Sleeving each arm was a mosaic of faded, undefined tattoos. This guy couldn't have been but thirty-three, but he looked *much* older.

"Ladies and gentleman," the bartender announced, "or *gentlemen* and gentlemen I guess ... it is the one and only *Jack Curry.*"

"'Bout time you faced the Devil," D'antre whispered to me.

Yeah ... 'bout time ...

"D!" Jack shouted, hobbling over to us. "What's shakin', hard rhymer?"

"How you feelin' J playa?"

"Better than I look, I hope. How you holdin' it, dawg?"

"Tucked into my sock, ya heard." They embraced forcefully and Jack took a seat on the stool next to me. "We missed ya at the service, kid."

"I don't do funerals," Jack answered. "Fuck alla that, son. I don't do churches as a rule. The six-six-six on my skull starts pounding and glowing and shit. Keem knows I love him. And I know he's looking down on me from above. Every time I try to take a shit or strangle the sea serpent. Filthy bastard."

"Jack, this here is Mikal Fanon."

Curry turned to me, looked me right in the eyes and offered the glad hand.

"Good to meet you, Mikal," he said smiling warmly.

How do you do it?

How do you drop twelve years of seething hatred all at once? How do you push it all aside? How do you control the wave of rage that crashes down on you? You don't. You don't drop it and you don't control it. But you *try*. Because you have to. I shook his hand and smiled back. And when I did there was no mistaking the bullet scars on both sides of his left wrist. Or the razor scars on his right.

"Um, yeah, good ... uh ... good to meet you too, Jack. Good to meet you too."

"Welcome to the ass-crack of the universe, dude."

"I've been up in it before."

"So what brings you to Blackchurch?"

"Mikal grew up here," D"antre said.

"Oh yeah?"

"Not exactly. I lived here from ... for a minute. But I'm up in Slow-lumbus right now. Just graduated from OSU."

"Aw, that's hip man," Jack said, slapping me on the back. "That's killer. Good for you. Dontell!" he called to the barkeep. "Get this man a Maker's on the rocks. On me. Man, that's something I always wanted to do, you know. Graduate from college. I was really into learning foreign languages. Wanted to be an interpreter or a translator or something. I just really got into the idea of being able to communicate with lots of different folks. You know? Weeeell," he chuckled, "so much for that shit."

D'antre looked at me. I thought he might call me out, but he didn't.

"See, Jack did his time at Warren County," D'antre said with a smirk. "That's an easy piece."

"Yeah, *easy piece* is right, muhfucka," Jack replied, "Easy piece my ass. You try being a cripple in lockdown and tell me if the sun is shinin'.""

"Boy," D'antre said rolling his eyes, "with all the cousins and shit you got who are locked up in that joint, going to jail's like a family reunion." We all laughed.

"You done time, Mike?" Jack asked.

"Just juvie."

"Yeah, I did juvie."

"So did I," D'antre said. "Juv was the first place and time I ever saw a dude jerk off another dude. I was all like, Y'ALL ARE SICK! and then I proceeded to spank it into a old sweat sock. Cuz see, I got *standards*."

"Well," Jack said stoically, "as long as the sock was a chick—"

"The sock was yo' mama." The whole bar laughed at that, and Jack called Dontell over and bought another round. *Yo' mama* snaps are round-worthy in these parts.

We talked and drank the night away. Spent a good piece talking about our wives: D'antre's ex, Jack's soon-to-be ex, my Darcy. *Never-to-be ex.* I had the sudden urge to call her in Boston. Make sure she was okay. See if she could come home early because I missed her. *Must be the booze. Alone time is good time ...*

At some point president George W. Bush appeared on the bar's decrepit black and white TV. A collective groan filled the room and grumbles of "white devil" were heard. Jack chucked a full basket of peanuts at the television.

"DIE YOU EVIL FUCK!!!" he shouted as the peanuts smashed against the screen and scattered all over the floor. No one so much as batted an eye. Dontell the bartender simply bent over and swept up the shells.

"So, Molotov," Jack turned to D'antre, cool and collected. "How's *Princess* selling, kid?"

"It ain't. Not really. Hedgehog Press got bought out by a larger publisher and they kinda don't know what to do with it."

"You writing something new?" I asked.

"Yeah."

"Is it about Blackchurch?" Jack asked.

"You know it."

"Sweet."

"Mikal's a writer too," D'antre said. "Just finished a book."

"F'real?"

"Well, it's not quite done," I said.

"I'd like to read it."

"Yeah. Okay. Sure."

Around 1:30 AM, after stopping by my parents' place to collect Igor, we stumbled back down Blackstone Street to Jack's house (his mother's house, actually). There we were greeted by Jack's soon-to-be ex Elaine, a quiet little hamster-faced girl with red hair and big hips. She seemed really nice and they appeared to be happy enough … but you can tell when a relationship is through, and theirs is most certainly over. That's just the way it is.

After gobbling up some delicious leftover potato salad Elaine had made for Rakeem's wake, Jack, D'antre and I sat out on the back porch drinking cheap red wine, smoking equally cheap hash, and daring the sun to rise. Three young old criminals shaking our fists at the night. Igor wrestled happily in the backyard with Jack's three-legged pit bull Araya and we collectively ignored the persistent sound of gunfire and crying sirens.

About 3:00 AM D'antre went into the house to try and call Madison, Wisconsin. It seemed a bit late to be making phone calls, but he was determined to talk to his daughter right then and there was no point telling him not to. BBC came on the radio with a report about the torture American soldiers had committed in Iraq and Guantanamo Bay. Jack shut off the radio.

"I can't deal with any more *torture*," he said. "It weighs on my mind too much."

"I feel you," I said.

"You a Public Enemy fan, Mike?"

"Aw hell yeah," I lied. He dropped *Fear of a Black Planet* into the CD player. It was pretty damn awesome. "Hey man, that's too bad about you and Elaine."

"That's life," he shrugged. "You take it as it comes."

"She seems like a real cool chick."

"Yeah, she is. It's not her fault, man. I'm not an easy guy to deal with. I mean, I only work twenty hours a week, I live with my mother, and I spend most of the day listening to right wing talk radio and screaming at the top of my lungs."

"Yeah, dude, that's pretty obnoxious."

"True that. I mean, I love her and all, but she can do better." He paused for moment, then said, "I *really* loved a girl one time. A long time ago."

"Yeah? What happened?"

"After I went to prison I never saw her again. That was my fault too."

"What do you mean?"

"I mean she wrote me like every other day. Came to visit me every week. But something always got in the way and she couldn't see me. I didn't want her to. There I was, with a big steel rod through my thigh. All gimped out and crippled, head shaved bald. That's no way to be."

"Yeah ..."

"I never even wrote her back. Eventually she moved away. The letters kept coming for years and years, well after I got outta the joint, and I never replied. Most I didn't even open. Finally they stopped. I loved that girl. But she couldn't love me back."

"Oh."

"I mean, she *did* love me, but not the way I loved her. She couldn't."

"Queer, huh."

"Yeah, I mean what can ya do? It's how she was wired. Even if she wasn't ... it wouldn't have worked. We were like twins, you know? From alternate realities. We weren't lovers, but we were soul mates, if that makes any sense at all."

"Sure."

"I told somebody one time that there are just a few people in the world who give off a great, shining light. The rest of us can only bask or burn ..."

"Blistering," I said, "blinded, trying to dance in it."

"Yeah," he said, looking at me askew.

"You still believe that?"

"I don't know. I think we're all fucked up and lost. All of us. Big or small. I mean look at Adolph Hitler. Yeah he was charismatic and yeah he had presence and rocked the stage like a true star, but when shit got hot he blew his own head off. He wasn't the man folks thought he was."

"I guess that's true."

"Lots of people were hung up on Niani. Lots. Men *and* women. They were *fascinated* by her. Thought she was a mystery or a puzzle to solve. But I knew her. She was just a girl. Beautiful, sure, and brilliant. Magnetic. But she was just a girl. A goofy, awkward, silly, clumsy girl. She never did her own dishes and she was always breaking shit by accident. And she could be a real prickly bitch sometimes. I was always cleaning up after her. But I guess ... she always cleaned up after me too. God ... I loved her."

"Whatever happened to her?"

"Last I heard she moved to Portland."

"Really?"

"That was a while ago. I don't know if she's still there. Wherever she is, I hope she's happy. I'm sure she is."

"Me too," I said. "Me too."

I awoke on Jack Curry's couch sometime around 8:30 AM. D'antre was asleep in the easy chair. No one else was about. I woke up Igor, who grumbled in protest, and I hooked on his leash. We crept quietly out of the house and out into the bright Blackchurch morning.

Down we walked, street after street, past churches, gun shops, liquor stores, weave boutiques, pawn shops, "checks cashed no questions asked," and house after boarded-up house. Each looked to be—and probably should have been—condemned, but none were. All occupied. Some with two or more families. *That's Blackchurch.*

One block from Will and Tanya's place I once again stepped onto the moving carousel. It spun me around and I fell into a lamppost. My head twirled like a top as I slid down the pole to the sidewalk, Igor whimpering and licking my face.

"Hey boy!" I opened my jittery eyes and looked across the street at an ancient black man sitting on a stoop smoking a cigarette and drinking a bottle of Wild Irish Rose. He flashed me a toothless smile and raised his drink. "Juth go on home and thleep it off, y'hear? You'll be a'ight."

I smiled back and pulled myself upright, the vertigo already subsiding. "I'm better already," I said. He cackled loudly and gave me the thumbs-up.

Back at the house I called Darcy in Boston right away. I expected to get the voice mail, but she answered on the first half ring.

"Mikal?"

"Hey sweetheart."

"Hey! How's the baby?"

"He ate a guy."

"Whole?"

"Yep."

"Cool."

"Yeah. How's everybody?"

"Good. Good. They're all asking after you."

"Give 'em all a kiss for me."

"'Kay. I miss you. Sooooo much. I want to come home early. What do you think?"

"You read my mind, Darce."

"Cool. Yeah, it was great catching up with everybody and all. But you know, they're my past. I'm ready to say good-bye to the past. I'm ready to come home. It's time to leave the past where it belongs. My future's with you and that's where I want to be."

"I couldn't agree more."

"Can't wait to see you."

"Can't wait."

"I'm catching the first plane back to Columbus."

"I'll be there waiting."

"I may get impatient and parachute out."

"I'll be there to catch you."

"I love you, Mikal."

"Hurry home and prove it."

I'm ready to say good-bye to the past. Good-bye, The Past. Good-bye, Blackchurch. Good-bye, old ghosts. Haunt ya later sometime. Good-bye old Mikal, young Mikal, whomever you are. Good-bye and good riddance to me.

And that was that.